Queer Looks

Queer Looks

Perspectives on Lesbian and Gay Film and Video

Edited by
Martha Gever, Pratibha Parmar,
and
John Greyson

Routledge
New York   London

Published in 1993 by
Routledge
29 West 35th Street
New York, NY 10001

Published in Great Britain by
Routledge
11 New Fetter Lane
London EC4P 4EE

Printed in the United States of America on acid free paper

LIBRARY OF CONGRESS CATALOGING IN PUBLICATION DATA
Queer looks : perspectives on lesbian and gay film and video / editors
    Martha Gever, John Greyson, Pratibha Parmar.
      p. cm.
    Includes bibliographical references.
    ISBN 0-415-90741-1. — ISBN 0-415-90742-X
    1. Homosexuality in motion pictures. I. Gever, Martha, 1947–
II. Greyson, John, 1960–   . III. Parmar, Pratibha.
PN1995.9.H55Q4   1993 '
791.43'653—dc20   93-9663
                       CIP

British Library cataloging in publication data also is available.

To Stuart Marshall

Contents

Favorite Aunts and Uncles

Acknowledgments

Special thanks to Ian Rashid, who came up with the idea for *Queer Looks* and jump-started it into existence; to Kobena Mercer, an early collaborator who helped shape the project; to Lachlan Brown and Bill Germano for support and encouragement; to the Ontario Arts Council, the Toronto Arts Council, the Gay Community Appeal, and the New York State Council on the Arts for assistance with writers' fees and translation costs.

Ray Navarro, "Eso, me esta pasando" appeared in the program notes for the 1990 San Antonio CineFestival and is reprinted with permission of Guadalupe Cultural Arts Center.

Jackie Goldsby, "Queens of Language: *Paris Is Burning*" appeared in *Afterimage,* vol. 18, no. 10 (May, 1991), pp. 10–11, and is reprinted with permission of Visual Studies Workshop.

Martha Gever, "Pictures of Sickness: Stuart Marshall's *Bright Eyes*" appeared in *October,* no. 43 (Winter, 1987), pp. 108–126, and is reprinted with the permission of MIT Press.

Charles Ludlam's "Manifesto: Ridiculous Theater, Scourge of Human Folly" is reprinted with permission from the Estate of Charles Ludlam, Walter Gidaly, executor.

Douglas Crimp, "Fassbinder, Franz, Fox, Elvira, Erwin, Armin, and All the Others" appeared in *October,* no. 21 (Summer, 1982), pp. 60–81, and is reprinted with permission of MIT Press.

Patricia White, "Madam X of the China Seas" appeared in *Screen,* vol. 28, no. 4 (Autumn, 1987), pp. 80–95, and is reprinted with permission of *Screen.*

Alison Butler, "*She Must Be Seeing Things:* An Interview with Sheila McLaughlin" appeared in *Screen,* vol. 28, no. 4 (Autumn, 1987), pp. 20–28, and is reprinted with permission of *Screen.*

Mandy Merck, "Dessert Hearts" appeared in *The Independent Film and Video Monthly,* vol. 10, no. 6 (July, 1987), pp. 15–17, and is reprinted with permission of the Association of Independent Video and Filmmakers.

On a Queer Day You Can See Forever

MARTHA GEVER, JOHN GREYSON, AND PRATIBHA PARMAR

On a queer day you can see forever. Or can you? Things move fast. Things move faster. When we started this book in 1989, three people from three cities, we knew we were living in three very queer places. Places of new possibilities and shocking repercussions. Places of unprecedented opportunities and unbridled repressions. In our particular cases: London, New York, Toronto. We knew from travel, from work, from networks of friends and colleagues, that there were lots of other queer places, north and south, east and west. Very queer places. Each particular, each idiosyncratic. Their experiences were nevertheless similar to ours.

1989. On the one hand, as film and video artists and critics, as people working in independent media pursuing lesbian and gay themes, the field had never seemed so ripe with possibilities. Funding, production, and distribution opportunities existed in ways that were unthinkable even five years earlier. The fields of lesbian and gay film and video were expanding, exploring, exploding. A critical mass of artists were producing, debating, challenging. A new militance in street politics was being cross-pollinated with a new rigor in queer critical theory. A significant moment to savor.

1989. On the other hand: Jesse Helms, Section 28, Canadian Customs . . . a gang of international thugs conspiring to create a significant moment to suffer. Then there was AIDS, continuing to devastate our ranks, a cruel tide with a vicious undertow, sweeping so many of us forever out to sea. The resurgent right wing was opportunistically using AIDS to declare a take-no-prisoners war on queer expression. Funding was slashed, screenings were censored, films were banned. What's to savor when we suffer so? Such queer places.

Things move faster. Things get more extreme. For the three of us, in our tale of three cities, it was certainly the best of times, the worst of times. The three of us decided to work on a book born of the moment: a book designed not to wallow in the grimness, but to fight back against it. We wanted to explore some of the things we were seeing, feeling, making, doing, some of the people we saw around us who made a difference. We wanted to make public some of the exchanges occurring between an ever-shifting network of artists, organizers, and activists that spanned several continents. We wanted to witness some of the coalitions and collaborations, efforts at a new type of politic, a new sort of image. We wanted to put down on paper some of the ideas being debated by this larger "we," this ever-expanding "we," this collective, communal "we" of lesbian and gay critics, artists, and audiences. We wanted a sassy, irreverent, open space to explore some of our differences, even as we would strive to make a difference, even as we could see we were making a difference.

1989. We were triggered by the profound dearth of critical theory addressing independent productions by lesbian and gay media artists. We were inspired by the groundbreaking (if sporadic) critical inquiry of the previous decade: special issues of *Jump Cut* and *Screen, The Celluloid Closet* by Vito Russo, the occasional panel at a cinema studies conference or gay film festival. We were dissatisfied with queer critics who endlessly analyzed Hollywood but ignored the independent sector. We were bored with tired seventies notions of positive role models, tired of boring seventies preoccupations with classic narrative structures. We were intrigued by the avant-garde canons of the twentieth century which disproportionately featured lesbian and gay artists yet disconcertingly bent over backwards to erase this sexual fact. We were committed to a wholesale interrogation of those canons, enraged by the gaps, absences, assumptions, and privileges that made those canons dominate official discourses. We were particularly influenced by the cross-disciplinary critical debates, both in the academy and on the street, that were contesting and deconstructing representations of race and gender, likewise refusing the authority of the tired old tropes that constitute official film and video history. We were eager to contribute a volume to the growing book-shelf of complementary projects that were in the works and would appear within the next two years: *How Do I Look?* by the Bad Object Choices collective (of which Martha was a member); *Now You See It,* by Richard Dyer; *The Woman at the Keyhole,* by Judith Mayne; *Inside/Out,* by Diana Fuss. We were empowered by the growing network of lesbian and gay film and video festivals on six continents which were building critical and enthusiastic audiences for queer media and queer debates.

Parameters? Independent film and video by lesbian and gay artists since Stonewall. An equal commitment to the voices of critics and of producers. An openess to wildly varied notions of the text and the image. An interest in contradiction. An excitement about exploring the edges of borders, the restricted zones of boundaries, the shadowy places where certainty isn't welcome and rules no longer apply.

1989. We wouldn't, couldn't, didn't expect the contrast between the good and the bad to get more extreme. It did. It is. Opportunities have both expanded and contracted exponentially. Funding has both blossomed and disappeared. Distribution for independent queer features is both red-hot at the box office and nonexistent. Distribution for queer video art has both mushroomed and ceased to exist. Lesbian and gay TV is going through the ratings roof; lesbian and gay TV is cancelled without adequate reason. Gay kisses and lesbian caresses are allowed one day in one city, censored the next in another. Pat Buchanan uses *Tongues Untied* to convince America that George Bush is soft on black gay men. (That's worth repeating: Buchanan uses *Tongues Untied* to convince America that George Bush is soft on black gay men. Helllllloooo?) Queer places. Queer looks.

We're in this together—that's what makes it slightly more tolerable, and definitely more exciting. Our inevitable regret is that this book isn't ten times bigger, ten times more inclusive, and ten times more provocative. This is an idiosyncratic collection of texts and images that come from our cities, our travels, our networks, the things that pull our political levers and push our aesthetic buttons, the things that we talk and care and fight about. Things are moving fast. Things are moving faster. On a queer day you can see forever, and ever, and ever . . . or at least, you can look.

What a Difference a Gay Makes

Lesbian and gay media, as much as it constructs the collectivity of our experiences, is just as often engaged in working against the grain, stressing the disjunctions where we differ, where we don't share, where we struggle. In short, we are often out of sync with the notion of a generic queer audience, and just as often the work we make speaks loudly about our differences. These are myriad, both overlapping and discreet. Whether it's Hammer's insistence on abstraction, Goldsby's celebration of drag queens' revolt against conformity, the desire of punk artists to really kill disco this time, Navarro's struggle with Latino homophobia, or Araki's refusal of limiting labels, an attitude of self-determination presents itself as sometimes the central content, center stage.

That Moment of Emergence

To be a lesbian means engaging in a complex, often treacherous, system of cultural identities, representations and institutions, and a history of sexual regulation. . . . Being a lesbian tests the meanings of sexual identity in ways that evoke intense, sometimes violent, social disapproval, while being straight is taken for granted as a neutral position from which gay folks deviate.
—Martha Gever[1]

For me being a lesbian is not only a fight against homophobia and the kind of homophobia we face everyday, but it's also a fight against the system that creates that . . . a class system as well as a system that is imperialist. It's a system that's responsible for the incidences of racism that all of my family and all of the people I know of Asian and African descent have had to go through in all of the Western countries, and I think its critical that we come together and bring all these experiences together and actually reach beyond ourselves. . . .
—Punam Khosla[2]

To be an artist, a lesbian and a woman of color engaged in mapping out our visual imaginations is both exciting and exhausting. The creative upsurge in black women and women of color's cultural production in Britain has not been given the spotlight and visibility that it deserves. Women of color have been organizing and creating communities which have inspired a new sense of collective identity, and it is only through our own efforts that we have ensured against our erasure as artists and cultural producers.

I don't think that this is because of a mere oversight or even deliberate conspiracy. I think it is much more to do with the persistence of a fantasy of what constitutes an authentic national culture, a fantasy which posits what and who is English. The dominance of the ideology of English ethnicity, although deeply ingrained in the cultural canons of British society and arts institutions, is and has been challenged by black artists and cultural producers through our work. We have been changing the very heart of what constitutes Englishness by recoding it with our diasporan sensibilities. Our ancestral as well as personal experiences of migration, dispersal, and dislocation give us an acute sense of the limitations of national identities. Some of us claim an English as well as a British identity, and in so doing transform the very terrain of Englishness and expose the ruptures in the discourses of

3

June Jordan (left) and Angela Davis in *A Place of Rage,* Pratibha Parmar

white supremacy. The fact that British national culture is heterogeneous and ethnically differentiated is something that still needs hammering home to those who are persistent in their view that to be black and British is an anachronism. Our visual outpourings are our referents for our "imagined communities" and utopian visions, which we seek to articulate and live and work towards.

By reflecting on my own working practices as a filmmaker and video artist, and in unfolding my personal and historical context, I hope to be able to contribute to the ongoing development of a general theoretical framework for discussing the cultural and political significance of black arts in postcolonial Britain.[3] It is a framework which differs from previous forms of cultural critiques because of the ways in which it seeks to centralize the black subjectivity and our experiences of difference. The more we assert our own identities as historically marginalized groups, the more we expose the tyranny of a so-called center.

I came into making videos and films from a background in political activism and cultural practice, and not from film school or art school. As an Asian woman I have never considered myself as somebody's "other," nor have I seen myself as "marginal" to an ubiquitous, unchanging, monolithic "center." But since my arrival in England in the mid-sixties, it has been a constant challenge and struggle to defy those institutions and cultural canons which seek repeatedly to make me believe that because of my visible difference as an Asian woman I am an "other" and therefore "marginal."

There is a particular history that informs the thematic concerns of my work as much as my aesthetic sensibilities. That history is about a forced migration to an England that is intensely xenophobic and insular, an England that is so infused with outdated notions of itself as the Mother Country for its ex-colonial subjects that it refuses to look at the ashes of its own images as a decaying nation, let alone a long-dead empire.

When my family, like many other Indian families, arrived in Britain in the mid-sixties, anti-black feelings were running high and "Paki-bashing" was a popular sport amongst white youths. It was in the school playground that I first encountered myself as an undesirable alien, objectified in the frame of "otherness." All those of us perceived as "marginal," "peripheral," and the "other" know what it is like to be defined by someone else's reality and often someone else's psychosis.

> We can read ourselves against another people's pattern, but since it is not ours . . . we emerge as its effects, its errata, its counternarratives. Whenever we try to narrate ourselves, we appear as dislocations in their discourse.
> —Edward Said[4]

I do not speak from a position of marginalization but more crucially from the resistance to that marginalization. As a filmmaker, it is important for me to reflect upon the process through which I constantly negotiate the borderlines between shifting territories . . . between the margin and the center . . . between inclusion and exclusion . . . between visibility and invisibility. For example, as lesbians and gays of color, we have had to constantly negotiate and challenge the racism of the white gay community, and at the same time confront the homophobia of communities of color.

What we have been seeing in recent years is the development of a new politics of difference which states that we are not interested in defining ourselves in relation to someone else or something else, nor are we simply articulating our cultural and sexual differences. This is not a unique position, but one that is shared by many cultural activists and critics on both sides of the Atlantic. We are creating a sense of ourselves and our place within different and sometimes contradictory communities, not simply in relation to . . . not in opposition to . . . nor in reversal to . . . nor as a corrective to . . . but in and for ourselves. Precisely because of our lived experiences of racism and homophobia, we locate ourselves not within any one community but in the spaces between these different communities.

Toni Morrison was once asked why she wrote the books that she did, and she replied that these were the books she wanted to read. In some ways, the reason why I make the films and videos that I do is also because they are the kinds of films and videos I would like to see: films and videos that engage with the creation of images of ourselves as women, as people of color and as lesbians and gays; images that evoke passionate stirrings and that enable us to construct ourselves in our complexities. I am also interested in making work that documents our stories and celebrates and validates our existence to ourselves and our communities. As a lesbian I have searched in vain for images of lesbians of color on the screen but I very quickly realized that they exist only in my own imagination, so one of my aims as a filmmaker is to begin to compile that repertoire of images of ourselves. The joy, the passion and desire embodied in our lives is as important to highlight and nourish as are the struggles against racism and homophobia. Desire for me is expressed sexually, but also in a need to recreate communities which are affirming and strengthening.

Experiences of migration and displacement, and the need to make organic links between race and sexuality, guide my desire to create works that throw up the contradictions of being "queer" and Asian. Images of Asian women in the British media have their root in the heyday of the British empire. The commonsense racist ideas about Asian women's sexuality have been determined by racist patriarchal idealogies. On the one hand we are seen as sexually erotic and exotic creatures full of oriental promise, and on the other as sari-clad women who are dominated by their men, as oppressed wives or mothers breeding prolifically and colorizing the British landscape.

The idea that many of us have our own self-defined sexuality is seen as subversive and threatening by the dominant white society in which we live, as well as by the majority of the Asian community. Within our communities our existence as lesbians and gays continues to be denied or is dismissed as a by-product of corrupting Western influences. In fact many of us are internal exiles within our own communities. This is despite the fact that there is an ancient history of homosexuality in India predating the Western history of homosexuality. This history is only now being uncovered by Indian lesbian and gay historians.

Unique to the British context has been the use of the word "black," which was mobilized as a political definition for peoples of African, Asian, and Afro-Caribbean descent. As different ethnic groups use "people of color" in North America, so in Britain a political alliance was formed using the word black. This united us in a fragile alliance against racism, since we experienced British institutional racism in very similar ways. However, in recent years this strategic use has lost its currency as questions of ethnic difference and national identities begin to take primacy.

The mid-1980s have seen a new generation of video artists and filmmakers emerging from the different black communities in Britain. This growth of independent film and video cultures has shown that there are many of us working not only to challenge harmful images but also to construct a whole new language of visual representation. Instead of allowing our marginality to impose a silence on us, we are actively engaged in making videos and films that have begun to redefine and recast notions of "mainstream," "difference," and "otherness."

It is important to create and proclaim assertive and empowering images which question and unsettle the dominant discourses of representation of people who are not white, male, and heterosexual, but it is equally important to move beyond the merely oppositional. Interrupting the discourses of dominant media with a strong counterdiscourse or corrective is sometimes necessary and has been an effective strategy used by some black filmmakers in Britain, particularly in the early 1970s. But one of the dangers with this has been the way in which perceptions of the black communities as a homogeneous group have been reinforced. Differences of class, culture, ethnicity, sexuality, and gender became subjugated, and the black communities were represented as an undifferentiated mass. Diversity, the multiplicity of our histories, experiences, and identities were reduced to "typical" and "representative" stereotypes.

My personal and political history of involvement in the antiracist movement in the mid-seventies, in feminism, and in lesbian and gay initiatives has given me the grounding for my work in film and video in many fundamental ways.

The development of cultural studies in the mid-eighties has been an important theoretical influence on my work as a filmmaker, and on the work of many other black filmmakers. As a postgraduate student at the Centre for Contemporary Cultural Studies at the University of Birmingham in the early eighties, I was involved with a group of students in writing and publishing the book, *The Empire Strikes Back: Race and Racism in 70s Britain.*[5] Our project was to examine the everyday lived experiences of black British people as culture. We developed critiques of the paradigms of race relations which had consistently pathologized black cultures and communities. We also critiqued white feminist theory and practice which did not acknowledge or grapple with the power dynamics around race and class. We rejected their Eurocentric bias and put forward our own analysis. We were the new generation that saw ourselves as both black and British, and, unlike the dominant communities, we did not see a contradiction between these two terms. Our alternative discourse around issues of race, gender, national identity, sexual identity, and culture marked a turning point. We, the children of postcolonial migrant citizens, were indeed striking back with no punches pulled.

As one of the founding members of the first black lesbian group in Britain in 1984, it was invigorating finally to find a community of lesbians of color where we could talk about our common experiences of racism and isolation within the white lesbian and feminist community, as well as share cultural similarities and a sense of integration. The collective empowerment that came as a result of this coming together was also crucial for our political visibility. The key point here was that my experiences as a woman, as a lesbian, and as an Asian person were not compartmentalized or seen as mutually exclusive; instead it was the ways in which I/we located ourselves within and between these differing subjectivities that gave us a sense of integration. This was against the duality that was constantly being either self-imposed or externally imposed upon us, so that the much-asked question of whether we were going to prioritize our race over our sexuality was made redundant. This claim to an integrated identity was a strategic claim inasmuch as many of us found political empowerment in a collective group identity and a heightening of our consciousness. Of course, in due course many of us also realized that "there is no real me to return to, no whole self that synthesizes the woman, the woman of color, and the (writer or the artist or the lesbian). There are, instead, diverse recognitions of self through difference, and unfinished, contingent, arbitrary closures that make possible both politics and identity."[6]

It was only in the late eighties that a rigorous critique of an "identity politics" was initiated, attempting to prioritize or create hierarchies of oppression. This revealed some extremely useful and positive insights, namely, that it is the constant negotiating between these identities that provides the framework for our cultural and political practice. Secondly, identities are not fixed in time and space, but what is valuable is the multiplicity of our experiences as lesbians of color, as women and as black people. June Jordan, the black American poet, writer, and political activist, has said, "We should try to measure each other on the basis of what we do for each other rather than on the basis of who we are."[7]

Indeed, some of the insights about the fluctuating nature of identities and a critique of identity politics have been pioneered and initiated by black feminists and feminists of color, and subsequently incorporated into writings on black cultural production.[8]

The choices I have made about what themes or issues to highlight in my work have also been about timing, funding, and how particular political moments have thrown up urgent issues. For example, I made the video *ReFraming AIDS* in the summer of 1987, when there were concerted and massive attacks both at the local and national level against lesbian and gay rights in Britain. This was at a time when the first government media campaign on AIDS fuelled existing antigay prejudices by representing AIDS as a gay plague. The antigay blacklash was vehement, and through the video

I wanted to create a space where different lesbians and gays could talk about the content of that backlash, for instance showing how black lesbians and gay men were being affected specifically around immigration and policing, and how AIDS was being used to further restrict the entry of black people into the country. By intercutting the government media ads with images and voices from the lesbian and gay communities, I also attempted to subvert the dominant images of the disease by linking ideas about racial difference, social difference, and sexuality in an historical context. The filmmaker Stuart Marshall was instrumental in allowing me to make these historical connections within the video.

One of the responses to my making *ReFraming AIDS* was that of surprise. What was I, an Asian lesbian, doing making a video about AIDS that did not have just black women's voices, but also the voices of black and white men? Why had I dared to cross the boundaries of race and gender? Underlying this criticism was the idea that, as an Asian lesbian filmmaker, my territory should be proscribed and limited to my very specific identities, and to my "own" communities.

It is such experiences that have reinforced my criticism of an essentialist identity politics as being divisive, exclusionary, and retrogressive. I would assert that our territories should be as broad as we choose. Without doubt we still need categories of self-enunciation, but we need them in a political and theoretical discourse on identity which gives us the space for the diversity of our imaginations and visions.

While it is crucial to acknowledge Stuart Hall's valuable insight that "it is important to recognize that we all speak from a particular place, out of particular experiences, histories and cultures," for me it is equally important that we are not constrained and contained by those positions . . . by fixed identity tags . . . that we do not get caught up in an essentialist "bantustan"[9] that decrees that you do not cross boundaries of your experiences. Such prescriptive thinking can be both creatively and politically stultifying.

One of my concerns as a filmmaker is to challenge the normalizing and universalizing tendencies within the predominantly white lesbian and gay communities—to assert the diversity of cultural and racial identities within the umbrella category of gay and lesbian. There is a need also to redefine "community," and just as there isn't a homogeneous black community, similarly there isn't a monolithic lesbian and gay community.

In my video *Memory Pictures,* and my films *Flesh and Paper* and *Khush,* I interrogate Asian gay and lesbian identities in ways which point to the complexities that we occupy as lesbians and gays of color. I explore our histories of diaspora, the memories of migration and upheaval, the search for an integration of our many selves, and the celebration of "us," our differences, and our eroticisms.

It is a condition of these postmodernist times that we all live heterogeneous realities, constructing our sense of selves through the hybridity of cultural practices, and this is inevitably reflected in the aesthetic form employed in my work. The form itself needs to be interrogated as much as the content, and by using a combination of styles and narratives—for instance, documentary realism, poetry, dramatic reconstructions, experimental, autobiographical— I attempt to enunciate the nuances of our subjectivities in my work. Furthermore, the influences of the mass media and popular culture inevitably find their way into the work in a self-conscious way. The four-minute video, *Bhangra Jig,* commissioned by Channel Four as a "television intervention" piece to celebrate Glasgow as the cultural capital of Europe for 1991, borrows unashamedly from advertising codes and pop promos.

In the film *Khush,* which I made for Channel Four's lesbian and gay series *Out on Tuesday,* one of my strategies was to use a diverse range of visual modes. So, for instance, my reworking of a classical dance sequence from an old Indian popular film utilizes the strategy of disrupting the given heterosexual codes. In the original film, the female dancer's act is intercut with a male gaze, but for *Khush* I reedited this sequence and took out the male gaze. I reused this sequence with scenarios of two Asian women watching and enjoying this dance. The gaze and the spectator became inverted. Clearly, postmodernist interest in reworking available material gives us an opportunity to use strategies of appropriation as an assault on racism, sexism, and homophobia. It is these politicized appropriations of dominant codes and signifying systems which give us powerful weapons in the struggle for empowerment.

This hybrid aesthetic, as it has come to be known, works with and against the "tools of the master" because these are tools which we, as cultural activists and artists, have appropriated and reformulated with our diasporic imaginations. In *Bhangra Jig* this was precisely my aim: to allude to Glasgow's history as the second biggest city of the British empire, as reflected in the city's architectural signs and symbols. At the same time I juxtapose against these memories of colonial carnage the vibrancy of our cultures of resistance: Bhangra music and dance as signifying practices of Asian youth culture, crossovers of reggae, soul, and traditional agrarian Indian music and dance. For *Bhangra Jig* to be shown several times within one week on British TV (known for its history of stereotyping and the invisibility of self-determined imagery of Asian people) not only disrupts dominant ideas of European culture but also offers new meanings of what constitute national cultures and identities.

Just as much as I distance myself from any notion of an essentialist lesbian or black aesthetic, so, too, do I reject the idea that I am forever relegated to the confines of an outsider looking in. Lesbians of color around the world are asserting our visions through film and video, and our creative efforts can only but grow in the twenty-first century as the map continues to be redrawn with our imaginations.

Notes

1. Martha Gever, "The Names We Give Ourselves," in Russell Ferguson et al., eds., *Out There: Marginalization and Contemporary Cultures* (Cambridge/New York: MIT Press and the New Museum of Contemporary Art, 1990), p. 191.

2. Punam Khosla, speaking in the film *Khush*, by Pratibha Parmar, made for Channel Four's lesbian and gay series *Out on Tuesday*, 1991.

3. See the writings of Stuart Hall, Paul Gilroy, Kobena Mercer, Lubaina Himid, and the journal *Third Text*.

4. Edward Said, *After the Last Sky: Palestinian Lives* (New York: Pantheon, 1986).

5. Centre for Contemporary Cultural Studies, *The Empire Strikes Back: Race and Racism in 70s Britain* (London: Hutchinson, 1982).

6. "Woman, Native, Other: Pratibha Parmar Interviews Trinh T. Minh-ha," *Feminist Review* no. 36 (Autumn, 1990) p. 73.

7. Pratibha Parmar, "Other Kinds of Dreams: An Interview with June Jordan," *Feminist Review* no. 31 (Spring, 1989) p. 63.

8. See Barbara Christian, "The Race for Theory," *Feminist Studies*, vol. 4 no. 1 (1988); *Charting the Journey: Writings by Black and Third World Women*, S. Grewal et al., eds. (London: Sheba Feminist Publishers, 1987); Pratibha Parmar, "Black Feminism: The Politics of Articulation," in Jonathan Rutherford, ed., *Identity: Community, Culture, Difference* (London: Lawrence and Wishart, 1990) pp. 101–126.

9. I thank Trinh T. Minh-ha for voicing this very apt analogy.

Working Round the L-Word

YVONNE RAINER

These musings began to take shape over a year ago in a lecture called "Narrative in the (Dis)Service of Identity: Fragments toward a performed lecture dealing with menopause, race, gender and other uneasy bedfellows in the cinematic sheets. Or: How do you begin to think of yourself as white when you've finally gotten used to thinking of yourself as an 'a-woman'?"[1]

I subsequently—a deceptively simple way to say it is: I subsequently became a lesbian, and accordingly revised both paper and title. Let me quote the revised title and beginning of the revised paper: "Narrative in the (Dis)Service of Identity: Fragments toward a performed lecture dealing with menopause, race, gender and other uneasy bedfellows in the cinematic sheets. Or: How do you begin to think of yourself as a lesbian—and white—when you had just about gotten used to the idea of being an 'a-woman'?"

"A young, white, artist-activist in New York City named Gregg Bordowitz begins a lecture on AIDS and safe sex with the words: 'I am gay; I am HIV-antibody positive; I like having sex with men'.

"Bordowitz inspires me to lay it—or something not quite like it—on the line: I am a white, menopausal lesbian, and, after many years of celibacy following decades of a heterosexual identity, I am once again—to borrow a phrase from the medical professionals—sexually active. You may well ask what prompts (what some might call) these embarrassing confessions, or why my sexual preference or sexual activity is anyone's business. Who wants to know? Not any of you, certainly, or, if you do, I feel under no obligation to reward such prurient curiosity. And why should I even mention the words 'white' and 'menopausal' in one breath as though they might in some way be equivalent, when in fact they denote contradictory relations to social privilege, and it is blatantly obvious that I am a middle-aged Caucasian? And if it is not so obvious that I am a lesbian (notwithstanding the short hair and lack of makeup that in some quarters might signify 'butch'), why is it necessary to state my sexual status so baldly?

"If you know anything at all about gay culture in the United States, you can conclude quite correctly from the foregoing that I am a novice at all this, an *arriviste,* newly 'come out', not from the closet, however, but from the sanctuary of heterosexuality, that hallowed site legitimated and regulated by the institutions of patriarchy, not the least of which is the family. Upon learning about my newly launched romantic attachment, a member of my family responded, 'It's wonderful that you're with someone, but you don't have to call yourself a lesbian'. An entire history of disavowal, repression, and persecution is contained in that simple declaration. 'You don't have to call yourself a lesbian'.

"So what does it mean to 'call yourself a lesbian' for the first time at the age of fifty-six? Outside of the usual requests on passport and bank account applications for age, gender, race, and citizenship, I never had to 'call' myself anything but dancer, choreographer, filmmaker, or teacher. I can even remember a time when I didn't question the benefits I enjoyed from being young, white, and middle-class, or the disadvantages that accrued from being female. As recently as six months ago I could describe myself as engaged in a struggle with the reductive nomenclature that defines desire, i.e., 'heterosexual, homosexual, bisexual', believing that by mixing up the terms that position us so implacably as dominant or marginal, privileged or unprivileged, protected or endangered, I could somehow invent a new position for myself, something along the lines of a 'lapsed heterosexual' or 'political lesbian', or even a utopian 'a-woman', the last derived from Monique Wittig's declaration in her 1978 essay, 'The Straight Mind', that 'Lesbians are not women'. If lesbians are not women, I persuaded myself, then I too could renounce the culture-debased designation, *woman.* 'A-woman' was the alternative I came up with. A-womanly. A-womanliness.

"But then, the first time I kissed my female lover on the street, I knew I was into a whole new ball game and that my previous wordplay had been a charade keeping me from acknowledging that—however dormant my sexual drive had been—I had been living in the safe house of heterosexuality, under the illusion that I was benefiting from all the security and legitimation that such habitation could offer, and not realizing that it is a protection system that does not serve everyone equally, especially women. One of the unspoken house rules is that after a certain age women have to move out; you're on your own. Many of us try to pass as young in order to prolong our residency. But the day of reckoning inevitably comes.

"Following from my new sexual status, to 'call myself' a lesbian is not only a statement of sexual preference, it is a way of pointing to where I— and others like me, for the same, also different, reasons—live: outside the safe house, on the edge, in the social margin. As a lesbian and aging woman, I reside in this margin. In contrast, as a Caucasian and successful artist, I reside in what Audre Lorde has called the *mythical norm,* that place in the United States usually reserved for those who are 'white, thin, male, young, heterosexual, Christian, and financially secure.'[2] As you see, I am still about forty percent safe."

In this context, if I'm going to distill out my lesbianism from those other markers of social status that comprise a heterogeneous identity, including lapsed heterosexual, political lesbian, and "a-woman," it might be worthwhile to start from scratch and ask, "What is a lesbian?" If calling myself a "political lesbian" was an attempt to declare solidarity, it was also an effort to challenge the notion of a fixed and closed sexual category. However, once my sexual life had undergone change, I was more than willing to embrace the category, come what may, to indicate my sexual preference. I welcomed and carefully noted every opportunity for formally or casually declaring my new sexual status. "Oh yes, my girlfriend lives near there," or "I'll either be here or at my girlfriend's house; here's the number," or "Now that I'm a lesbian . . . ," and so on. I've already noted the family response. Most people congratulated me on my newfound felicity, but I was amazed to learn that in some quarters lesbians would, like my family members but for different reasons, be reluctant to accord me *lesbian* status. You may be sleeping with a woman but you're not a lesbian.

Hey! what is this? A club or something? I eat pussy just like you. Just 'cause you've been doing it longer does that make you more of a lezzy than me? Well, evidently. Unlike the term "gay man," the word lesbian— at least to some who identify as such—carries more than a sexual meaning. A man comes out and no one questions his credentials as gay. If you're out and a man and have sex with men, then you're gay. But a woman doesn't necessarily become a lesbian by changing the gender of her sleeping companion. In those quarters you have to earn your stripes, have been on the barricades, taken shit, and certainly you must have foresworn men as sexual partners.

OK, OK. I'm not the pushy type. I'm perfectly happy with my neologisms, for the time being, anyway. And I have a strong survival sense: while trying to get into the club I didn't burn my bridges; I didn't give up my identity of a-woman, lapsed heterosexual, and political lesbian. So next year I'll simply reapply. After all, my résumé does contain some impressive data—I marched in the Gay Pride Parade before ever applying for admission to the club, and some of my best friends are lesbians. As for pussy-eating, you'll have to take my word for it.

Yes, I mean to be a bit silly here; forgive me if I strike the wrong note. One thing I find unsettling is that in the gay and lesbian public sphere I am being paid attention to as a lesbian *before* doing any work that identifies me as one. It's not that I wish to preserve privacy, far from it, but as a former member of the dominant sexual category I can still see it as odd that the gender of the person one has sex with is a determining factor in public recognition. This, of course, is a view that a gay person can afford to sustain only in the best of all possible visions of a world. In the world we know, where same-sex preference is a signal for exclusion, ridicule, persecution, and neglect from individuals and institutions that don't have to name their sexual bias, only point to ours, our relegation to weirdo-freak-queer marginality if we do name ourselves still demands that we exceed the bounds of polite address and scream our name. Fundamentalism and essentialism aside, I therefore call myself a lesbian, present myself as a lesbian, and represent myself as a lesbian. This is not to say that it is the last word in my self-definition. "Lesbian" defines not only a sexual identity but also the social "calling," or resistance, made necessary by present societal inequities. I must keep in mind that "white" and "aging woman," as markers of both social privilege and social stigma, form other parts of this identity, and that my status as aging lesbian, however stigmatized in daily life, is not equivalent to the experience of people of color.

On the other hand, whatever my sister-in-law or I or other lesbians call or don't call me, the dominant culture is definitely going to call me a lesbian. The specific negative consequences of this have yet to make their appearance. So far, my life as a lesbian has been filled with satisfying work and unpredicted pleasures. I find myself, however, suddenly in a unique position from which to examine the social benefits I have derived from being a heterosexual for so many years. There is no doubt in my mind that the extent to which I can currently be called a successful artist can be directly traced to a life as a white heterosexual. I doubt if Jill Johnston's championship of my dance work in the early sixties would have been a sufficient impetus to my career without the influence of the white, male artists who also supported it. It is interesting to note that at that time I knew of only two lesbians connected with the Judson Dance Theater, where many of my early performances took place, and their relationship was an object of destructive gossip or detachment on the part of the straight women, and outright harassment by male artists. It is also interesting to speculate about how my career might have fared if the content of my work—both dance and films—had focused on lesbian subjects and subject matter throughout the sixties and seventies.

Yes, I have to say that I enter the arena of lesbian sex with less risk than I might have twenty-five years ago. Beside the career factor there is also the consideration of my age. Because older women are not relevant to dominant sexuality, they can become lesbians with less fear of discrimination. To paraphrase one of the interviewees in *Privilege,* we don't have to please straight men anymore.

It's time to talk more directly about representation. Much has been said to me about Brenda, the lesbian character in *Privilege.* First of all, she is played by a straight woman, one who I belatedly discovered was somewhat homophobic. When we first meet her in the film she has no name because

Jenny, the narrator, has forgotten it. She is the object of a sexual assault and is therefore required to speak generally *for women* and not specifically for lesbians. Later she articulates a questionable psychoanalytic theory aligning people of color and women as victims, which, though contested by the African American documentary filmmaker Yvonne Washington, puts Brenda in the position of crackpot theorist. In her last appearance she is seated on the other side of the desk of an assistant district attorney, confronting him with a quote from Joan Nestle's *A Restricted Country* about an erotic interaction between two women. It is a powerful moment—the DA is dumbfounded—but it is yet another instance of the lesbian character's not being allowed to be seen *in her own life, as a lesbian.* The justification might be that Brenda is a peripheral character seen through the eyes of Jenny, the straight protagonist. But so were the African American and Puerto Rican characters in the film, and yet I managed to place *them* both within the story and outside as commentators on their respective social conditions. This, in fact, was the whole point of the flashback. Unlike these characters, the only opportunity given to Brenda to detach herself from the diegesis and address the camera is her recitation of a short poem by Judy Grahn. I now think that, coming at the end of an intense interaction with her alleged attacker, this was too brief a moment to establish an autonomy and savviness comparable to that of the other characters.

After seeing the film, Geeta Patel, who teaches Indian literature at the University of Iowa, said, "I was impressed by certain omissions, particularly the omission of the lesbian's subjectivity. It suggests that one subjectivity, or its representation, always excludes another." Admittedly, there is a trade-off of subjectivities operating in *Privilege,* but I don't think it need necessarily be the case.

And I don't think one has to be a lesbian to make a film about lesbians. The question arises: How—let alone why—should one speak the struggles of those with whom one does not have precisely the same things at stake? Stated so baldly, the why part of it seems almost like a dumb question, one that must be put into perspective by further questions: If you are no longer of reproductive age, do you drop out of the fight for abortion rights? If you are a man, do you not speak out for women's right to control their bodies? If you are not HIV-positive do you not take a stand against the government's foot-dragging policies around AIDS? If you are white do you not express your revulsion at the neocon defense of white racist behavior on university campuses parading under the First Amendment?

The answers to the above are self-evident to anyone who sees her or himself as a progressive. The ticklish part is when those in more advantageous positions—white, First World, with more money, behind the camera, rewarded, institutionally legitimized—represent the "struggles of others."

Brenda (Blaire Baron) and Carlos (Rico Elias) in *Privilege,* Yvonne Rainer

The debates around documentary and ethnographic film have amply deline-ated the problems inherent in the invisibility and supposed neutrality or objectivity of the filmmaker, who is *ipso facto* empowered. As for fictional scenarios, it has become painfully clear to me that when peripheral fictional characters are used to represent people who are also peripheral in white-dominated society, those characters must be given their day in court. Overall, this is not news to me. As I indicated before, I have been more than theoreti-cally aware of the dangers in using marginalized people casually, that is, without making reference to their particular marginalized positions. In re-sponse to criticism about Brenda that followed screenings I attended before becoming a lesbian, I would agree on the specifics, but then justified her characterization on the basis of her *feminism.* I maintained that she spoke for both feminists *and* lesbians. This would have been fine if her lesbianism had had a more complete airing *vis á vis* scenes in which she would not have had to be *accountable to heterosexuals.* As things now stand in the film, Brenda is the patsy. The mistake is telling: Jenny, the straight, white protago-nist, is concerned about her racism, not about her homophobia. Her last line is a portent of things to come in the life of her creator, namely me. When Yvonne Washington asks her if she ever "made it with Brenda," Jenny replies, "Hell no, I was terrified of women."

Brenda confronts the Assistant District Attorney, *Privilege,* Yvonne Rainer

So, on to new cultural work. In closing I shall relay some scenes and notations for a new film that as yet has no story.

Possible opening: An almost-deserted beach, maybe Coney Island, slightly garbage-strewn, very wide shot. The theme music from Jaws *is heard. Steadicam begins to meander toward two figures who cannot at first be identified as the focal point of the shot. Two white women in their early sixties are seated in the sand, leaning against a sea wall (San Francisco?) or against a support under the boardwalk. One is huddled under a blanket, speaking while the other listens. As we approach we begin to hear their conversation.*

WOMAN #1: So what's it like?
WOMAN #2: What's *what* like?
#1 *(laughing)*: Whadya mean "what?" Sex of course.

We are now in CU on Woman #2's face, which is in three-quarter or complete profile.

#2: *(after thinking for a bit she delivers line with a cunning smile)*: You know something? Never in my wildest dreams, my most far-out fantasies,

did I ever come close to imagining that I would one day be able to say—
with the utmost conviction—"*I love eating pussy.*"

My mother, far into her dotage, was looking at a photo of Marilyn
Monroe. She said, "What beautiful breasts she has." My brother later remarked—in disbelief—"She sounded just like a man!"

Conversation between two white women in their seventies:

#1: . . . and they had this wonderful old dog named Emma . . . Emma . . .
G, begins with a G . . .
#2: Goldman.
#1: Emma Goldman. And she had this great trick. She had two . . . two . . .
she would fetch a blue or red . . . (gesticulating wildly)
#2: What?
#1: She would fetch . . . what you throw in the air . . . you know . . .
(gesticulating)
#2: frisbee!
#1: Yes! frisbee!

*Lesbians #1 and #2 are lying nude at opposite ends of a bed. One lies with
her feet resting on the breasts of the other. Her toes play with her lover's
nipples. They are engaged in a serio-comic discussion around "What constitutes a lesbian?"*

#1: Well, *your* credentials as a bona-fide lesbian have never been in question.
#2: No, that's not true. My old girl friend always said I wasn't the real thing
because I had been married. . . . Not only that but I'd had sex with men.
#1: You mean she never fucked a man, even once? That's pretty extreme,
isn't it?
#2: I'd say it's fairly common.
#1: Oh Christ, then they'll never let *me* in, after my lifetime of copulation.
And here I had thought all I had to do was give up wearing two earrings.
But I don't even know if I *want* to be in the club! I don't want to be a
professional lesbian.
#2: I don't know about the professional part, but really, do you have a
choice? You're a lesbian, like it or not.
#1: How do you *know?*
#2: I don't sleep with straight women.
#1: I was straight when you first got involved with me.
#2: No you weren't. A straight woman wouldn't have behaved the way you
did.
#1: You mean, at the Clit Club? How did I behave? Tell me again, my love.
Tell me about the rabbits and the chickens.

#2: (*laughing*): The way you came on to me. Only a lesbian would have behaved like that.

#1: OK, I'm a lesbian. I'll take your word for it . . . for now.

C's STORY: I fell in love with a woman in Australia. I had always known it was a possibility. I was there for six weeks. She was wonderful. Then when I came home I let her come visit me, and it was a dreadful mistake. I couldn't stand the social thing. As a heterosexual I don't have to say I'm heterosexual or be known as something special, but as a lesbian I would be put into this category and I couldn't stand it.

N's STORY: After my divorce seven years ago, which was very ugly and nightmarish, I vowed I would never get involved in something like that again. So I've been pretty much alone since then. In feminism it's a big problem here [Germany]. Lesbians have their own conferences and culture. Feminist conferences include lesbians, but the differences are never talked about. And much of the organizing wouldn't happen without the lesbians because they are the most active and energetic and advanced in their thinking.

Notes

1. This essay is based on a talk delivered at the Lookout Lesbian and Gay Television Festival on October 13, 1991, at Downtown Community Television in New York City.
2. Audre Lorde, "Age, Race, Class, and Sex: Women Redefining Difference," in *Out There: Marginalization and Contemporary Cultures,*" Russell Ferguson et al. eds. (Cambridge/New York: MIT Press/The New Museum, 1990) p. 282.

1993

On the Make: Activist Video Collectives

CATHERINE SAALFIELD — DIVA TV
member

for Raymond Navarro

This paper could have been written by a group of people. In all but the most basic sense, it was. As I draw upon experiences of people in "real-life activist video collectives," this insider's view is not the result of an un-collective process. I want to discuss the underpinnings of our work, the fuel for it, the subjects and the products, and the relationship between those things. After I explain this endeavor, one collaborator turns her head, looks at me from the side of her face, and says, "I really don't think twenty pages will be enough." Sure. But we have to start somewhere. So, true to collective process, the first thing on the agenda is to set the agenda.

Setting the (Alternative) Agenda

During the last few years, gay and lesbian and AIDS-activist video collectives in New York City have caused a chain reaction of grassroots production. Often there's no office or telephone. Often the members meet a lot of times, with not enough time, anytime, and, when the crunch is on, all night long. Some persevere, continuously producing clips like a radical newsreel. Others make one tape, get a little exposure, and then procrastinate or get distracted by other productions, with members regrouping in another collective with a different acronym. All get at least a little bogged down in bureaucracy, but maybe only for a moment before getting back in gear.

Across these variations, no one gets anywhere without an agenda. Besides, an agenda—whether to foreground activists with AIDS protesting their own limited access to health care, or to represent lesbians and gays of color in an empowering and insightful way—is usually what brings the group together in the first place. Often more than one agenda, of the personal and historical type, crowd the room, and never do just a few remain hidden. Whether the problem is a peculiar editing style, previous sexual involvement with someone in the group, authoritarian ego, dogmatism, or political desperation, collectivities often bury their motivations in irrelevant and frustrating cat fights or frantic forays into distracting topics. Just as we bring our temperamental dispositions and frequently humorous mood swings to a shoot, we can't hang our desires like a jacket at the door when we get together to edit. The impetus for this work is passion, and lust haunts many a move.

It's time to chose a facilitator, even though not everyone's here yet and the meeting was supposed to start half an hour ago. Someone's on the phone in the other room. Someone's on the other line in another bedroom. Someone's piling more beers into the overstocked fridge. Someone's hanging out with a unaffiliated housemate, and to everyone's distraction, someone's cranking the stereo volume and gyrating with the fantasy partner of Queen Latifah.

Rule number one: the facilitator and the host cannot be the same person. As we narrow down potential nominees for the job, a harried member whisks in with papers falling to the floor and his shoes untied; "Sorry I'm late, but my *other* meeting ran over." On his backpack there's a pin which reads, "Process is for cheese." I pour more diet coke into my coffee mug.

The facilitator uses the back of an old party invitation to scrawl out an agenda, as the topics are listed. The final order (and does anyone have a problem with this?): introductions, announcements (gotta be short), counter-surveillance at upcoming demonstrations (when are they?), the current tape (screening of rough cuts and then half an hour of discussion), distribution initiatives (fifteen minutes), cable group update (another fifteen), speaking engagements and presentations (ten minutes, to be continued by subcommittee), future projects (will we ever get this far?).

Exchanging Names and Numbers

All right, we've allotted five minutes for introductions. Newbies first. Who you are and what you do.

The most recent effort in New York City of more than two inverts getting together to make a video about queer issues is House of Color. This group was the brainstorm of Robert Garcia, who, fantasizing about an explosive mix of lesbians and gays of color from various backgrounds, invited everyone to a meeting. In this case, "invitation only" presumes a shared ideology, a shared goal. The premeditated nature of House (as it is called by its intimate relations) sets it apart from other collectives discussed here. Ultimately, their work is about the web and weave of dynamics within the group and how the experience of working on their tapes affects and empowers other gays and lesbians of color. Their main focus is not necessarily the interaction of their work with a viewing audience.

Robert Mignott, Jeff Nunokawa, Pamela Sneed, Jocelyn Taylor, and Julie Tolentino all joined what would become House of Color because they were Robert's friend—or roommate: "I really say no way of getting out of it." They also live with a double-edged invisibility of being people of color in various queer communities and being queer in various communities of color. They found the final member, Wellington Love, at a swinging downtown benefit for a different group with overlapping membership.

Although it's the most closed collective of the bunch, House exemplifies the political urgency and upbeat confidence common to all. Their original project was to produce three-minute blips with commentary on any range of issues, which would be interspersed during mostly milky-white programming on gay cable channels. Their first deadline narrowed this intent, and they produced the five-minute *I Object*, which glimpses at, and simultaneously revisions, exoticized and eroticized people of color as icons of beauty. In *I Object*, intermittent remarks by the producers break up what otherwise might feel like commercial TV, or like the inside of some mainstream fashion

I Object, House of Color

magazine: (white) face after (white) face, skimpy (white) women running around in next to nothing. Next page, (black) women, skimpy as well, and running around in next to nothing too, but with a different, sometimes almost subtle, exotic quality. Maybe it was the leopard skin underwear.

I Object has been described as "spunky," a term apropos of rapidly successful upstarts. Given that very few of the members of this collective had any background in video, the tape represents a powerful combination of suggestive shots, rhythmic editing, political savvy, excellent tunes, and great looks. Shot on borrowed equipment, in collective members' homes, edited at work after-hours, and finished a couple of minutes before its premiere in a video marathon at a popular nightclub, *I Object* is an origin story of sorts, one that aptly describes the nativity of many collectives.

Clearly a predecessor of House, the Paper Tiger Television Collective (PTTV), was the brainstorm of a few media agitators who were interested in exercising the democratic mandates of public access cable TV in the early eighties. Since then, the Paper Tiger production philosophy has influenced the evolution of many New York City video collectives and should rightfully be credited as a model for much quick-and-dirty media that evolved later in the decade. As an urgent response by, for, and about the ever-present medium of television, PTTV demonstrates a methodology by which to reinterpret cultural misrepresentations using the very same tools of their production. Cofounder DeeDee Halleck has noted, "There was a very conscious effort to make *Paper Tiger* a model for cheap television, to think about what those elements are in television that make television what it is."[1] House of Color continues the tradition of calling to question the racist, sexist, and homophobic backbone of network television that posits all "special interest groups" as such.

Paper Tiger's weekly shows—aired citywide on public access television, with roll-ins—have a handmade look and an immediate message. By challenging network forms of television, it represents alternative TV, and can be watched not only at home but also in community centers and galleries, in schools and organizational meetings. Fundamentally, the group maintains that people "should be able to work in media, so they can be critical of the mass media and not victims of mass culture."[2] Whereas network TV perpetuates the hierarchical structure by which it is produced, the collective nature of the particular alternative media at issue here redefines a long, profit-guided history of nonparticipatory forms of TV production.

True to form, the PTTV collective is completely open to volunteers, so most progressive video producers in the city today, at one time or another, either have worked on a Paper Tiger tape, spiritually guided one, or been a commentator who deconstructed a propaganda mechanism of the information industry for one of their programs. Paper Tiger encourages anyone who already knows (or is willing to learn) about a certain topic, to investigate relevant documents, organize a script, paint a backdrop, put the headphones on, and get behind a camera. In PTTV, producers are encouraged to research, analyze, and represent social and political issues despite (and at the same time, because of) their own race, gender, class, age, and sexual identity.

Between its New York City headquarters and Paper Tiger/Southwest, a San Diego affiliate, the fluid group of lesbians, straights, and gay men that comprise PPTV—more or less in that order—has produced four of the earliest activist documentaries pertaining to the AIDS crisis. In *PWAC Talks Back* (1988) the late Max Navarre of the People with AIDS Coalition (PWAC), discusses the organization's unique publications *Surviving and Thriving with AIDS* and *PWAC Newsline,* a monthly newsletter. In *Simon Watney Speaks about Clause 28* (1988) the author of *Policing Desire: Pornography, AIDS and the Media* provides a scathing critique of homophobia in the UK by closely reading the mainstream media coverage of England's repressive legislation against queers. Like Jesse Helms's parallel amendment to a bill on AIDS education funding, Section 28 limits government support for "materials which promote homosexuality."

Then the San Diego crew came out with *Transformer AIDS* in 1989, which features University of California, San Diego graduate Bob Kinney illustrating the vacuity of Ronald Reagan's lip service to the AIDS crisis. Two years later the same queer crew again occupied the university's in-house studio and graced us with *The Silence that Silences,* which calls into question "pictures without context." Kinney examines desolate, desperate, lonely photographs of people with AIDS taken by Rosalind Solomon and Nicholas Nixon, and sees not the implied "AIDS victim," but rather a manipulated image of people living with AIDS who seem to lack agency and voice, unlike many people with HIV who are vehemently fighting with their lives, for support, love, family, friends, lovers, and themselves. Like other activist collectives, PTTV/Southwest also used footage of protests in its half-hour reformulations of mistaken, mainstream dictum, changing a documentary into unapologetic agitprop.

Such informal linkages as those between the Paper Tiger collective and ⟵ House of Color similarly inform the history of another early, collectively produced tape on the AIDS crisis, *Testing the Limits: NYC.* In spring 1987, the Testing the Limits Collective (TTL) turned out their half-hour documentary about what some people living with AIDS were saying and doing about the dominant heedlessness of government and medical officials. Notably, the gay and lesbian liberation movement was the genesis both for this collective video work and for the earliest activist responses to the AIDS crisis. After taping demonstrations against the 1986 *Bowers v. Hardwick* Supreme Court decision, which upheld state sodomy laws, a few folks got together in the familiar networking-the-circle fashion to record the growing AIDS activism in New York City. The early TTL members were lesbian, gay, and straight: David Meieran, Gregg Bordowitz, Hilery Joy Kipnis, Sandra Elgear, Robyn Hutt, and, later, Jean Carlomusto. In 1986 and 1987, they spent six more months covering various demonstrations of ACT UP (the AIDS Coalition to Unleash Power). Subsequently, they completed the tightly edited and well contextualized *Testing the Limits: NYC* about the swirling hellhole of AIDS deaths, panic, misinformation, and governmental bigotry that the city had become.

TTL attracted many other eager video jocks from the paisley of ACT UP's energetic band, many of whom created DIVA TV (Damned Interfering Video Activist Television), which targets ACT UP members as its primary audience and makes videos by, about, and, most importantly, *for* the movement. Nine folks founded DIVA: Ray Navarro, Jean Carlomusto, Gregg Bordowitz, Bob Beck, Costa Pappas, Ellen Spiro, George Plagianos, Rob Kurilla, and myself. All TTL members were immediately considered members of DIVA, because we thrive as a loose affiliation that chronicles the commotion around City Hall, at the Stock Exchange, inside the Department of Health—some key

Transformer AIDS: Bob Kinney Looks at Media and Governmental Response to AIDS, Paper Tiger TV Southwest

targets of ACT UP/NY. By its very definition, DIVA stands in opposition to closed or hierarchical groups. As DIVA Peter Bowen writes, "Rather than having a fixed membership, a bank account, a solid identity, DIVA floats freely, making tapes with the money, technical resources and labor that is available at any one meeting. . . . I learned firsthand the political effects of such a democratic production schedule. Borrowing a camera for one ACT UP demo, I learned to shoot video. Abandoned in the editing room one afternoon, I learned to edit it."[3]

Ah, if it *were* that easy. DIVA, like all activist collectives, functions best when the folks involved are excited about a given project, the end and the means of it, and the process of creating. But sometimes the flurry of the moment puts us all out of control. The saying "too many cooks spoil the broth" comes to mind. We can't continue to have one group initiate and outline a given show, and then have three newcomers responsible for editing the segments together. Our last tape wallowed a year in postproduction for this reason, even though each week we renewed our collective commitment to get the piece out. A rational remedy looms before us: no more middle-of-the-show crew reorganization; at least one production team must remain in place from the beginning to the end of each project. Furthermore, never forfeit the essential goal of inclusivity, with open lines of communication among collective members for expressing opinions and offering analyses. Here protest is the process, communication is our form of resistance, and everyone has a say.

A sense of urgency propels DIVA through personality clashes, busy schedules when we'd all rather procrastinate, people competing, moving on, burning out, and arguing. And we have persisted through the loss of two of our most spirited members to AIDS. Actually, it's hard to specify how much that hinders our process and how much it thrusts us headlong into grinding production. In any case, when ACT UP organizes a demonstration, DIVAs organize to be there, document, provide protection and countersurveillance, and participate. The final products, needless to say, vary wildly. Since DIVAs like to interview (hyper)activists mid-arrest and are often themselves learning how to run the rig mid-shoot, the images aren't always steady. With all the hullabaloo in the background, the comments aren't always perfectly audible. Still, we're in good company, since the quick-and-dirty model has existed since the invention of the moving image.

Julio Garcia Espinosa begins his influential essay, "For an Imperfect Cinema," "Nowadays perfect cinema—technically and artistically masterful—is almost always reactionary cinema."[4] This isn't to say that any tape with low production values, glitches, and jerky camera movement is a progressive and deserving piece of work. It's a question of priorities. "Armed propaganda" goes nowhere if bogged down by corporate approaches to the technical aspects of logo manufacturing and the unfathomable cost of crystal-clear images and sound. Plus, "perfect cinema" remains fundamentally incompatible with the unpredictable and spontaneous activist approach towards life-and-death situations.

Announcements

Announcements often serve as a reality check. They tie us and our concerns into a larger context of innovative community-based groups and individuals confronting traditional modes of representation:

> One of the many aims of an AIDS-activist cultural practice is to explore and expose the gaps between such rhetorical terms as "the nation," "the family," or "the community," and the complex reality that they mask. Such gaps are especially significant in a time of crisis, when one may well discover that one's very life counts for extremely little. . . . How can one explain this to other people in such a way that they might be able to identify with one's desperate situation, and be empowered to act collectively on the basis of their new perceptions? Of what might such action most effectively consist?
>
> —Simon Watney[5]

> Information exchange among imagemakers and activists is vital. Video activists should organize among themselves, whether producing a collaborative project, looking out for each other at an event, or coordinating complete documentation. Organizing insures that important events get recorded.
>
> —Ellen Spiro[6]

> Art *does* have the power to save lives, and it is this very power that must be recognized, fostered, and supported in every way possible. But if we are to do this, we will have to abandon the idealist conception of art. We don't need a cultural renaissance; we need cultural practices actively participating in the struggle against AIDS. We don't need to transcend the epidemic; we need to end it.
>
> —Douglas Crimp[7]

> It was the early representations of AIDS and the "Don't do it"-type posters, coupled with the Tory posters: "Young, gay, and proud," "Policing the classrooms," and "Sex education taught in schools" and so forth—a whole hidden agenda specifically around race and sex. . . . I tried to combat it through *This Is Not an AIDS Advertisement,* which is an ad for gay desires. I'm being a propagandist, using images and representations of sexuality to celebrate love and desire. . . . *Testing the Limits: NYC* . . . has a very politically activist agenda, but asks: how can you describe loss of friends

or the total re-direction we are taking in our identity, which we all have to negotiate now? Our tapes take a stance; there's an edge to them.

—Isaac Julien[8]

So the fight is for, let us say, representation, but in new forms; forms that are bound up more with participation than delegation, dependent on significant associations of people rather than recorded majorities, moving towards the development of a non-representative representation: the achievement of modes of presentation and imaging and entertainment and argument that are the realizations of collective desires, group aspirations, common projects, shared experience.

—Stephen Heath[9]

Who's Got the Power

Next on the agenda is countersurveillance, because there are demos this week that need to be covered; those activists committing civil disobedience and risking arrest are counting on us. Originally, DIVA TV came together because the cops who patrol our protests and arrest us like to do it with a heavy dose of gratuitous force. We need to protect our fellow activists by providing synchronized countersurveillance at the Centers for Disease Control, at the Post Office, on the Brooklyn Bridge, and in front of abortion clinics threatened by antichoice Operation Rescue fanatics. Whatever measures we can take to guard our folks—who handcuff themselves to desks, hang banners off the scaffolding of city buildings, interrupt the Stock Exchange—are always welcomed. So everyone in ACT UP who has a camcorder, some experience, or a desire to participate in a demonstration in a new way, can come to a meeting. ACT UPers with camcorders still bump elbows on the front lines but now at least we know each other's names.

Do we have camerapeople going to the protest in West Harlem at St. Luke's Hospital? They're closing Women and Babies Hospital. Will someone do demo support for the folks picketing at the trial of the Stop the Church defendants? Suzanne Wright and Gerry Albarelli will be covering Saturday's needle exchange on the Loisaida.

Sometimes our raw footage seems redundant, obligatory; more often it is sensational, if only because demo-graphics brighten even the most boring concrete edifice in the midst of a parking lot. All the rugged bods getting thrown around certainly look impressive, but, importantly, this footage has also served as evidence in court. After a big demo, the phone rings off the hook with demonstrators who need shots of their arrests. After we stormed the National Institutes of Health in Bethesda, Maryland, one ACT UPer faced a trial for assaulting an officer. He was acquitted after showing the judge footage of himself passively resisting arrest (that is, refusing to stand up for the cop, which *is* resisting arrest, not assaulting an officer). We've got an image bank of cops bending peoples' wrists to the breaking point, of cops slamming protestors on the back and shoulders with billy clubs, of cops trying to intimidate AIDS activists with big yellow dishwashing gloves, of cops threatening nonviolent protesters with trumped-up charges of assault.

While compiling our first production, *Target City Hall,* which chronicles ACT UP's March 28, 1989 demonstration against then-mayor Ed Koch and his hideously neglectful administration, the late Costa Pappas came to a meeting with a half-inch, glitch-filled, brilliant, nine-minute segment complete with stop-motion images and a musical interlude. He had crash-cut this gem on two home VCRs. We promised to get him a new cassette for the next day's action, since he always used every inch of tape, recording more originals on the heels of a master edit. In the clip, Costa trails one affinity group, CHER (Cathy Has Extra Rollers or Concerned Homos Espousing Reality), for the entire day.[10] He shows them deciding when to enter the fray, chanting and bouncing into the middle of the Brooklyn Bridge off ramp, being dragged away in stilled frames cut to a folksy '60s song, and finally processing their varied perspectives on the jail experience at the party afterwards.

The treasured alliance which emerges in this pragmatic approach to media production never ceases to amaze me. Street activists looking to us for technological confidence understand the process involved in, and thus the potential for, alternative television. They not only flock to screenings to see themselves and their ex-lovers going limp for the women and men in blue, but now they come to us during the planning stages.

By exploiting the mass production of consumer format equipment, we manage to rig several DIVAs, usually in pairs, for each event. We garner a lot of strength from sharing resources, costs, technical expertise, information, and editing facilities. We have created for ourselves a viable production community which gathers after-hours at the various nonprofit media centers where some of us work during the day as professional TV and video producers. Teams of two or three edit each segment at different locations, such as Gay Men's Health Crisis, Electronic Arts Intermix, Testing the Limits, Downtown Community Television Center, Paper Tiger, as well as the ad hoc production centers that several of our own homes have become.

The AIDS Crisis Is Not Over

It's time to talk about the current work, the tape which exists in pieces at the fingers of the team now laying control track, turning dials, monitoring sound levels, and typing titles in the editing suite. Scanning demo reels for dramatic arrest images, good statements by onlookers, and useful cutaways, we spend countless caffeine-induced sleepless nights with cottonmouth from too many salty pretzels. For these reasons, this section was allotted thirty minutes, more than anything else on the agenda.

Although the working styles of TTL and DIVA were born from the same principles, the two groups have veered in opposite directions, partly as a reaction to each other's choices and to account for the diverse challenges we face. TTL received considerable pressure to produce a powerful and useful sequel to their first piece. But they couldn't have foreseen all the dimensions of their popularity and significance. The choice presented itself: institutionalize and prosper, or stick to principles more attuned to the quick-and-dirty approach—limited audience, inconsistent participation by collective members, and more process than product. Following some philosophical disagreements and divisions over these options, the remaining members decided to set up an office. Consequently, grant money must be earmarked for office rental and phones, applications to foundations must be processed efficiently, and precise scheduling takes the place of phone tag in assembling a crew. TTL became a formal group of three producers: David, Robyn, and Sandra; assistant editor Lisa Guido; scattered ad hoc camerapeople; and volunteer fund-raisers. Upon completion of *Voices from the Front,* TTL remains a vital component of the New York AIDS community, and they still generously share their impressive activist archive and three-quarter-inch off-line editing system.

Watching TTL evolve into an institutionalized organization reinforced DIVA's commitment to working as a collective. We remain fluid, make decisions with whomever comes to a meeting, and resist assigning a treasurer by dedicating any income to buying tape stock. Yet, despite the structural differences, many of the same processes endure in all of the collectives.[11] People are supposed to bring in rough cuts or raw footage, either of segments (DIVA), shows (PTTV), paper edits (TTL), or interviews (House). This is what holds us together: the material we've mulled over since the previous meeting. For DIVA, edited segments appear according to very strict deadlines. Whatever appears on the night chosen for rough cut previews may get minor revisions, and then goes into the completed show. That the sections connect coherently speaks to a shared vision of the uses of radical media: how to make it, stretch it, challenge it, change it. And the enormity of the AIDS crisis dictates the passionate approach. On the other hand, the fact that the segments are also stylistically distinct speaks to the influence of television. We either act in entertained accordance with or in critical opposition to the tube. For example, some producers are comfortable rapidly chopping shots to house beats, while others who don't like voice-over narration favor talking heads.

After *Pride '69–'89,* (about the weekend that lesbians and gays spent commemorating it), DIVA churned out *Like a Prayer,* an assembly of five- to seven-minute perspectives on the ACT UP/WHAM! demonstration Stop the Church at St. Patrick's Cathedral, on December 10, 1989. Protesting Cardinal O'Connor's deadly policies on AIDS, homosexuality, abortion, and safe sex, activists demonstrated ingenuity of costume (clown noses and fluorescent wigs), posters and slogans ("Cardinal O'Condom"), and commentary (including lesbian and gay ex-Catholics expressing their disgust with Catholic bigotry).

The wafer group met at Craig Paull's off-line office equipped with half-inch editing equipment. Craig set up his hi–8 camera on the tripod to interview ACT UP member Tom Keane, who was responsible for "desecrating the host." His was the story that garnered the most media attention, and crumpled wafers evolved into a raging public debate perpetuated by political personalities casting about for votes. Another section is presented as a fable, centering on an evil sorcerer who speaks to his people, "filling them with ignorance and blinding them with lies." The promotional shorts which

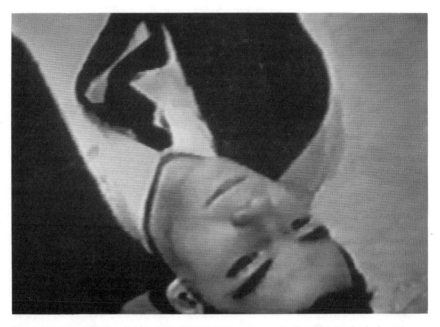

A protestor participating in the ACT UP/WHAM! action at St. Patrick's Cathedral, New York City, in *Like a Prayer,* DIVA TV

advertised Stop the Church in advance are incorporated to provide a thread. In one, the late Ray Navarro, playing his favorite role of Jesus with a crown of thorns, toga, and jimmy hat, tells the audience to "be sure your Second Coming is a safe one. Use a condom, every time."[12] Shot with the same cruddy camera, faulty mic, and desk lights, another has apples being bagged in condoms to the tune of "New York, New York." Parodying a simple safe-sex dictum, it ends with Ray's nimble fingers topping off a statuette of the Empire State Building with a condom, Christoesque, wearing its politics on its sleeve.

We dedicated *Like a Prayer* to Costa, a DIVA supreme and a fierce AIDS activist who died of AIDS-related complications on December 26, 1989. We used footage from different demos where he was shooting or dancing, always wearing his DIVA press pass, and, once, expounding on the pleasures of being a DIVA. *Target City Hall* is dedicated to Steve Zabel—an unassuming man who single-handedly stocked the most thorough video archive of lesbian, gay, and AIDS activism in New York—who was murdered in his apartment on February 28, 1989.

Making memorial tapes collectively has been one of the only revitalizing aspects of grieving. The memorial tape for Ray Navarro stands on its own and was spontaneously produced by an ad hoc group of his close friends: John Greyson, Gregg Bordowitz, Jean Carlomusto, and myself. We had worked in different combinations on videos before. We had worked on deadline before. But faced with Ray's death, the four of us found ourselves conceptualizing a reservoir for our friend, a reservoir which turned out to be the power of collective action. For two days we were there, exorcising, purging, processing, crying, giggling, and longing for an image to last forever, or better, to come back to life. We scoured the raw material of many videographers. Looking through footage of the Thanksgiving dinner before he got sick and the demo at the FDA, pausing for Ray's wide grin at a midnight gathering in his studio, trying to identify him at the takeover of the Sixth International AIDS Conference in Montréal, searching everywhere to find even the back of his head or his elbow, we plotted to preserve and to persevere. The finished tape was ultimately for the people who would crowd into his memorial service the next day. But for us, it was a defense, our last word about losing a collaborator, a lover, a best friend.

Spreading the Word

The facilitator gets nudged from poring over today's paper. "Let's go on to distribution. Two announcements. ACT UP needs more VHS copies of *Target City Hall* to sell at the Monday night meetings. And we gotta get volunteers to answer these calls for tapes and mail preview copies. Now a report from the cable group. We've got fifteen minutes for this, so let's rock and roll through this section."

Instead, a new guy raises his hand, talking at the same time: "What audience are these tapes directed to? Who are we making them for? Should we address them to people who don't know the meaning of all the acronyms in the alphabet soup?" The old members want to know if the constituency of ACT UP isn't reason enough for our efforts. The shows function as propaganda for empowerment and recruitment, for education and enjoyment. None of the allotted time takes into account this unexpected inquiry into our theory and practice. We have to vote to extend this section by five minutes. After ten minutes of discussion about the vote itself, the proposal to go on another five minutes passes unanimously. We can see the future projects section getting bumped to next week, again.

Originally, we needed imagery by, for, and about us. People with suppressed immune systems never speak at the same time *about* themselves and *to* other seropositives on TV, and activists don't know how dishevelled, vulnerable, and strong they look after all the heat and fury of an action has passed. DIVA shares with House of Color a quality of "amongness" between the producers and the audience. We make work for the people featured in it and formed our collective identities from talking to each other. When the producers in House were asked after a screening who their second tape, *Probe,* was directed to, they made the point that, insofar as no images like the ones in their videos exist anywhere else, they create these images for anyone who will look.

The *Living with AIDS Show,* Channel L, and *Out in the '90s* have screened completed DIVA productions and used unedited demonstration footage for their weekly cablecasts in Manhattan. NBC, CBS and ABC have each called to request "whatever we have," and we've sold it to them. Sometimes they become insistent and belligerent about our duty to further their beneficent intentions; other times they coax us with endearments and then ridicule and manipulate our material for their own, biased stories. We have to fight about this every time. What constitutes an intervention? When does a DIVA credit alter an image which is immersed in a barrage of unsympathetic coverage? When does earning a couple extra bucks make us feel OK about denigrating our work?

Suzanne had rare footage of the Church demo because she went inside as a regular activist while the acknowledged media mavens were corralled into a distant corner. Sleazy-tabloid station Channel Eleven offered to buy it and give her DIVA credit, but they never even replaced her tape stock and the only credit she received was being the butt of a joke. When our name appears, the newscaster says, "Activists turned holy mass into a holy mess." We incorporated a part of this distortion into *Like a Prayer,* which deconstructs the entire media mishigas and, at least, empowers DIVA producers through the act of decoding.

Of course, when we rip off *their* imagery, it's a different matter altogether. Gran Fury, another collective in ACT UP, which concentrates primarily on poster campaigns and public art projects, has produced a series of thirty-second public service announcements (PSAs) that mimic the ubiquitous advertisements for the "United Colors of Benetton." Likewise featuring a multiracial cast, the Gran Fury PSAs consist of same sex couples smooching in every thinkable combination. Originally intended for MTV, they haven't been aired except on scattered pay cable shows and in public access slots. Nonetheless, they've been in several shows, including a program of music videos that travelled across the country, as well as in film festivals and art galleries.

The tapes of DIVA, House, PPTV, and TTL are used in teach-ins and at fund-raisers. They are programmed in galleries, museums, and video festivals. Italian TV station RAI subtitled a segment from *Target City Hall* for a news program. Tapes are made available free of charge to other ACT UP chapters and sold at Monday night meetings for only twelve dollars, a compromise between our anarchistic desire to give them away and the needs of ACT UP/NY's fund-raising committee. The tapes provoke varied reactions from all kinds of audiences, and ultimately demonstrate *for* us in different settings.

Show and Tell

People in these collectives speak well, speak through many media, and speak a lot. But this section of the meeting should take only about ten minutes. We have a few upcoming speaking engagements and presentations. City University of New York, Wesleyan, Harvard, and Cooper Union have invited a bunch of people to screen tapes and talk shop. At Brown, they put a tube on a table in the snack bar and looped *Target City Hall* all day for the rotating, munching crowds. For World AIDS Day, 1990, the Institute of Contemporary Art in Boston ran our three half-hour productions continuously.

DIVA is sponsoring a benefit for ACT UP at Brand Name Damages gallery in Brooklyn, under the Williamsburg Bridge, and no one can find a flier. "Who's got the flier?" asks Rupert, who just seconds ago passed it around. "I swear to God I don't have it," says a guilty, overtired facilitator. "But we need help coordinating this event. Who can we call to do outreach . . . ?"

Everyone then suggests the person: "She's not here anymore, so she can do it."

As we all expected, future projects have been tabled until next meeting. Also for next time, think about DIVA T-shirt imagery. We've been offered free silk-screening. If no one comes up with any more ideas, we'll have to decide between color bars—activist video in jail—or Lady Liberty with a camcorder leading the people.

Is this meeting adjourned?

Notes

1. DeeDee Halleck stresses this purpose in an interview with Judith Mayne and Lucretia Knapp, "Feminisms Does Media Activism: An Interview with DeeDee Halleck," *Feminisms,* vol. 3, no. 3 (May/June 1990), p. 4.

2. *Ibid.* p. 3.

3. Peter Bowen, "Collect Yourself," *Outweek,* no. 52 (June 27, 1990), p. 108.

4. Julio Garcia Espinosa, "For an Imperfect Cinema" [1969] in Coca Fusco, ed., *Reviewing Histories: Selections from New Latin American Cinema,* (Buffalo: Hallwalls, 1987), p. 167.

5. Simon Watney, "Representing AIDS," in Tessa Boffin and Sunil Gupta, eds., *Ecstatic Antibodies: Resisting the AIDS Mythology,* (London: Rivers Oram Press, 1990), p. 174.

6. Ellen Spiro, "What To Wear on Your Video Activist Outing (Because the Whole World Is Watching): A Camcordist's Manifesto," *The Independent,* vol. 14, no. 4 (May, 1991), p. 24.

7. Douglas Crimp, "AIDS: Cultural Analysis/Cultural Activism," *October* 43, (Winter 1987), p. 7.

8. Isaac Julien and Pratibha Parmar, "In Conversation" in Boffin and Gupta, p. 100.

9. Stephen Heath, "Representing Television," in *Logics of Television: Essays in Cultural Criticism,* Patricia Mellencamp, ed. (Bloomington and London: Indiana University Press and BFI Publishing, 1990), p. 298.

10. An affinity group usually coalesces for the planning stages and the duration of a demonstration in order to carry out specific, small, group actions. As many as twenty coordinated affinity groups have participated at one time in a large ACT UP protest.

11. Other activist video collectives, with multiple overlapping memberships, complement the work discussed here. For example, Media Against Censorship (MAC Attack) was founded by Dean Lance, Maria Beatty, and Branda Miller in August 1990. The group is a collective of video artists and media activists documenting acts of and protests against censorship. In May 1991 they produced a one-hour documentary, *State of the Art/Art of the State.* ReproVision, the video collective affiliated with WHAM!, was founded by Julie Clark, Dolly Meieran, and Dana Nasrallah. In September 1991 they produced *Access Denied.*

12. Arch-conservative Reverend Donald Wildmon got his hands on a copy of *Like a Prayer,* and he searched for a way to connect it with his attempts to embarrass the National Endowment for the Arts (NEA). He discovered that the Second Coming clip played in

New York's lesbian and gay New Festival as part of Ray Navarro's memorial tape. His frantic and skewed call to arms included the following bit of hysteria: "Considered most shocking of all was the fact that twelve hundred dollars of Council money paid for the Festival's movie guide which promoted the film, *Jesus Christ Condom,* produced by militant gay activists who call themselves DIVA-TV." In response, the NEA drafted a fact sheet about DIVA: "That organization, a small group working in media-based AIDS awareness programs, never received a grant from the NEA." And we probably never will.

Eso, me esta pasando 1990

RAY NAVARRO

I am an HIV-positive Chicano gay man from Simi Valley, California. By looking at me you may not be able to see any of these things. You will also not be able to tell that I am college-educated, a videomaker, and scared to death of my own culture. For the last several years I have grown comfortable with my gay identity, I have marched on the streets, go-go danced in bars and wept at the death of people I respected who died from AIDS (Acquired Immune Deficiency Syndrome). So now I am also an AIDS activist. Full-time.

When I was nineteen I remember walking into a Latino drag bar in Los Angeles. There I saw many lesbian and gay people. Each one looked like they could've been my aunt or uncle. It shocked and thrilled me to see so many Latinas and Latinos expressing their sexuality openly, defiantly—but it dissatisfied me that the only safe place to do this was in a dark bar off of Santa Monica Boulevard.

To be "gay" was not a reasonable option for me as a teenager. Gays were supposed to be white men with buzzed hair who lived in West Hollywood, not Chicanos. When I sought out my preferred way of expressing myself sexually it was under conditions of extreme secrecy. I was afraid of rejection by my friends and family, not to mention terrified of having my ass kicked by "the dudes." As a "man-child," being queer did not fit comfortably into what I knew was expected of me: college, wife, kids, the English language, in short, assimilation. The only Spanish word I knew that described my sexual feelings was a bitter insult: I was a *puto*.

Being HIV seropositive (I have human immunodeficiency virus antibodies in my blood) has ushered me into a kind of second "coming out." Around two years ago at the Los Angeles Lesbian and Gay Film Video Festival I encountered a remarkable video tape, *Ojos que no ven* by José Gutíerrez and José Vergelin (shown during CineFestival 1988), which dealt with AIDS from a Latino perspective. I was so impressed by its telenovela form that I could even picture my great-grandmother watching it in her bedroom, where a Spanish-language soap opera marathon ran constantly. Right there and then I became determined to seek out other media works which spoke directly to the Latino community and to people of color generally.

Independent video and filmmakers have responded with particular passion to the AIDS crisis. Working with low budgets and often collaborating with local social service agencies, these artists have proven that entertainment, education, politics, and sexuality can be interwoven into remarkable audiovisual tools. My own collaborative efforts in producing AIDS media have driven home lessons I originally encountered in viewing the grassroots performances of El Teatro Campesino. Clearly, art and activism are comfortable bedfellows in the Chicano community, and have been for years.

There are several films and videotapes currently available to Latino communities (though still too few) which address the issues of HIV infection and AIDS. But rather than merely describe them to you here, I would like to provoke you somewhat, and inform you about the menace on the horizon. You may be surprised to know that the menace is not, in my view, AIDS itself, or HIV. I am not going to recite statistics, although I assure you that they are grim where Latinos are concerned. It is true, the virus is lascivious and stupid, and the opportunistic infections which attack the person with AIDS are swift and merciless. But what is more threatening to our community is what Amber Hollibaugh so appropriately names "The Second Epidemic" in her videotape of the same title. This is an epidemic of discrimination, fear, bigotry, and homophobia, which will certainly damage the Latino communities in a way that will have deeper effects than HIV ever can.

I can only compare this to the legacy of the Conquest of Aztlan itself. We withstood that, didn't we? Our language survived, our culture thrives, but the scars run deep and the memories are painful. And the psychological, social, and economic effects of this racist violence permeate our very souls. This is AIDS. It began with a lethal lie: that AIDS only affected gay, white men. Homophobia was wielded as a misguided defense against a virus which would travel only by certain routes, primarily through blood. Addictophobia was also called in—misunderstanding and intolerance for substance abusers and intravenous drug users prevented us from reaching out to people who needed understanding and drug treatment, not moral condemnation. Haitians were blamed for the spread of the disease, a racist conception which distracted us from the growing numbers of Latinos and blacks affected. Women were told they were not at risk. A tradition of antisex propaganda was resurrected, the "safe" means of having good sex were withheld from teenagers, women, lesbians, and gays. A perverse antilogic reigned as Reagan-era antidrug hysteria pushed the community leaders into adopting shortsighted positions such as: "Instructions on clean needle use should not be offered to addicts; it will promote drug use." How many addicts' lives could have been saved had they learned to shoot safely, had they been educated about treatment and recovery instead of left to die at heaven's gate? More shortsightedness: "Teenagers should not be taught about responsible condom use because it will promote premarital sex." How many adolescents have transmitted HIV who could have been helped? (God knows they had sex anyway!) We learned the hard way that "just say no" doesn't work for sex, drugs, or AIDS. But Latino communities are learning even more lessons. AIDS accentuates the lack of access to health care for poor people in this country. It underscores the economic discrimination enacted by insurance companies and the shocking lack of primary health care in communities of color. Already overcrowded emergency rooms explode under the AIDS caseload. Understaffed social agencies find themselves unable to handle the burden of inquiries from the community. Children are dying—thousands of them.

Finally, we are able to conclude that the AIDS crisis is part of the larger social agenda of an insensitive government. That old enemy *La migra* is even in on the act, as HIV-positive immigrants are refused their residency status or are threatened with deportation due to their HIV seropositivity. Women are forcibly sterilized before being allowed to participate in clinical trials for experimental AIDS treatments. These same clinical trials routinely exclude Latinos from admission. A crude and familiar justification is offered: that we fail to meet the "cultural criterion" necessary for collecting accurate data. This begins to sound more and more like Uncle Sam's traditional line.

CineFestival has demonstrated a firm commitment to fighting this crisis by helping to arrange a series of discussions, workshops, and screenings of Latino AIDS media. The importance of these different venues cannot be overstated—part and parcel of these tapes and films is that they be viewed in many different contexts, not only in dark theaters but in brightly-lit *clinica* waiting rooms. I hope that you will be able to attend and participate, to debate the significance of AIDS for Latinas and Latinos both locally and nationwide. The videotapes being offered to you, the Latino communities, at this year's CineFestival provide a wide range of perspectives from which to view AIDS. As a legal, sexual, cultural, and political issue, the menu is diverse because this pandemic is complex. Here are political analyses, protest images, sexy scenes, angry young men, defiant feminists, and *gente*. You will be hard-pressed to find an "AIDS victim." Rather, we are Latinas and Latinos living with AIDS.

"Filling the lack in everyone is quite hard work, really . . ."

A roundtable discussion with:

JOY CHAMBERLAIN, ISAAC JULIEN, STUART MARSHALL, AND
PRATIBHA PARMAR

After several months and weeks of agonizing attempts to get together Isaac Julien, Stuart Marshall, Joy Chamberlain, and myself for a roundtable discussion, we finally managed to coincide with our respectively busy schedules. I enticed them with promises of a wonderful brunch and champagne, and so, one sunny Saturday morning in May 1991, we gathered at my house in North London to rap about our desires, pleasures, and problems as filmmakers.

Stuart Marshall is an educationalist, writer, and independent video and filmmaker. Joy Chamberlain directed the lesbian drama, *Nocturne,* and works both as a freelance film director and as an editor. Isaac Julien is a video and filmmaker, a former member of Sankofa Film and Video Collective (London), one of the first black film and video workshops in the UK. I am a writer, activist, and filmmaker.

—Pratibha Parmar

PRATIBHA: I thought we could start off by talking about what we are trying to do individually, in a very broad stroke. What is our agenda in our film and video work? It would also be interesting to talk about how we decide to work across and within different genres. Most of us, with the exception of Joy, began by making experimental artwork, and now all of us are involved in doing mainstream films. Is this a transition, or is this a decision to work in a variety of styles and traditions? Are we moving away from trying to do work that's shown in galleries or exhibition spaces and reaching .out to a much broader audience? Does this mean compromising to institutional demands as well as revising or rethinking the question of form and content?

Why don't we start with something quite specific about our latest film projects. Isaac, can you talk about *Young Soul Rebels,* since you just completed it?

ISAAC: In terms of talking about different audiences for my work, in the case of the *Young Soul Rebels* there's an obvious switch. I had to have a certain budget to make that kind of switch, but behind the decision to find the money for the project is a decision to make a work that is more of a narrative. And behind that there's a political imperative, which is that I want to make work which gets seen by more people and which questions more people. In all the work that we've done to date in Sankofa [a London-based, black, filmmaking collective] we were talking to a converted audience. That began to worry me, especially after *Looking for Langston.*

However, I do think that it's important to do work which acts as a catalyst for change or resistance for different communities of interest and different audiences. But what I realized when I was showing *Langston* at a cinema in central London [the Metro] was that the audience for the film was mostly white men. (In the US, I think the audiences were more hybrid.) That was a problem. Still, I know the film was seen by lots of black gay men and black lesbians and was also seen by a rather broad audience, because it was shown on television twice. But you never know about television audiences, because you're not in direct contact with them.

With *Young Soul Rebels,* I wanted to see if I could get back to some of the questions we were trying to deal with in *Passion of Remembrance.* That meant engaging with a black audience as well as a gay audience. Once you do try to grapple with different audiences, you have to think different film vocabularies or film languages, to communicate that as ideas. That then suggests using certain genres. I think the problem of genre is how you can best articulate the points you want to address: are you compromised by working within certain genres? Of course they're all constructions, and we can deconstruct them . . . de-la-de-da-de-de. I was interested in working with certain genre conventions in order to undermine them. But once you do that, you alienate audiences. Then again, you want audiences to think. These problems are quite unresolved for me.

JOY: I think those of us working in Britain at the moment are at a turning point. In terms of filmmaking, we're coming out of the gay ghetto, because larger budgets are becoming available. I started off making campaign documentaries in the early seventies for Women Against Rape, the Grunwicks strike, and then various films for and with teenagers, one of which Isaac was in [laughter]. That work was very much about being politically directed and thinking in terms of a specific audience, and not reaching a larger audience. Underneath these political considerations, there are also personal considerations. People become filmmakers because they love that particular medium. I've come to a point where I really want to make films with lesbian characters that I think are interesting and engaging; for me, that means making narrative films.

I started working in the mainstream around about 1975 as a film technician, mainly because I'd just seen so many agitprop gay and lesbian films that were very badly made—out of focus, unintelligible sound, and so on. Clearly, those technical problems can be attributed to financial problems. But I also thought that this may have to do with feeling so estranged from society that we didn't feel that we had access to training. That is why I worked as an editor for film and television—to acquire certain technical skills, so that I could make something that had a political agenda but at the same time was polished and professional. Having reached that point, though, raises a lot of questions about how much we can move out of our particular ghetto, what sort of audience we keep in mind while making a particular film or even conceiving the ideas behind a film.

I actually like working in traditional genres. I'd like to see gay and lesbian characters across the board: you turn on a television and you want to see gay, lesbian, and black characters. That's a basic step. There's been a lot of talk over the last ten years about deconstruction, and I think it is very useful as an analytic tool, but I don't think it works as a tool for making an interesting film. The film medium is about empathy, it is about catharsis, it is about being drawn in, and identifying with the characters and with the story.

PRATIBHA: How do you create empathy with lesbian characters?

JOY: Well, not by thinking this is a lesbian character and she has to be an ideal character. When you create a character who has all good qualities and doesn't have any complications, then you've created a boring character whom no one will identify with and think, "Oh, that's a lesbian character." Whereas if you have a character who conveys the richness of a whole person, who has conflicts, then people become interested. That also allows them to transcend the label. They're not thinking, "This is a lesbian character." They're thinking, "That's a character."

STUART: I was thinking about what you said about deconstruction and the history of avant-garde political work in this country, since I've come out of that movement. I have a certain kind of loyalty, maybe a nostalgia, for that period. One of the reasons why our work has been at the cutting edge is because that whole project of deconstructive practice which bloomed in the late seventies and early eighties collapsed when the problem of pleasure came up. There was so much suspicion of cinematic pleasure. If one experienced pleasure when one watched a film, then one was being ideologically manipulated. It's no coincidence that the collapse of the debate coincided with the founding of Channel Four, when money became available in a way it hadn't before. People started to struggle individually in order to get funding. Maybe this is a bit cynical, but I think all the fine community politics fell to pieces when there was money. But that's incidental.

So much of that work was informed by two things: a particular kind of politics of film form, and certain ideas coming out of feminism around

Nocturne, Joy Chamberlain, director

representation—ideas which were profoundly suspicious, about representation of sex and sexual pleasure. Now that's the point where we—lesbian and gay filmmakers—took off, because our pleasures had never been spoken about. We wanted to speak about our pleasures in a way which was very difficult, say, for heterosexual feminist filmmakers. And I think for me that's been the most problematic issue that I've been trying to negotiate: how to make work that is still politically critical in the way that you're talking about, but would produce pleasure, a pleasure that is very confirming for lesbian and gay audiences.

Isaac: I feel like something of a Jekyll and Hyde after making *Young Soul Rebels,* because I see myself very much as a part of an avant-garde tradition. In my mind, you don't know how much conventional genres are imprisoned or fixed in their meanings, so it's a skill to try to manipulate genres to achieve political ends, to make your own kind of political statements and at the same time not totally pull the mat from underneath the feet of the audiences who are watching.

At the same time, I think about the useful corruption of Channel Four. Having money and being able to make work is a fantastic opportunity. But these opportunities have produced a number of anxieties, for instance, the continual questioning of the political implications of what you're doing. Programs like *Out on Tuesday* give access to different audiences, and we're in an enviable position since different kinds of people get to see the work of lesbian and gay filmmakers in this country. It's good political intervention. But this also produces a downside: competitiveness and a breaking down of solidarity in terms of people making images and representations.

PRATIBHA: For me, the *Out* series has been an opportunity to not only work with decent budgets but also produce work around South Asian lesbian and gay subjectivities. The half-hour film *Flesh and Paper* which I made for the second series in 1990, on Indian lesbian poet and writer Suniti Namjoshi, was the first time that British television audiences saw an Indian woman in a sari talking about being a lesbian and Indian in a way which was not apologetic or explanatory. This was a deliberate choice, and it was quite thrilling to know that nearly a million people watched that program. One of the unique things about this series has been the way in which many of us who have worked on it have engaged with the question of pleasure. The one thing that shines out is the sense of both visual and emotional pleasure in some of these programs.

STUART: The notion of pleasure is something to be struggled with and contested. In terms of the funding agencies, be they the British Film Institute (BFI) or Channel Four, they've got a particular idea about what pleasure is: it hinges on this notion of a completely homogeneous audience who all sit and look at a piece of work and respond in exactly the same way. However, I find an enormous perverse pleasure as a gay man in seeing the ideological structures of our society undermined and subverted. I have a grudge that is being played out.

PRATIBHA: Because you're not just then talking about pleasure as purely an aesthetic engagement with the form, but you're talking about pleasure in terms of your hidden agenda of disturbing the status quo.

STUART: Right. I've had the experience of watching films with different audiences, and they've become different films because of the way the audience responded. An example would be the first time I saw *La Cage aux Folles* in San Francisco. It was a ninety-percent gay audience. The next time I went with friends to see it in London at Notting Hill Gate, with a ninety-percent heterosexual audience, and it was a different film. People laughed at different things. The straight audience was profoundly uncomfortable at certain moments, whereas in San Francisco the audience had been screaming with pleasure. The way you see an audience divide and shape around those issues is fascinating. As we talk about moving more into the mainstream and dealing with government agencies who can provide large amounts of money, but always with their own agenda, that for me is the area of greatest risk. One could end up losing one's loyalty to that more perverse notion of the way pleasure is produced.

ISAAC: The more you move into a large budget arena, the more you begin to lose control of a situation where executive producers want to have an input. Ultimately everyone thinks they're trying to make a film that is going to be pleasurable for people to watch. But we've got different agendas from most of those executive producers.

PRATIBHA: In a way you're an exception, because I can't think of another lesbian or gay filmmaker who has received the kind of funding that you did for *Young Soul Rebels*. It's a historical precedent. And I think it would be useful to learn from that, not just in terms of audiences, but also your personal feelings and experience. Would it be true to say that without an avant-garde independent milieu in which you could flourish and learn and explore, you wouldn't be doing what you're doing now?

ISAAC: Absolutely. The context for my work is dictated by two conditions. There is an institutional agenda, which one should always be healthily skeptical about, and then there's my own, which has to do with not being marginalized economically, because I need the finance to make the political statements I want to make. In any big project, there are vested interests—those of the commissioning editors and executive producers, as well as our own as scriptwriters or directors. There is a contestation in relationship to power and control. The bigger the budget, the greater that contest. Gay representation is something that some people are attracted to because they

Mo Sesay (left) and Valentine Nonyela in *Young Soul Rebels*, Isaac Julian, director

think it's transgressive. But you may not agree with their ideas of transgression.

In *Young Soul Rebels,* I made the gay theme so central to the plot that if anyone tried to remove it, the script would fall to pieces. It was during discussions of the script with commissioning editors that resistance to representations of the black and white gay characters began to appear. This also factored into the struggle to get finance; *Young Soul Rebels* was put back a year because of that difficulty, and was four years in the making. When we began editing, the issue of control came in again. People wanted to cut the gay sex scene. They didn't want it to be as long as it is. And then there were compromises made in order to adhere to genre conventions. By having a long sex scene does it take away from the plot? Ultimately, you make these decisions in terms of the audience.

JOY: For lesbian filmmakers, these issues must be seen against the background of the early feminist movement in the seventies, which was a situation where women became politicized, but very much from a position of powerlessness. Which is partly real powerlessness but partly also that women were brought up to feel themselves as powerless. There are more lesbian filmmakers who don't want to intervene in the mainstream than there are gay men who feel the same way. And I think this comes still from a fear of being swallowed up and a fear of not having the power to actually hold your own in that situation.

But that's where the risk comes. Because to not intervene, to stay in a separate ghetto, is playing it very safe. You won't make any mistakes if you do that, and you won't come up against any contradictions. You're also not really going to change very much in the long term. So in a way it's very important for us to take those risks, but we always have to be aware that we are taking risks. Sometimes we will make mistakes, and sometimes we will fail. For instance, I know my films will go out to a mass audience, and I have no control over who that audience is going to be. Some will be a gay audience who'll respond sympathetically, there will be other people who'll respond sympathetically, there will be some people who will be voyeurs. But I still think I've got to take that risk.

ISAAC: There's a more pedagogic aspect, in terms of audiences, in making narrative films. Black straight audiences see *Young Soul Rebels,* and they're confronted with gay characters. But the flip side to that is that one still needs to produce work that encourages a critical understanding within the community that you're a part of. In gay communities, I find a lull in the process of asking political or theoretical questions.

PRATIBHA: Can you say some more about that?

ISAAC: For example, Stuart's first film for broadcast television, *Bright Eyes,* was for me very important in terms of people thinking about representations for ourselves. Then take the more recent *Longtime Companion* as a counter-point. That film was primarily made for a straight audience. When you make this kind of intervention, do you make films for a primarily straight audience? When that's the case, I don't think those pieces of work are particularly engaging or important.

STUART: *Bright Eyes* was made before there was a lesbian and gay television slot, i.e., *Out on Tuesday*. It did attempt to address, quite clearly, a gay audience with what was supposed to be an empowering representation, but was also supposed to be critical. The specificity of its address was one of the problems. It was broadcast at eleven o'clock at night, in December, 1984, to a general audience that had no idea how to relate to it. That's why I have since changed the way in which I've been making films for television. Now we've got the *Out on Tuesday* slot, which does specifically address a lesbian and gay audience. But the channel also needs to have a large heterosexual audience watching, and there has been a slight pressure to generalize *Out on Tuesday's* form of address. I don't think you can use the experimental forms that *Bright Eyes* used.

PRATIBHA: When filmmakers make the move from documentary to fiction, they find that there's more artistic freedom as well as conceptual freedom in fiction. As a fiction filmmaker, you can say what you want to say through your characters, whereas with documentary you've got the subject matter but you've also got the subjects, and you can't put words in their mouths. Sometimes I find that frustrating, because I want to put words into their mouths. That's when I start questioning myself. Why am I making this? Is it because I want the subject matter to be saying this in this way? I imagine that's partly why documentary filmmakers want to move into drama.

ISAAC: With drama you can end up with more layers of meaning. You've got a story and the variety of possible identifications with the characters. These forms can produce all sorts of effects and meanings which deserve analysis.

JOY: In some ways you have more control, because there's a script and the actors read your lines.

PRATIBHA: Would either you or Joy, now having worked within a main-stream fictional genre, want to or have any desire to move back to documen-tary filmmaking?

JOY: I don't enjoy documentaries any more. It's not so much a political question, it's that I don't feel that's what I'm best suited for. I'm not very good at interviewing people and getting them to say what I want them to say. But I do feel comfortable working with actors and thinking in terms of stories.

ISAAC: I'd like to do something similar to *Langston* soon, rather than com-partmentalizing interests in terms of fiction and documentary. I see all these things as a construction really—even documentary work. There is a pretence of realism, but all documentaries are about constructions and manipulating, in one way or another, what people say.

STUART: It was very interesting to see *Memory Pictures* next to *Khush* at the National Film Theatre last week. How much was the fact that *Memory Pictures* is not a conventional documentary to do with its being made with Arts Council funds, and therefore you had a certain space to work, while *Khush* was made for television?

PRATIBHA: Formally, I don't see *Khush* as a conventional documentary. Sure, there are talking heads, but there are also dramatic scenarios, performance, dance, and archive footage, used not as wallpaper but in and for themselves, as different kinds of voices and different modes of telling.

STUART: It's more conventional in its address than *Memory Pictures*, though, isn't it? I'm just establishing a gradation.

PRATIBHA: I think you are right in that *Memory Pictures* does use a more fragmentary, multilayered address that requires shifting subject positions, whereas *Khush* is more specific in its address. Undoubtedly, there is a tension when you are making work for television as opposed to the art gallery circuit. When we produce work for prime-time television we have to be mindful of audiences who may not be familiar with work by experimental filmmakers.

Nevertheless, when I made *Khush* I was trying to do something quite different from *Memory Pictures*. I wanted the oral history testimonies from South Asian lesbians and gay men to be heard. All the women and men who speak out in this film are coming out for the first time, publicly or to their parents. Many of them found it an empowering experience being involved in this film. When we refer to conventional documentary filmmaking, we understand that to mean talking heads, but talking heads are ok for me. It really depends on who is doing the talking and what they are talking about. Talking heads can be transgressive if they belong to individuals who have never been given the space on prime time television.

JOY: I would like to give a practical example of working in a traditional genre in relation to *Nocturne*. When we first had the script of *Nocturne*, I had to decide how to interpret and direct it. I was leaning very much towards trying to use a lot of the conventions of film noir. But in making that decision I spent a period of time really studying that genre and looking at what the implications of it were. In the traditional film noir story, you have a heroine who doesn't fit into the role of the passive woman: She's seen as a very dangerous woman; she's active; she's usually a criminal. At the end of the film, the hero, who's always a man, is usually redeemed, and the dangerous heroine is either imprisoned or killed. What I tried to do with *Nocturne* was to turn the genre on its head by starting off with a heroine who is very repressed but who passes through ordeals of the soul to become dangerous.

PRATIBHA: I would like us to talk about what it means to be identified as a gay or

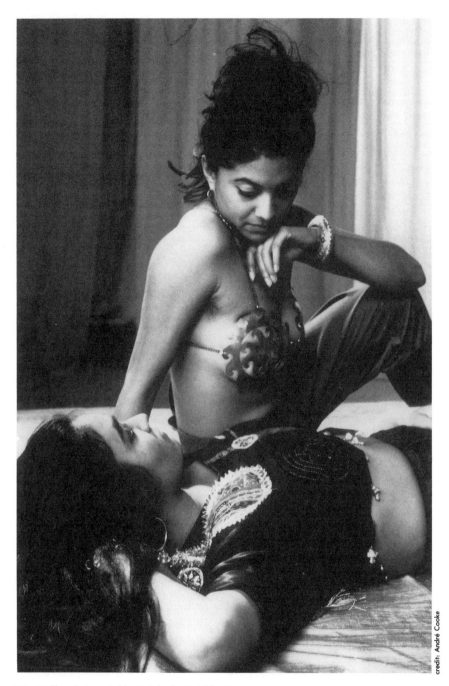

Rita Wolf and Anna Ashby in *Khush*, Pratibha Parmar

a lesbian filmmaker. There are expectations from the particular constituency about what your identity is supposed to represent. There is a tension both in terms of the audience but also for yourself—the burden of representation that is thrust upon you. And then the critical reception, that any piece of work that you may make is seen in light of that particular identity.

JOY: You get that even more from our own community. For instance, taking *Nocturne* around I've noticed when I'm interviewed by a gay writer, they will always want to write about it as a lesbian film. And they always want to talk about the implications of sexuality in it. The recent National Film Theatre screening was the first time I actually had questions that were about *Nocturne* as a film—about the genre, the way we made it, and the artistic elements of it. As a filmmaker, that's an important validation.

ISAAC: I've found as time goes by that the notion of a specifically gay audience becomes more and more impossible. In the course of making my last three films, the questions of difference within the community around gender, race, sexuality, become more important. There's a notion that there is a homogeneous audience which is being addressed. But that becomes more and more impossible to sustain. It's a fiction. That's what I object to most when talking to most of the commissioning editors.

STUART: When commissioning editors talk about homogeneity they're talking about your work being understandable and accessible to an ideological notion of an audience that is their lowest common denominator. Anything involving textual complexity or interrogation of the television text on the part of the audience is seen to be problematic. So they say, "Oh, can you make this a bit more explanatory? Can you use a commentary here to explain this?"

ISAAC: But who's kidding who? Who watches *The Eleventh Hour* at eleven o'clock at night? We know about audience ratings; they're about scheduling.

STUART: This is a question for all of us. Why does a series like *Out on Tuesday*, which is a very mixed bag—entertainment to analysis to straight agitprop—have the kind of ratings that it does? Why is it so popular?

PRATIBHA: When we say it's popular, we've got to put the ratings in context. The figures are one million, which is good in terms of the comparison with, say, *The Late Show*, which tends to get around six hundred thousand. We're still talking about a very small percentage of the population, if you compare it to *Coronation Street* [a soap opera]. About half the population of the country watches *Coronation Street* at any given time.

Having something like *Out on Tuesday* on mainstream TV at prime time is also about creating an audience, not simply assuming an audience exists. That's really crucial when you're talking about trying to get your work out and seen by as many people as possible. Working in this context, I've thought about audiences in terms of the actual form I use for the first time.

STUART: And the relationship to the audience is so removed, so different

Comrades in Arms, Stuart Marshall, director

from the situations that we've all known in the past, when we're there with the work and there's a debate and you begin to understand the way people relate to the work. I found when I made *Bright Eyes* and it was broadcast, that I was actually unable to make any work for two years afterwards, because I was so confused by the fact that I'd put a year of my life, energy, and creativity into making a piece which was then shown on Channel Four one night and disappeared; it was gone. It was two years later when it started to be shown in the States on a video-political art audience circuit that I started to get any kind of feedback whatsoever. Until that time I was almost completely immobilized because I'd produced something and not understood the consequences, so I couldn't move on. How do others feel about that?

PRATIBHA: For me, having my work seen on the lesbian and gay film festival circuits, especially in the US, has been an absolute lifeline. The feedback has really kept me going, and winning the Audience Award for *Khush* as the Best Documentary Short at the Frameline Festival in San Francisco in June was a thrill. All the nightmares of shooting illegally in India suddenly became distant memories when I watched the film with the audience at that festival. It was a very special moment. To get that validation from your own peer group mattered much more than getting a great review from a critic. That kind of nurturing is very important. It's what's kept me going. But it's only in recent years that we have had access to television audiences.

STUART: It is something that all of us have worked hard to create for a long time, though. It also means that it's opening a space that other people can benefit from.

ISAAC: It's something which is undergoing change as well. Will there be another *Out on Tuesday* series, for instance? Everything that's produced in terms of lesbian and gay film culture at the moment on Channel Four is directed more or less towards that series. In the process, the possibility of having different forms of film or video work become less.

There is a liberal tokenism around the funding of our work. In terms of *Young Soul Rebels* having been given a fairly large budget by the BFI, it's unlikely that they will fund another film dealing with lesbian or gay issues for a number of years. They'll say, "Oh, we did it already, with *Young Soul Rebels.*"

JOY: I've seen that already. I have a project which I've been trying to do for ten years, which is based of the life of Romaine Brooks. We've finally got a really good treatment together and started sending it out, beautifully packaged and everything. We've had some very nice letters back saying it's a very interesting proposal, well handled, and so on, but so far as we have no solid prospects. I'm afraid it's too much like *Portrait of a Marriage,* which went out on BBC earlier this year. In fact, my project is nothing like *Portrait of a Marriage,* either in terms of the story and the style.

I have the same worries that you do, Isaac. I think it's very good that there is a gay series. I think *Out* has created a potential audience and has given our community much more visibility. But there's always a point where people can turn around and say, "Okay, we're doing gays and lesbians; we have a gay and lesbian series." There's very little money for the series, so most things are made with very low budgets, therefore most of the stuff is in a current affairs format, because that's the cheapest way to work, which is a kind of tokenism—they provide the series but only give enough money to do it in a certain way.

ISAAC: But that's the way in which Channel Four has dealt with all minority groups.

STUART: And you don't think we're going to see the BFI fund another film on anything having to do with gays or lesbians?

ISAAC: To an extent, institutions do have expedient positions. But at the BFI there has been a lot of resistance to supporting serious lesbian or gay work. There has also been a shift as well in the priorities concerning the form they're willing to consider—a shift to the right. At the same time, there's ambivalence; in the past few years the BFI has produced two feature films and one short made by three gay men: *Young Soul Rebels*, Ron Peck's *Strip Jack Naked*, and Chris Newby's *Relax*.

STUART: Then maybe you're disagreeing with me. Are you saying a space has been opened up?

ISAAC: It's contradictory, because politically there's been a shift to the right, but that doesn't explain their support and promotion of these three films. In the current political climate, where there has been a complete move to oppression of gay male sexuality in particular, that seems like an extreme contradiction.

STUART: But I think the two are connected. It's no coincidence that the first *Out on Tuesday* series was funded at the same time that Section 28 was proposed and passed. The swing to the right may be the major context, but I then there's a liberal opposition to that within Channel Four and the BFI. And, in a sense, we've cashed in on that.

JOY: But it's not really so much cashing in. We did the groundwork in the seventies.

STUART: At the time when the Independent Film Makers Association was around, in some ways there was less rivalry because nobody had much funding. People were working together politically much more. People lobbied for years to get Channel Four set up and to make sure that there was an independent film and video section. And a lot of the people who are now in positions of power at Channel Four and the BFI actually come out of that same background we do.

ISAAC: I've done these things for *The Eleventh Hour;* I've done work for *Out on Tuesday.* But as far as Channel Four is concerned that's no track record. They're very ambivalent about their commitment to the kind of work we were doing anyway. Their hearts lie much more in realist, journalistic type of programs. They want to be seen as commissioning editors that have as much clout as other commissioning editors and have audience figures.

PRATIBHA: It horrified me that six months ago a woman director said to me, "Isn't it awful that you have to think about what you're making with a view to your next commission?" In fact, she had made a short film with a view to her next commission. I guess I'm naive about the film industry, but that horrified me. I only make things that I feel a certain passion or desire for. But maybe you have to learn this "war of maneuvres" if you want big-time funding.

ISAAC: It's about career.

JOY: On the other hand, even if we see ourselves as having more integrity than that, how much can you afford to ignore those practicalities?

STUART: I think it's a very individual thing in how you work it. It's about your own borderlines.

PRATIBHA: I agree, it's about your own political and aesthetic borderlines and how you negotiate them.

ISAAC: And that's a very personal decision. But because we come from a left background and involvement, we are so used to a certain kind of policing in our own ranks that there's a tendency to get defensive.

JOY: In terms of the two features I've done for Channel Four, I haven't yet made something that I haven't had to compromise on. *Nocturne* came about because Tash Fairbanks, the writer, took the idea to Channel Four. They then asked me if I was interested in directing it, and I tried to put some kind of stamp on it afterwards.

To learn to make the kind of films I want to make is a very long learning process as well. With *Domestic Bliss* I was doing it half blind. *Nocturne* presented an opportunity to learn another level of directing skills, and to be able to do something that was a coherent piece, where I could see and visualize it before we started. The greatest achievement for me was that it turned out looking ninety percent like what I visualized before we went into preproductions. Having done *Domestic Bliss* and *Nocturne,* I now feel that I have the skills to do something that is more personal and close to my heart.

STUART: When you take on a commission for a television film, whether documentary or fiction, you're constantly aware of the fact that you're learning through that process. It reminds me of the situation when I was doing a lot of video installation work, and I could never get all the equipment together at any one moment in time to see what the piece was going to be like. I had this fantasy about what the piece was going to be like. When I finally got all the equipment together, it never was quite how I imagined.

But it was really very difficult because I saw other people around me working on pieces where they'd got the means of production there within their control, and they could go through that learning process in quite a private way in their studio. I find that a terrific tension—to know that one's learning in this fantastically public medium.

PRATIBHA: I find that really frightening and scary. I particularly feel the lack, because I've not got a film background, and I didn't go to art school. I come from a community activist background and a theoretical academic background. I feel that every single thing that I've worked on, I've learnt another level of directing and technical skills. It's scary because you're judged on what the audience sees. They don't know that you had to do the camera at one point, or you had to do the production managing and the off-line editing and everything else that you did on your own. And it's the first time you've ever done it, and you've had to learn it as you go along. You've been nodding away, Isaac [laughs]. Did you feel that with making *Young Soul Rebels?*

ISAAC: There's a problem if you are interested in theory and have a theoretical background. These questions impinge on you more, because the critical element of theory is about dissecting and deconstructing images and their workings. When that's placed in relation to an audience, then that is a bigger avenue of inquiry; people are doubly critical. People will always judge, and they have lots of expectations—I think, in a way, rightly so, because you're talking about desire to a certain extent. But filling the lack in everybody is quite hard work really [laughter]! The burden of representation weighs on each of us quite heavily. The different backgrounds which we come from are not properly acknowledged, and the critical apparatus which is then pushed on us is undifferentiated. There's not a lot of space for making mistakes in public. It's uncomfortable.

STUART: It's interesting in terms about background that none of us has gone through a traditional film training, and, Isaac, you actually turned down a place at National Film School a long time ago didn't you?

ISAAC: Yeah. The woman who directed *Oranges Are Not the Only Fruit* was in the same year that I was accepted, and she's just been offered a big picture deal in Hollywood. The National Film School allows you to learn in private, and that's where you also get the contacts.

PRATIBHA: But also there's an ideological underpinning within that institution.

ISAAC: They really want you to work in a certain way.

PRATIBHA: And mold you in a certain way. When I went for my interview I had a very heated discussion with the head of documentary, because they were into a particular form of documentary filmmaking, whereas I wanted the space to explore.

STUART: You have to accept the whole ideology of that institution, but we've all positioned ourselves outside those institutions because we're suspicious for a variety of reasons.

One of the things that I have found so distressing over the last few years, is that critics, for want of a better word, in the seventies would have seen themselves as being part of an independent filmmaking culture, with an understanding of the problematic issues it was taking on, and played a supportive role in relation to what we were doing. But by the eighties, those critics didn't see themselves having any relation to that movement whatsoever. In contrast, one of the most marvelous things about the early days of Channel Four was that people were able to make mistakes in public, because there was a possibility of a critical dialogue. It brought television alive in a way, rather than adhering to these grossly fetishized notions of professionalism. I find the current split between the critical support system and the production system very distressing.

JOY: What I find particularly disturbing is that most critics younger than me have come straight out of film school, or not even film school—some are just out of university—and have no knowledge of the history of independent filmmaking.

STUART: None at all.

ISAAC: There is a personal resentment that one doesn't really like to make public. But I think it's important to say that when you have struggled for years to make certain things possible, that you'd at least like some acknowledgment of what you've had to go through to get to that point— not individually but as a community. Aside from that, it's very dangerous to ignore history. I think that's one of the things that comes out so clearly in your work, Stuart.

PRATIBHA: That's also one of the ramifications of certain kinds of political and social movements having to do with film culture in Britain. In the eighties, and for the generation coming up now, a number of questions have been taken for granted—questions of feminism, for example.

STUART: Critics don't identify with a film movement and a politics, so they don't see themselves as having a role in creating a legitimacy for a set of political filmmaking practices. They approach it purely as a group of individuals who are disconnected from the history of that movement and the history of those problems of production.

PRATIBHA: If there were film critics writing in London who had a knowledge of the history of film culture in this country over the last twenty years, I think we could get much more positive feedback. By positive feedback I don't mean someone saying, "Your film is wonderful," but a critical analysis that you can actually engage with.

ISAAC: It's very much about Thatcherism, isn't it?

PRATIBHA: Last week I picked up a copy of *Vogue* and saw an article on British black filmmaking, with a beautiful photograph of Isaac, Reece Auguiste and John Akomfrah [from Black Audio Film Collective], and Karen Alexander. The article was talking about black filmmaking very much as a style that's come out of the black experience in Britain. I can't imagine that *Vogue* would have done anything like that at the beginning of the independent filmmaking movement back in the seventies or the eighties. What do you think about black British filmmakers being taken up by style magazines like *Vogue?* What is their interest?

ISAAC: I think it's about commodification. There's a way in which one does want to make an intervention into those spaces, but on one's own terms, and that's very difficult. For *Vogue* to do a piece on black filmmaking is probably more about Cynthia Rose [the writer] approaching the magazine with an idea for a piece on black practices in Britain, rather than *Vogue* initiating it. The spaces to talk about work are very few. Also, profiles of who we are and what we do within a certain kind of public space that is not just left magazine culture is also important. At the end of the day, it's about trying to get certain ideas across to different types of audiences. I read it as such. Politically speaking, some of the things that are said in the article are interesting, although it is debased by making it pleasurable. Pleasure makes the threat acceptable. If you trivialize it, you don't have to take it seriously, because we can't really have black politics being spoken about in *Vogue,* which we know is a racist magazine.

PRATIBHA: It's also about asserting some notion of black culture as entertainment.

ISAAC: Yes, and it is also something to do with fashion and music, as well as media types realizing that they have to keep up with trends and that trends are not necessarily vested within high culture. If you're in the business of making films and wanting people to see your work, then it seems to me that's the risk that you run; you get contaminated along the way.

STUART: Sankofa and Black Audio have produced some of the most interesting work to come out of the independent sector. It seems less restricted by traditional forms than a lot of the other work that I've seen coming out from England from white groups and workshops. How much of that do you think comes out of the fact that all of you come from art school backgrounds?

ISAAC: I think that's got a lot to do with it. Dick Hebdige has written about art school students. He says they're people who don't quite know what to do with society. The other thing which is not really spoken about is not shying away from intellectual rigor. Many filmmakers shun certain questions around representation. I find, for example, that a lot of lesbian and gay filmmakers are content to make films for a lesbian and gay audience. This is something that I feel uncomfortable with, because that's not my only identity. This is true for Pratibha, as well. You have to ask yourself lots and lots of questions which, in many ways, white lesbian and gay filmmakers take for granted.

STUART: Identities are constructed through and by images, as much as by words, so it's getting hold of the signifying practices and manipulating them. There's a certain pleasure in doing that, which produces a certain unpleasure for different audiences.

PRATIBHA: You take those risks if you're positioned marginally anyway, in terms of your access to power or self-definition. Even when you become engaged in the process of self-definition through a particular practice (in this case we're talking about filmmaking; it could be literature), you can break the codes of those practices and of the dominance of those practices.

JOY: One of the things I find extremely frustrating is that people seem to give up so easily, to feel that things aren't possible and, therefore they're not even going to try. We've got a fantastic opportunity here—having fun with gay and lesbian film. It's ever so important that we don't just let it stop.

ISAAC: We need a more utopian way of thinking about things politically. Gay and lesbian filmmakers need to ask the question, "Who is the work for?" What we're talking about is work that has a life after it's been shown on television. Which is why I object to the grand narrative of Channel Four as the first and last cause of what we do.

JOY: One of the things that pleases me is that *Nocturne* has provoked controversy and that people leave screenings talking about it. For some, it brings out things in their own lives; for others it brings up political questions. I think that's because I have taken risks with it. It's not just about being gay; the core of it is about power in sexual relationships. It's also about class differences and racial difference. Within the lesbian community there has been an ideal that we're all supposed to have equal relationships. But anyone who has ever been in a relationship knows that there are always power differences. Some have to do with personality, some have to do with class, and some have to do with race. I decided to direct that script because I thought it was important to expose some of those questions.

PRATIBHA: What interested me is that the part played by the black actress wasn't written as a black part.

JOY: No, it wasn't.

PRATIBHA: Don't you think that the film to a certain extent neutralizes those differences. Many black women have criticized the film on the basis that it infantalizes the black woman.

JOY: I don't know about neutralize. In retrospect, that casting decision may have been slightly naive, although I like to think of it as idealistic. I was looking at black and white actresses for a lot of the parts, and I thought I wouldn't make up my mind beforehand, although once I started casting I did try to work through the implications for the film. Obviously if you've got a small cast and you end up with one black actress, then it's the same as if you have one lesbian character. That person is then going to be seen inevitably as some kind of representative. And I was doing a film where no single character was ideal enough to be a representative. All the characters have negative sides to them, and they're all acting out power games. Basically it's a situation where, in some ways, you're hung whatever you do.

I decided to go ahead and face that, partly because I'd seen Karen Jones, who plays Ria, doing some improvisations, and her improvisations were the Ria character. That's how I cast her for the part. My reading of the film is that the two young girls, Sal and Ria, are fairly equal in their relationship, but when they go into Marguerite's house, they have to survive on their wits. Some people say that I infantilized the black character, because when Sal and Ria make Marguerite lose control and power by enacting her childhood fantasy, Ria plays Marguerite as a child. But I don't see that. That's an association that applies in a society that sees black people as children; then you're going to see that as being racist. I hadn't realized how many people think it still applied. What I was more worried about—which maybe comes from my own history—was I thought it would be more problematic to cast Sal as a black character, because she was role-playing the governess. Half of my family comes from the South [in the US], where until recently upper- and middle-class white people were often brought up by black nannies. Also, the film is about the breakdown of Marguerite's middle-class Englishness and her subsequent liberation, and I thought casting a black actress to reenact Marguerite as a child was an allegory to the multiculturalism of Britain.

ISAAC: One of the things that I have realized from making a number of black films is that the grip of realism surrounding black characters in films is very strong. I mean it grips the throat in a certain way, in terms of articulation, because of the barrenness of the repertoire of images.

PRATIBHA: I think it's also about the kind of baggage and preconceptions that different audiences bring with to these films. In *Flesh and Paper* I had an Indian classical dancer who functions as an icon and a symbol of the poet's desire. I've had a variety of criticisms about that, ranging from people saying, "You're in danger of presenting an exotic image. You're replicating a particular exoticization of Asian women, in the way she looks and the fact that she's dancing and being alluring." I don't see her as an exotic image but as a particular icon coming from my particular cultural background.

ISAAC: That kind of criticism says a lot about the critic, because critics never declare their identity interests. They're always assumed to be universal. Until crisis declare their own specificity, there is always going to be a lack in what's articulated.

The Cost of Love

RICHARD KWIETNIOWSKI

In a diner one night . . .

Sam asks for matches.

Inside is a phone number, sender unknown.

"Why not try it?" says his mischievous flat-mate.

Sam dials & makes a rendez-vous.

After a night of indescribable bliss, Sam asks for his name.

"You have my *number,*" he is told.

But it is answered by a busy freight company. "What do you want?" they say . . .

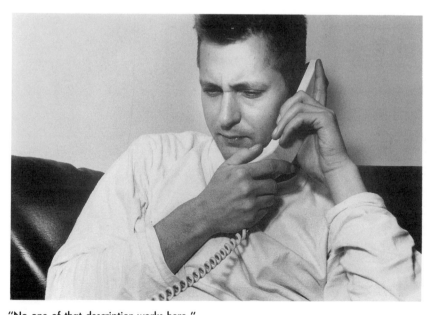

"No one of that description works here."

Back at the diner, the waiter explains: "I wrote the number, for a friend with a parcel . . .

. . . You must have misdialled it!"

His flat-mate explains there are over a million ways to misdial the number.

Together they work out a system.

One month later, the phone bill arrives.

But Sam hopes the search will never end.

For he has fallen in love with his flat-mate, & his head for figures.

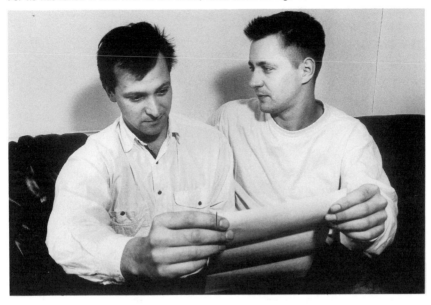

photographs: Tony Clancy

This proves beyond a doubt that the cost of love *can* sometimes be calculated, after all.

The Politics of Abstraction

BARBARA HAMMER

As an experimental filmmaker and lesbian feminist, I have advocated that radical content deserves radical form. In 1979 I had my first screening outside the supportive lesbian feminist community when Terry Cannon, then programmer at Film Forum in Los Angeles, asked me to show my films in a venue of experimental films. I had already completed several experimental films of lesbian feminist content and had shown them regularly in the Bay Area of San Francisco. They were also distributed by early women's film cooperatives. In both cases I was called upon to explain my unorthodox form and content. To the feminist community, I introduced my films in light of the formal concerns of experimental filmmaking. To the experimental film community, I spoke about the importance of unrepresented content.

It is my belief that a conventional cinema, such as classical narrative, is unable to address the experiences or issues of lesbian and gay perceptions, concerns, and concepts. When an audience awaits the image on the screen it expects a heterosexual narrative to unfold, and the audience is not disappointed. Even if the characters are lesbian, the script projects lesbian characters within a heterosexual world of role-playing, lovemaking, and domestic and professional life. The numerous films that purport to be "lesbian films" have failed to address me as a lesbian spectator. The romance, the on-screen gaze, the plot, the character development are all situated within a heterosexual life-style or a Hollywood imaginative life-style made for the cinema. Certainly the women I have seen on the screen, their issues, the story, and the mise-en-scène do not relate to the personal experiences I live and have lived as a lesbian woman for twenty-three years in the Western world.

Lesbian cinema is on an invisible screen. By the "the invisible screen" do you mean pictures drawn in lemon juice backwards that when heated can be read through a mirror? asked a friend. It has been that difficult to see lesbian representation in cinema. The lesbian imaginary is carried in a back pocket inscribed in invisible lines until heated by the projector lamp.

How could this be, in an age where we have films like *Desert Hearts,*

Lianna, and *Personal Best?* These are films where the on-screen space is filled with seeming "lesbian representation." But my reading of these films is that there is no lesbian to deconstruct, as the discourse of the gendered subject is within a heterosexist authority system. The lesbians act out heterosexual gender roles and positions rather than claiming any difference, and even sexual practices are situated within heterosexuality.

As a runaway from the political regime of heterosexuality, I and other lesbian filmmakers began to construct a lesbian cinema in the early seventies. Visibility was the central concern for lesbians making cinema at this time, for the simple and profoundly sad reason that there were few or no pictures, images, or representations available. The screen space, on and off, was blank. Not just marginalized, but not there. There was no cinema to deconstruct. There was no gaze to analyze. Lesbian image-makers in the seventies were forced by critics into the "camp of essentialists" because of the extreme urgency of their need to make lesbian representation. A marginalized and oppressed group must make a mark first, define a form, and make a statement that they exist. As we began to make films of lesbian representation, we were categorized by the emerging feminist semioticians and theorists (newly emerged themselves from French studies with Christian Metz) as "essentialists." Because we made representations of lesbians, the false assumption was made that we invested these representations with biological, essential "meaningness" separate from ideology or social construction.

I, for one, as a lesbian cineaste, take a more eclectic and I hope eccentric view of the lesbian representations I made in the seventies. The lesbian women I imaged in film were constructed by the general and dominant society, as well as the marginal society of the lesbian community. In the process we also discovered who we were, as we stepped into the void, the invisible, the blank screen, and named ourselves "lesbian." That was the first step. There could be no semiotics if there were no sign. The lack we felt as we began this early naming process was not the lack of a phallus but the singular and significant lack of any representations. The image did not exist, the picture was not made, the word scarcely heard in discourse nor seen in text.

Until recently the dominant discourse of feminist criticism has not addressed this issue but has continued to ignore it, and by doing so perpetuates the invisibility and repression of lesbian cinema. To dismiss the early naming and identity films with the highly charged and emotive term "essentialist" further removes the opportunity for discourse in a climate where deconstruction, Marxist, psychoanalytic, and Lacanian theories prevail.

The reidentification of a lesbian self through lesbian sexual experience is but one part of lesbian representation. There are many parts and practices of lesbian experience to be represented. In physics, light can be understood through wave and particle theories at the same time. So too can there be multiple, coexisting, and different theories and understandings of "lesbianisms" through a variety of readings. One of these readings is experimental cinema: the cinema that makes its own construct where form and content are inseparable. I don't think one can make a lesbian film using a patriarchal and heterosexist mode such as the conventional narrative. Plot points are male points. We are radically changing people, and we cannot reproduce that radicality using conventional forms.

I have chosen images rather than words for the act of naming myself an artist and a lesbian because the level of meanings possible for images and image conjunctions seemed richer and held more ramifications. I have broken rules, studied the construction of norms, and questioned restraints since I was a little girl. It was not strange that I chose to practice in the longtime artistic tradition of breaking or modifying the status quo in an attempt to advance the dialogue. Generally speaking, my films made in the seventies, *Dyketactics, Multiple Orgasm, Double Strength, Women I Love,* and *Superdyke,* as well as others, were made with this intention that grew from an unconscious impulse to a conscious insistence on lesbian naming.

Superdyke, Barbara Hammer

Once named, and identities established as artist and lesbian, I wanted to get on with other areas of expression that I had left unexplored. The second ten years of my nonnarrative film production focused on my perceptual interests. In my early films I chose "realism" by using the camera as an eye, capable of defining form, outline, and depth to depict the lesbian body. The social realism of the scenes were contrasted with the dreamlike, metaphoric, and imaginative images of freedom. In the urgency to make lesbian imagery, I neglected my thrill of simply projected light even without images, and my love for abstraction.

Abstract or nonrepresentational art appeals to me for several reasons. I have deeper emotions when I'm working beyond realism because there are no limits, and I enter and engage with the dialogue between light and form. I am not presenting a statement or an essay, but a more amorphous work which allows the maker and the viewer the *pleasure of discovery*. Meaning is not apparent at first glance, and often requires repeated screenings, promising *challenge*. The *satisfaction* that comes from study and understanding of a complex work of *multiple references* and *perceptual insights* is a very rich fullness that can't be compared to linear journalism or narrative. Film allows me to express perceptual, intellectual, and emotional configurations that provoke pain and give pleasure.

The contributions of postmodernism have challenged the singularity and

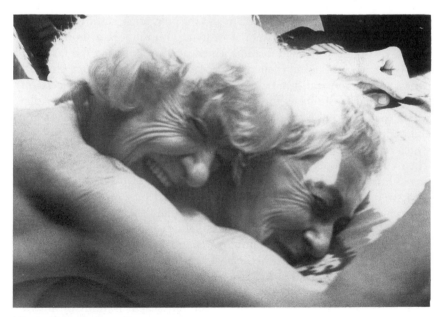

Nitrate Kisses, Barbara Hammer

uniqueness of individual expression through the "utilization of forms over and above content due to the production of works in concrete historical circumstances."[1] The forms I choose are marked by the historic period in which I live, but the content of my work has not been remarked upon by modernists or postmodernists. Lesbian difference is ignored by both schools of theory. While I may enjoy the multiplicities of abstraction in form, it is still continually necessary to state my difference in content in my films, videos, performances, and writing. It is true that I bear the mark of the construction of perception by the social forces and institutions in which I live. Architecture, advertising, educational systems, family rearing, and Hollywood movies have all shaped my construction of knowledge and perception.

All these authority systems have "authorized certain representations while blocking, prohibiting or invalidating others".[2] So even while I find pleasure and ambiguity in the formal characteristics I select for my films, I am still compelled to work from my experience from which my "subjectivity is semiotically and historically constructed."[3]

As a working lesbian artist, I am using abstraction not only for the perceptual pleasure and multiple possibilities of meaning, but also because I believe the viewer must be active. The supposition I have made is that participatory behavior in one area can lead to participation rather than passivity in another. The passive reception of nonchallenging visual media— broadcast television, commercial film and the pulp press, static or moving— encourage passivity in other modes of living (on the job, at home, in the streets, in politics). An active audience engaged in "reading the text" will also be active in making their own decisions about campaigns, elections, issues, and demonstrations. I also use abstraction because of the uncertainty principle that is the locus for a certain type of play. There is linear play, where each person accepts rules of behavior, dialogue, and dress, such as children playing nurse and doctor. Then there is an abstract kind of play which requires the active imagination, where the only rule is: anything goes. There can be abrupt changes of scenes and locations, gender, names, and all possibilities of expression are possible. This form of play for children or adults requires a strong sense of self. In abstract play, everything around you can be turned upside down, the most unimaginable combinations of words might be spoken; the disruptions, flights, costumes, and fantasies will swirl around you. You must know you won't be destroyed by letting go. Similarly, in letting the abstractions of light and texture, image and voice swirl around you and carry you into a filmic experience, you become aware of what you are experiencing. The active audience members don't lose a sense of themselves while engaging in the physical sensations of abstract cinema, but feel more the possibility of being.

Finally, multiple readings, understanding, and namings are promoted by abstractions providing richness, diversity, and complexity. If it is any worldview we need right now to allow for preserving difference, it is a worldview that embraces flexibility, possibilities, and multiple understandings of phenomena. There is not a feminism but feminisms, not a lesbian cinema but lesbian cinemas, and there is not abstraction but multiple manifestations of abstraction.

Notes

1. Craig Owens, "The Discourse of Others: Feminists and Postmodernism," in Hal Foster, ed., *The Anti-Aesthetic: Essays on Postmodern Culture* (Seattle: Bay Press, 1983) p. 58.

2. Owens, p. 59.

3. Teresa de Lauretis, *Alice Doesn't: Feminism, Semiotics, Cinema* (Bloomington: Indiana University Press, 1984), p. 182.

George Kuchar: Half the Story

MARK FINCH

George Kuchar grew up in the Bronx, largely at Loews Palace cinema. In the same year Barbara Stanwyck starred in *All I Desire,* his mom gave him and twin Mike an 8mm camera. They mounted mini-melodramas like *The Naked and the Nude* and *I Was a Teenage Rumpot* on the roof of their tenement. Unwittingly, the Kuchars were part of a more extensively documented underground gay scene: Kenneth Anger, Jack Smith, Ron Rice, and Ken Jacobs. But George was the only one who wanted to make high-strung dramas like Douglas Sirk's. He groomed his high school pals for stardom, switched to 16mm and moved to San Francisco, where he still teaches at the Art Institute. His 1976 classic, *A Reason to Live,* is a tribute to the movies he was raised on as much as a melodrama about his then-lover and star Curt McDowell. His films are giddy, thoughtful accounts of how dangerously distraught women and largely unappealing men cope with the problems of love and of the lower intestine; many also have a meteorological theme. Today his favorite movies are *Making Love* and *Maurice,* and he mostly makes videos—virtually reinventing the diary form with his Sony 8 scrapbook. He does not identify himself as a gay filmmaker, and he frowns upon the intolerance of some gay audiences. His work (which includes writing and painting) can't be called camp—he's too engaged with popular culture to enjoy the distance camp requires. He is the epitome of charm and of ingenuousness. He loves America and only reads one newspaper, *The National Enquirer:* "The *Enquirer* asks people which stars they like, and which they don't like. Then they run more of what people want, and trash the others. It's kind of human, you know. It's got all the good parts of being human, and all the lousy parts too." He was born in 1942.

Filmmaker Dresses, Undresses, Suffers Wind

"You know, I made the movies as a review of my friends—I wanted to make them stars. I'm doing the same with the tapes, only my friends don't have to dress up. I think the films dressed up feelings for the screen. The tapes don't need to do that. I used to give people [in the films] parts of my clothing to wear, and I'd also design the people. But in the tapes I don't do that. I always had a feeling that you never want to know too much about anybody—it takes away the mystery. . . . I can go back and reguide the tape after I've filmed everything. If there's anything I think shouldn't be seen, I take it out. There's gotta be a little mystery. It's like a burlesque show. When it comes to editing, there are many considerations. You can be vain and say, eh, that's a horrible shot of me and I don't want it seen. Or you can be in a funny and nasty mood and want to show those horrible things. I often take out shots or moments where [other] people sounded or seemed bad. I have bad skin problems, wind, diarrhea attacks. I keep that stuff in the tapes so my friends look better. For me, I'm always a removed character—it's not me, it's my TV. I laugh sometimes; then other times I think oh my God."

Hold Me While I'm Naked (1966) 16mm, 15 mins.

George is a filmmaker frustrated by a leading lady who runs away with one of her costars. He is unable to find a suitable replacement because all his pals are having sex in their showers. He himself takes a shower, interrupted by his mother's call to dinner. Faced with a plate of overcooked beets and other burnt offerings, George wonders whether there is indeed anything worth living for.

Laments Lack of Finance, Toilets

"I've developed a language in my movies almost like shorthand. Some people don't know what the hell is going on. In fact, what is going on does interest me to an extent, but it doesn't interest me to show where people are or how they got there. I want the big scenes, the essence of what's happening. When you've been in movies for many years you begin to

16mm films by
George Kuchar:

CORRUPTION OF THE DAMNED (1965)
HOLD ME WHILE I'M NAKED (1966)
LEISURE (1966)
MOSHOLU HOLIDAY (1966)
COLOR ME SHAMELESS (1967)
ECLIPSE OF THE SUN VIRGIN (1967)
THE LADY FROM SANDS POINT (1967)
KNOCTURNE (1968)
UNSTRAP ME (1968)
HOUSE OF THE WHITE PEOPLE (1968)
ENCYCLOPEDIA OF THE BLESSED (1968)
THE MAMMAL PALACE (1969)
PAGAN RHAPSODY (1970)
PORTRAIT OF RAMONA (1971)
THE SUNSHINE SISTERS (1972)
THE DEVIL'S CLEAVAGE (1973)
BACK TO NATURE (1976)
A REASON TO LIVE (1976)
LA CASA DE CHORIZO (1977)
KY KAPERS (1977)
WILD NIGHT IN EL RENO (1977)
FOREVER AND ALWAYS (1978)
MONGRELOID (1978)
BLIPS (1979)
AQUEERIUS (1980)
THE NOCTURNAL IMMACULATION (1980)
YOLANDO (1981)
CATTLE MUTILATIONS (1983)
UNTITLED MUSICAL (1984)
THE X-PEOPLE (1984)
ASCENSION OF THE DEMONOIDS (1985)

discard those details. Also, the expense is too high, you want to get right to the point. Finance isn't always on my mind, but I did develop shortcuts. With video, I can enjoy the mundane, but add meaning to it. I can do bathroom shots, faucet close-ups, what you ate, stuff like that. Also, this is the kind of stuff I was deprived of in movies. You know, the trouble with TV is there's no toilet scenes."

Eclipse of the Sun Virgin (1967) 16mm, 13 mins.

College graduate George struggles with Catholic guilt, a domineering mother, and his overweight sisters, who are always dancing and doing their hair in the kitchen. He is pursued by fantasies of muscular men. On a date with a girl, he wears a black leather jacket and keeps his distance on the sofa. Later—after a domestic accident involving his mother, a coffee cup, and *Teenage Love* magazine—George invites a young man to watch his collection of medical instructional films. There is tension in the air.

George Kuchar (right) in *Eclipse of the Sun Virgin*

Binges: A Four-Day Plan

"People want different things, different shades and grada- tions. The world of sex is based on how you were brought up, other peculiarities. I've been to that world. There's an incredible driving power, it gives so much energy. It's also funny to see it masked in mainstream films—it will always surface, and you can read it, you can get the message. People are driven by sex. It'll drive you crazy. Everyone knows if you hump before making a picture, you lose that spark. You have to clean yourself up before you make it work. You have to go to the steam room, get the poison out, the vices. Then you make a picture about the vices, but you have to be clean to do it. And then the process makes you pent up. I was never really able to merge the two. My pictures are mostly about the binges, the vices."

Mongreloid (1978) 16mm, 9 mins.

A tale of unrequited love, George's salute to his pet dog, Bocco. George asks Bocco if he recalls past adventures; when the animal is unforthcoming, George fills in with flashbacks set to a delirious sound track celebrating the United States of America. In vacation footage, George and Curt McDowell muck about with Bocco. Finally, the dog's bio comes up to present-day, with his move to California from the East Coast: "You like to piss on palm trees, don't you? And you make kaki all over San Francisco, America's favorite city."

"He Told Me It Was Gay"

"*Eclipse of the Sun Virgin* was the follow-up to *Hold Me While I'm Naked,* in which I try to get into the character's mind. The character was me of course. I did it in a more dreamlike way. *Naked* was about the experience of what's happening; *Sun Virgin* was more enigmatic. When it first came out, no one could make head nor tail of it, but now people understand it—which scares me. I didn't totally get it 'til years later. Someone saw it and said this is a gay picture, and I thought, he's right. I had no idea at the time, twenty years ago."

San Francisco Art Institute productions:

DESTINATION DAMNATION (1972)
CARNAL BIPEDS (1973)
I MARRIED A HEATHEN (1974)
THE DESPERATE AND THE DEEP (1975)
I, AN ACTRESS (1977)
THE ASPHALT RIBBON (1977)
ONE NIGHT A WEEK (1978)
PRESCRIPTION IN BLUE (1978)
THE POWER OF THE PRESS (1979)
REMEMBER TOMORROW (1979)
SYMPHONY FOR A SINNER (1979)
HOW TO CHOOSE A WIFE (1980)
THE WOMAN AND THE DRESS (1980)
OCHOKPUG (1980)
BOULEVARD KISHKA (1981)
THE ONEERS (1982)
MS. HYDE (1983)
CLUB VATICAN (1984)
THE LEGEND OF THELMA WHITE (1985)
MOTEL CAPRI (1986)
LA NOCHE D'AMOUR (1986)
PRC MUSICAL (1986)
INSANITORIUM (1987)
SUMMER OF NO RETURN (1988)
LA VERBOTENE VOYAGE (1989)
VILE CARGO (1990)
FALL OF THE HOUSE OF YASMIN (1991)

L.A. Screening Workshop [1988] video, 30 mins.

George is in Los Angeles for a presentation of his tapes, staying with friend Virginia, who works for Bud Yorkin Productions ("Bud's son is very hot"). He prowls around her home and dinner party with his Sony, and the next day, almost uncomfortably, films her getting dressed for her executive job. George seems restless, bossy. He meets Ainsley, Curt McDowell's leading actress ("she managed to stay dressed throughout his movies—practically unheard of"); now she writes kids' books and volunteers at the Braille Institute, which he visits. Back at Virginia's, GK pops in on her stranger Hungarian neighbor ("she's a creature of anthropological interest") and annoys Virginia's boyfriend by calling him Fat Boy.

Love, American Style

"*Forever and Always* often gets buried, but I like it a lot. It's a series of portraits of a crumbling marriage, with people posed against fixed backgrounds to get that postcard tone and to accentuate what they're feeling. There's no dialogue, just music. But the movie didn't start out like this. Two women gave me fifty dollars because the city was having a "Hooray for Kids" festival, down near Fisherman's Wharf. It was supposed to be a celebration of children on this huge pier. There was all sorts of stuff for them to play in, but they were mainly ripping it off. I went to make a documentary record, but I thought, how about planting an actress and inventing a sequence of events? So I asked this woman friend who had two children to come in and act like she was having a breakdown amidst this mob of people. Then I filmed some surrounding material explaining why she was cracking up, showing her husband going off to some tropical paradise with a glamor queen. . . . I was pleased with it. I think that mothers really understand this picture. . . . The funders saw me taking pictures of seagulls and got a bit worried. At times it was a little embarrassing. Finally, they demanded to see the movie. One of the women caught me at the bank as I was standing in line to cash a check. I think she liked it. But, anyway, what the hell is fifty dollars?"

Point 'N' Shoot [1989] video, 5 mins.

GK's handsome friend John invites him to visit another pal's apartment in Marin. It's plush and tasteless. George's camera enjoys John's body, and even manages to get him in the jacuzzi while they chat about real estate.

Shocked by a Sofa

"I had fun photographing *A Reason to Live*—it was all done with a Bolex, and the sound was dubbed in later. Plus I loved designing Marion Eaton, although she was horrified at the result; because it was black and white, I wanted the lipstick to look just right, to stand out, and I had to redesign her eyebrows. I liked the way the sofa looked when you took the cushions off—you could see the shapes of the springs underneath. Marion couldn't understand why I'd want such a horrible-looking sofa in the film. I explained that this movie was about a relationship falling apart, about disillusionment, I guess."

Videos by George Kuchar:

POINT 'N' SHOOT (1989)
WEATHER DIARY 5 (1989)
CHILE LINE STOPS
   HERE (1989)
A PASSAGE TO
   WETNESS (1989)
WEATHER DIARY 6:
   SCENES FROM A
   VACATION (1990)
LETTER TO BOB (1990)
THE BIG ONES HURT
   (1989–90)
SNAP 'N' SNATCH (1990)
A ROCKY INTERLUDE (1990)
CURSE OF THE
   KURVA (1990)
KISS OF THE VEGGIE
   VIXON (1990)
THE WARMING OF HELL
   HOUSE (1988–90)
ORBITS OF FEAR (1990)
SCARLET DROPPINGS (1990)
THE SAGA OF
   MAGDA (1990)

Curt McDowell in *A Reason to Live*, George Kuchar

Weather Diary 1 (May 1986) video, 80 mins.

George arrives at Oklahoma's Motel Reno during storm at nearby Edmonton. The water in his bathroom sink doesn't drain too well. George befriends a dog he calls "runt." After some calm days, another major storm hits. More days pass; George catches a TV documentary about weather watchers. "These people are lucky, they get to go to cocktail parties and eat *hors d'oeuvres*." George eats at Dairy Queen. His sink starts to get scummy; meanwhile, TV weather celeb Gary Englund hosts a special, *Those Terrible Twisters*. George gets a headache from the background disco music. Insects infest his bedroom; George shows us his mosquito bites, throws up. On Memorial Day George celebrates with a MacDonald's breakfast, then lunch at Pizza Hut—only they've run out of the giveaway Gary Englund Storm Map. Satiated, George interviews Ruth, the motel's owner, whose daughter Gloria's husband has just left her. "Time to go," announces George, "I met new, interesting, and squat people. I like Ruth and her husband Roy a lot—they're decent people. Decent enough to try and convert me to Christianity."

Teen Employs Polaroid, Theaters for Sex

"*Thundercrack!* was designed as a porn film to make money. But halfway through, I told Curt that everything I'd worked on hadn't earned money. He said, well, how come you're telling me now . . . ? I used to be hungry for porn. I always wanted to go to Copenhagen, where porn was freely available. I sent money to a man in Washington who sent me gay films. He wrote back to me that he was so impressed by my sincerity and trustfulness in sending him money! Before that, my father—he was a truck driver—often brought home porn films, which he borrowed from other drivers, and he let me watch them. They were black and white, and the men had funny hairstyles and the women looked a bit dingy. I used to take porn pictures of myself with a polaroid. But I preferred dressing things up. I didn't want to see the actual thing. I wanted to see some gloss on it. I went to the movie theater. You know, I always found it interesting that there was more bathroom action at the regular theaters—were they weren't showing porno films—than at the porno theaters. I think people ought to make something of that. If more theaters showed porno films, or if more films had sex in them, there might be less action in public spaces. Something like that."

Weather Diary 3 (May 1988) video, 30 mins.

Back in Oklahoma, George reflects on the escalating heat. He espies football players through a hole in a fence, jerks off in motel shower. Another guest arrives—Mike, who sports a National Severe Storm Lab T-shirt—and an affectionate but tense relationship develops.

"Everyone Wants to be a Stripper"

"I did *Weather Diaries 1* and *2* and they were an hour and a half, and I was back in the same hotel room and I thought I hadn't dealt with these other problems. I felt harsh. So I aimed the camera at something I hadn't filmed before. . . . I had no visitors, until that guy Mike turned up, and then I thought, well that sexual tension would be interesting. Each time you make a tape you like to approach it from different angles. . . . Some people don't want to look at that stuff. I went to the School of Visual Art, and I took *Weather Diary 3*. I was testing out the color before we began, and suddenly that scene came on where I'm pissing, and I looked around and saw this look of horrible distress on a nice girl's face, and I thought, oh my God, these poor people might not want to see this. And other people get a big kick out of it. That's what they want to see. But sometimes they're having problems of their own. Other times they have the same feelings. . . . I heard that the boy from *Weather Diary 3* saw it in his class. The guy's teacher showed it. Before the lights were turned up, he ran out of the room. It might have been embarrassing for him. Also with that nude scene in *Weather Diary 3*, I thought I'm getting old, I'm nearly fifty. Everyone wants to be a stripper, but if you don't do it now, you'll go to your grave bitter. That's how I felt. What could be better in your past than a nude scene? It's a dream come true. We all want a scandalous past— it's what Hollywood pictures were always made about. I think it's the dream of our nation, to be a person like that."

Love Me True (Spring 1989) video, 30 mins.

(1) At Jeff and Suzanne's wedding reception, George loiters by the outdoor bathroom, interviews guests. After lots of badgering, J & S finally cut the cake. (2) GK is with Suzie and Carlos, a bored and boring couple, who grudgingly show George their engagement gifts ("You want to see our juicer?"). (3) George attends spoof I-Married-a-Werewolf wedding outside City Hall. (4) His pal John [from *Point 'N' Shoot*] shows off a new car and chats about a recent wedding at which he was a guest. (5) Behind the scenes on a student production; George competes with director Amy over instructing the cast, who are playing typically tortured lovers. (6) In his office, George hears a student's pitch for a new movie: "I want to follow around somebody for two weeks and examine their excreta—to get at our fear of bodily fluids. Can I use yours?" GK says he needs to sleep on it. To John: "I'm going to be in a constipated mood from now on. Let's talk about wholesome things—the car, the wedding."

Likes Straight Guys

"I don't see myself as a gay filmmaker. . . . I don't think other people see me as a gay filmmaker either because certain of my films don't deal with that—and because I don't grab my student audience and fondle them on the side. Curt felt the gay scene was a ghetto. He loved mixed crowds because he liked straight guys. Another friend of mine, Dan Turner, was saying how he liked interchange situations. That's where I come from."

The Thursday Album: Video Album 5 (1987) video, 60 mins.

George reads Curt's obits, then attends one of the regular Thursday soirees. Back home, George shows his mom Curt's funeral pics—"Doesn't he look good?" he asks. "He doesn't look that good to me." All about Curt: a filmfest tribute is intercut with Curt's family by his bedside. At Mike and George's, a friend from Brooklyn is visiting. GK works on a student Sasquatch movie and attends a Greek-themed celebration out of town. He comes back to Curt at the end: "I sometimes wish that the clock would turn back again so I could once more get that stupid look on my face."

Sex Adventures and Representation

"*Rainy Season* was pretty pent up. I had all these clues left under the bed. This guy came over to my house for dinner and I said, Hey you wanna get on the bed and let me kiss you? That tape was about the seedy side, and then that image of us in bed with the cat was the appealing, attractive side. I don't like things that are painted too brightly—I always found calculated representations of life-styles—gay, black, Christian, whatever—stilted. My characters aren't role models. You would never want to be one of my characters. They're composites. Life is a rich hodgepodge, it'll make your hair stand on end. There are people who want a positive image—hey, we all want to look good. But when you get into what everyone's actually thinking and it's a cesspool, you know—which is part of the tragedy of being human, I guess. That's what interests me. Nowadays, of course, to present that is like a slap in the face. . . . I realized all this years ago, when I embarked on my sex adventures—that I had to buy the sex paper, and I had to answer the ads, and I had to make the telephone calls, and I had to be there in person, and I had to turn up at the motel, and I had to be on the streets. You just have to do it. Otherwise you live it vicariously, and I was sick of living vicariously, and I was sick of just looking at dirty pictures—I wanted to be in them. If you're desperate enough, you can make the dream come true. How can you find something true and genuine if you're not dirty first? Sometimes, atrocious deeds pay off—a genuine thing comes out of it."

Taste

"I don't have the best taste in the world. Sometimes my taste is a little off kilter." (All quotes by George Kuchar.)

An Unrequited Desire for the Sublime:
Looking at Lesbian Representation Across the Works of Abigail Child, Cecilia Dougherty, and Su Friedrich

LIZ KOTZ

In recent years, issues of lesbian representation and of the lesbian spectator have become nagging questions posed to feminist theories of film, which have become codified around semiotic and psychoanalytic discourses and, to a lesser extent, the study and critique of traditional narrative film. In many instances, this has represented a closed system, one open neither to new lines of analysis nor to works which don't fit the predominant theoretical models.[1] Now, however, both the rapid production of lesbian and gay media in the community, and the recent legitimation of lesbian and gay studies within the academy, have begun to shift these agendas for feminist film theory, as have, on other levels, the emergence of postcolonial cultural criticisms and Third World feminisms.[2]

Drawing on the contributions of postcolonial cultural theory to unravel some of the contradictions of contemporary North American lesbian experience, Martha Gever notes:

> My experience has taught me a few things. Above all, it has taught me that to *be* a lesbian means engaging in a complex, often treacherous, system of cultural identities, representations and institutions, and a history of sexual regulation. This is not a unique status nor a form of privileged consciousness; everyone is implicated in these systems.[3]

As Gever's quote suggests, the terms within which we understand and discuss questions of lesbian representation have undergone a fundamental shift. Recent work on marginal sexual identities has focused on the process of their formation as *cultural* identities, located in specific social and representational histories.[4] Challenging previous tendencies within feminist criticism and lesbian and gay studies, which theorized lesbian and gay experiences as somehow "outside of" or apart from the structures of the wider, "patriarchal" culture, these contemporary analyses insist on the importance of understanding how lesbian and gay identities and cultural practices are articulated within and in relation to their cultural and historical contexts.

These contemporary approaches to gay media acknowledge cultural hybridity and syncretism as central processes in the formation of marginalized cultural forms. Therefore, they implicitly question models of lesbian representation which claim to articulate "autonomous" or "authentic" forms of lesbian sexuality or desire in relation to filmic discourse. Such an approach starts from an understanding that the "dominant culture" is never unitary or entirely monolithic, and suggests that what is dominant in a given context assumes different forms and offers a range of possibilities for subversion, resistance, or resignification.

Tendencies by lesbian and gay critics to posit heterosexuality as far more monolithic than it is, and "marginal sexualities" as far more "oppositional" than they may be, may actually reinforce dominant cultural beliefs in the inherent and essential separateness of lesbian and gay sexuality and desire, rather than challenging these dyadic terms.

Much recent critical work, for instance, has argued against such claims to autonomy or specificity, suggesting, instead, how a reading of the relationality of lesbian sexuality and desire could insist on their capacity to displace or dismantle hegemonic, heterosexual norms. Reflecting discomfort with the regulatory aspects of identity categories, these efforts explore how gay practices are structured in part by the very dominant heterosexual codes they resist and reinscribe, and suggest that models of reinscription and proliferation can offer provocative and necessary sites for lesbian cultural practices. As theorists such as Judith Butler have insisted, such *structuring* of identities never fully determines them, nor is such relationality or reinscription ever only one-directional.[5] Instead, such models offer frameworks for considering how lesbian, gay, and other marginal sexual cultures themselves continually contest, inform, and reshape the dominant culture.

The current popularity of Butler's project of resignification and reterritorialization suggests the extent to which it offers a theoretical articulation for a range of practices which have emerged since the early eighties. Clearly, such theoretical models do not come out of a vacuum. It's in this context that I'd like to look at questions of lesbian representation in the experimental film and videomaking of three contemporary artists: Abigail Child, Cecilia Dougherty, and Su Friedrich. Working out of distinct aesthetic and formal traditions, their films and videos offer provocative ways of looking at lesbian representation which go beyond the boundaries of the still largely accepted agendas of "realist representation," "positive images," and highly codified forms of "explicit lesbian content." Their work centrally interrogates marginal sexual identities not only as subject matter but also as *stance,* as a *process* of reinscription, as a way of situating oneself in relation to sets of images, experiences, and historical formations.

Such a shift in perspective is reflected in my own choice of terms, which assumes a field of inquiry of "lesbian representation" and "lesbian media" which is considerably wider, less stable, and less clearly defined than a more realist-defined (and purely content-oriented) model of the "representation of gays and lesbians," "images of lesbians," and so on. Such a choice is strategic, aimed at opening up questions of lesbian representation within a wide range of works with greatly varying political, aesthetic, and representational agendas, many of which exceed or question our existing theoretical vocabularies. These works inevitably destabilize a category like "lesbian media," suggesting that such a term can't describe any stable unity, any body of work that is "out there"; instead, it offers us a different map of the vast activity of film and video, with new sets of fault lines, continuities, and lines of flight.

The work of New York-based experimental filmmaker Abigail Child[6] excavates the ways Western cinematic forms figure masculinity and femininity, and artfully probes their subliminal articulation in an array of pop cultural artifacts. Her seven-part series *Is This What You Were Born For?*[7] (1981–1989) combines found footage and recreated elements of film noir, pornography, soap opera, early cinema, and home movies, in its relentless interrogation of gesture and the body. Coming out of a tradition of structural filmmaking and cinematic minimalism, her work represents a feminist project located partially within the legacy of historically male, formalist practices,[8] one which adapts their rigorous attention to structure and materiality, and reinscribes these from a conviction that the cultural meanings of images and materials *do* matter.

Child's short, dense, and highly poetic films work to destabilize familiar images, sequences, and tableaux, insistently exploring the artifices which structure narrative, and probing them for moments of rupture and excess. Her focus is on the body, as visually and corporeally enacted (and gendered) through gait, gesture, rhythm, and repetition. Influenced by the strategies of language poetry and the musical work of John Zorn, Christian Marclay, and Zeena Parkins (all of whom have collaborated on her films), she uses found footage, reenactment, and multilayered sound cutting to reframe and reposition familiar sequences, images, and materials. Contrapuntally rechoreographing these fragments of action, gesture, and ritualized movement ("that array of corporeal theatrics understood as gender presentation"[9]), Child makes a kind of music out of this "noise."

Mayhem, Abigail Child

Child's engagement with cinematic melodrama can be traced to her 1984 film, *Covert Action*. The short found-footage work is made from salvaged home movies of two heterosexual couples on holiday in the 1950s; the two sequences, with the same men but different women, appear to date from different years. In Child's film, the scenes are intercut and fragmented, suggesting a range of possible story lines. The focus is on questions of gesture, the formalized mating rituals and games that read as a form of dance, and the theatricalized roles of the men and women. Chipping away at the repetition and exaggeration within these home movie sequences, Child denaturalizes their heterosexual rituals, replaying them as what Butler has termed "an incessant and panicked imitation"[10] of their own phantasmatic ideal, engaging a viewer who is alternately fascinated and horrified.

Child's 1987 film *Mayhem* most centrally explores questions of specifically *sexual* roles and representations; along with *Both* (1989), it most explicitly engages questions of lesbian representation. Child describes the film as:

> Perversely and equally inspired by de Sade's *Justine* and Vertov's sentences about the satiric detective advertisement, *Mayhem* is my attempt to create a film in which sound is the character, and to do so focusing on sexuality and the erotic. Not so much to undo the entrapment (we fear what we desire, we desire what we fear) but to frame fate, show up the rotation, upset the common and incline our contradictions towards satisfaction, albeit conscious.[11]

The film opens with a classic noir scenario: a woman in forties' attire waits in a darkened room. Her face is barred by diagonal shadows, created by the light through a venetian blind. The music suggests fear, foreboding. She looks up, startled, awaiting an intrusion. The film then cuts to a scene of two men peering, menacingly, suggesting malice—except that the sequence is lifted from a postwar spy thriller. Veering between historical periods and locales, the film catalogues types of actions, codified gestures, ways of representing the body. Men and women shift positions constantly: watching, being watched, looking around, flight. Two men pursue a woman through an urban landscape; just when things threaten to get menacing, she turns around to glimpse them as they suddenly embrace, introducing slippages between hetero- and homosexual desire that reverberate through the film.

Yet simply describing sequences risks misreading the film, for *Mayhem* is a deeply kinetic work, one in which the images slip from the viewer's grasp before she or he can fully register them—a strategy which heightens their subliminal apprehension, their capacity for slippage and deferred action. As the film continually sets up and then redirects its melodramatic encounters, *Mayhem* plays on the fine line between threat and fascination. Rather than attempting to separate out pleasure and danger—or "lesbian" and "straight" fantasies—what is frightening or pathologized becomes reworked as sources of excitement and arousal. In this messy nexus of fear and desire, the film's densely layered and surgical editing strategies are designed to open up what is seamless, or, in Child's words, "to have the pleasure but be aware of the dynamics and origins of this pleasure."[12]

As film scholar Madeline Leskin has noted, "*Mayhem* meticulously employs the language of noir: the lighting, the camera angles, even the latent sadism, but takes noir to the next level by drawing the connections between sex and violence."[13] Using its found-footage materials as a very partial and idiosyncratic archeology of sexual scenarios, Child sets up erratic lines of flight and echoes within the text: a brief scene of a woman resisting a man's embrace reverberates off an earlier sound fragment, where a woman's voice stutters "no, not so close." Later, another intones, "no no quiere," as the sound track shifts from fragments of Hollywood film scores to a Mexican soap opera. Looking at the postures and behaviors of romance, the film implicates itself within these representations and the ways that they construct desire, even as it also pulls back and lays bare some of their workings. As the film catalogues and explores contradictory fantasy scenarios, and constructs multiple points of identification and desire, Child locates herself *within* these contradictions, within the erotic interplay of anticipation and suspense.

As the four primary actors (two male, two female) shift roles and positions, the film embraces sexual ambiguity and the relationality of sexual identities. Clearly, Child draws from available theoretical models, yet complicates and expands them—interrogating lesbian desire *and* heterosexuality, the female body *and* the male body (her final film in the series, *Mercy*, explores normative constructions of masculinity). Combining a multiplicity of gazes and forms of desire, the collisions between them give *Mayhem* density and movement. There is a loose progression in the film, from sequences of fear and foreboding towards more playful and comic scenes; this parallels a movement from strictly heterosexual scenes to more mixed encounters, but the film does not lend itself to reductive or utopian readings about lesbian or gay sexualities. Instead, like the collage and theft-based strategies of the gay fanzines that critic Matias Viegener has written about,[14] Child's found footage and reconstructed materials offer a strategy of appropriation and erotic reinscription of pleasurable *and* problematic images from an array of sometimes deeply misogynistic mass cultural sources—a strategy based on reconstructing and refiguring these images, rather than trying to produce an "affirmative image" of female or lesbian sexuality.

The potentially threatening ambiguity with which this works can be seen in the porn sequence that ends the film, a sequence which provides a sort of epilogue or coda to it. These final scenes, taken from a 1920s Japanese porn film, feature two women furiously making love, who are interrupted by a thief-voyeur, who masturbates to the women's lovemaking and is then "forced" at gunpoint to join in. As the voyeuristic dimension of noir are enacted, very literally, the conventions linking sex, violence, and control are stripped bare. Yet as a representation of lesbian sexuality, it is far from reassuring. It offers no safe place, no nostalgic retreat, from the voyeurism and entrapment of dominant cinematic codes. Instead of offering reassurance, or the illusion of an uncorrupted sphere of representation, the sequence seems to propose a series of questions which reflect back on the film as a whole: Who was this meant for? Who is the intended audience? Who is turned on? What kinds of images are disturbing? What is erotic?

By closing on such a "corrupt" lesbian image, one not "free," but completely embedded in histories of oppression and resistance, *Mayhem* implicitly questions the production of sexual identities that are "stable, natural, and good"[15]—as well as questioning the privileged position of a feminist "critique" which seeks to authorize its own status as rational analysis, somehow outside such histories of distortion, entrapment, and desire. In contrast, it presents a kind of alternate map through its idiosyncratically assembled film history, offering a *proliferation* of sexual identities, pleasures, and dangers. It's a strategy that locates lesbian desire *within* the romantic and voyeuristic interplays of cinematic representation, rather than claiming to articulate a new, distinct language or an autonomously defined lesbian sexuality. As such, it refuses to isolate or compartmentalize lesbian desire; it positions it as always already a part of these systems of desire, deviant and subversive, to be sure, but not separate.

A more pop-cultural approach to positioning the lesbian subject can be seen in the work of San Francisco-based videomaker and photographer Cecilia Dougherty.[16] While Dougherty's earlier videotapes addressed marginal and stigmatized aspects of lesbian experience, engaging in a project of demystification and self-definition, her later work has departed from this mode of direct contestation. In *Grapefruit* (1989), Dougherty takes a different, seminarrative tact, staging an all-female video reenactment of Yoko Ono's account of life with John Lennon and the Beatles. Like *Mayhem,* it is a work that constructs a mode of lesbian representation based on stance and subversion—the entry into and impersonation of dominant cultural materials—rather than employing explicit content or straightforward representation. As Dougherty has described her project, her work "is not *about* lesbians, it *is* lesbian."[17]

Dougherty has stated that this strategy resulted from her frustration with the reception of her previous videotapes, *Kathy* (1986) and *Claudia* (1987). Intended by the artist as statements about banality and the everyday, they were nonetheless often read—in art settings—as "transgressive," due to the fact that both contain explicit depictions of lesbian sexual acts. (In lesbian and gay festival contexts, ironically, they were often read as unsuccessful porn—as not "erotic" enough.) This reception set up a "problem" for Dougherty: how to create lesbian visual representations that would not be immediately annexed into the category of the "transgressive"—and the very problematic duality between "normalcy" and "transgression" it reinforces.

Dougherty's choice was a circuitous reengagement with popular memory, reworking seventies icons and contemporary nostalgia for them. Drawing on both mass culture and sixties-style Pop Art, *Grapefruit* intentionally confounds distinctions of "high" and "low," of pop-cultural "original" and appropriated "copy." The very couple John and Yoko (played by two women) becomes a sign for this marriage, of the aggressively heterosexual pop-cultural mythology of the Beatles, and the much campier, much queerer

Grapefruit, Cecilia Dougherty

art-historical mythology of Fluxus, Pop, and underground performance. As deeply steeped in these avant-garde traditions as in its ostensibly more rock-and-roll narrative, *Grapefruit* aggressively opens itself up to different, intersecting cultural histories. Lackadaisical and decompressed, the video aims to produce a Warhol-like mode of distracted attention; with its Day-Glow colors, horizonless visuals, and deadpan nonacting, the tape evokes Pop and the legacies of 1970s performance and conceptual art. These influences, encoded visually, also structure the viewing experience the video creates. For the most part it is plotless and intentially "flat," without clear hierarchies in meaning, inviting its viewer to focus in and out of attention or to seize on particular details or twists.

With its mix-and-match music, costumes, and performance styles, *Grapefruit* plays with the inevitable distance and disalignment between historical "truth" and contemporary "reenactment." Working as a subversively lesbian parody of straight material, the video relates to the past by ignoring historical accuracy, and instead reinvesting historical figures from an idiosyncratic contemporary point of view—one which draws as much on art school as on mass culture. Rather than making any claim to realism or to some more rationally grounded critique of pop culture, the tape locates itself within the realms of popular fantasy and the open-ended manipulation and reinterpretation of cultural history.

The cross-gender and cross-race casting further destabilizes any sense of conventional "realism," continually reinflecting the past with new, unanticipated twists and meanings, both cultural and personal. Lesbian writer Susie Bright plays Lennon to performance artist Shelley Cook's Ono. Malaysian-born videomaker Azian Nurudin, as the easternly mystic George Harrison, reads her lines off index cards with varying accents and inflections. The sequences are colorized with garish pseudo-psychedelic video effects. Historical scenes, such as the Lennon-Ono "bed-in," are recreated, songs are lip-synced, actors forget their lines. Off and on throughout the tape, Dougherty's voice is heard coaching the actors, or directing their loose improvisations. Constantly embracing artifice and distortion, simulation is not even an issue.

Within the tape's layerings, manipulations, and subversions, the complex mapping of the lesbian subculture onto the heterosexual mythology may not be read by all viewers. The video is not explicitly "lesbian," in terms of realist representation or content. Instead, it functions more analogously to a form of "camp," working with impersonation and quasi-parodic imitation to reappropriate mass cultural figures and reinvest them with lesbian fantasies and desires. While the jokes about conceptual art (with Cook restaging Yoko Ono's Fluxus-like performances) may not register with everyone who watches the tape in the context of lesbian and gay film festivals, the quasi-Warholian play with subcultural celebrities, images, and interactions creates a range of openings and identifications, depending on the audience.

In lieu of a linear narrative, the video's involvement in a shared pop-cultural history serves to orchestrate these fragmented cultural references and allow them to play off one another. Its reinscription of the past grounds itself in the trashy discards of seventies pop culture and television. As the tape concludes, with a long scene of John and Yoko at home, talking, eating, and shooting up, it evokes a sense of the intertwined boredom and sadness of everyday life which is nonetheless quite moving. The sequence itself is aggressively banal, even boring, as *Grapefruit* works to simultaneously resituate its stars within the everyday, and restore banality to the hyped-up mythologies of pop-cultural history. Its innovation, I think, lies in its insistence on locating lesbian subjectivity within this popular sphere, setting up a *tension* between mass cultural and subcultural elements which is never allowed to resolve itself into a polarity or neatly compartmentalized division.

Dougherty's question, in more ways than one, is how to locate lesbian subjectivity within the larger culture. In her most recent work, *Coal Miner's Granddaughter* (1991), Dougherty uses a semiautobiographical narrative to replay the "coming-out" story form. The feature-length video, shot mainly on a Fisher-Price toy camera, depicts a young woman's coming-of-age in the late 1960s and early seventies. Starring video artist Leslie Singer, the tape focuses on the violence and rebellion at the center of a working-class American family. Like *Grapefruit, Coal Miner's Granddaughter* aims more for emotional truths than historical ones; casually acted, it plays on anachronistic details and historical slippage. Yet its coming-out narrative both is, and is not, conventional; the heroine leaves the repressive constraints of the home, but, except for a first exuberant brush with sexuality, the tone is far from upbeat. The women she meets as she moves West (to San Francisco, the promised land of gay liberation) form a series of awkward and sometimes painful encounters, and the ending is at best open-ended.

A step away from "video art" toward a more direct engagement with narrative, *Coal Miner's Granddaughter* uses more familiar formal structures, but continues to inflect them with a deeply personal, and culturally marginal, perspective. The strategy Dougherty's work offers—to place lesbian experiences within popular cultural landscapes—has certain parallels with the Pop Art and punk-inspired work of such fellow San Francisco-based artists as Singer and Nurudin, or the gay rereadings of popular narratives performed in Robert and Donald Kinney's recent videos. With their cross-gender and cross-race drag, celebrity impersonations, pop cultural references, and adulterated genres, these artists, like Dougherty, locate marginal experiences within the discards of contemporary mass culture, questioning both the implied boundaries between "marginal" and "mainstream" and those between "true" reproduction and "distortion."[18]

The New York based filmmaker Su Friedrich[19] has the longest involvement in the development of lesbian media. Coming from a background in photography and avant-garde filmmaking, in recent years Friedrich has shifted from the silent, nonnarrative strategies of *Cool Hands, Warm Heart* (1979) and *Gently Down the Stream* (1981), to incorporate dramatization, narrative, and documentary techniques in her films *The Ties That Bind* (1984), *Damned If You Don't* (1987), and *Sink or Swim* (1990). Working to reopen and expand the traditions of American avant-garde filmmaking, Friedrich's work has brought a poetic and deeply lyrical style to questions of female identity and lesbian desire. Situated in the interpenetration of personal family history and public events, Friedrich's films probe her relation to the legacies of Catholicism, German fascism, and postwar destabilization, through her own experiences and those of her parents. While often loosely autobiographical, Friedrich refuses to fetishize "the personal" as the locus of meaning in the heavily codified manner of much American "personal filmmaking" of the 1960s and 1970s. Instead, her films locate the individual in a web of intersecting histories and narratives, chance events, and fantasies, in which forces of empowerment and entrapment cannot be fully separated.

Gently Down the Stream, Su Friedrich

Gently Down the Stream uses hand-scratched texts and rephotographed imagery to intercut memorylike shards of sexual conflict, troubled relationships, and Catholic guilt. Based on dreams Friedrich recorded in her journal over a number of years, the film meditates on moments of anxiety, doubt, and everyday trauma. The texts are scratched word by word into the emulsion, leaving the spectator in a state of waiting and uncertainty: "I/wake/her/She/is/angry/Smears/spermicidal/jelly/on/my/lips/No!" "I/draw/a/man/Take/his/skin/Get/excited/Mount/it/ IT'S/LIKE/BEING/IN/LOVE/WITH/A/STRAIGHT/WOMAN." As the film progresses, the anxieties take shape, offering different glimpses of Friedrich's psyche and identity. The ambiguous trauma of the first sentence, for instance, is illuminated by and reverberates through the second text. The images are also offered like glimpses—feet walking, water from a boat, figures of the virgin and Christ, a woman rowing. Enigmatic and richly suggestive, the film's disconcerting impact proceeds by this back-and-forth movement of ellipsis and illumination, as clear pictures form, change shape and dissolve, both conceptually through the text, and visually through the rephotographed and reframed images.

The film's form is itself fractured and disturbed; bits of white leader and punched-out holes insist on the vulnerability and incompleteness of the material substrata. Series of images shift from full-frame to reframed presentations in irregular patterns and rhythms; their relation to the text is not illustrative but more suggestive and oblique, intersecting erratically to create new sets of associations or subjective impressions. The structure of *Gently Down the Stream* is highly permeable, allowing a sense of random and unpredictable encounters that approximate a kind of dream logic, as the film proceeds in a stream-of-consciousness flow with constant interruptions and eruptions of unprocessed, sometimes obscure, dream material.

If *Gently Down the Stream* situates the conflicts between lesbianism, heterosexuality, and Catholicism within the realm of interior psychic experiences, *Damned If You Don't* restages these as a narrative story between two characters, "the nun" and "the other woman." Like Friedrich's previous films, its quiet and acutely nuanced flow combines elements of dream structure, private fantasy, and personal memory. But it expands on these to engage with more traditional narrative forms, drawing in sequences from the 1947 Powell-Pressburger film *Black Narcissus,* and texts from Judith C. Brown's *Immodest Acts: The Life of a Lesbian Nun in Renaissance Italy.* Collaging scraps of documentary and narrative materials, personal testimony, and enigmatic images of Catholic rituals and vestments, the film performs an informal, loosely historical investigation of nuns as embodiments of suppressed and displaced female desires. Friedrich weaves in and out of secular and religious worlds to create poetic associations between contemporary and historical narratives. Her selective samplings focus the viewer's attention as much on the artifice and excesses of their baroque and frequently melodramatic forms as on the tales they tell.

The highly compressed presentation of *Black Narcissus* flattens the film into a comic duel between moral absolutes, accentuating the codes of cinematic melodrama and the repressive sexual politics of the original. Friedrich condenses the story into a conflict between the "good" nun, played by Deborah Kerr, and the "bad" nun, who descends into the world of lust and men. Stylized and aggressively "amateur," with its rolling scan lines and black-and-white TV reproduction, the appropriation delights in the melodramatic excess of the original, while intimating an unstated erotic bond between the two women. The convent becomes an almost allegorical site of repressed desire, with death as the punishment for transgression. In Friedrich's own narrative, of course, this scenario is replaced by the temptations of other women—and the outcome is reversed. As the sexy "other woman" silently pursues the tortured nun, Friedrich weaves in fantastic tales from the seventeenth century trial of Sister Benedetta (recorded in Brown's *Immodest Acts*) and a friend's reminiscences of a Catholic school girlhood. The pleasures of voyeurism and the intrigue of concealed sexuality play a hide-and-seek game within the film, which slowly reveals its own narrative progression. Friedrich describes the contradictory legacies of Catholicism embedded in the film:

> With *Damed If You Don't,* I found myself wanting to tell a story, and
> again one which I thought of as a moral tale. I was ready, I thought, to
> crucify once and for all the Catholic Church, and rescue a poor nun from
> its clutches. But I found myself unable to be as censorious as I'd imagined;
> I wanted some of the characters and places and objects to function as a
> tribute to certain sensual aspects of Catholicism. . . . I had to admit that
> there were some experiences growing up Catholic which I still valued.
>
> Perhaps the most subtle manifestation of that is simply in the way the
> film is shot and edited. It isn't easy for me to articulate how it works, but
> I'm convinced that my upbringing, with all its repression, idealism and
> sense of an unrequited desire for the sublime, has had a direct effect on
> my way of shooting and editing.[20]

Turning the tables on the symbols and structures of institutionalized
repression, the film gently eroticizes the religious vestments as covers hiding
potential pleasure and abandonment, as played out in its final seduction
scene. Lyrically composed and sensuously edited, Friedrich's enigmatic visual
images serve as indirect projections of the repressed desires and longings
acted out in the narrative. Sensuality and physical pleasure seep into the film
at every turn, as the nun is unable to escape her desires; for example, she
flees her pursuer to visit to an aquarium, only to be confronted by a pair of
beautiful white whales twisting through the water. Throughout the film, the
implicit sensuality and perversity of the baroque Catholic iconography is
used against itself to create an erotic fascination with concealment and
repression. The other woman finally accomplishes her seduction through a
gift, a small needlepoint image of Christ with only the mouth embroidered,
which she leaves in the nun's room—an eroticized *detournment* of the
religious icon.

The underlying strategy of the film revolves around recovering—for pleasure, for suspense, for fantasy—the mechanisms, anxieties, and twisted representations of the oppressive culture. Rather than questioning the "truth"
of its assembled documents—the exoticized intrigues of *Black Narcissus,* the
wildly fantastic testimony of Sister Benedetta's accuser—Friedrich probes
their pathologized narratives as sources of both history *and* fascination,
documents whose aesthetic excesses and ambiguous powers can be undermined and resituated in a modern tale of girl gets girl. The very structure of
the film works to appropriate filmic clichés—voyeuristic pleasure, female
sexuality, happy endings—into its highly personal and even humorous meditation on lesbian erotic pursuit and guilt-drenched lust. Rather than using
its fragments to create a new fiction of the "natural" or the "true," the film
plays itself out on the level of suggestion and allegory. Perhaps more than
anything, it is about fantasy, and the processes by which repressive experiences and traumas are replayed and transformed into turn-ons. Like the

dream structure of *Gently Down the Stream, Damned If You Don't* explores the subjective processes of memory, anxiety, fantasy, and desire.

In this alternation between critical and almost nostalgic stances, Friedrich's film explores how a modern lesbian subject is positioned in relation to these representations. Like *Mayhem* and *Grapefruit,* Friedrich's film seems to revolve around the possibilities for creating pleasure in the discards of a repressive and highly constrained past, and of moving beyond feminist critique to selectively reinvest these images and memories with private and erotic meanings. With its sensual and suggestive intercutting, *Damned If You Don't* probes the complex interplays of voyeurism and identification, guilt, pleasure, and shame, at work in their cautious reappropriation. As Scott MacDonald notes in his discussion of Friedrich's films:

> *Damned If You Don't* . . . energizes feminist deconstruction by locating it within a context of at least two forms of (redirected) film pleasure: the excitement of the melodramatic narrative and the sensuous enjoyment of cinematic texture, rhythm and structure. Friedrich's decision not only to include a representation of female sexuality but to use it as the triumphant conclusion of the film is central to her new direction. Friedrich has cinematically appropriated the pleasure *of* women *for* women.[21]

In these films and videos from the past several years, Child, Dougherty, and Friedrich offer strategies for situating the lesbian subject within and against the narratives of the past, within and against the inherited materials of the dominant culture. It's an ambiguous position—situated within the culture, structured in part by it, and yet deviant. There is perhaps a danger involved, of loss of identity and loss of autonomy, in abandoning the codified cultural practices of a more ghettoized community. Yet this tension, this troubled and troubling instability that comes from engagement with the codes and artifices of the wider culture, is also a potent source of pleasure. These works offer their viewers, not the pleasures of a well-consolidated lesbian subject position, reassuring in its stability and autonomy, but something else: the pleasures of *exploring* cinematic pleasure, of challenging and unsettling our relations to these materials. Actively engaging with this ongoing process of repetition and reinscription, such work opens a space for exploring the imprecise boundaries of contemporary sexual identities.

Needless to say, many of these strategies no longer seem as controversial or as disturbing as they once did. And perhaps, as they lose their power to shock, they may also lose a certain intensity of impact, as viewers and practitioners alike develop critical languages to describe and in a sense defuse their disruptive reworkings of familiar images, materials, and cultural memories. From the time this article was first drafted, in the spring of 1990, to the time of its publication three years later, a major shift in theoretical discourses and critical expectations has indeed taken place. Concepts of "parodic imitation" and "subversive repetition" have proliferated, to the extent that even Judith Butler, with whose work such terms are most closely associated, has come to question and problematize their blanket usage. Clearly, not all forms of parody are subversive or disruptive. As a number of recent works attest, parodic strategies can serve to reiterate, consolidate, and renaturalize normative relations of power and sexuality in some contexts, and work to destabilize and disrupt them in others. What constitutes effective reterritorialization is always open to question, challenge, and reappraisal.

Yet this expanded field of critical discourses with which we understand lesbian media, and feminist cultural practices more generally, is crucial. Work such as Child's, which was long marginalized for its "failure" to align with stable or identifiable identity categories, or to produce an unambiguously "affirmative" or "critical" position towards its assembled materials, now appears almost prescient. And with a renewed attention towards aesthetic strategies, including those from avant-garde and experimental traditions, such work refreshingly and productively challenges the straightforward and often deeply reductive focus on "content" that plagued much feminist and gay media criticism of the past decade.

Indeed, the strategies evident both in contemporary lesbian media and critical theory could be conceived "simply" as lesbian reengagement with some of the most classic avant-garde and poststructuralist practices—a series of intersections with a long, if often suppressed, history, one which is anything but simple. Without calling for any kind of renewed formalism, I'd like to propose that works such as those of Child, Dougherty, and Friedrich suggest the reopening of questions which have long been marginalized from media criticism and the world of professional film studies, centering around issues of aesthetics, formal strategies, and what works as "art." These questions may have far more relevance than we expect to ongoing discussions of lesbian subjectivity, feminist media, and political complexity and effectiveness.[22]

Notes

1. The implicit closure of many psychoanalytically-based feminist theories can be seen, for example, in Constance Penley, ed., *Feminism and Film Theory* (New York: Routledge, 1988), Laura Mulvey, *Visual and Other Pleasures* (Bloomington: Indiana University Press, 1989), and in some of the earlier work of Teresa de Lauretis in *Alice Doesn't: Feminism, Semiotics, Cinema* (Bloomington: Indiana University Press, 1984). Subsequent efforts to open feminist theories of film to questions of lesbian representation can be found in de Lauretis's *Technologies of Gender* (Bloomington: Indiana University Press, 1987), and

Judith Mayne's *The Woman at the Keyhole* (Bloomington: Indiana University Press, 1990), as well as in articles by Chris Straayer, Martha Gever, Patricia White, and others.

2. Although very differently located, such approaches share a common grounding: the questioning of the unity of the category of "women" and the adequacies of analysis based solely on gender.

3. Martha Gever, "The Names We Give Ourselves," in Russell Ferguson, et al., eds., *Out There: Marginalization and Contemporary Cultures* (Cambridge/New York: MIT Press and the New Museum of Contemporary Art, 1990), p. 191.

4. As British writer Stuart Hall suggests, in relation to the representation of postcolonial ethnic identity: "Perhaps instead of thinking of identity as an already accomplished historical fact, which the new cinematic discourses then represent, we should think, instead, of identity as a "production," which is never complete, always in process, and always constituted within, not outside, representation. But this view problematizes the very authority and authenticity to which the term, 'cultural identity', lays claim." Stuart Hall, "Cultural Identity and Cinematic Representation," *Framework* no. 36 (1989), p. 69.

5. See Judith Butler, *Gender Trouble* (New York: Routledge, 1990), and "Imitation and Gender Insubordination," in Diana Fuss, ed., *Inside/Out: Lesbian Theories, Gay Theories* (New York: Routledge, 1991). See also Liz Kotz, "Interview with Judith Butler," *Artforum,* (November 1992).

6. Critical writings on Child include Marjorie Keller, "Is This What You Were Born For?" and Charles Bernstein, "Interview with Abigail Child," *X-Dream* (Autumn, 1987); Maureen Turim, "Childhood Memories and Household Events in the Feminist Avant-garde," *Journal of Film and Video* no. 38 (Summer/Fall 1986); Barbara Hammer, "The Invisible Screen: Lesbian Cinema," *Center Quarterly* (Spring, 1988); and Dennis Barone, "Abigail Child," *Arts Magazine* (September, 1990); as well as Child's book of experimental writings, *A Motive for Mayhem* (Hartford: Potes & Poets Press, 1989). Child's 16mm films are distributed by Filmmaker's Cooperative and the American Federation for the Arts in New York City, Canyon Cinema in San Francisco, Canadian Filmmakers Distribution Center, and the London Film Co-op. *Mayhem* is also distributed on video from the Video Data Bank and the Kitchen.

7. The title is an inversion of that of the Goya etching "This Is What You Were Born For," part of the *Disasters of War* series.

8. Analogously to classic minimalism in art history, structural filmmaking has, in progressive analyses, often come to represent the epitome of a straight, white, male aesthetic, deriving from a reading of minimalist practices as based on the denial of subjectivity, the suppression of cultural associations, and the evisceration of content. A classic articulation of this position can be found in Anna C. Chave, "Minimalism and the Rhetoric of Power," *Arts Magazine* (January, 1990) pp. 44–63. Such a reading of minimalism of structural film is clearly complicated by the current proliferation of feminist, gay, ethnic, and postcolonial work reappropriating and reinflecting classic minimalist strategies. See, for instance, Kathryn Hixson, "The Subject Is the Object: Legacies of Minimalism," *New Art Examiner* (May, 1991) and " . . . and the Object Is the Body," *New Art Examiner* (October, 1991); Laura Cottingham, "Interview with Adrian Piper," *Journal of Contemporary Art*, vol. 5, no. 1 (Spring, 1992); and my own "Complicity," on work by Abigail Child and Lutz Bacher, in Roma Gibson and Pamela Church Gibson, eds., *Dirty Looks: Women, Power, Pornography* (London: British Film Institute, 1993).

9. Butler, "Imitation and Gender Insubordination," p. 28.

10. Ibid., p. 23. Butler's work offers a number of concepts that are quite provocative in relation to Child's films, particularly her conception of heterosexuality as a compulsive and compulsory repetition, a panicked imitation of its own phantasmatic ideal, which can potentially be destabilized by the parodic and imitative effects of gay identities, as well as her notion of "subversive repetition," of exploring the moments of rupture within heterosexual repetition, as potentially productive strategies for lesbian and gay cultural practice.

11. Abigail Child, "Program Notes: *Is This What You Were Born For?*" San Francisco Cinematheque (February 22, 1990).

12. Madeline Leskin, "Interview with Abigail Child," *Motion Picture* vol. 3, no. 1/2 (Winter, 1989–90). Reprinted from *Skop* (West Berlin, February, 1988).

13. Ibid., p. 39.

14. Matias Viegener, "Gay Fanzines: There's Trouble in That Body," *Afterimage* (January, 1991). Expanded and republished as "Kinky Escapes, Bedroom Techniques, Unbridled Passion and Secret Sex Codes," in David Bergman, ed., *Camp Grounds* (Amherst: University of Massachusetts Press, 1993).

15. Ibid., p. 12.

16. Critical writings on Dougherty's work include Valerie Soe, "Cecilia Dougherty/*Grapefruit*," *Cinematograph* no. 4 (1991) and Liz Kotz "Interrogating the Boundaries of Women's Art: New Work in Video by Four Women," *High Performance,* no. 48 (Winter, 1989). Dougherty's tapes are distributed by the Video Data Bank (*Grapefruit* and *Coal Miner's Granddaughter*) and Frameline (*Sick, Kathy*).

17. Interview with the artist, San Francisco, January, 1991.

18. Coming from a younger generation of videomakers, most of whom were directly or indirectly influenced by the punk movement, this rejection of liberal and gay-assimilationist mandates for "realist" representation has parallels with the cultural scavenging and anti-aesthetic disruption of the gay fanzine circuit. See Viegener, "Gay Fanzines: There's Trouble in That Body," and his essay in this volume.

19. Critical writings and interviews on Friedrich's work include Scott MacDonald's "Interview with Su Friedrich," *The Independent* (December, 1990); Martha Gever, "Girl Crazy: Lesbian Narratives in *She Must Be Seeing Things* and *Damned If You Don't,*" *The Independent* (July, 1988); Scott MacDonald, "Reappropriations," *Film Quarterly* (Winter, 1987/88); Bruce Jenkins, "*Gently Down the Stream,*" *Millennium Film Journal,* nos. 16/17/18 (Summer, 1986); Stephanie Beroes, "Interviews with New York Filmmakers," *Cinematograph* no. 2 (1986); Barbara Kruger, "*The Ties That Bind,*" *Artforum* (October, 1984); and Lindley Hanlon, "Female Rage: The Films of Su Friedrich," *Millennium Film Journal* no. 12 (Fall–Winter 1982–83). Friedrich's films are distributed by Film-makers Cooperative, Women Make Movies, and the Museum of Modern Art in New York City, Canyon Cinema in San Francisco, and the Canadian Filmmakers Distribution Center.

20. Su Friedrich, statement from the panel, "Does Radical Content Deserve Radical Form?" *Millennium Film Journal* no. 22 (Winter/Spring 1989–90) pp. 122–123.

21. Scott MacDonald, "Su Friedrich: Reappropriations," pp. 41–42.

22. The writing of this article was supported by a New Writings in Art Criticism grant from San Francisco Artspace. It was initially given as a talk at the Whitney Symposium on American Art in March, 1990. Much thanks to Erika Suderburg for comments on drafts on this paper, and to the artists for extensively discussing their works with me.

Girlfriend in a Coma: Notes on the Films of Gregg Araki

DARYL CHIN

Asian-American films have been typed as being about socially progressive Asian-American subject matter. Most gay films are narrative love stories: two men or two women fall in love, with results that are either happy or unhappy. Gregg Araki is an Asian-American who does not make Asian-American films. He is a gay filmmaker whose films do not configure solely gay concerns.

Araki is a young, Los Angeles-based filmmaker whose first two feature films, *Three Bewildered People in the Night* (1987) and *The Long Weekend (O' Despair)* (1989) are highly unusual. They are unusual not just because

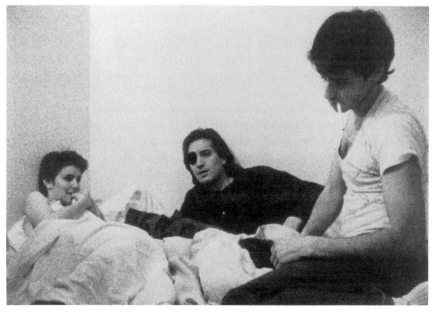

Left to right: Alicia (Darcy Marta), David (Mark Howell), and Craig (John Lacques) in *Three Bewildered People in the Night*, Gregg Araki

Left to right: Bretton Vail, Nicole Dillenberg, and Maureen Dondanville in *The Long Week-end (O'Despair)*, Gregg Araki

his budgets are extremely low, but because his approach is artisanal in that he wrote, directed, and produced these narrative features while also acting as cameraman, chief sound recordist, and editor on both projects.

Araki was born in Southern California in 1959. He received his B.A. in film studies from the University of California, Santa Barbara, in 1982, and his M.F.A. in film production from the University of Southern California in 1985. Given his background and education, Araki's choice to pursue dramatic filmmaking seems logical. What sets Araki apart, however, is his refusal to satisfy the expectations associated with such an endeavor.

Most of the Asian-American media produced in Southern California depicts social and political issues pertaining to the Asian-American community, or traces the maker's personal Asian-American heritage. In concrete terms, this translates into documentaries about Angel Island or the internment camps, interviews with parents and grandparents, or fictional narratives dealing with the immigrant experience. When attending film school, Asian-Americans are encouraged to move in that direction.

Another pressure is applied as well: the pressure to adhere to motion picture industry standards. Narrative filmmaking serves as the sole model of filmmaking practice, and most students attend such schools in order to become proficient in this mode of commercial production. As a result, the filmmakers produced by this system often attempt to create the kind of narrative transparency favored in Hollywood. After graduating from the film production course at USC, for example, the young filmmaker has been indoctrinated in the style (or stylelessness) of apparent seamless continuity, smooth editing, and polished camerawork.

Araki is the antithesis of all this. His two films concern the psychosexual problems of Los Angeles postgraduates, who are often embroiled in intensely solipsistic love relationships. *Three Bewildered People in the Night* presents a study of a few days in the lives of a young woman who is a video artist, her boyfriend who is between jobs and confused about his sexuality, and her best friend, a gay male performance artist. To describe the "plot" in this way is to overstate the case, because the film itself does not explicate any of the above in overt terms. A typical scene is one near the beginning of the film, in which the young woman returns late from a night of editing. She opens the door to find her boyfriend sitting in the dark, staring out of the window. The scene is played out in a series of cross-cut shots in which each character is never placed in the center of the frame but always off to the side and surrounded by a great deal of empty space. In a typical shot of this kind, the boyfriend appears at the left of the frame, staring to his right and speaking to his girlfriend who is off-screen right. Although he looks towards where she would logically be positioned, his gaze is slightly averted, not direct. Both characters remain isolated, even when engaged in dialogue, which consists of evasive non sequiturs that echo the visual effect.

In *Three Bewildered People in the Night,* suspense revolves around the ambiguity of the relationship which develops between the two male characters. Moments of stasis, ennui, and depleted action—which are certainly plentiful—are nevertheless haunted by the possibility of sexual interest, although the film ends without a resolution. As a result, *Three Bewildered People in the Night* could be called an almost-love story, which flirts with sexual expression but never makes it to consummation. The film teases viewers with the promise of narrative closure, and plays on the reliability of gay film stories to conclude with the fulfillment of sexual desire. Frustrating that fulfillment, however, the film throws desire into relief in the same way that recurring stasis in the film throws the idea of narrative movement into relief.

In *The Long Weekend (O' Despair)*, Araki ups the ante by multiplying the interactions between characters. This film is populated by three couples: two men, two women, and one of each, who gather for a weekend reunion. However, the increased number of characters demands a greater emphasis on plot than in the earlier work, and the tension of narrative displacement which sustained *Three Bewildered People* becomes dissipated in this film.

Still, the two works are similar in many respects. Like *Three Bewildered People, The Long Weekend* is not easy to watch. Again, Araki drains his narrative by presenting scenarios of attenuated inactivity, while the audience is asked to endure minute-by-minute reports of the angst afflicting the various characters. Over time, however, these moments become emblematic of the search for genuine contact with the reality of present-day Los Angeles. In the later film, there is more contact than occurred in *Three Bewildered People,* with more scenes where the characters crowd into the same space, framed together in the cramped surroundings of small apartments and un-fashionable clubs which make up bohemian L.A. Still, the sense of isolation prevalent in Araki's earlier film persists, because these characters, too, rarely look one another in the eye.

Most low-budget feature films attempt to recreate the illusions of realism common to commercial cinema, but with smaller budgets. Not Araki. Recognizing that his movies are not commercial, he allows for intentional stylistic roughness in order to emphasize the qualities of grit, contrast, and disjunction that underscore his characteristic portrayal of a generation adrift. His narratives do not flow. Rather, they proceed through ellipses, blockages, emptiness, devices which break the continuity to allow for breathing. There are notable similarities between this aspect of Araki's method and earlier cinematic precedents. Araki's use of temporal extension to invoke an awareness of the conditions of the filmmaking practice was one of the strategies employed by Andy Warhol in a film such as *Blow Job* (1963), where Warhol uses the metaphor of sexual consummation to define narrative continuity—but teasingly, outside the frame. In many respects, Araki tries to position his work in this arena, stretching time to reveal the seams in the work. Like Warhol, he wants to remind the viewer of the fact of the film, provoking an illusion and then holding that illusion up to scrutiny. Although Araki's films distend time, however, they do not exhibit Warhol's interest in issues of real time and spacial continuity. Instead, Araki hews to narrative continuity, a significant departure from the simple sequential order that characterizes Warhol's film work before *Chelsea Girls* (1966).

Visually, Araki's films are immediately arresting, with a compositional boldness that is always enticing. He is attracted to the quality of light within the artificially lit urban landscape—buildings and streets pierced by the sharpness of neon lights. Shooting with black-and-white, 16mm Tri-X stock, which can record photographic images in very low light, Araki surveys a variety of locations in and around Los Angeles, wandering the streets at night to render compositions that reveal the particular architectural dissonance of that city, with its mismatched styles and insistent decorative touches. Araki's images often have the quality of charcoal smudges, with the film's graininess causing shades of grey and black to bleed together. In contrast, the rhythms that Araki establishes though editing are often choppy, emphasizing discord rather than continuity, and eliciting discomfort. The erratic pacing suggests a narrative trope, as editing disjunction evolves into narrative disjunction and tension builds through elision.

It seems too easy to categorize Araki's achievements, to try to tame the jagged edges of his work through interpretation. For example, it would be easy to claim that the frustrated sexual desire in the films can be read in terms of the lack of acknowledgment of the validity of homosexuality in mainstream society. It would be easy to claim that the dislocation of desire which motivates the actions of his films can be extended to include the dislocation of identity through the inequities of race in American society. Taking Araki's films as metaphors for social conditions is tempting, but that temptation should be resisted, since interpreting these works according to an imposed sociopolitical agenda denies their tendency toward autistic self-enclosure. Ironically, it is precisely this quality that accounts for much of their appeal: Araki's films at once invite and negate the prospect of audience involvement. His work disdains easy pleasure and so provides a friction which rivets attention at the same time as it mobilizes wariness of the obstacles to pleasure which he constructs.

In a far less literary way, Araki also want to provoke self-consciousness about forms of media presentation. Elongating dramatic time, he reestablishes contemplative time. Similarly, there is a certain conscious decision to frustrate narrative and dramatic conventions in order to promote the audience's critical awareness of the limitations of what's on the screen. Unlike Godard, Straub and Huillet, and Fassbinder, who all used formal restructuring of narrative to engender such self-consciousness, Araki remains ambivalent about his negations of and resistances to narrative convention. This ambivalence then finds a correlative in his depiction of frustrated desire.

Although singular, Araki should be counted as a full member of the community of independent feature filmmakers. As a one-man production company of feature-length narratives, his process is similar to Jon Jost's. As a gay filmmaker experimenting with narrative, his work is related to that of Todd Haynes, Jack Walsh, Su Friedrich, Peggy Awesh, and Gus Van Sant. As an Asian-American filmmaker working with nontraditional subject matter, he has affinities with Roddy Bogawa, Trinh T. Minh-ha, and Jon Moritsugu. What is unique about Araki's filmmaking, though, is the combination of his artistic ambitions. Gregg Araki has already proved himself to be a challenging artist. The hope is that he will develop into an artist of continual provocation.

Queens of Language

Paris Is Burning

JACKIE GOLDSBY

"If money wasn't important in the world today to survive, I guess I wouldn't want anything but what I have now," Octavia St. Laurent muses as she readies herself for a photo shoot. "But since money does, I hope that the way I look puts money in my pocket." A model-perfect beauty with smooth cocoa complexion, beckoning green eyes, a pouty but playful mouth, a mane of hair that bobs thickly just above her shoulders, and firmly muscled legs and tightened torso that do serious justice to a two-piece bathing suit, Octavia St. Laurent has reason to be confident about the value of her appearance. But her ambitions can only be realized once her self is completed; as she confides to filmmaker Jenny Livingston in the documentary *Paris Is Burning* (1990), Octavia St. Laurent hopes "to become a full-fledged woman of the United States" by having a sex change operation in the near future.

If the world according to *Paris Is Burning* seems disorienting, that's because (wo)men like Octavia St. Laurent defy simple categorization. What Livingston accomplishes in this, her first feature documentary, is to record how Octavia and her coterie recode conventional meanings of race and class through their representations of gender. *Paris Is Burning* bursts open another closet door, leading into New York City's black and Latino drag society, and the culture of Harlem's drag balls, where gender-fuck is not just a theoretical concept but is, first and foremost, a way of life.

Establishing a stable life is a priority for the gay men, transvestites, and transsexuals who are citizens of the ball world. Disowned by their families of origin because of their sexual orientations, the "children" (the term house members use to refer to themselves) flock to the piers fronting the Hudson River near Christopher Street where, as Cherríe Moraga would say, they "make familia from scratch," finding safer refuge in cliques or family units known as "houses." Adopting the name of either a famous haute couture corporation—such as St. Laurent (hence Octavia's surname), Chanel, or Armani—is one way houses identify themselves. The other is to take on the name of the most powerful member of the group, the "mother" of the clan:

the houses of Pepper Labeija, Angie Xtravaganza, and Willi Ninja are three that are featured in the film. In the world of *Paris Is Burning,* a house is not a home; the film reconstitutes what that fabled term means. It certainly shakes up Daniel Patrick Moynihan's black-woman-as-head-of-the-house-hold-is-necessarily-pathological thesis. Here, (wo)men of color raise and nurture each other, not only to provide a measure of protection against the violent dangers facing them as sexual outcasts in Manhattan, but also to groom themselves to become "legends" at the balls.

To be a "legend," one must "walk" or compete in—and win—a drag ball. If personal reputation and community stature are on the line, so is one's very sense of identity, because in the ball world drag goes beyond female impersonation. Every conceivable form of identity becomes subject to (re)interpretation. Contestants—hand-picked members from various houes—battle for honor, glory, and six-foot trophies in a bevy of categories that would make Bert Parks's head spin: Femme Queen Realness, Butch Queen Realness, Military Realness, Executive Realness, Town and Country, High Fashion Evening Wear, and Butch Queen First Time in Drag Realness, to name an easy-to-decipher few.

Angela Jendell walking as a futuristic femme queen in *Paris Is Burning,* Jennie Livingston

The critical term here is "realness," which is the aesthetic imperative defining the ball and its culture. The point of the competition and the categories is not only performance but, more importantly, the re-presentation of self—to re-form a cultural ideal, to erase the signs of difference, and to be(come) an ultrafeminine "Virginia Slims" girl/ a *GQ* hunk/ a decorated army hero/ a Merrill Lynch trader/ a Ralph Lauren pseudo-aristocrat gone black or brown/ a Lincoln Center-going society matron. The trope of "realness" derives its charge from the gesture of erasure precisely because the marks of race, class, and sexuality limn these image(s) indelibly and cannot be suppressed no matter how hard the children try. At the same time, the improbability of the synthesis that is drag reframes just what is liminal in the terms of the ball world. Dislocating the oppositions of male/female, colored/white, power/disenfranchisement, margin/center, the aisle-cum-runway at the Imperial Elks Lodge (where many of the competitions were filmed) becomes a path into the psyche of ball culture; its logic unfolds in subversive splendor.

Credit for the exposition of the political critique implied in the social practices of the ball world goes to director Livingston and editor Jonathan Oppenheim. From the def(t) resurrection of Cheryl Lynn's late-seventies flash-in-the-pan hit record *Got to Be Real* as an aural leitmotif to the smart cutaways counterpointing the "real" world of white, heterosexual culture to the ball world, the film's narrative structure dissolves any notion of "authentic" experience.

The relationship between terminology and imagery underwrites the film and gives it its narrative drive. To begin with, Livingston couldn't have happened upon a more wittily critical, verbally dexterous group of folk if she tried; these queens serve up delicious dish and incisive commentary at a moment's notice (though, as Livingston jokingly confides in an essay that accompanies the press packet, they were notoriously late for interviews). Though the participants love the camera and play to it (the close-up is, after all, what their culture is about), they also relax and let Livingston and her crew record them as they are. At one point, each of the main participants— Pepper Labeija, Dorian Corey, Willi Ninja, Venus Xtravaganza, and Octavia St. Laurent—sheds his or her facade and names what it is he/she wants most—fame, a "normal" domestic life—with a shuddering of the shoulders, a bittersweet closing of the eyes, or a pang of resignation that is testimony to the trust Livingston formed with them over the course of two years of filming (1987–89).

Linking the portraits of the individuals and the spectacle of the competitions is language, which, along with the notion of performance, structures both the ball world and the film. The film unfolds conceptually, initiating visual understanding of the culture through its linguistic signifiers. Title cards flash periodically—"BALL," "HOUSE," "REALNESS," "VOGUEING," "READING," "SHADING," "MOPPING"—as if to drill the viewer into learning the ball world's lexicon. In this way, *Paris Is Burning* becomes a kind of talking book, a radically updated and resituated version of Raymond Williams's classic historiography of language, *Keywords*.[1] Williams attributed language's slippery fix on meaning to its subjection to political contexts. *Paris Is Burning* projects a similar critique, specifying the body as both subject to and the instrument of re-vision because of its (dis)engagement with commodity culture.

Two legends, Pepper Labeija and Dorian Corey, recall that, at their beginnings during the 1960s, the balls trophied "*big* costumes, feathers, and beads," or the Las Vegas showgirl look. In the seventies the ball world was enamored with movie stars. By the Reagan eighties it was appropriating the symbols and personae of the nouveaux riches as well as their plebeian underside: supermodels, captains of designer fashion, oil barons, and junk bond kings crossed competitive paths with "bangee girls" and "bangee boys"—"you know, the ones who tried to rob you on your way to the ball," an MC jokes. That the children, legendary or not, want what these life-styles represent is entirely explicable; indeed, their desires are wholly logical within the scheme of consumer capitalism. They should want to be Alexis Colby and Blake Carrington (or Ronald and Nancy Reagan, for that matter) precisely because they are of color, poor, and queer, living in one of the most class-conscious cities in the country. Why shouldn't they want out of their reality?

Once the ball expanded the categories available for competition, its critique of identity politics and consumer culture deepened. Equating identity with symbolic constructions, the children take consumerism to its logical conclusion: identity is nothing so much as a commodity fetish. Placing *Town and Country* on a par with either bangee type demystifies the system of values that produces and defines these as socially meaningful categories. Drag, for these black and Latin queens (femme and butch alike), disrupts the economy of desire and difference, the identification of self with objects meant to represent self, that fuels consumerism. By "mopping" (stealing) the clothes and accessories necessary to effect their look, or by buying breasts, reconstructed noses, lifted chins, and female genitals, the children turn traditional ideas of labor around: far from being alienated from some true self by such exchanges, the children who opt to re-produce themselves through cosmetic applications or surgical procedures find meaning and a kind of freedom in their actions. When Brooke Xtravaganza announces that her "transsexualism" operation is complete and that she is, as she exults, "as free as the wind on this beach," she declares an independence, one that calls the material and ideological bases of identity into question.

The ball world recycles commodity culture, much as rap music samples

Left to right: Octavia Saint Laurent, Freddie Pendavis, Kim Pendavis, Pepper Labeija, Dorian Corey, and Willi Ninja in *Paris Is Burning*, Jennie Livingston

from the musical gene pool. In their respective recombinations, both insist upon a sense and system of referentiality that mitigates the ahistoricism of much poststructuralist aesthetic theory. As we ask of rap, What is that riff; who performed it first, and when? so we should ask of the balls, Who is that persona; what are its social origins; whom does it represent and from what era? Indeed, the critical challenge posed by (and confronting) the ball world comes down to a question of origins, namely, when is borrowing not appropriation, and/or when does appropriation become co-optation? Or, in other words, what does it mean that the ball never ends?

It means that when *Paris Is Burning* cuts to 1989, vogueing enjoys its Warholian moment and becomes the featured entertainment at a benefit sponsored by the Design Industries Foundation for AIDS. The film borrows clips from news broadcasts that, predictably, conceal the true roots of vogueing by using that generic signifier of blackness, "Harlem." Vogueing's move downtown raised over three hundred thousand dollars to provide assistance to homeless people with AIDS. However, that the film does not pass comment on the obvious irony of the event leaves the politics of charity and compensation open to query. As we learn in the film, house members earn their income through low-paying jobs, hustling sexual favors, or performing as "showgirls." Could the participating houses really afford to donate their labor to this event? Is the hot light of the media sufficient payback? Though the film doesn't tell whether the houses were paid for participating in the benefit, its silence on this point suggests that levels of exploitation exist in even the most worthy of circumstances.

It means that Madonna can convert vogueing into excess (the film correctly depicts the dance form as just one category to be walked in a ball) and into a cultural cash crop, banking on the ball world's invisibility and its inability to publicly claim vogueing as its own. Hence the power of her visual remix of the song *Vogue* at the end of *The Immaculate Collection* video (1990). The original studio version was shot in black and white. In Madonna's live, color performance at the 1990 MTV awards, the scene is dramatically reset: the poseurs are arranged as if in a tableau vivant, corseted and bewigged in eighteenth-century French court fashions. In consuming a representation of Paris, a dying Paris (Madonna reportedly bought the gown worn by Michelle Pfeiffer in *Dangerous Liaisons*), is Madonna (figuratively) burning it? Is Paris burning? Reasoning through the logic of Madonna's performance leads us (or me, anyway) to revise the title of Livingston's film, which is named after the most important ball of the season.

The social divide that privileges Madonna to enter the ball world and exit with its cultural goods in tow, and that also impedes the ball world from rebutting her move, was described in an earlier time (1903, to be exact) by W. E. B. DuBois.[2] He called it the "veil." Then DuBois believed that the veil symbolized the problem of the twentieth century, "the color line." Now, however, in the late twentieth century, the conversion of the veil into a commodity (how else to explain the growing media attention to racially motivated police brutality and public enthusiasm for "crossover" rap?) suggests that African American theories of cultural alienation and economic disenfranchisement are in need of revision.

Paris Is Burning and the ball world play back and rework concepts of community and culture sacred to African-American discourse. In a truly grand diva move, the children restitch the veil to mean something other than socially imposed, self-abnegating denial, since, in the ball world, veils allow illusion, which allows self-expression, which allows self-fulfillment. "Home" no longer stands as the unproblematic site of Black cultural salvation it represented for DuBois; it is, instead, a fount of homophobia that damns difference and sponsors rejection, which, in turn, inspires the rebirth of the "house."

That the difference between "house" and "home" transcends the semantic points toward the children's swiftest step; signifyin' on the theory of signifyin(g) as they work the ballroom floor, they walk straight into the halls of black academe.[3] In the ball world the children clarify the workings of power in signifyin(g) exchanges because they split the notion into two forms: "reading" and "shading." Where the former is an insult that occurs between dissimilarly advantaged speakers, the latter happens when two similarly positioned speakers square off to spar verbally.

For example, the film catches a femme queen's encounter with a group of black teens. The confrontation is clearly hostile. When her humanist appeal to defuse the danger fails—"If you cut me, I bleed, just like you"—she "reads" them, taunting the girls in the group as being her "sisters" and "bulldaggers" and claiming the boys as her "boyfriends." To "throw shade," on the other hand, one addresses an equal on the sly. As Miss Dorian explains it, for two black queens to call *one another* "black queens" is "*not* a read, but a fact." Shading casts unflattering light on flaws and foibles through insinuation. When, for example, David Xtravaganza is ejected from the men's evening wear competition because he is wearing a woman's fox coat, that is, as an audience member observes, "shady." Signifying, traditionally conceived, assumes that such language contests are racially motivated— black folks talking back to white folks. However, the ball world makes it clear that blacks can read each other too. The fact of the matter is that black heterosexual culture—from assimilationist to nationalist—exercises the power and privilege to exclude and silence its (queer) own.

Yet, as much as the film opens the ball world to our view, it also betrays its subjects. The film's form as documentary—even if it becomes a *Roger and Me*-like media splash—is inimical to the participants' desire for glamour and mass fame. For example, simply by representing Octavia St. Laurent, the film exposes the fiction informing her "realness." She'll never become the supermodel she hopes to be. Not surprisingly, it is Willi Ninja, with his butch looks, who crosses over into *Village Voice* feature stories and Malcolm McLaren music videos.

But therein lies the dilemma. The documentary is probably the only genre that will acknowledge this world as it is: colored and queer. Interestingly, Marlon Riggs's *Tongues Untied* (1989) depicts drag queens as pathetic, lonely figures, who are ultimately silenced by the subjectivity of Riggs's narrative "I" (and by the voices on the sound track of singer Nina Simone and poet Essex Hemphill). If the din of voices heard throughout *Paris Is Burning* leads us to ask why Riggs quiets his queens, we can—and should—

also ask what it means for Livingston, a white woman, to give the members of the ball world a public voice. Though Livingston herself dismisses such discussions by recounting the acceptance she earned within the ball community, and the hostility she faced soliciting funds from straight black and Latino communities, the point remains: she can tell this story because her identity is not implicated in it, clearly not in the same way as is Riggs's. This is not to say that Livingston shouldn't have made the film, or that a "black" film necessarily would have been different. It is to suggest, though, that the cultural and social privilege of the filmmaker is inscribed into the film, however unobtrusive she strives to be. That Riggs silences drag queens is the obverse of Livingston's authority to accord them speech.

But I am thankful that she did, because never has speech, as performance and oral text, been so irresistible to my eyes and ears. In a way, finally, *Paris Is Burning* is about writing; it documents the impossibility of archiving identity in gendered or racial terms. Which makes the final vocabulary flash card so apropos: the words "PIG LATIN"—the dissimulation of language by reversing the pronunciation of words—signal that we can't know this world fully. Levels of signification and understanding amongst the children remain that, like their bodies, defy translation.

Notes

1. See Raymond Williams, *Keywords*, rev. ed. (New York: Oxford University Press, 1985).

2. See W. E. B. DuBois, *The Souls of Black Folk* (New York: New American Library, 1969).

3. Signifyin(g) is, as Henry Louis Gates Jr. and numerous others have described and argued, a form of verbal parody. Folk address and redress power imbalances in the occasion of dialogue through a strategy of indirection; the point is to level critique by inference. An example: A white person enters a crosswalk just as the light turns red. The motorist, who happens to be black, waits for the pedestrian to reach the opposite curb safely, but not without shouting, "You better run!" The warning could be interpreted two ways: it is a blunt but caring injunction meant to hasten the pedestrian out of harm's way, and an equally blunt cut acknowledging the pedestrian's lack of power in the moment. See Henry Louis Gates Jr., *The Signifying Monkey: A Theory of Afro-American Literary Criticism* (New York: Oxford University Press, 1988).

"The Only Haircut that Makes Sense Anymore":
Queer Subculture and Gay Resistance

MATIAS VIEGENER

One could quite reasonably trace four strains of gay culture and representation after 1969: social realism/activism, spirituality (New Age, radical fairy), drag and punk, the last two especially marked by an interest in fashion, provocation, and style. This last category is the one most resistant to critical analysis, partly because within itself abstract ideas are unarticulated and there is a distrust of speaking "reasonably" at all. And also, one cannot speak of a gay "punk" visual media without recognizing that, perhaps more than most gay aesthetics, this one is formed by specific communities for whom punk is far more than a style, but a practice embodying a philosophical and political position in the world.[1] This is a subculture to which punk plays the role that existentialism might have played for the Beats or William Burroughs, grounding them in a sense of futility in the world, a resistance to bourgeois values, a certain (moral) seriousness, and a zealous commitment to the act of negation. While this seriousness might lead in existentialism to an affirmation of the necessity for individual action and political commitment, the more anarchist strains of punk turn towards forms of self-efface-ment, deliberate provocation and (in place of individual "enlightenment") towards pleasure, usually in forms not sanctioned by the larger culture.

Although the original punk movement seemed to have little tolerance for gays and lesbians, its edginess proved ready-made for a new generation of queers.[2] The work I've chosen to examine shares the aesthetics of a post-punk generation, using techniques of shock, antigrammaticality (a muscleman wearing a bra), and negation (often tearing objects and people apart). Its gestures of provocation, juxtaposing seemingly disparate objects and styles, and blurring the boundaries of art and everyday life, is of course shared by sixty years of the avant-garde; and yet much of the work I'll discuss can be read as both populist and avant-garde.[3] However, what motivates these artists is rarely an art-historical agenda, but a cultural one, which makes any look at queer, punk, film and video production as much a project in sociology as in film aesthetics. What characterizes these works is an energetic opposition to mainstream gay *and* straight culture. What it probes (and provokes) is the difference within difference and the tendency of cultural minorities to divest themselves of their extremities.[4] The insistence on difference is in direct opposition to what one might find in the love triangle in *Making Love*, for example, where the gay lover, almost a mirror image of the protagonist, is just as "respectable" as the faithful wife.

Contemporary gay punk, in distinction to seventies British punk, tends to consider issues of sexual orientation and gender identity—marked especially by its affiliations to drag. In records of seventies punk such as the documentaries *D.O.A.* (1981) and *Decline of Western Civilization* (1980), one is struck by the retrograde sexual role-playing (as with most of rock, performers are male while audiences are feminized) perched alongside punk's obvious gender ambiguity and androgyny.[5] Lech Kawalski's *D.O.A.* is structured around footage of Sid Vicious and Nancy Spungen, the Adam and Eve of punk. In the interview, the passive Sid is stoned to the point of incoherence, while Nancy irritably tells him what he ought to be saying: they are already a parody of the putrefied heterosexual couple, frozen between adolescence and senility; they are also a study in ironic role reversal, an aggressive female with a passive, anesthetized male. In contemporary gay punk, the gender dysphoria lurking behind Sid and Nancy is brought screaming into the foreground.

> *I discovered punk around the same time I discovered my own queerness so the two are forever intertwined, providing days of endless euphoria and frustration. In my foolish younger years I believed that any guy who sucked cock was cool, just cuz it made him a faggot. I found out pretty quick that you don't have to be het to be expendable. There are as many boring stupid homosexuals as there are heterosexuals.*
> —*Letter in* Homocore, *no. 5.*

Perhaps gay punk isn't punk at all. The primary argument to substantiate calling it punk lies in the antecedents this queer subculture claims—which are more straight than gay. What gay punks reject most rigorously is "nice," post-Stonewall gay culture, as it is manifested in disco, gay marriages, *The Advocate*, polo shirts, David Leavitt's fiction, and Calvin Klein advertisements. The gay world as it is found in *Desert Hearts, Parting Glances*, or *Personal Best* is rejected on two counts, political and stylistic: for every direct or declarative challenge queer punks make against social hegemony, another indirect one is lodged in terms of style.[6] This usually involves a tacit recognition of the commodification engendering mainstream gay representations, by which the original function of the *Advocate*, for example, can be read as marketing gay culture as a saleable commodity while also creating a gay consumer who could buy his way into social legitimacy.[7] In promoting dissident cultural formations, punk encouraged cultural consumers to seize the means of production. Anyone with a guitar, a bass, and drums can start a band. Anyone with a Xerox, a Magic Marker, and an Exacto knife can start a magazine. And anyone with a video camera can be a filmmaker. This has some rather radical, empowering implications, linked especially with punk's original connection to anarchism; the erasure of barriers between audience and artist is demonstrated by such implosive phenomena as performers hurling themselves into the audience.[8]

Gay punk communities tend to be specific and local, centered in San Francisco, Toronto, and Los Angeles, among other cities, placed willfully beyond the "mainstream."[9] Clubs such as L.A.'s Club Fuck, Cafe Hag, the Sissy Club, and Sit & Spin are characterized by in-house videos (found footage, numbers from old musicals set to new music), local bands, as well as offbeat sixties and seventies records and, often, live dancers. San Francisco's pioneering Uranus (brainchild of Michael Blue, creator of Club Chaos) features scantily clad boys and girls "chained" in little cages, climaxing in a striptease, a drag, or a domination scene with bizarre paraphernalia. Composed of a mutating number of members, the Bay Area's Popstitutes (a play on substitute and prostitute, which is how at least one member makes a living) usually play at the weekly club, Clubstitute. Other bands in the queer punk community are Mighty Sphincter, The Dicks, the Nip Drivers, Aryan Disgrace, Fifth Column, MDC, ASF, and The Apostles.

Characteristic of this community's decentralization is that the bands they follow are not famous and almost seem to be disqualified once they pass a certain threshold of success—quite different from the heterosexual monomania around the Sex Pistols, for instance. Groups frequently disband and mutate into other groups; dancers take up instruments (which has its historical precedent: the Sex Pistols said anyone in the audience could play the guitar as well as they could, *and that was the point*), writers make videos and musicians publish fanzines. Some of the more visible groups are organized around these fanzines: the *Homocore* group in San Francisco, the people clustered around *J.D.'s* and *Bimbox* in Toronto, around *My Comrade/Sister* in New York, and around *Sin Bros.* and *Fertile LaToyah Jackson* in Los Angeles.[10]

Gay punk film and video production, like the work that appears in the fanzines, opens up all kinds of questions about correctness, about feminist models of representing women (especially lesbians, a sticking point for traditional feminism), and the gay models of representation as established in such mainstream publications as the *Advocate* or the Gay and Lesbian Alliance Against Defamation (GLAAD) *Newsletter*. Indeed the work covered here could be used to compile a pocket inventory of "unacceptable" gay characters: narcissists, criminals, self-loathing nihilists, sadists, masochists, and resentful children. But a point worth stressing here is that these representations are made by and for gays and lesbians, and that there is little contradiction in supporting activist policing of the media while protecting the freedom of all queers to depict themselves as they like; such a distinction requires a nuanced examination of inside-outside dynamics.

Made by a collective and produced by Laurie Light, the *Snatch* (1990) video is set in a bordello, a San Francisco Victorian house which aspires to be a kind of lesbian island paradise, while still negotiating with gritty, urban, economic necessities. All the johns are played by women in drag and all are murdered by their prostitutes, who range in style from butch to femme, in a kind of revisionist *Arsenic and Old Lace.* "We do what we want," one of the voices in the background says, while overall the film resists setting a political manifesto; indeed, the overt politics are anarchist.[11] While a leather aesthetic prevails, the women are arrayed in every flavor on the menu of sexual role-playing. Both the play of sexual stereotypes and the aestheticization of violence explicitly defy previous formations of "feminist" art; this revision sets up a postfeminist, postliberal paradigm, in which it is conceivable that one might want to court danger, get tied up, or be objectified in someone's gaze.

An old hippie john, after rambling about peace and equality for women, persuades the prostitute to try a yoga position with him; she quickly ties him upside down to a man-sized peace symbol, inverts it into a crucifix, nails his hands and feet to the cross and immolates him. This sardonic Nietzschean commentary implies that New Age ideology is merely an inverted Christianity, equally as oppressive; its destruction is celebrated in a victory of flesh over "spirit" and masquerade over essence. Another client, a repressed librarian type, comes to be abused by a dominatrix, who makes him/her erect (the penis is part of an inflatable, black, rubber girdle), and makes him reveal that he is wearing his wife's camisole. After having him crawl on the ground and bark, she becomes the puppet incarnation of a *vagina dentatis,* constructed from false teeth and hair held between two legs, and murders him. This revenge against gynephobia is both literal and symbolic, animating (as an engine of social change) the symbolic figure of the all-consuming vagina.

For a long time punk hasn't exactly opened its arms to queers even though the visual aesthetic was so close that lots of straight punks were being fag-bashed! It happened all the time, these women with shaved heads, who were maybe straight, got called dykes on the street, they wore leather jackets and tattoos and just didn't fit into the feminine role.
—Mary Ann Peacott and Pam Nicholas,
"Where Are the Punk Dykes?" Rock Against Sexism.

Another john is a manipulative, patriarchal, Freudian analyst who is repulsed by the overt sexual play of the prostitutes in the outer room, and especially offended by an old tampon soaked with blood; he is both attracted and repulsed by the females he takes as his object of interpretation, turning his knowledge into a form of domination. Flustered that they refuse to heed his proclamations, he rejects all of them and goes to take a shower in a bathroom covered with nasty, dyke graffiti. After hesitantly undressing and entering the shower, he is murdered in a shot-by-shot reenactment of the motel murder in *Psycho*. This scene plays on the transvestite murderer in the original film: it isn't the murderer (a woman portraying Norman Bates dressed as a woman) who is sick, it's the "normal" (cross-dressed) psychoanalyst, who in Hitchcock's film functioned to bluntly decipher Bates's maternal psychosis; the blond woman is not the victim who kind of asked for it, but the killer. This critique of gender difference and sexual proscription (and the vertigo of revenge) is set against a utopian backdrop of the prostitutes talking and caressing each other in the main room. Clearly these prostitutes prefer each other to their "men"; the "goods" have gotten together in a world in which men are expendable and women's exchanges are, as Irigaray puts it, "without identifiable terms, without accounts, without end."[12] The anarchist utopian impetus here is inseparable from the dystopia of the decaying urban economy with which the women are obliged to negotiate.[13] Yet as in much punk work, there is a guileless reluctance to universalize and a preference for the glow of the image over the logical grid of analytic language.

It is instrumental to compare *Snatch*'s relationship to punk with that in Monika Treut's film, *Virgin Machine* (1988). Packaged with a slick photo of the director in S-M leather, Treut's film reveals itself to be no more than another coming-out scenario in which punk, S-M, and drag are only three more interchangeable styles among many; Treut's ingenue comes to America to shop for a sexual identity. What gets confused here? Leather and camp are styles or philosophies, whereas S-M (which one must be careful not to confuse with punk) and drag are practices. Punk (how antithetical to this movement to delineate and delimit!) blurs the boundaries between style and practice.[14] This embodies a rejection of the binarism at the heart of a bourgeois rationalism which demands that one be either inside or outside the culture—and signals the way in which gay punks are *both* inside and outside three cultures: heterosexual, homosexual, and punk. The ambiguous relationship of punk to bourgeois notions of identity are manifested in its emphasis on gender as a (reluctant) performance and in subcultural rituals as a means to subvert the bankrupt identities available to cultural consumers. In the context of particular gay communities, punk often functions to question "identity politics," the strategy by which post-Stonewall gay liberationists demanded the rights accorded to other minority groups.[15] In independent gay films with aspirations to hipness, such as *Virgin Machine* and Stephen

Frears's *My Beautiful Laundrette,* punk cynically becomes a ready-to-wear fashion, a style in the service of entrepreneurship. The vector of (confused) punk/S-M style in *Virgin Machine* is Shelly Mars, as the club dancer who fucks (in a vanilla way) the freshly come-out ingenue, later revealing herself as a prostitute when she sends the surprised ingenue her bill. The prostitutes in *Snatch* short-circuit this kind of entrepreneurial economy: they kill their johns.

When I or my friends walk through the Castro ('mainstream gay' neighborhood) in punk-type drag we get nasty looks and under-the-breath muttering, like I'm a fag-basher or something. It is assumed that 'all gay people' look a certain way, and if you don't you start out at a severe disadvantage.
    —Story reported from Maximumrocknroll, *in* Homocore *no. 5*

John Yahnke's *Shower* (1988) is a narrative involving a disenchanted, bleached-blond main character who is mortified at having to go to his sister's wedding (real, "straight" footage of which is hilariously cut, almost guerrilla-style, into the tape), while also curious about her fiancé. The wedding is criticized more for its tackiness than for its role in enforcing compulsory heterosexuality; the complaint is lodged in terms of *style.* John sits in the bathtub with his female friend, and they bitch about weddings in general, about boys, and about being too old: the male character and the girl shave his chest because he wants to look sixteen (he feels sad that he hasn't "come further" at twenty-two). The sister, who has run out on two weddings before this, runs from this one as well and comes to sit in the tub to have a nervous breakdown. The main character and his female friend later run outside to roll in the grass, and cut each other's clothes off with a knife, in a kind of double displacement or deliberate antigrammaticality. Whereas one might interpret such a scene in a sixties film as suggesting sexual liberation, here it becomes an idiosyncratic musing on what boys and girls might do to each other with knives. Underlying this is a commentary on the depleted menu of post-AIDS sex acts and a sense of the deeper-lying fears of (same-sex) sex that AIDS taps into. Like other works of Yahnke's, this tape criticizes the complacent hetero world of "breeders," without offering a recourse to any contemporary gay social formations. Whatever possibilities remain for sexual identity and desire are negotiated between specific individuals whose queerness is a matter of conscious choice, not inexorable compulsion.[16] Sid and Nancy, whoever they might be, change roles at will: they become subject positions, and there is nothing essential in either identity.

"We're like the new Lost Generation," a lesbian character in Gregg Araki's film *The Long Weekend (O' Despair)* (1989) tells us. While more narrative than Yahnke's tape, Araki's film shares its bleak postadolescent gloom; they are similar to the world evoked by gay writer Dennis Cooper, and such imitators as Bret Easton Ellis. Six college friends, two gay men, two lesbians, and a straight couple, meet for a reunion in an angst-filled, uneventful, yet tumultuous weekend; their disillusionment is palpably related to their sense of betrayal at the revolution fraudulently "sold to them by Patti Smith and the Sex Pistols," as Araki puts it in his press release. Shot mostly at night on grainy stock with a hand-wound Bolex camera, this inverted *Big Chill* tends to put off its audience with flat, naturalistic acting in which all the characters sound alike and say the same kinds of things. While it tends to be heavy-handed in its stress on the characters' less-than-profound alienation, what the film emphasizes is a crisis in identity in which both neoconservative mainstream values and accepted gay alternatives fail to serve as a road map for a new generation. Araki wants to blur the lines between gay, straight, and bisexual, offering us people who act and desire "without regard for which set of genitalia they prefer."

In all the work discussed here, there is a conspicuous absence of the coming-out theme so characteristic of mainstream gay filmmaking. Gay political scientist John D'Emilio argues that there has perhaps been "an overreliance on a strategy of coming out" in gay representation, which has "allowed us to ignore the institutionalized ways in which homophobia and heterosexism are reproduced."[17] What this work represents is less a retreat into the closet than a playful engagement with sexual identity that often flies in the face of accepted liberal notions of gay identity. Homophobia and heterosexism are teased out through deliberate techniques of alienation, often through those familiar to the experimental film audience: the hand-held camera, deliberately unfocussed images, often filled with ambient noise, shots framing body parts rather than full fronts, and establishing shots eschewed in favor of plunging midstream into the narrative. Another primary characteristic of punk film aesthetics is the fast and often brutal edits, which are often contrasted with almost unendurable long takes. This kind of work does not appear out of a vacuum, but is of course descended from the avant-garde. Its history, particularly its gay history, is distinguished, ranging from Warhol's films, the work of Kenneth Anger, Werner Schroeter's films, such as *Maria Malibran,* Ulrike Ottinger's *Freak Orlando,* some early Lothar Lambert and Fassbinder, Jack Smith's iconoclastic drag classics, Sandy Daley's *Robert* [Mapplethorpe] *Having His Nipple Pierced,* and even the *Rocky Horror Picture Show.*[18] What is notable is that, like the work examined here, few of these historical antecedents, pre- or post-Stonewall, are concerned with the theme of coming out; the figure of the closet can be seen in the close confinement of much of this work, its fascination with costume and the spectacular performance of gender.[19]

In contrast to Yahnke's work, Azian Nurudin's video work is oddly minimal and microscopic in its focus. Her *Malaysian Series 1, 5, & 6* (1986–

87) feature Nurudin, wearing a motorcycle jacket over a floral-print sarong (a comment on the collision of cultures in a postcolonial diaspora of identity), whipping various inanimate objects, from a stove with a television sitting on it, to a bouquet of flowers beaten against a chair back, to an inflatable male dummy (who we are told is being beaten to death for smuggling drugs). Mostly shot in single long takes, the whippings are carried out with all the frenzy of the opening scene of Sam Fuller's *Naked Kiss*. The sensationalized female anger (rather than the anger against the female in Fuller's film noir) shocks the viewer into considering both the constructed nature of the object and the "female." In hitting the stove, it is as though the slave is beating the prison warden, enacting her revenge on the commodity; Nurudin, in her frenzy, is oblivious to the camera, and yet the presence of the flickering screen on the television is a kind of synecdoche of the viewer him/herself. Nurudin's allusions to domesticity function, for critic Liz Kotz, to generate a perpetual sense of disalignment. "Clearly feminist and yet not 'feminist,' these post-punk works probe how to construct a position while avoiding the available vocabulary of politics or dissent. In their place is an odd kind of silence, a *dis*-articulation of positions."[20] The strategy of negation and the alignment of filmic and aural elements in the *Malaysian Series* work at articulating Third World experiences on the grid of post-punk aesthetics, as Kotz points out—the objects being destroyed are more often than not objects of Western consumer technology. Since the object usually remains intact, Nurudin "dismantles" it through repetition, making the gesture of negation commensurate to negation itself. Commodification is connected synecdochically to identify through the gesture of refusal, calling into question any kind of essential truth about the other or the self.

Similar issues of race, sexuality, and representation are very differently articulated in the video works around Vaginal Davis, products of a collective group including John O'Shea and Keith Holland. A six-foot six-inch, black drag queen raised in Watts, Vaginal has long been at the center of a thriving underground punk-drag scene in Los Angeles, crystallized in her magazine *Fertile La Toyah Jackson*.[21] Unlike drag queens of an earlier generation, such as Candy Darling, Jim Pearce, or even Dustin Hoffman in *Tootsie*, the measure of success is never how close the man comes to seeming a woman, but how provocatively the difference manifests itself. While sharing the problematization of representation that is an earmark of the avant-garde, there is something shocking in the realization that, in another sense, these tapes are without irony; like much subcultural work, they *mean it*. In *It All Started in Black* (1987), Davis's muscular arms and shoulders contrast with her blond Marilyn wig, setting the mark for the dialogue that follows: "Can you handle the charms of a beautiful black woman?" Davis asks the viewer. In bed, she tells us that sleeping with a white man is just like sleeping with a white woman; after having campy sex with an unidentified white man, she sits in a tub of bubble bath and toys with the viewer's wanting to *know* her/him; "you *want* to know, but there's only so much you can know." This is not masculine power disguised by feminine costume or an object lesson in being a woman, but a play on sexual identity that disputes dominant cultural values.[22] Putting gynephobia, homophobia, and racism into play through vacillations between manic and depressive, narcissistic and dialogic, this tape toys with what has been called "the grave doubt resulting from homosexual desire: *the doubt about which self to adore.*"[23]

The gender dysphoria parodied in such work is usually discussed under the rubric of camp, in an analysis inaugurated by Susan Sontag, who ignored both its political and erotic aspects.[24] Like blackface, drag also has a specific culturally policed function (demonstrated by Dustin Hoffman or Milton Berle, for instance, whose drag is arguably all about enforcing gender roles), which in these works is countered by the infusion of punk aesthetics, gender-dysphoric eroticism and (basically anarchist) politics. The fusion of punk and camp, two once-antithetical aesthetics, works to unravel some of the cultural contradictions in which queers find themselves.[25] Post-Stonewall identity politics do not seem to hold sway when they are dis-articulated through the engagement of subcultural style, particularly because the whole way the subject is constructed is called into question. To the camp doubt about which self to adore, punk aesthetics and the eros of abjection and negation also prompt oneself to doubt which self (the bourgeois, the libertine, the demimondaine?) to despise.

> I know no punks who are either lesbian or gay, all literature, 'zines is either punk or gay, the two never coincide. Even a lot of the so-called sussed punks here are homophobic—me, my girlfriends and some friends got beaten up in London by anarchists wearing animal rights T-shirts 'cos we were kissing at the bus stop.
>
> —Letter in Homocore no. 3

In her video *Nancy's Nightmare* (1988), Nurudin depicts a hard-core, lesbian S-M sex act in full leather regalia. Tightly framed and occasionally shot in split-screen, the film begins after the sex has begun and ends while it is still underway, situating the viewer discomfortingly inside the work, which is deeply resistant to a psychoanalytical reading of spectator identification (the gaze) and against the particular feminist baggage of such a reading.[26] The soundtrack segues from Nancy Sinatra's *These Boots Are Made for Walking* to Megadeath's cover of the song. Played end to end, both versions seem campy and sadistic, and both invoke masquerade: they highlight the way style both makes and unmakes subcultural identities. The "nightmare" is Nancy Sinatra's, and it reflects the determination of queers to inhabit a culture of their own inside the unspoken parts of straight culture. The shock effect of this work lies in its spectacular S-M drama and its technological intervention into another world, creating tension between the outside of the subculture and its inside representation; the bourgeois audience's discomfort is generated by displacing the "leisurely" consumption of the film with radical (interior) pleasure.

One commentator on the original punk movement states that the petulant, self-conscious, amateurish style of the music and the fanzines are mechanisms of self-effacement within subcultural identity:

> The punk mindset presents us with a paradox. It combines the hatred of apathy and a sense of urgency concerning everything related to punk culture, with an acute awareness of sociopolitical impotence, a belief that actions were inconsequential, that an improvement of self or society was at best elusive and at worst utterly futile. . . . Self-effacement is a constant theme in the fanzines.[27]

In terms of gay and lesbian punk, where identity is still at issue, I would argue that self-effacement is never the definitive goal because there is always a play between effacement and revelation (which I'd hold distinct from coming out). In Nurudin's work, this is manifested in the discontinuity

Nancy's Nightmare, Azian Nurudin

between sound and image and the performer's obliviousness to the camera. In Bruce LaBruce's more narrative *No Skin Off My Ass* (1990), there is likewise conspicuously unsynchronized, overdubbed dialogue and music. Moreover the main character's object of desire, a maybe-straight, maybe-gay skinhead, pretends to be mute for most of the film; his muteness seems to evaporate (we are never sure) once he agrees to have sex with the main character. One need only compare these works to the pivotal seventies documentary *Word Is Out* (1977) to see the transformation of the role of talking in gay identity; every interview is a kind of talking cure, centered around coming out: "I am gay" became a confirmation of identity, not just sexuality.

No Skin Off My Ass opens with the main character watching television, showing Sandy Dennis walking in a park behind the titles for Robert Altman's *That Cold Day in the Park,* the story of a spinster teacher who falls in love with a teenage delinquent. The spinster is the object of identification for the main character (played by LaBruce), a sort of mod Kewpie doll hairdresser. Wearing eyeliner à la Mapplethorpe and speaking in a breathy voice, the lethargic aesthete is only one of several gay "types" repossessed here. The hairdresser goes to the park and picks up his own (mute) object

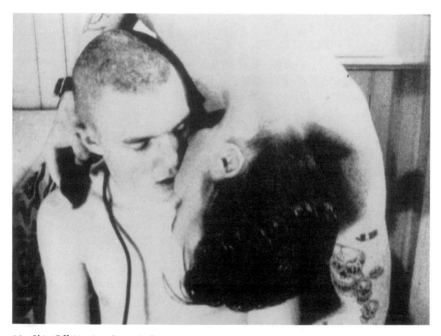

No Skin Off My Ass, Bruce LaBruce

of desire, a skinhead who sits freezing on a bench. The hairdresser explains that he's done "research" on skinheads, later reading from Nick Knight's book, *Skinhead*. "Of course I don't always agree with your beliefs," he says, "but then I've never been a very political person. I guess it was always an *aesthetic* question for me." He gazes at the skinhead, whose shaved head, the hairdresser tells us, is "the only haircut that makes sense anymore."

In the younger character's odd silence, what follows is a kind of reading of the skinhead, playing first of all with the confusing subcultural indexes of punk and skinhead, straight and gay: how does one distinguish the straight from the gay skinhead? The in/visibility of the nonidentifiable gay person collides with what Hebdige calls punk's blankness, the refusal to speak or be positioned.[28] As with much of the work discussed here, this points up the shortcomings of psychoanalytic, subject-based, interpretive models in favor of subcultural and postcolonial sociological ones, especially since the relations pertaining here are ones of power and class. We learn that the skinhead is actually middle-class, from a "perfectly normal" background (his sister wants him to be a punk) and not working-class, as most skinheads are. He chooses to be a skinhead, and though he has sex with the hairdresser at the end, he refrains from identifying as a fag.

In its history as a white, middle-class movement, gay liberation may be said to have fashioned gay identities suited to the bourgeoisie. If, as Roland Barthes tells us, the bourgeois is a man "incapable of imagining the Other," then the homosexual bourgeois, short of turning color, has the powerful option of choosing the identity of a gay or lesbian *other*.[29] If one of the first stages of gay identity formation (from the Mattachine to the Stonewall generation) was to be an other *just like* the bourgeoisie, then a subsequent gesture is to be an other unlike the bourgeoisie; this can both signal difference and reclaim pathologized queer identities, thereby placing oneself outside the purview of the bourgeois imagination. A similar question about the articulation of race, gender, and class exists in the history of rock in general, as white musicians and audiences identified with black music. Are these cases of "genuine" resistance or of assimilation? In the panorama of gay punk subcultures, "assimilationist" gays (different but the same) are the same as straight "breeders," and the essence of difference resides in the distinction between marginal and mainstream queer. The interplay in LaBruce's work between self-effacement and self-revelation stresses the importance within these gay subcultures of being seen over being heard; referential or analytical language is distrusted. Style functions to seduce one into a world of images in which language and speech (demonstrated by the disjunctive soundtrack) are secondary to the reign of the index and the icon over the sign.

A subsequent dream sequence engages this reformulation of gay identity and desire. Accompanied by an uncanny rendition of the German national anthem, LaBruce's hairdresser dreams about handcuffing and harnessing the skinhead, forcing him to lick his boots and then having both of them in turn raise their arms (full-frame, facing the camera) into a "Heil," albeit with one marker of difference: the hairdresser flips his limp wrist down after saluting. The references to Nazism are commonplace in both skinhead and punk subculture and are usually dismissed, after some enlightened head-shaking, as merely a flirtation with cultural taboos in order to remind society of its brutality.[30] Discussing the Sex Pistols' song *Belsen Was a Gas*, Greil Marcus makes short shrift of the question by saying it implied that "fascism had won the Second World War: that contemporary Britain was a welfare-state parody of fascism."[31] While undoubtedly one function in both works is to *épater le bourgeois*, their appeals to fascism are neither parenthetical nor innocent. This imagery plays the conscious frisson of Nazi paraphernalia and the fetishizing of enslavement and capture against the more unconscious erotic functioning of the violent and the forbidden.

The erotic charge of fascist iconography in *No Skin Off My Ass* mounts a further challenge against the 1980's gay gentrification of sexual identity. It stakes a claim against sexual essentialism, against a conservative psychoanalytic model of sexuality consisting of natural libidinal drives and their cultural restraints. Michel Foucault argues that desires are constituted in the development of specific and historical social practices. The fact that new sexualities are constantly being produced is his substantiation for the generative quality of the social construction rather than its repressive functions. Sexuality is constituted in society and history, not biology. By focussing on fascism's external trappings at the expense of its biological essentialism, *No Skin Off My Ass* stresses the constructedness of fascism, its stylization and masquerade, a reminder that our sexuality is likewise a structure of desiring and seeing. And yet, what is one to make of Nazi style in a gay context? Certainly, the specter of masquerade is not evoked merely to be dismissed. The Nazi dream represents a vision of the law driven to its zenith, a fascism whose identity politics of blond families and proud burgers have their flip sides in leather uniforms and absolute discipline; cast in their most intense light, these aesthetics come around full turn to meet those of a historical gay underground, the postwar gay leather culture perhaps best captured in the work of Kenneth Anger.

Shot in a recalcitrant style reminiscent of Godard's early films, *No Skin Off My Ass* has the same relation to gay mainstream film that Godard's work had to Hollywood of the fifties. In severing the image of domination from the political context, LaBruce's work suggests, first of all, that the political context has been collectively forgotten—only to be called to consciousness within a dream. The eroticization and decontextualization of the "oppressor," furthermore, serves to mark this subculture's discomfort with liberal identity politics and old New Left radicalism. An earlier scene has the skinhead run out on the hairdresser, who had locked him into a room, to visit his sister (played by G. B. Jones, also a filmmaker and coeditor with LaBruce of the fanzine *J.D.'s*). Working on her (actual) guerrilla film, *Girls of the S.L.A.*, based on the Patti Hearst story, Jones sits with the cast while they listen to a sixties speech by Angela Davis. Instead of listening, Jones reads a pulp novel and muses (as a model of terrorism) that in the same week Davis was both on the cover of *Life* magazine and on the FBI's ten-most-wanted list. While Jones can show her boredom with Angela Davis's puritanism, she isn't rejecting the project wholesale; her fascination is as much with revolutionary style as with revolutionary politics.

With its critique of the puritan seriousness and the denial of pleasure in radical politics, *No Skin* suggests an entirely different economy: one of gays and lesbians whose political engagement is more anarchist than liberal, and whose practices promote pleasure in the service of dissent. In a late-capitalist culture dominated by the commodification of pleasure, the subversive power of pleasure (fundamentally ambiguous, if it exists at all) seems to exist in a form of allegory. As Jameson puts it, the proper political use of pleasure must "always involve a dual focus, in which the local issue is meaningful and desireable in and of itself, but also *at one and the same time* taken as the *figure* for Utopia in general, and for the systemic revolutionary transformation of society as a whole."[32] The outstanding marker here is the limp wrist as the exclamation point to the hairdresser's fascist salute, an apostrophe of difference that disrupts the fascist machinery. What the dream sequence rehearses is both the colonization of the gay political unconscious and its resistance to or (a queer) reterritorialization of a fascist world.

After the dream, and after the skinhead visits his sister (who urges him to fuck the hairdresser), the two are reunited and finally have sex. They record their first fuck with a super 8 camera, whose readjustments cause the hairdresser to continually interrupt fucking. "But it was worth it," he says in a voice-over, while we watch them from the perspective of the 16mm camera. "I knew I'd never show it to anyone," he tells us, in a conceit. "It was just too personal." Within this fetishization of the camera (also manifested by the sister), with its history from Vertov to *Blowup,* there is a double play of the private camera with the social or utopian one—an inscription of pleasure which serves as an allegory for revolutionary dissent, not bourgeois commodification; in this sense it shares a project with other youth subcultures.[33] The question looming over the work of Jameson and his allies is whether there are nodes of resistance within the all-devouring paradigm of the postmodern: "(think of punk or pornography)," he tells us parenthetically. Like all the work discussed here, *No Skin Off My Ass* provides a model of cultural resistance by fragmenting the pervasive imagery of dystopia into utopian change through local pleasure.

This instance of pleasure is perhaps closest to the frenzy of teenage rock fans, radically untheorizable and also demonic, a Nietzschean pleasure in destruction. For us to read it and make use of it calls for an entirely different artistic and critical practice, informed by the strategies of punk and camp, based far from the traditional intellectual (who represents the interests of the ruling class) *and* the organic intellectual (who supports those of a rising or oppressed class). It no longer suffices to merely identify the Western homosexual with a position of poverty or victimage. This is doomed because it misconstrues "the real utopian desires of 'class victims' to identify with abundance" and to create a culture of abundance and destruction that is beyond simple Frankfurt School critical negation; if we continue to build a cultural politics around the theme of oppression and alienation, we will never learn to speak, "in a radical accent, the popular language of our times, which is the language of pleasure, adventure, liberation, gratification and novelty."[34]

The super 8 set to record what the audience's camera sees redoubles the distance into a strange intimacy. The actors aren't really performing *for* the super 8 camera, which is for themselves, and comes to stand for a kind of insider's view, for what is seen from within the subculture. While hearing the wound-up spring of the super 8 wind down, we are still caught in the liminal specter of the image, in the seduction of grainy, black-and-white film. But our kind of pleasure—which Jameson calls a by-product (pleasure itself never being attainable of itself in capitalism)—is supplemented by another. The pleasure of the hairdresser and the skinhead is not "reasonable" and hardly containable in our critical language. Desire, sexuality, and libidinal cathexis are subsumed in fucking, in performance; identity, especially sexual identity, becomes framed in terms of style and attitude, not essence; and "speaking" punk is concerned less with its own vocabulary than the negation of the transcendence and rationality of *language*, its metaphoricity and tropes.

Notes

1. I've placed punk in quotes and hope to keep the term in suspension here; some gay critics [cf. Liz Kotz] will use the term "post-punk." Straight or traditional punk (how queer to etymologize words younger than we are!) is marked by the rise of a few bands, the Sex Pistols foremost among them, in mid-seventies London, arriving on the tails of the working-class skinhead movement in a time of economic distress. See Tricia Henry, *Break All Rules: Punk Rock and the Meaning of a Style* (Ann Arbor: UMI Research Press, 1989);

Dave Laing, *One Chord Wonders: Power and Meaning in Punk Rock* (Philadelphia: Open University Press, 1985); or Virginia Boston, *Punk Rock* (New York: Penguin, 1978).

2. Punk is infamously laced with homophobic, misogynist, and racist associations. Rosa von Praunheim's *Armee der Liebenden* (1978) includes a segment on a demonstration following the murder of a gay man by a group of punks in San Francisco.

3. Andrew Ross identifies the punk moment as one in which "it became inescapably clear that the traditional concerns of the avant-garde would henceforth be addressed and worked through in relation to popular culture." "The Rock 'n' Roll Ghost," *October*, no. 50 (Fall, 1989) p. 116.

4. "That's so true, when you come out you think that you're going to find all these lesbians who think like you do. Then you realize that you're a subcategory of a subcategory!" Mary Ann Peacott and Pam Nicholas, "Where Are the Punk Dykes?" *Rock Against Sexism*, no. 4 (1990–91) [P.O.B. 390643, Cambridge, MA 02139], n.p.

5. Interestingly, while British punks went out of their way to play down sexuality (at least in its commodified forms) and particularly homosexuality, the word "punk" once meant "a boy (often a novice) who gets fucked," among other things. See Wayne Dynes's *Homolexis* (New York: Gai Sabor, 1985) p. 118.

6. These are Dick Hebdige's indispensable terms. See Hebdige, *Subculture: The Meaning of Style* (London: Methuen, 1979) pp. 17–18.

7. See Michael Bronski, *Culture Clash: The Making of Gay Sensibility* (Boston: South End Press, 1984) pp. 144–59.

8. See Jon Lewis, "Punks in LA: It's Kiss or Kill," *Journal of Popular Culture*, vol. 22, no. 2 (Fall, 1988) p. 92.

9. See Craig Lee, "Getting Down with the Third Sex: Gay Post-Kids Build a Scene of Their Own," *L.A. Weekly* (July 20, 1990) pp. 55–57.

10. See Matias Viegener, "Gay Fanzines: 'There's Trouble in That Body,' " *Afterimage*, vol. 18, no. 5 (January, 1991) pp. 12–14. See also Mark Leger, "The Drag Queen in the Age of Mechanical Reproduction," *Out/Look* (Fall, 1989); and Dennis Cooper "Homocore Rules," *The Village Voice* (Sept 4, 1990) p. 92. More journalistic are Bill Van Parys, "Fag Rags Come of Age," *The Advocate* (November 6, 1990) pp. 70–72; Wickie Stamps, "Queer Girls with an Attitude," *The Advocate* (Nov. 20, 1990) pp. 56–7; Adam Block, "The Queen of 'Zine," *The Advocate* (Nov. 20, 1990) p. 75.

11. The "a" in *Snatch* is written with the anarchist symbol, the "a" in a circle, only in this case it is modified by a + underneath, feminizing the symbol. *Homocore* editor Tom Jennings has come up with a queer anarchist logo with the "a" in a circle over an inverted pink triangle.

12. Luce Irigaray, "Commodities Among Themselves," *This Sex Which Is Not One* (Ithaca: Cornell University Press, 1985) p. 197.

13. Further works in this domain are Carol (Scarlet Harlot, prostitution-rights activist) Leigh's *Die Yuppie Scum* (1989), a documentary about the Anarchists' Convention in San Francisco; and *Live Nude Girls* (1989), a documentary by Petra Mueller and Elizabeth Dewey about strippers at the Market Street Cinema.

14. What distinguishes a subcultural identity like punk from a more general (though marked) fashion like leather lies in the interior distinction between doing (affecting the appearance and rituals of punk) and being punk. See Widdicombe and Wooffitt, " 'Being' Versus

'Doing' Punk: On Achieving Authenticity as a Member," *Journal of Language and Social Psychology,* vol. 9, no. 4 (1990) pp. 257–277.

15. A concise critique of gay "identity politics" can be found in Dennis Altman's *The Homosexualization of America* (Boston: Beacon Press, 1982); see pp. 118–120.

16. *Homocore's* Tom Jennings states that "One thing everyone here has in common is that we're all *social mutants;* we've outgrown or never were part of any 'socially acceptable' categories. You don't have to be gay . . . any decision that makes you an outcast is enough." *Homocore,* vol. 1 (1988).

17. See p. 111 of John D'Emilio's "Capitalism and Gay Identity," in Ann Snitow et al., eds., *Powers of Desire: The Politics of Sexuality* (New York: Monthly Review Press, 1983) pp. 100–113.

18. Richard Dyer points out that gay underground film from 1940 to the sixties was a place for the expression of gay people because of its emphasis on the personal, and that such work was more "personal" than "gay." This makes it an "anathema to collective notions of identity," such as those proposed in the more social realist films made after Stonewall. Richard Dyer, *Now You See It* (London: Routledge, 1990), p. 173.

19. Michael Moon's "Flaming Closets," *October,* no. 51 (Winter, 1989), examining Jack Smith's filmography to tease out the theory and praxis of drag in the pre-Stonewall closet, is indispensable to my argument. Abject drag and symbolic appropriations of the Hollywood "feminine" function to project gay subjectivity within the psychological-political realities of the closet against a screen of fantasy for collective recognition and analysis.

20. Liz Kotz, "Interrogating the Boundaries of Women's Art: New Work in Video by Four Women," *High Performance,* Los Angeles (Winter, 1989) p. 38. I'd like to thank Liz Kotz for calling the *Snatch* tape and the work of Azian Nurudin to my attention.

21. See *J.D.'s* no. 7 (1990), for a letter from Vaginal Davis.

22. See Elaine Showalter, "Critical Cross Dressing; Male Feminists and the Woman of the Year," in Alice Jardine and Paul Smith, eds., *Men in Feminism* (Routledge: New York, 1987), pp. 116–132, for a discussion of this problem in *Tootsie.* See also Carole-Anne Tyler, "The Supreme Sacrifice? TV, 'TV', and the Renee Richards Story," *differences* 1:3 (Fall, 1989), an issue devoted to male subjectivity.

23. Leo Bersani, *A Future for Astyanax: Character and Desire in Literature* (Boston: Little, Brown, 1976) pp. 306–307.

24. "Camp is a certain mode of aestheticism. It is one way of seeing the world as an aesthetic phenomenon . . . not just in terms of beauty, but in terms of degree of artifice, of stylization." Susan Sontag, "Notes on Camp," in *Against Interpretation* (New York: Dell, 1967) p. 277.

25. This manifests itself in the work of Robert Mapplethorpe; even in the first triptych greeting the visitor to his censored show, *The Perfect Moment,* one photo is of him in butch leather, the second in boy-model makeup, and the third a profile shot in full drag. See Doug Ischar, "Endangered Alibis," *Afterimage* (May, 1990) pp. 8–11.

26. It is easily recognized that this piece and the *Malaysian Series* owe no small debt to earlier feminist work, such as Barbara Hammer's sex tapes or Martha Rosler's *Semiotics of the Kitchen.* This continuity of feminist rage is often unacknowledged in the newer work, and the denial of this debt is part of the baggage of post-punk aesthetics.

27. Tricia Henry, p. 97.

28. "In punk, alienation assumed an almost tangible quality. It gave itself up to the cameras in "blankness". the removal of expression (see any photograph of any punk group), the refusal to speak and be positioned. This trajectory—the solipsism, the neurosis, the cosmetic rage—had its origins in rock." Hebdige, p. 28.

29. Roland Barthes, *Mythologies* (Editions de Seuil: Paris, 1957) p. 239.

30. "Swastikas, for instance, were not worn to indicate that punk was in agreement with fascist philosophy, but rather to remind society of the atrocities it permits." Tricia Henry, p. 80.

31. Greil Marcus, *Lipstick Traces* (Boston: Harvard University Press, 1989) p. 118. Marcus's "secret history" of the twentieth century quickly dispatches women and queers, barely accounting for sexuality, sexual identity, and gender crisis to celebrate the boy moment of punk-anarchist jouisance and its apocalyptic macho posturing.

32. See Fredric Jameson's "Pleasure: A Political Issue," in *Formations of Pleasure* (London: Routledge and Kegan Paul, 1983) pp. 1–14, p. 13.

33. There is an ongoing debate about the political meaning of punk, whether it is "the final modernist capitulation to decadence, irrationality and despair or . . . a completely recalcitrant stance against the bland conformity of mass society and the naturalization of consumption within it." David James, "Poetry/ Punk/ Production: Some Recent Writing in LA," in E. Ann Kaplan, ed., *Postmodernism and Its Discontents* (London: Verso, 1988) p. 167. See also Robert H. Tillman, "Punk Rock and the Construction of 'Pseudo-Political' Movements," *Popular Music and Society,* vol. 7, no. 3 (1980) pp. 165–175; Dave Laing, "Interpreting Punk Rock," *Marxism Today,* vol. 22, no. 4 (April, 1978) pp. 123–128; Simon Frith, "Beyond the Dole Queue: The Politics of Punk," *Village Voice* (October 24, 1977) p. 77–79; David James, "Hardcore: Cultural Resistance in the Postmodern," *Film Quarterly,* vol. 42, no. 2 (Winter, 1988–89) pp. 31–39.

34. Andrew Ross, "The Rock 'n' Roll Ghost," p. 115. For camp, see Andrew Ross, "Uses of Camp," *The Yale Journal of Criticism,* vol. 2, no. 1 (Fall, 1988).

Bodies in Trouble

EXCERPTS FROM A VIDEO BY MARUSIA BOCIURKIW

Her body is contested territory. First of all, does it exist? Second of all, is it dangerous? If so, how to contain it? And who has jurisdiction?

In an act of total but involuntary submission, she spreads her legs and arms. A uniformed man slowly and insolently traces her body with his rod. Her shoulder: (pale and mole-covered, beneath her shirt). Her breast: (small, pear-shaped, a hardened brown nipple). Her cunt: (a triangular thicket surrounding purple lips).

She gets across. She boards a plane. She's afraid she'll be found out. She looks suspiciously like k.d. lang.

. . . On the street, our bodies change shape, grow hard against the watchfulness of others. You no longer recognize me. I no longer recognize you . . .

She makes love. The night of the Montréal massacre she goes to the bar. "Feels like there's a war going on," she says. "There is a war going on," says her lover. "In a war, people get killed . . . "

When they talk on the phone, it's the outline of her lover's body she's trying to grasp: lines of protection that create the meaning of her white skin, and the place from which she grieves. Their bodies lean towards each other; helpless with grief or guilt, powerful with anger, solidarity, desire.

The bar gets raided, the woman leaves. She dreams. . . .

. . . that their tongues taste of oranges, and that their bodies smell of sweat and leather. Their bodies press against each other, they leave marks, they say: this is what it's like. Remember, during the spaces in between . . . In between, I close my eyes and the image of women's bodies burns into my vision. I live in the throat of fear . . .

CHARACTERS:
Woman/1   Naomi Riches
Woman/2   Martha Judge
Man (on plane) David McLean
Security guard Brent Cehan

Woman/1 is sitting in an airplane, next to a man. They have never met before. The man looks over at her frequently, as though about to speak. She reads her paper and tries to ignore him.

MAN: You Know who you look like?
WOMAN/1: (*Wearily, not looking up from newspaper*) No, who?
MAN: You look like . . . Oh, geeze, I can't think of her name, and you look just like her. She's a singer . . .
WOMAN/1: I don't sing.
MAN: She's about five foot seven. Big-boned kind of gal. She's from Alberta . . . Where are you from?
WOMAN/1: Saskatchewan.
MAN: Well, anyway, you look just like her. She's kind of androgynous . . . you know what I mean? (*nudges Woman/1 meaningfully*)
WOMAN/1: No.
MAN: Oh, c'mon. She's won a lot of awards. She's . . . different. Doesn't wear makeup, only eats vegetarian food . . .

WOMAN/1: (*Feigning alarm*) Vegetarian?
MAN: Yes.
WOMAN/1: Well, I give up.

Airline attendant's hands appear, offering dinner.

WOMAN/1: No thanks. I don't eat meat.
MAN: (*Thoughtfully*) Hmm. That must be it.

Cut to Woman/1 in profile against airplane window, clouds floating by. As the voiceover begins, the lighting changes and dims, until she is in silhouette and her features are invisible.

VOICEOVER: Her otherness is like a second skin. It's smooth, it's cool, it's the razor edge between danger and pleasure, it's the thrill of just barely escaping recognition, it's the look she passes to other women who are outlaws too. It's the way they recognize one another, it's the way they touch one another, it's the subtle privilege of invisibility. It's the pleasure of slipping across the border like this—until one (or more) of them gets caught.

Woman/1 is talking to a security guard.

SECURITY GUARD: What's the purpose of your trip: business or pleasure?
WOMAN/1: Both.

Cut to an image of women at a demo, with the word BUSINESS *keyed in over top, followed by an image of two women kissing, with the word* PLEASURE *keyed in over top.*
Cut back to Woman/1 and Security Guard.

SECURITY GUARD: Can you step into our office for a moment? We'll just be asking you a few simple questions. (*They continue talking, silently*)
VOICEOVER: Border crossings are always trouble. First of all, who's in control? Second of all, is it dangerous? And finally, do you have the courage to go across?

Woman/1 and Woman/2 are seated on a living-room couch, facing the camera, holding cups of tea.

WOMAN/1: Honey, there's something I've been meaning to tell you.
WOMAN/2: . . . Yes?
WOMAN/1: Darling . . . I'm carrying your baby.
WOMAN/2: Oh, no.
WOMAN/1: Yes, they did the ultrasound yesterday. It's . . . it's . . . a lesbian.

Freeze Frame

VOICEOVER: Everyone freezes. There is a commercial break.
We're floating in the present.
We're kicked out of history.
We're stuck
in the here and now.

Cut to a medical diagram of a woman's body. A hand is drawing weather patterns and the names of right-wing groups—REAL Women, National Citizen's Coalition, Citizens for Foreign Aid Reform, the Progressive Conservative Party—over the diagram.

VOICEOVER: The right wing advances like a growing storm.
You think you're safe
Because you can't get pregnant.
You think you're safe
Because you're invisible.
You think you're safe
Because you're loved.
You think you're safe
Because your eyes are closed.
It only takes one border crossing to remind you: the only thing that will make you safe is courage.

BODIES IN TROUBLE
written and directed by Marusia Bociurkiw
videography: Kim Derko
sound recording: Paula Fairfield
on-line edit: Dennis Day
music: Ingrid Stitt and Mary Margaret O'Hara

Favorite Aunts and Uncles

Much contemporary queer culture uses lesbian and gay heros from the past to speak to our contemporary struggles with identity and community formation: Marshall recruits Hirschfeld, Yukhananov resurrects Fassbinder, Julien looks for Langston, Diamond outs Emily Carr, Bordowitz wants to fuck Ludlam, Tartaglia makes love to Genet, and Ottinger fearlessly invents an entire boatload of lesbian heroines. Such tributes to our perverse parents (both textually and cinematically) demonstrate how history can construct our present, but only if we construct our history.

The Third Body: Patterns in the Construction of the Subject in Gay Male Narrative Film

THOMAS WAUGH

Prelude: Victorian Gay Photography and Its Invisible Subject

Nineteenth-century homerotic photography established a constellation of three types in its construction of the male body. The three bodies can be glimpsed through the photographs of Wilhelm von Gloeden, the Prussian aesthete and archetypal gay Victorian who worked in Taormina, Sicily until his death in 1931. Two objects of the homoerotic gaze, the ephebe and the "he-man" (the adolescent youth and the mature athlete, respectively) constituted polar figures in his work. The ephebe, Ganymede, was by far the most popular body type in the erotic repertory of the Victorian gay imaginary. He reflected both cultural justifications derived from the classical pastoral model, and economic and social realities of the period. The ephebe in drag was an important subcategory: cross-gender motifs offered not only an image of nineteenth-century sexological theories of the "Urning," or the "third sex," a biological in-between, but also a matter-of-fact acknowledgment of the marketplace scale of erotic tastes. The cross-dressed ephebe may also have functioned as an alibi for that homosexuality that dared not fully assume the dimensions of same-sex desire, a reassurance for the masculine-gendered body and identity of the discreet spectator (not to mention the producer and censor).

The ephebe was predominant in von Gloeden, and there were only occasional appearances of the "he-man," the Hercules who substitutes maturity for pubescence, squareness for roundness, stiff, active untouchability for soft, passive accessibility. Apparently not von Gloeden's cup of tea, the he-man was nevertheless very popular with other Victorian photographers, and omnipresent in other cultural spheres, from the Academy to the popular press and postcard industry, that is, in media that were on the surface more respectably homosocial than homosexual.

These two bodies together predicated in turn a third body, an implied gay subject, the invisible desiring body of the producer-spectator—behind the

A rare convergence of ephebe and he-man in the photography of Wilhelm von Gloeden

camera, in front of the photograph, but rarely visualized within the frame. The third body, the looking, representing subject, stood in for the authorial self as well as for the assumed gay spectator.

The Victorian homoerotic pattern of visualized objects and invisible subjects replicated those structures of Otherness and sexual difference inherent in all patriarchal Western culture. In fact, in gay culture, as we shall see, those structures seemed even exaggerated, as if to offset the sameness of the same-sex sexual relation, to unbalance the tedious symmetry of the Narcissus image. The ephebe addressed the phallic spectator as older, stronger, more powerful, active, just as surely as the female photographic object addressed

Self-portrait of von Gloeden as a Christ in disguise

its gender opposite, the heterosexual male spectator. At the same time, the he-man object addressed the more "feminized," passive body of the homoerotic spectator. As for all the other variables entering Victorian gay iconography, from implied distinctions of class, age, and gender role to Orientalist and classical trappings, these clearly accentuated and elaborated on the basic built-in structures of difference.

In Victorian gay photography the third body, the gay subject, became visible only in the minor genre of the self-portrait. Von Gloeden and his American contemporary Holland Day, both adopting the drag of Christ, anticipated the element of costume and disguise in the gay self-portrait in its later photographic manifestations of our century (think of George Platt Lynes and Robert Mapplethorpe).

Twentieth-Century Gay Cinema and Its Visible Subject

In the twentieth century, it is gay male filmmakers, competing with photographers as prophets of the homosexual body, who most definitely take up the job of constructing the gay subject. In the gay-authored narrative cinema, as gay themes become more and more explicit after the Second World War, filmmakers replace the alibis of their photographer precursors with an agenda of self-representation and self-definition. At the same time, they unfreeze the iconicity of the photographic body with the identificatory drive of narration and characterization. From his obscure corner in the photographic corpus, the third body finally enters the foreground of the image, alongside the ephebe and the he-man, the objects of his desire. In the new configuration of character types, the cinema provides two points of entry for the gay spectator: a site for identification with the narrative subject, and a site for specular erotic pleasure in his object.

Within a gay narrative universe that remains remarkably constant across the seventy-five-year span of my cinematic corpus, 1916–1990, the gay subject consistently accomplishes twin functions. On the one hand, he enacts a relationship of desire—constituted through the specular dynamics basic to the classical narrative cinema, the diegetic and the extra-diegetic gaze—and on the other, he enacts certain narrative functions that are more specific to the gay imaginary. These functions often have a literally *discursive* operation within the diegetic world. To be specific, the gay subject takes on one of, or a combination of, several recurring social roles, namely those of the artist, the intellectual, and/or the teacher. In other words, to complete the mythological triangle, Ganymede and Hercules are figured alongside, and are imagined, represented, and desired by, a third body type that is a hybrid of oracle, centaur, mentor . . . and satyr.

The gay subject looks at and desires the object within the narrative. As artist-intellectual he also bespeaks him, constructs him, projects him, fantasizes him, in short, *represents* him. He fucks with him rarely, alas, seldom consummating his desire as he would within the master narrative of the (hetero) patriarchal cinema built on the conjugal drive. The dualities set up by both photographers and filmmakers—mind and body, voice and image, subject and object, self and other, site for identification and site for pleasure—these dualities remain literally separate. For the most part, narrative denouements, far from celebrating union, posit separation, loss, displacement, sometimes death, and, at the very most, open-endedness. Yet, at the same time, the denouement may also involve an element of identity transformation or affirmation. In fact the assertion of identity, the emergence from the closet (to use a post-Stonewall concept), is often a basic dynamic of the plot, usually paired with an acceptance of the above separation, and signalled by telling alterations in the costumes that we shall come to in a moment. Through all of these patterns, the same-sex imaginary preserves and even heightens the structures of sexual difference inherent in Western (hetero) patriarchal culture but usually stops short of those structures' customary dissolution in narrative closure. In other words, the protagonists of this alternative gay rendering of the conjugal drive, unlike their hetero counterparts, seldom end up coming together. We don't establish families— we just wander off looking horny, solitary, sad, or dead. Or, as I said with denunciatory fervor along with everyone else in the seventies, gay closures are seldom happy endings. (Waugh, 1977)

Costumes

The physicality of the gay subject is cloaked, like Grandfather von Gloeden, in various corporal, vestimentary, and narrative costumes, which are in sharp contrast to the sensuous idealized bareness of his object, whether the he-man's squareness or the ephebe's androgynous curves. The third body puts on costumes as readily as the objects of his desire take them off. The element of costume has several resonances. Firstly it is obviously a disguise, a basic term of homosexuals' survival as an invisible, stigmatized minority. Secondly, it operates to desexualize the subject within an erotophobic regime in which nudity articulates sexual desirability. Finally, costume is a cultural construction, which sets up the nudity of the object as some kind of idealized natural state, but at the same time acknowledges the historical contingency and discursive provenance of sociosexual identity, practice, and fantasy.

The costumes of the gay subject are familiar markers from the repertory of cinematic realism, drawing singly or in combination from a roster of

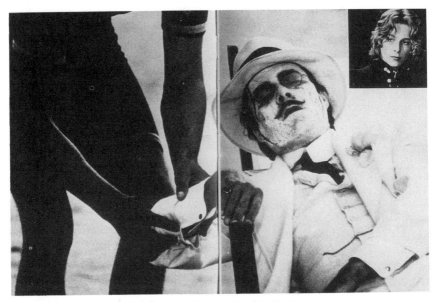

The disguise and mortality of the gay subject in *Death in Venice*

attributes, each attribute predicating its opposite in the narrative object of desire. Thus we have:

A) *age* as opposed to the greater *youth* of the object (e.g. *Mikael* or *Montreal Main*);

B) *class privilege* as opposed to *peasant, proletarian* or *lumpen* affinities (e.g. *Ludwig* or *Ernesto*);

C) *cultural-racial privilege* as opposed to identities that are *less white*, or *less European* (e.g. *Arabian Nights, Prick Up Your Ears,* and *Mala Noche*);

D) *clothing* connoting all of the above, as opposed to *nudity* (e.g. *A Bigger Splash* or *Flesh*);

E) *bodily condition*, by which I mean markers such as eyeglasses, makeup, obesity, disease, and mortality, as opposed to *beauty, strength,* and *health* (e.g. *Death in Venice, Caravaggio*);

F) *gender role* as opposed to its complement (this pair is a reversible term: if the subject is feminized, the object is often masculinized, and vice versa, with narrative oppositions of active-passive or powerful-submissive assigned either in the traditional gender configuration (e.g. *Flesh, The Naked Civil Servant*); or

G) its *inverse*, that is, with the object exerting control over the subject (e.g. *Querelle, Sebastiane*).

Shifting Ground

All of these narrative functions and layers of narrative costumes constitute a mosaic of the gay self, the third body, which subtends the corpus of the gay-authored narrative cinema from the First World War to the present. Certain films stand out as prototypes of successive generations of the gay imaginary. Under the shadow of the German civil rights campaign of the Scientific Humanitarian Committee (1897–1933), the pair of films based on the gay novel *Mikael*, by Mauritz Stiller (1916) and Carl Dreyer (1924) respectively, together with the German social-reform narrative feature *Anders als die Anderen* (1919), produce the jilted artist and the violinist blackmail victim as the first gay subjects of the cinema.

In the considerably more repressed period after the Second World War, the works of Anger, Fontaine, and Warhol elaborate obliquely on the pattern. They tease out heightened and ambiguous tensions with spectator voyeurism and construct a gay subject that is partly obscured, displaced, or off-screen. In the early seventies, Visconti's *Death in Venice* and Pasolini's "Trilogy of Life" converge as a final celebration of a departed (fantasized?) sexual regime, as if to deny the rumblings of Stonewall (not to mention the women's movement) on the other side of the Atlantic. Their younger contemporaries, like Larkin, Hazan, Peck, Fassbinder (*Germany in Autumn*), and Benner situate the gay subject within a complex, curiously antiseptic universe where visions of post-Stonewall affirmation are often achieved at a cost. Interestingly, in all of these latter films, the gay subjects' strong nonsexual relationships with women rival the inter-male subject-object sexuality for dramatic space.

Finally, the flood of 1980s updates—the British pair *Caravaggio* and *Looking for Langston* dispelling the shadow of Section 28, the Canadian *Urinal*, the Dutch *A Strange Love Affair*, the Spanish *Law of Desire*, the numerous American entries from *Abuse* to *Torch Song Trilogy*—are all eclectic, postmodern renditions of the traditional configuration of the gay artist-intellectual, situated on various strata of the cultural hierarchy and in different relations to gay subcultural constituencies. These entries of the last prolific decade all reflect (implicitly or explicitly) shifting sensibilities and cultural-political strategies in the face of the antigay backlash and the Pandemic. Significantly, all reclaim the sensuous Pasolinian eroticism which the Stonewall pioneers had somehow downplayed.

As for the object types, Victorian iconography has undergone a radical shift as twentieth-century gay male culture has evolved. The predominant icon of the modern gay erotic imaginary, the he-man (in his postwar ghetto incarnations as "trade," "clone," and bodybuilder) has gradually supplanted the ephebe, in both his straight and "in-betweenist" shapes. Aside from some important exceptions, the ephebe is now relegated to stigmatized specialty tastes within gay culture. When young Thomas Mann imagined an ephebe at the center of his novella *Death in Venice* in 1911, he was in stride with his generation, but when old Luchino Visconti translated that vision literally onto the screen sixty years later, it now seemed nostalgic and anachronistic within the rapidly changing gay cultural context. It is symbolically apt that the professorial protagonist of *A Strange Love Affair* supplants his original ephebe object with the latter's decidedly bearish old dad. The decline of the ephebe stems perhaps from the tightening taboos on pedophilia within sociomedical-juridical discourse, but no doubt more fundamentally from changing conceptions of the economic role and sexual identity of the child, and the emergence of youth culture with its (post-)pubescent subject. No doubt as well, the gay imaginary has dared more and more to desire (and represent the desire for) objects with no alibi of femininity, but the trend away from the ephebe was clear well before Gay Liberation took hold. One perhaps symptomatic development of postwar gay sensibilities is the emergence of a hybrid object, the body of the he-man with the mind of the ephebe, incarnated archetypally by (Little!) Joe Dallesandro and the cowboy hustlers of *The Boys in the Band* and *Midnight Cowboy* (the last decade may have mercifully reversed that trend). Regardless, the object type of our dreams may have fluctuated, but the figure of the artist-intellectual remains an all-embracing constant.

The Queen

One important variation of the gay artist figure is the queen, whether aggressively lustful or passively pining. Though the queen does not always have the obvious discursive narrative function of the artist-intellectual, no one will deny that she discourses in her own active way in the construction of gender, body, and identity. The queen inherits gender markers from her Victorian third-sex precursor, the ephebe in drag, but these markers now adorn the gay subject rather than the gay object. In some manifestations, the queenly subject may even push gender markers into the realm of biology, whether real or silicone, whether as transvestite, transsexual, or even as heterosexual woman, all incarnating to a greater or lesser degree the desiring gay male subject. Though Molly Haskell (1974) and Pauline Kael (1981) thought they'd cleverly unmasked the insidious phenomenon of gay men hiding in the bodies of heterosexual heroines in Tennessee Williams and George Cukor respectively,[1] in fact the most vivid recurring example in the corpus comes from the Warhol-Morrissey oeuvre. Here, queens as biologically diverse as Taylor Meade and Holly Woodlawn join "real women" Jane

Goforth and Viva in playing the gay male subject, often competing for (though never obtaining) the films' limp and sleepy dreamboat objects like Joe Dallesandro.

The Artist

What does it mean for the gay subject to be translated so often as a figure operating diegetically as a discursive agent, namely as artist or intellectual or queen? No doubt many factors are in play. On the one hand, two ideals are inherited from precinematic gay literary traditions: firstly the ideal of pedagogic Eros, the Socratic intergenerational initiation (the two silent adaptations of *Mikael* present a mentor relationship where the sexual object is simultaneously artistic apprentice and model), and secondly the aesthete or dandy, member of a refined and sensitive elite. Wilde's *Picture of Dorian Gray* may not have been the first work to posit artistic representation as some kind of metaphoric analogue of gay identity, and the artist-intellectual as the gay prototype, but it is undoubtedly the Ur-text of the third body narratives.

On the other hand, a documentary dimension to the artist figure is also significant insofar as he embodies a sociological acknowledgment of a sector where gays traditionally are disproportionately visible, sheltered, and nurtured. More specifically, an autobiographical discourse can be read on a quite literal level. What else to make of Visconti, in his sixties, undertaking his final progression of portraits of aging artistic figures: composer, patron, and connoisseur, respectively in *Death in Venice, Ludwig,* and *Conversation Piece?* The autobiographical possibility is dramatically foregrounded in that small group of "avant-garde" words, mostly nonfiction, by Werner Schroeter, R. W. Fassbinder, George Kuchar, Rosa von Praunheim, Derek Jarman, and Curt McDowell, where the filmmaker plays himself as gay artist literally integrating sexual expression and artistic creation. Of course, Pasolini's performance as artist in two installments of his trilogy is a unique and sublime variation of this pattern in narrative fiction. The autobiographical reading of the gay artist figure may be better understood by comparing it with the important role of autobiographical writing in the cultural affirmations of other disenfranchised groups, from women to blacks.

Another perspective on the artist figure assumes an analogy between the Romantic moment of artistic inspiration/crisis and the gay ritual of coming out. Pasolini's *Teorema* does exactly that, when aspiring painter Pietro has sex with Terence Stamp and calls into question his entire vocation: Action Painting becomes Piss Art (Stamp as homoerotic object has had a similar devastating impact in other films as well, from *Billy Budd* to *Far from*

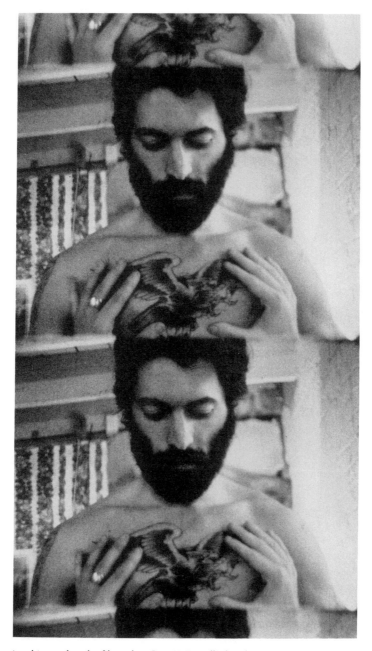

Autobiography: the filmmaker Curt McDowell's hands in *Loads*

the Madding Crowd, and his androgynous compatriots, Dirk Bogarde and Michael York, have shown similar propensities—there's a thesis in there somewhere).

Perhaps at a more profound psychosexual level is the issue of empowerment, both individual and collective. Does the artistic control of model and scenario, guaranteed by professional protocol, social status and/or class privilege, translate into a fantasy of general sexual empowerment in a hostile social setting? Does specific sexual control of the body of the loved one represent a symbolic victory over repression?

The incarnation of the gay subject as artist connotes a sense of presence in the world that is one of thought and feeling as opposed to action; of desire rather than consummation; of representing as if in revenge for the nonrepresentation of gayness in official culture; of observation as if in retaliation for the increasing surveillance we have been subjected to from the start of this chronology.

Narrative Role: The Look and the Voice

Sexual looking is, of course, a highly charged activity in out culture, all the more so for the same-sex look that ventures outside of certain carefully controlled areas (such as sport). The artist figure, then, at the most pragmatic level, has recourse to a traditional high-status alibi, and thereby legitimizes sexual looking and representation. Furthermore, the artist-intellectual is traditionally an outsider type in our culture (as is the queen in her simultaneous embrace and rejection of disguise). The artist's outsider vantage point fuses with that of the sexual outlaw in patriarchal culture. The image of Caravaggio watching the goings-on of the papal court, or of Aschenbach on the porch of the Venice hotel, is that of both the alienated artist charting the machinations of social power from the wings, and the gay man tuning into the sexual undercurrents of his surroundings. The gay artist figure exposes and concentrates the networks of sexual looking and being-looked-at within gay narrative and within gay culture, and, in fact, within Western patriarchal culture as a whole.

Two interesting variations in the scenario of the look must also be noted:

1. *The return of the look of the sexual object.* The subject's model, initiate, or sexual object looking back can be a key moment in the narrative of the third body, hinting tantalizingly at the possible union of subject and object. Remember Tadzio's complicit look back as *Death in Venice* draws to a close—a look of acceptance and reciprocity, perhaps a challenge to the act of voyeurism as well (this look back is incidentally a key addition that Visconti brought to the Mann novella). In some cases, the returned look of

the object can so dominate or unsettle or overturn the narrative structure that an entirely new narrative mythos emerges, the object as subject—as in Fassbinder's groundbreaking *Querelle* or its realist precursor *Fox and His Friends*, or in Derek Jarman's *Sebastiane*. More literal instances are those moments in 1980s works like *Looking for Langston* and *Law of Desire*,[2] where the object looks directly at the camera and the spectator, thus subverting both the subject-object dynamic and the narrative syntax of voyeuristic pleasure.

2. *The voice of the subject.* In many cases, the look of the gay subject is activated by or signified by his voice, namely through the mechanism of disembodied voice-over narration. It might be argued that the preponderance of voice-over narrations in gay fictional cinema reflects only the low-budget artisanal level of the production, as in *My Hustler* or *Loads*, or in physique movie mogul Dick Fontaine's overdubbing of his classic erotic shorts with a giddy voice-over by queenly commentator Glory Holden. However, the voice-over has lingered as an aesthetic strategy in nonartisanal cinema, throughout entire films such as *Looking for Langston* or in key moments such as the porn-dubbing opening sequence of *Law of Desire*.

The voice-over, emitting from the body of author-subject as he retreats once more behind the camera, may impart a level of retroactive self-reflexivity, as in *Caravaggio* and *Loads*. This voice may also enact a simultaneous sportscasting relationship to the erotic action of the camera's gaze, as in *My Hustler*, or the gay cable video genre represented by a mid-eighties New York work like *How to Seduce a Preppie* (Rick X). With both options, the effect is to amplify the outsider status of the gay subject, to cement the irreconcilability of subject and object, and to indulge in a deliriously self-conscious game of voyeurism that at the same time problematizes and exults in the subject's look. In *Langston* and *Querelle*, external and literary voices engage in a multivocal address of and by the gay subject. The often disembodied quotations and overlapping voices create a distancing, multivalent effect.

The Erotic Cinema

Many of the foregoing titles, because of the oblique or direct eroticism of their address, call for a momentary digression to consider how the third body pattern pertains to that disreputable mirror of the narrative cinema, the erotic cinema proper. Since no gay fiction is far from the erotic impulse that is central to all gay (popular) culture, it is not surprising that the third body makes an appearance in the erotic cinema as well, yet with an important inflection. Here, the gay subject is both absent and present: absent as in the erotic photograph, even in the pinup layout's narrative modes, for the gay subject seems invisible and is assumed to be off-screen. Yet the gay subject is also present, in the sense that subject and object within the diegesis are often fused, and these roles are dispersed interchangeably among all the bodies within the frame. It is a question, to paraphrase Mingus, the legendary, pseudonymous, porn reviewer of the *New York Native*, of confusion and ambiguity between the men we want to be and the men we want to love, in other words, between subject and object. Mingus goes on to argue that this confusion emerged with what I've called the decline of the ephebe, which he situates in the late fifties, before which there was a clear dichotomy between adolescent object and "dirty old john over thirty" (the exact point of this historical threshold needs further study at the very least). Nevertheless, this current (con)fusion of subject and object is highlighted by the artist-intellectual figures who people the porno formulas. For they are indeed stock characters in erotic gay film, including the writer-researcher (usually of porno novels), the photographer, and the journalist. The list expands if one includes the porno world's variations on the Socratic mentor: the track coach, the sex doctor, and the Marine officer. With these figures, who are homoerotic objects as well as subjects, most of the tensions of difference that structure the licit fiction disappear; artist and model, subject and object, self and other, he-man and third body, become all but indistinguishable in bodily construction (except for the occasional differences in race, age, body, consciousness, and sometimes other factors that recall but usually don't replicate the original structures of opposition). In this minimization of difference, it is interesting to locate gay eroticism's most essential distinctiveness alongside heterosexual eroticism, in whose narrative world difference is always visualized at its most extreme form, that is, as *gender* difference.

Positive Image/Happy Ending, or the Failure of Gay Liberation Criticism

The foregoing attempt at a taxonomy of gay-authored narrative cinema as a transhistorical, transcultural corpus, this project of defining the gay subject as third body, as incarnation of difference and enactor of representation, is not without methodological stresses. Aside from the dangers of gay essentialism lurking in any cross-cultural and transhistorical study, does this taxonomy in fact constitute genre criticism without a genre (in the sense that the necessary continuing dialogue between genre author and genre audience would seem missing with this retroactively constructed discontinuous corpus that is the gay art cinema)? Is this auteur criticism without an auteur (in the sense that they gay author is constructed collectively and retroactively on the basis of thematic consistency and biographical knowledge that in many cases are invisible to the ordinary spectator)? Or is this a structuralist inventory of narrative archetypes and functions without the necessary mythological coherence of a discrete host culture (unless the international network of gay subcultures that are the pillar of the "art cinema" constituency can be considered a coherent "culture")? (Of course, these problems tend to dissolve with the 1980s corpus, since the new breed of young gay directors have been very much plugged into their gay constituency, and the international circuit of gay festivals has begun to consolidate something like real gay genres, gay audiences, and gay authors, arguably for the first time in our history.)

What is clear amid this methodological tentativeness is that traditional gay liberation criticism, as exemplified in the post-Stonewall decade by the ethic-aesthetic of the positive image, would see, and has usually seen, the foregoing corpus as irredeemable traffic in negative stereotypes. A familiar litany of "bad images" can readily be drawn up from the films I've discussed: the young, silenced, and objectified sex object, attracting but never reciprocating the lustful gaze of the aging, bourgeois, libertine predator; the sensitive yet self-destructive artist; the wilting pansy; the dead queer.

In short, the "positive image" perspective founders before this corpus assembled around authorship and sexual orientation, and has no power to explain the irresistible attraction by gay authors to images that seem harmful in the viewfinders of movement ideologues. Is the attraction to the "negative image" by the gay author simply a question of self-oppression, as we assumed in the 1970s? Or is it a kind of existential reappropriation of stigma, a Genetesque, defiant inoculation against the denigration of the stereotype? Is it a preference for the exclusive marginality of the damned, rather than the anonymous absorption entailed by the civil rights/gay liberation platform? Is it a Pasolinian refusal of the consumerism and conformism of the liberal utopia? Or is it simply, as Dyer would have it, the adaptation by an invisible minority of the only available system of coding for self-definition? ("Film Noir," 1977) All of these possibilities no doubt enter into play, but too often we have avoided them, relying instead on reductive moralism instead of criticism.

For all of the indisputable magnitude of the late Vito Russo's contribution to gay cultural history, as a populist polemicist he did have certain blind spots around gay authors of the art cinema. Russo's famous "Necrology" of the cinema's dead queers in *The Celluloid Closet* contains not a few gay authors (though several obvious entrants have inexplicably been sifted out, such as Fassbinder and Pasolini). His dismissal of *Ludwig* ("Sleeping with a stable boy rots your teeth") is a scandalous rejection of one of the few serious, gay-authored works to attempt to imagine nineteenth-century cultural and sexual sensibilities. (Russo, 1987, 336) But Russo was not alone: remember the fierce polemics in many gay community newspapers around Fassbinder's *Fox*, around semi-mainstream films, from *La Cage aux Folles* to *Kiss of the*

Spider Woman, and around Dyer's and Jack Babuscio's useful articles on "camp."[3] (Dyer, "Camp," 1977; Babuscio, 1977) Even Dyer seemed to contradict his own sensible discussion of stereotypes and a social typing strategically useful for the gay liberation project of self-definition by his later uncharacteristically moralistic broadside against Pasolini's *Arabian Nights*. ("Stereotyping," 1977; "Pasolini," 1977) My own record is by no means spotless in this regard: I still cringe when I remember my 1978 denunciation of *Sebastiane* for its "cloyingly pompous stylization, visual and dramatic vacuum," and "tawdry jumble of s-m formulae," with the parting shot that "the only thing that distinguishes *Sebastiane* from the realm of the soft core is the honesty of the latter." In short, while the positive-image gay critic has usually been dead-on in his targeting of the *Cruising*s of the (hetero) patriarchal entertainment industry and has effectively revolutionized the reception of mainstream media within gay culture, he has too often gunned for the fragile butterflies of gay expression within the art cinema as well, and with counterproductive effect. Of course, feminists, too, have had to grapple with the negative image issue: for example, over the past decade, New York lesbian independents Lizzie Borden, Sheila McLaughlin, and Su Friedrich have insisted on dealing upfront in their films with previously "negative" iconography of woman as victim, sex worker, butch/femme, and nun respectively.

Our uneasy relationships with the tragic or ironic sensibilities of the great gay art-house filmmakers of the post-Stonewall generation continue—from Visconti and Pasolini to Fassbinder and Almodovar (our relationship with cult gay authors from Morrissey-Warhol to Waters has been only marginally better). Our reluctance to become the gay constituency they deserved has been due in no small way to the failure of a whole generation of gay critics to understand the contradictions of the international art cinema marketplace within which so many of these authors were circulated.

The institution of the art cinema stalled the development of a discrete gay constituency in two ways: through the ambivalence of its discourse, and through the crossover constitution of its audience. Textually speaking, the art house/film festival product usually offers a something-for-everyone blend of intellectualism and ambiguity, and an aura of recuperable marginality. The "exotic" articulation of taboo desire alongside its simultaneous disavowal, this cinema hovers on a tightrope between high-cultural status and subversive subcultural chic. Gay cinephiles are offered a mixed package, just the right blend of melodramatic catharsis, social justification provided through visibility alone, and finally an adequate dose of skin, albeit ultimately frustrated through the forever-receding closure of the open ending.

The demographic mosaic of the art house audience also enters the picture. If the gay spectator cements his identification with the gay subject through the voyeuristic sighting of the gay object, non-gay spectators, one can speculate, attach their voyeuristic fix on the gay subject himself, shaped through discourses of stereotype, freakshow, and pathos/victimization. For non-gay constituencies and critics, gay directors' tragic sensibilities seemed a tautological adjunct of marginality. Meanwhile, straight critics actively stifled gay discourses around these films, either through homophobic panic, liberal tolerance ("I'm so matter-of-fact and cool that sexual orientation doesn't have to be mentioned"), or allegorical exegesis ("This film is not about gayness, it's about fill-in-the-blank"). If the built-in ambiguity of the narrative codes of the art cinema allowed gay authors space to create, it denied them the chance to nurture a continuous and coherent gay audience. Instead, we remained invisible and covert spectators, a divided and discontinuous audience.

The inadequate critical context set the tone for the expectations and tastes of gay audiences in the rare moments when they were constituted as a discrete group, most often through the gay festivals that started cropping up in large markets in the 1970s (a similar abdication of critical responsibility affected the other discrete gay market, the porno scene). Even seasoned gay festival audiences still lean towards the happy-ending, positive-image standard, with a preference for *intimiste* domestic or romantic melodramas with open— but not *too* open—endings—and this after almost two decades of gay programming. Some post-Liberation gay filmmakers have excelled within the melodrama genre—think of Frank Ripploh, the late Bill Sherwood, the late Artie Bressan, or Quebec's Michel Tremblay (in his screenwriter's hat)— namely through developing strong and authentic emotional hooks on lifestyle issues within the ghetto. The melodrama's validity as a format of gay popular culture is without question, having delivered some of the 1980s' undisputed masterpieces. However, the development of the gay melodrama hardly constituted the appearance "at last" of *the* gay cinema, as each successive new work from *Taxi Zum Klo* to *Longtime Companion* was greeted by both gay and straight blurbists. As for the Pandemic's impact on the mythic landscape, ACT UP's exemplary cultural politics may have stimulated a new creative energy in the cultural margins and on community levels, but the health crisis's impact on feature-length independent fiction has been largely to enrich this important melodrama tradition—think of *Buddies, Death in the Family,* and *Parting Glances,* all precursors of that mother of all melodramas, *Longtime Companion.*

Reinventing the Third Body/Gay Subjects in the 1980s and 1990s

Aside from this healthy melo current, the third body pattern maintained its currency at the end of the 1980s, and is still in the process of being reinvented by the young, post-Stonewall authors (who are still incidentally far ahead of their critical constituency for the most part, though the gap may be closing). In another context, Richard Dyer describes this work as "post-affirmation," "films that manage to deconstruct without auto-destructing, that leave behind without anguish the fixed identifiers affirmed by earlier films, that seem to enjoy the struggle with definitions of identity as an ongoing process." (1990, 284) In the recent renditions of the third body films, the separation of subject and object is no longer a given, nor is the fixity of observer status, the immutability of difference, or the infinite deferral of closure. The gay subject emerges now dialectically, for example, as a comic subject rather than tragic, through parodic quotation or through reversals. Risks are taken with "dangerous" or negative imagery (I am sure that for Almodovar the concept of the positive image is an inscrutable aberration of Protestantism), sexual pleasure is reclaimed and celebrated as much as it is problematized, humor and anger are as characteristic as the melancholy of yore.

Fassbinder's relentless exploration of the subjectivity of the object and the power dynamics of desire in *Fox, In a Year of Thirteen Moons*, and *Querelle*, and Jarman's not-dissimilar experiment in *Sebastiane*, have now proven to be prophetic of a whole spectrum of work, from the haunting *L'Homme Blessé* (Patrice Chéreau, 1983) to the infuriating *A Virus Knows No Morals*. Meanwhile, Jarman's idols Genet and Pasolini reawaken as the presiding spirits of the end of the century.

Jarman's two non-white compatriots Hanif Kureishi and Isaac Julien both explode the patterns of subject-object difference predicated on white, middle-class subject and racial Other, superimposing contradictory grids of identity, involving race, class, gender, and sex, and making new connections and coalitions from grid to grid. Julien goes further than Kureishi's fundamentally populist, realist framework to disperse the subject, and yet collectivize him at the same time, disallowing the individualist readings encouraged by art cinema's fetishization of psychological realism.

While Julien reclaims the gay subject from buried racial, cultural, and sexual history, John Greyson reclaims dozens of them, offering his historical reconstructions of everyone from Aschenbach and Kipling to Foucault and (Rock) Hudson. This video artist offers essayistic hypernarrative formats, matter-of-factly peopled by self-conscious and lascivious gay artist-intellectual subjects from the pre-Stonewall era, who have come back to haunt the post-Liberation gay sensibility. Is this recuperation of gay history or a tongue-in-cheek postmodern version of the old gay community ritual of citing the famous fags of history from Plato to Liberace (a self-affirming ritual which in any case has undoubtedly been more responsible for the momentum of the "third body" narrative than I have acknowledged)? Whatever, in *Urinal*, Greyson's first feature film, Sergei Eisenstein tries to seduce not an object type but another subject, Langston Hughes. More at home in the toilet stall than the art house, he squints through a glory hole, not at an ephebe or he-man, but at the parade of gay artist subjects who now become recycled as postmodern pastiche, at the ferment of sexual politics in the cultural horizon of the present, at the collapse of the public and the private, and, at the same time, happily, at the still-undiminished, infinite, and delirious possibilities of the (homo)sexual body.

Three of Greyson's subjects are lesbian artists, sketched with his traditionally impeccable gender parity. Greyson however certainly did not invent the lesbian third body narrative. In fact the sudden emergence of a flood of lesbian-authored variants of the form in the mid-1980s, each with its own incarnation of the artist-intellectual subject, made a major contribution to its reinvention. The list includes works by Su Friedrich, Patricia Rozema, Elfi Mikesch, Lizzie Borden, Sheila McLaughlin, Léa Pool, Chantal Akerman, and perhaps Sally Potter, with associate status for Liliana Cavani and Jill Godmilow (for her non-lesbian-authored, nonsexual Gertie and Alice). Donna Deitch has a place, albeit tenuous, in our category as well, since *Desert Hearts* occupies the borderland between art film narrative and pop romance, and Helen Shaver's status as an intellectual is more a question of script exposition and wardrobe than of narrative function. Léa Pool's *A Corps Perdu* (*Straight to the Heart*, 1988), her follow-up to *Anne Trister*, may also belong as a lesbian-authored version of the gay male third body narrative, with the subject this time a photographer. This is not to say that the specularization of eroticism, the problematization of subject-object relations, or the autobiographical resonances in the lesbian films are identical to the gay male formulations—far from it. Whether the lesbian films constitute a transmigration or spontaneous combustion, whether or not they confirm the pattern as a basic cultural structure of same-sex sexuality, or as just a genre of art cinema with a new lease on life, they clearly second Greyson's demonstration that the third body narrative—the subject as artist-intellectual and gender transgressor—is large and flexible enough to absorb each generation's and each constituency's particular mythic projection and political challenges.

The continuous thread from von Gloeden and Stiller on through Jarman and Greyson is of course neither as continuous or as threadlike as might be inferred. The new breed of the 1980s notwithstanding, the battles are far from over. The spurts and starts sometimes seem as uneven as ever, especially as the crisis in non-Hollywood film financing deepens around the world, gay or straight, and the flourishing gay festival circuit still can't finance a single feature budget. The lures of success are also as insidious as ever (will the *Poison* of today become the *Tie Me Up Tie Me Down* of tomorrow?), and the bowdlerization of gay history in the mainstream biopic seems as obnoxious as ever (was Charlton Heston's Michelangelo in *The Agony and the Ecstasy* really any worse than the recent Canadian Whitman travesty *Beautiful Dreamers* or the Hollywood "straightening out" of Sir Richard Burton in *Mountains of the Moon?*). Still, for all the continued lurching back and forth, in and out of the closet threshold zone of self-censorship dictated by state-supported art film financing, for all the occasional rubbing thin of the "third body" thread, it shows surprisingly little danger of unraveling in the 1990s. For gay and now lesbian artists and audiences, the narrative art cinema, poised halfway between the quagmires of Hollywood and the uncompromising nontheatrical fringes of the radical avant-garde, continues to be an indispensable forum for confronting the world and ourselves.

The Third Body: A Select Filmography of the Gay Male Subject as Artist, Intellectual, and Queen

(Titles are in approximate chronological order; works are presumed gay- or bisexual-authored, with authorship sometimes defined to include scriptwriter or, in the case of adaptations, author of original source material).

Mauritz Stiller, *The Wings (Vingarne)* (Sweden, 1916); sculptor—first adaptation of Herman Bang's gay novel *Mikael.*

Richard Oswald and Magnus Hirschfeld, *Anders als die Anderen (Different from the Others)* (Germany, 1919); musician.

Carl Dreyer and Herman Bang, *Mikael* (Germany, 1924); painter—second adaptation of *Mikael.*

Jean Cocteau, *Blood of a Poet* (France, 1930); *Orphée* (1949); *Le Testament D'Orphée* (1959); more-or-less autobiographical variations on gay artist as subject.

S. M. Eisenstein, *Ivan the Terrible* (USSR, 1944–46); Czar as proto-gay subject/looker, body-guards as objects.

Kenneth Anger, *Fireworks* (US, 1948); hybrid formula includes photo-object protagonist.

Dick Fontaine (US, 1950s–60s); physique narrative shorts, many with artist subjects, some narrated by queen voice-over.

Andy Warhol and Paul Morrissey, *My Hustler* (US, 1965); queens compete for object.

Lonesome Cowboys (US, 1968); queens compete for cowboy object.

Flesh (US, 1968); hustler object surrounded by queens and photographer.

Trash (US, 1969); queen and hustler.

Pier Paolo Pasolini, *Teorema* (Italy, 1968); episode around painter/son Pietro.

"Trilogy of Life" (Italy):

The Decameron (1971); PPP as Giotto.

The Canterbury Tales (1972); PPP as Chaucer.

Arabian Nights (1974); episode around Arab poet Abu-Nuwas, etc.

Luchino Visconti, *Death in Venice* (Italy, 1971); composer.

Ludwig (Italy, 1973); patron.

Conversation Piece (Italy, 1974); connoisseur/collector.

John Schlesinger, *Midnight Cowboy* (US, 1969); hybrid melodrama includes gay object as protagonist.

Sunday Bloody Sunday (UK, 1971); hybrid melodrama includes doctor/art-lover as gay subject.

R. W. Fassbinder, *Beware the Holy Whore* (Germany, 1970); filmmaker.

Fox and His Friends (Germany, 1975); prole underdog as object-protagonist surrounded by subject types.

Germany in Autumn (Germany, 1978); RWF episode has real-life filmmaker as subject.

In the Year of Thirteen Moons (Germany, 1978); transsexual.

Querelle (Germany, 1982); sailor as object-protagonist, officer as subject/representer/looker.

Frank Vitale, *Montreal Main* (Canada, 1974); photographer and ephebe.

Jack Hazan, *A Bigger Splash* (UK, 1974); painter and model.

Ryan Larkin, *A Very Natural Thing* (US, 1974); a romantic melodrama with both photographer and teacher as protagonists.

Derek Jarman, *Sebastiane* (UK, 1976); hybrid includes centurion as gay subject and martyr as gay object/protagonist.

The Tempest (UK, 1979); magician/impresario.

Caravaggio (UK, 1986); painter.

Richard Benner, *Outrageous* (Canada, 1977); *Too Outrageous* (1988); drag performer.

Arturo Ripstein, *A Limitless Place* (Mexico, 1977); drag queen subject.

Jack Gold and Quentin Crisp, *The Naked Civil Servant* (UK, 1977); queen.

Ron Peck, *Nighthawks* (UK, 1978); teacher.

Rosa von Praunheim, *Army of Lovers or the Revolt of the Perverts* (Germany, 1979); documentary author as subject.

Guy Hocquenghem and Lionel Soukaz, *Race d'Ep* (France, 1979); episodes around von Gloeden and Hirschfeld.

Salvatore Samperi and Umberto Saba, *Ernesto* (Italy, 1979); student subject, autobiographical core.

Curt McDowell, *Loads* (US, 1980); documentary author as subject.

Frank Ripploh, *Taxi Zum Klo* (Germany, 1980); domestic melo with teacher subject.

Werner Schroeter, *La Repetition General* (France, 1980); documentary author as subject.

The Rose King (Germany, 1986); mother and son compete for ephebe.

Arthur Bressan, *Abuse* (US, 1982); filmmaker and ephebe.

Paul Verhoeven and Gerard Reve, *The Fourth Man* (Netherlands, 1983); writer.

Gus Van Sant, *Mala Noche* (US, 1985); countercultural subject and Chicano ephebe.

Hector Babenco and Herman Puig, *Kiss of the Spider Woman* (US/Brazil, 1985); queen/cinephile as gay subject.

Takis Spetsiotis, *Meteor and Shadow* (Greece, 1985); poet.

Eric de Kuyper, *A Strange Love Affair* (Netherlands, 1985); film studies teacher and ephebe.

Stephen Frears and Hanif Kureishi, *My Beautiful Laundrette* (UK, 1985); entrepreneur.

Bill Sherwood, *Parting Glances* (US, 1986); musician, editor, porn writer.

Michel Tremblay and Jean-Yves Laforce, *Le Coeur Découvert (The Heart Exposed)* (Québec, 1987); domestic melo, teacher and actor subjects, child object?

Stephen Frears and Joe Orton, *Prick Up Your Ears* (UK, 1987); non-gay adaptation of playwright's diaries.

Pedro Almodovar, *Law of Desire* (Spain, 1987); filmmaker.

Isaac Julien, *Looking for Langston* (UK, 1988); poet.

John Greyson, *Urinal* (Canada, 1988); Eisenstein, Mishima, Hughes, Wilde, etc.

Harvey Fierstein, *Torch Song Trilogy* (US, 1989); drag performer.

Marlon Riggs, *Tongues Untied* (US, 1990); autobiographical elements, poet persona.

Texts Cited

Dyer, Richard. "Homosexuality and Film Noir," *Jump Cut* no. 16 (1977), pp. 18–21.

———. *Now You See It: Studies on Lesbian and Gay Film* (London: Routlege, 1990).

———. "Pasolini and Homosexuality," in Paul Willemen, ed., *Pier Paolo Pasolini* (London: BFI, 1977) pp. 57–63.

———. "Stereotyping," in Dyer, ed., *Gays and Film* (London: BFI, 1977) pp. 27–39.

Haskell, Molly. *From Reverence to Rape: The Treatment of Women in the Movies* (New York: Holt, Rinehart and Winston, 1974).

Kael, Pauline. Review of *Rich and Famous*, in *The New Yorker*, October 26, 1981, rpt. Kael, *Taking it All In* (New York: Holt, Rinehart and Winston, 1984) pp. 247–48.

Mingus (pseud.). *The New York Native*, undated, untitled clipping, c. 1985.

Vito Russo, *The Celluloid Closet*, revised ed. (New York: Harper and Row, 1987).

Waugh, Thomas. "Films by Gays for Gays," *Jump Cut* no. 16 (1977), pp. 14–16. "*Sebastiane*," *The Body Politic* (March, 1978).

Acknowledgments

This article was first presented in embryonic form on the panel "The Sexual Representation/ Appropriation of the Male Body," chaired by Peter Lehman, at the 1990 Society for Cinema Studies. I am grateful to José Arroyo for inspiration and criticism and to John Greyson for input and ideas in the editing process of the final version.

Notes

1. Both critics follow earlier attacks in the 1960s by mainstream theater critics on the pervasive and insidious influence of homosexuals in the theater, focussing most notably on Williams and Edward Albee.

2. I am indebted to José Arroyo's analysis of *The Law of Desire* in a forthcoming article.

3. For example: Bob Cant loved *Fox*, Andrew Britton hated it (*Gay Left* [London] no. 2, 3, 1976; rpt. *Jump Cut* 16, special section "Gay Men and Film" [1977], pp. 22–23). *The Body Politic*'s Gerald Hannon loved *Cage* (no. 56, Sept. 1979) while *Gay News*'s Jack Babuscio found it a "reactionary farce" (undated clipping, c. 1981). *Gay Community News*'s longstanding critic Michael Bronski favoured *Kiss*, for which he was thoroughly tongue-lashed by op-ed reader Kenneth Hale-Wehmann (August 10, October 26, 1985). Britton was responsible for "For Interpretation: Notes Against Camp," a tirade against Dyer and Babuscio, *Gay Left* 7 (Winter, 1978–79), pp. 11–14.

Storming the Lull, or It's a Lesbian Heat Wave

SARA DIAMOND

Section One: An Interview with Sara Diamond

EDITORS' NOTE: We received this unlabelled audiocassette in the mail, with no return address. It appears, from the preponderance of references to British Columbia, to be an interview with the Canadian feminist, video artist, and theorist Sara Diamond, (*not* the American, feminist, writer, and theorist Sara Diamond). Surprisingly, the identity of the interviewer is never disclosed. Indeed, the interviewer's voice is so similar to the interviewee's that at times we couldn't tell when the questions ended and the answers began.

INTERVIEWER: What is the Women's Labour History Project?

DIAMOND: It is a nonprofit production society which I began in 1978, committed to documenting, representing, and critiquing the representation of working-class women in British Columbia's work force, community, and domestic life. It concentrates on the instrumentality and consciousness of those women. The initial impetus, which was to contruct a set of histories, which no one at that time had valued or even posited, has since expanded to include a consideration of issues of representation: what sources are there from which to make evident this history, what is the history "writing" process, what is fictional, what factual about historical construction, and so on? How can we imagine documents, films, photographs operating in relation to these women within the historic context, and how do they function when recontextualized now?

Since 1978 I have collected a large number of oral histories, produced a research bibliography, a series of articles about the history for a range of publications—from union newsletters to academic journals—developed a photo exhibition about the ways that photographers represented women at work in the province, and finally, have produced an ongoing series of videotapes—fictional, artumentary, documentary—on this history.

INTERVIEWER: Tell me a bit about these women? Were you interested in their activism? Were they exceptional?

DIAMOND: I looked for paradigms, networks, specific resistances, and ordinariness. How did women express agency? What was their relationship to existing structures of resistance, such as unions? How were they constituted

in terms of any group identity? What made women work to change circumstances, what inhibited? The activists tended to be "different," although
circumstance intervened enough to make one aware that it is continually an
historical factor (that is, who fortuitously sits next to whom at lunch—
although one could read causality into even that). Anyhow, heterosexual
women who were activists were either "single," had strong family support
(husband, brother, dad), had child care arrangements if they had kids, usually
in the form of a live-in grandmother, and often faced intensive personal
crises as a result of their activism, which in turn led either to withdrawal
into more appropriate activities, or else single status and with that a primarily
professional identity. There were many divorces, some battering, and lots of
personal pain attached to women's militancy.

INTERVIEWER: What about lesbians?

DIAMOND: Well, some of the purportedly "single" women might have been
lesbians or have become lesbians after they left repressive marriages. I did
not interview anyone who described herself as a dyke. Although two lesbian
war-workers were mentioned to me, they were not available or interested in
interviews.

INTERVIEWER: Were activist women individualists? You have spoken primarily about their home life.

DIAMOND: No. Women were part of networks which helped to sustain their
activism: networks of other women, friendships, unions where they formed
enclaves, political organizations like the Communist Party, which encouraged women's membership, or the Cooperative Commonwealth Federation.
With a few exceptions, who functioned alone or with male acknowledgment
and support, women were almost always a part of a network.

INTERVIEWER: What about their personal lives? What happened there—were
these women sexually active? Were any of them married? Were any of them
lesbians?

DIAMOND: What do you mean "personal lives"? I can't accept that division,
because both realms were so intertwined in terms of motivation and permission for these women. But there's also a kind of protocol, that it's not
acceptable, even for the historical record, to talk about emotional issues or
to talk about really articulated differences. These things were noticeable
when I was younger, really younger, and the distance loomed large between
us.

In reality, many of them could not sustain ongoing activism as well as a
family. They were forced to choose: their husbands would not stick around—
the men were threatened. Some women alluded to "female friendships," as
it could be euphemistically stated, and several coworkers who were "manly"
women. Then there were the women I interviewed who were married and
seemed about as butch as one could get, women who "wore the pants in the

family." Were they latent? Were they hiding? Was there a gap, as is often the case, between image and desire? It's fascinating. Now that I'm older I would like to go back.

INTERVIEWER: Could you talk about the translation of all this research into artwork? Your work crosses a line between fictionalizing, documentary, fantasy.

DIAMOND: There are several series of videotapes which I have made about this social history. *Keeping the Home Fires Burning* is a videotape in two parts, about women and war work and war-working women and unions. It cites agitprop theater and deconstruction as a methodology, where the purely documentary character falls apart into very thin workers' theater sequences.

Then there is *Daughters Have Courage, Mothers Take Heart*, a series about the 1930s. *Ten Dollars or Nothing* looks at the gap between archival imagery, such as fishing industry films and photos, and the testimonial stories of actual women, done retrospectively in order to create instrumental fictions about their lives. At the same time, it provides certain glimpses of the historical process of working in the canneries. The images are very automated.

Finally, there is the four-part television coproduction *The Lull Before the Storm*: a two-part experimental drama and a two-part documentary, complementary to the drama. The documentaries decline the drama into a potential actuality. The fictions are about a small, miserable, nuclear family: George, Dorothy, and Bobby Sanderson. It uses genre after genre of recreations from the era to trace the deeply immobile character of their relationship with its masculine hierarchy.

INTERVIEWER: So what is the plot?

DIAMOND: Nothing much changes in the video, while Dorothy, the maternal figure and wife, moves deeper and deeper into commodity fetishism and George, the father, into assembly-line regression. Bobby gets larger. George won't let Dorothy work, and Dorothy yearns for her former working life, her ex-lover (male), and her pinkish, soft-radical past. While Dorothy remains at home scrubbing the floor, there is a constant framing by an materialized voice-over narrator (Mr. Grey) and a series of mostly ironic panel discussions about the changing status of women. All this fantasy is intercut with exemplary historical footage from the times in question. The relationship between Dorothy's motivation and ideological practices is hopefully placed in question. The dramas are written as antinarrative, or at least there is no catharsis in them, just lots of hysteria.

The family dramas are intercut with fantasy dance sequences which double as ads. The voice-of-god narrator is a flexible fellow who comments on the family's dilemmas, narrates the ads, and chairs public affairs panels. The dramas are also intercut with historical footage. While the dramas are intended as metahistories, the documentaries are located in a specific, Vancouver Island logging community, and follow the experiences of women who were loggers, from a white, European background or from a Sikh background.

INTERVIEWER: You're a lesbian right?

DIAMOND: Yeah.

INTERVIEWER: Well, why are there no lesbian characters? It's not like there is overt heterosexism in the film, but there isn't a clear lesbian position in any way.

DIAMOND: No, there is a lot of space for the lesbian viewer to feel self-satisfied. After all, the piece is a vindication of women's autonomy, and the importance of feminine desire. I am looking at certain icons within the culture of the times, and it would have been difficult to play with the signifiers in the same way if one of the central characters had been a lesbian. It would have been an interesting project, but not the one that compelled me at the time: constructing the signifiers for working-class heterosexual, family life, and underlining their impossibility.

INTERVIEWER: You sound rather sadistic to me. Why are you bent on forcing your lesbian audiences to submit? Isn't it enough that most of them grew up in a straight family? No—maybe you're a masochist—hoping beyond hope that you will rile your viewers into acts of humiliation and rage against you?

DIAMOND: Gee, I never thought of it that way . . .

Section Two: Letters of Consolation

EDITORS'NOTE: We received this packet of letters in the mail, the day after the audiocassette. Again there was no return address. We are printing them for their historical interest, since to our knowledge these constitute the first time that the famous Canadian expressionist landscape painter and writer Emily Carr (1871–1945) ever explicitly addressed issues of lesbian subjectivity. Naturally, some will question the veracity of the correspondence—for instance, some wonder whether Carr would have actually used the phrase "What a babe." Similarly, others have noted that Diamond was born at least a decade after Carr's death, making ongoing correspondence between the two somewhat improbable.

Dear Emily:

Sorry to hear about the recurrance of your tuberculosis. I hope that Sophie will come to visit you while you are convalescing. Victoria is so lovely this time of year, it would be wonderful if you could take the air while in recovery.

Now about your note: Yes, you did hear the latest gossip. Even though I carefully cited Michel Foucault in my last installation, lots of women got to the Lacanian phallus and stopped dead in their tracks. So much for an anatropic image! Lots of recognition and no fascination.

In any case, I am wandering . . . Word in this town says that no lesbian in her write mind (or perhaps minds would be more apropos) would quote psychoanalysis. It's as unpopular as communism round about midnight. And how do you feel about your beloved Canada becoming more balkanized than those Balkans?

Please, don't get depressed. Enjoy those begonias! And please be careful when you paint in the woods, and stop trying to adopt everybody's babies.

Love, Sara.

Dear Sara:

Now that we're pursuing this, let's talk about writing and the location of relevant knowledge. Dorothy, fragile cipher that she is, seems to carry with her your lover's family, your coworkers' families, and, to my surprise and at times chagrin, my family. What's more, the difference that is lesbianism does not preclude women identifying with either your George or your Dorothy.

Now what *about* George—you always go for those boy-girl-boys, don't you honey, those horrid brutes that occupied the Vancouver Art Gallery in '38, profaning that sacred house of history. And here he is again, the logger, the tough but vulnerable soldier you turn into a disappointed couch potato whose placating wife runs tighter and tighter circles around him. What man

The Emily Carr Appreciation Club meets, *The Lull Before the Storm,* Sara Diamond

would want to identify with him? But you know, Sara, women have told me that they identify with George.

As for myself, much as I love your letters, I am more interested in the forest than the film. I must get up North again to paint. Of course, the mosquitoes are deadly this time of year, and the rain unbearable, but the light, the color, the trees hanging low from the weight of wet, that wet coast wet that seems always to drip. And of course I long again to share the spiritual simplicity of the forest with her inhabitants. I have just come from seeing my beloved Sophie, her husband is quite morbid and I fear for her. I will be in the Queen Charlottes soon my dear, so don't expect a swift response . . .

Dear Emily:

How nice of you to rise from the dead for me, how flattering, your letter was charming, although quite anachronistic, all that nonsense about "the primitive" and the power of the Natural, you really were an insistent little modernist weren't you?

And thank you for not dismissing my concerns. It's true what you say, half the people in this town developing neopsych media crit are dykes (and another quarter are bisexuals). But that makes me boil inside even more! Without even seeing the piece, some women are mad at me for writing a script with a straight woman central character—they assume that there's no room for the lesbian viewer. As though being a lesbian could make me lose my fascination with that formative but resurgent monster, that reproductive force of compulsory heterosexuality, the nuclear family. Isn't the correlative that, because I'm a dyke, I have no right to consider heterosexuality as an institution.

I am fascinated by the ways that you represent a different era, for in your time expressionism on the west coast of Canada was quite a courageous venturing forth against realism. Ironic, isn't it, that video, that most modern of media, should so inherit a mid-nineteenth-century aesthetic, and all the surrounding expectations. But, *The Lull*, I assure, is neither a realist fiction nor an expressionist catharsis. Rather it's subject is interruption (for its subject is femininity)—it's about available fictions that circulated around lesbians *and* straight women in the 1940s and 1950s.

In any case, we both acknowledge that there's a larger-than-life need for alternate culture(s) based on lesbian identities. After all, here I am, outing you of all people. Well, as in your case, those identities are not fixed, and especially when dealing with history. That's another reason why it may well be valuable for dykes to run our commentary about race, class, and location, location, location.

You know, the way that gays and lesbians have always overrun dominant cultural icons—well, we assert our space within discourses as well. Even if the *subject* is not lesbian identity, its object may well be.

Dear Sara:

I'm back from the Coast and feeling quite ill, but I hauled myself out of bed and went, monkey and parrot in hand, to greet my dish of a letter carrier today, hoping that there would be some communication from you. I know you wrote several months ago and I didn't reply. All those run-on sentences! You know my philosophy: why use a big word when you can use a little one.

I was tired, and thinking of you, and I lay down for a moment on the couch. Surprisingly, I fell asleep. In my dream, I was giving a lecture to a group of frowning young women with lawn-mower haircuts, inventive tattoos and a range of leather artifacts. I was shocked at their public demeanor. I have always believed that women should wear skirts or dresses and a proper hat in public. Their appearance so dismayed me that I turned by back on them and began to speak.

Perhaps I was defensive as I began, "I want to respond to the review of my acquaintance Sara Diamond's recent videotape. This scandalous piece of writing is entitled, "Hidden Heterosexuality Erupts in Diamond's Stormy Drama: Weathervane Points to Closet," by De La Dyke, *Victoria Colonist*'s arts critic. I will begin by quoting the review:

'Sara Diamond has done it again. Her recent video series doesn't say the word "lesbian" once? Historical investigation is crucial for emerging feminist identity: womyn need to know our past. We need to reclaim our possible older sisters, such as Emily Carr or Rosa Bonheur. There are enough straight feminist cultural historians, especially of the socialist variety. I'm personally tired of maternal desire and phallic displacement being assigned to every ounce of female creativity. It's time that each and every lesbian stands up for the truly "hidden from history," each other! Diamond had better spend some fictive time and energy on the lesbian community if she wants its support. Let's have Dorothy leave George in the next round of narrative negotiations. . . ."

I guess that there's nothing more dangerous than overstating your enemy's position, for all those horrid young women were cheering, whistling, and stamping their feet. In any case, I had prepared a disclaimer, refusing to be associated with my name being used against you, and I proceeded with it.

I felt a sudden shocked silence in the room. Turning, anxious to respond to questions, I saw that the room was completely empty, I awake startled, the monkey is sitting on my chest.

Dear Emily:

Thank you for your attempted rescue. Your dream sure states the question. Who's the superego in this story, or am I walking some weird high-low line? Is it the straight museum world or broadcast which edits my scripts in my head, or the lesbian community, or some strange tension between both? Do I need the approval of my subcultures to continue to feel good about my own praxis? *Yes.*

By the way, can I borrow your car? How many people made that joke to you, you old cowpoke bulldyke you? You know, its fun to slip lesbian references into my social (and I mean social) history videos. Take *Keeping the Home Fires Burning.* Remember the sequence where the men are playing (water sports no less) on the logs? The guy falls off into the water just when the singer croons, "I heard that that romance fell through . . .," and then the image cuts to these two women, one a femme and the other a butch, both in overalls, on a log boom. The butch is lighting the femme's cigarette while the singer continues, "it's nice to see you again." Get it? The lesbian double entendre. Really, I prefer to code in ways that are slippery: where one thing seems to be happening, but the other reading is standing on the surface just begging to be taken.

Emily, you of all people should not chide me for some implied "biology is destiny."

Dear Sara:

Thanks for the historical information about Canadian lesbians during the Second World War—it was just at the end of my time and heavens knows my interest was mostly in protecting my collection . . . that was my Final Conflict. I didn't realize that there was so much harassment in the Canadian Women's Army Corps.

My curiosity about your lesbian viewers still remains. There is certainly much ado (too much for my taste) in *The Lull* about issues of class, race, and being a woman, that have little to do with preference but could still be a source of identification and pleasure. Then there's that militant little cutie, Mrs. Coldwood the journalist, what a babe—as Mr. Grey would say, "a real tomato." And then there are the line dances, waltzes, and rumbas. A little old-fashioned voyeurism goes a long way: your lesbian could dance with Dorothy.

Dear Emily:

You, of all people, know that the theorization of the gaze and the male franchise on visual pleasure can make us into rebellious little pleasure-seekers. Let us say that women are positioned as viewers as much these days by the economy of that discourse, which solidly links anxiety and fun, as by any inherent activity of matching. Lesbians are notorious for outperforming the marathon run between the masochistic feminine passive and the sadistic masculine, in asking, whom do I identify with anyhow, in cross-identification and subversion.

Well, in *The Lull*, the omniscient narrator, Dr. Spark/Mr. Grey, the fatherly voice of reason that so dominated capitalism's postwar boom, uses both discourse and his look to construct masculine "knowledge" and thus a favorable exchange of power, but a power which is always referenced and named. This is a gaze that demarcates discourses of social class as much as of gender, holding up examples of working-class social problems to the scrutiny of the historically middle-class documentary audience. The narrator plays another role—he is there to extricate anyone in the audience who slips into believing these fictions. After all, how can you believe in a ploy so large that you can trip over it?

If the narrator too literally looks in on the drama, the viewer can overtake his gaze, allowing both distance and identification. Ideally, we are allowed to both share his authority and refuse it (an argument for a willful lesbian identity if I ever heard one). And after all, it is Dorothy who rolls the diegesis slowly forward.

I ask you: are you watching from a lesbian position? Does the fact that I, a lesbian, made this work mean that I write from a lesbian position? But what *is* a lesbian position? (I know many, but that's another discussion . . .) Do you say to yourself and your date, "If Dorothy was a lesbian she would have left for sure!" Don't be so sure. . . .

I keep coming back to this issue of pleasure, to the ability or inability to read sexuality through an art work. Your work is disturbing and compelling: its content constructs a romantic modernist vision of Nature; it idealizes the supposedly dying culture of the West Coast Native, the primitive Other, and in doing so, it reproduces hierarchies of colonial domination, no matter how altruistic your written intent. But your canvasses! They are filled with giant phallic trees and vaginal passageways through the forest, with a passionate and thick application of paint: a veritable panorama of feminine fetishism. It is work that can be taken over, assigned to a subcultural identity perfectly appropriate to your individualistic life-style, filled with good women friends and a menagerie of creatures. I think I had the sequel to your dream last night.

Section Three: Dream Sequence

The following text arrived the day after the Carr-Diamond letters. Again, there was no return address. We have two theories: either this is a transcription of a taped session between Diamond and her psychoanalyst, or this is just possibly an excerpt from the infamous Diamond Dream Diary (of which we've heard many rumors). Unfortunately, we have been unable to confirm or deny the existence of an actual Lesbians from Hell Content Committee—all we know is that they aren't listed in the phone book.

In the dream I am watching the news when it was interrupted by a pirate broadcast. There I am, tied to a chair in front of a computer. A young women dressed in a stunning, pink, evening gown stands at a floor microphone. She clears her throat and delivers the following rhetorical message:

"Lesbian artist, Sara Diamond, having been held for ransom by the Lesbians from Hell Content Committee, has made the following retraction and renunciation of her previous work."

The camera cuts to a medium close of me. I say, "I am intrigued by the idea of reworking my postwar family antidrama into a lesbian fiction, playing around with the problem of seducing a little someone who is straight (or so they claim), or has never had a lesbian affair, but who pines for one.

"What might happen if Dorothy had a particular penchant for female friendship? Perhaps she would have had an affair with a woman instead of with Bill, maybe a Billie or Wilhemena, during that long, dark wartime hiatus of drawn blackout curtains. They might have met on the job and danced in an underground club, or even better, openly, at an assumedly innocent Women's Royal Navy dance. There no men would be allowed, and the socials were considered to give the gals some exercise without the seductive dangers of a mixed event. Just imagine, Dorothy and Wilhemena pressing their bodies together in all the right places, oh so subtly, whispering coyly to each other, and giggling with the ingenuity of the situation.

"In later life, when old George was a bore, Dorothy's dream time would turn to yearning for her Wilhemena. Better yet, George would never suspect and she could even continue to see Wilhemena during the weekly poker game that she played in her very own kitchen with her old wartime buddies.

"How would this work in the drama? Would Wilhemena function as "difference," as the utopian Other, never alighting into the real, the stuff of fiction and fantasy, the classic position of the androgyne. This lesbian Ideal might never be allowed to enter the neurotic terrain of daily discourse, the Sturm and Drang of George and Dorothy as currently inscribed: one long struggle after another. It has its appeal: a lonely and romantic figure to cut. And what would the narrative be from Wilhemena's position: attached to a feminine that continues to align itself to heterosexual privilege—is this not the classic narrative of the lonely lesbian? Or if Dorothy and Wilhemena start to fight, as well they might, given the circumstances, then we truly arrive at soap: two embattled couples restating the familiar emotional stakes of love and jealousy.

"But that is not the story I wanted to explore . . . so let's try another bend

Dorothy dreams of the delectable Georgette in *The Lull Before the Storm*, Sara Diamond

in the river . . . Maybe *The Lull* needs to be a full-blown lesbian melodrama. In this instance, George would be Georgette, Dorothy would still have Bobby, her son, having "tried" the straight life. George would be at war; Dorothy and Georgette, working as lumberjills. The latter could pick up where *Keeping the Home Fires Burning* left off, proffering a cigarette to the lovely Dorothy, while resting on a log boom. So could begin a classic butch/femme relationship."

As I speak, a small assemblage of Lesbians from Hell has entered the studio. One of them, wearing a candy-striped hospital uniform, pipes up: "No way." I look at her, gathering that she is a butch in femme clothing. She continues, "Enough with this stereotyping. Surely you are reducing lesbian history to the most coded images that we retain. Please be more subtle."

"Forget it!" I pout, using the last resort of the imbecile, "I'm the writer."

Another one of my captors speaks: "The metaphor fails, it's like apples and oranges."

"Now come on girls," I say, "After all they're both fruits."

The entire assemblage moans. Finally, a small blond in the corner pipes up, "The point is, that we can't afford to start with the hegemonic, with dominance, we have to start with our *own* subjectivities. We *are* different."

George contemplates Dorothy's deception, *The Lull Before the Storm,* Sara Diamond

"Well then, that's easy," say I, "Then they are indeed a butch/femme couple."

I become distracted, tuning out from the discordant sounds around me. I muse out loud, "Where could I work some lesbian dialogue into the rest of the script. Of course, the poker game *is* perfect: they could all flirt with each other, the antipathy between Susan and Nicola could be because of competition for Dorothy. That much of the current dialogue is about feminine solidarity on the picket line translating into feminine solidarity within the household against errant husbands would be lost. Small sacrifices to produce a piece for *my* community . . .

I could have had one lesbian (a token) in the poker game. But would that not have simply peripheralized her in relation to the other women? Wait, the video could well have been about that peripheralization, about the ways that their conversation about husbands and their laziness marginalizes her ability to participate without duplicating their circumstances (and this, the masculine or feminine position for the partner in relation to housework), *or* she could have provided an ideal other for her friends (like the time I came out to my female friends on the Left, and they all said, "Well that's fine for *you*, but *we* still have to deal with men," inferring that I was cheating), and assumed the margin that way.

Suddenly I begin to type at my keyboard. The camera cuts to the screen.

"I met Dorothy when she was a waitress working on the skid road. I was a waitress too—we shared a station. The boys were down for the fire season, all the logging operations were down, and out of the corner of my eye I watched Dorothy serve them.

"She was great with the old-timers, the way she'd slip them an extra large piece of pie and a wink.

"I'll never forget the day that Bill and his buddies were trying yet again to get into her pants. She poured an ice-cold pitcher of water into Bill's lap, never skipped a beat. Then she said to the rest of them, 'OK boys, what would *you* like?' You could have hear a crumb drop to the floor.

"I was so impressed. Sometimes, our eyes would meet and she would trip with the coffee pot and blush, my heart would race from my head to my toes. I just had to ask her out . . ."

As I keep writing narration, I muse out loud: "It's so easy to get diverted! Most of the dialogue between Dorothy and George is fighting, and I mean fighting. Translate that into a lesbian relationship and let me tell ya, its totally possible, but, *wince*, I mean in *public*??? It would be an act of resolute antinarrativity on the other hand to write a lesbian relationship where there is no conflict, in which Georgette and Dorothy happily manage the family budget, little Bobby's socialization, and all the postwar pressures to be married, feminine, and domesticated. Yawn. Whoops, sorry. Where's all that melodramatic pleasure that we thrive, thrive, thrive on??? This tale would be a perfect remedy for lesbian conflict junkies."

I turn to the young women, "Is that what you lesbian critics really want?"

"No," I continue, "the possibilities would more likely be these:

"The skirmishes about money that plague George and Dorothy might just as easily rear their heads in a lesbian relationship. One partner might earn more and the other less. There might be pressure in the 1940s and 1950s, depending on just *how* butch Georgette was, for Dorothy to stay home, both from Georgette from and their subculture. On the other hand, Dorothy might pressure Georgette to improve her job, *or* Georgette might want Dorothy to get out of the house and a get a job, knowing how underpaid women, even those doing work equal to men, were on the west coast of Canada and everywhere else."

As I speak the studio dissolves into a group of women and men working on a green chain.

"Many women worked in the wood industry, a few in the forests, and many more in timber and paper mills or box factories. Women were favored if they were single and harassed, even dismissed, if they married. You got pregnant, you got out. So it could be a lesbian enclave. It was a tough subculture, with lots of harassment and competition with men. The economy got bad and they'd try to boot you out of the work force, union or not.

"I know of lesbians in the late fifties who drove lumber trucks, piloted scows and worked in other wood-related occupations. Appearances are deceiving. I don't know of any long-term lumber gals who didn't look butch; the image came with the territory, and many of them were "happily" married with children. Which is only to say that lesbians would be comfortable as all heck in the wood industry in and after the war. Which in turn is only to say that Georgette has one steel toe firmly planted in some historical possibilities, with one hand firmly holding her IWA membership card and the other her lunch bucket, full of Dorothy's delicious sandwiches.

"You could bet that Georgette and Dorothy's relationship, idyllic though its beginnings may have been, could have run into many of the same problems that their straight counterparts faced. Problems compounded by the closet or ostracization. Problems of long-term boredom in both the space of conversation and the bedroom, of sexual pleasure requiring imagination and openness, of being surrounded by images of an unaffordable lifestyle. And Georgette's capacity to bottom out on the bottle, like old George there, coupled with a parallel ambient aggression, could be as much a part of a lesbian couple's life as G. and D.'s. And is the solution to George and Dorothy's problems for them to be queer?

"It's likely, as well, that Georgette and Dorothy would have their own rivers to cross. They might feel the need to pretend that they are just "friends," "cousins," or "sisters." Imagine if they met at work and kept working together all those years. Or they might be "out," accepted as the "special" aunties by the family, or treated as subhumans by them and by workmates. Still, there *was* a community in Vancouver, centered around the Vanport bar and dinnertime social groups. They may well have had close dyke friends, including other women with children, in their lives. They would be deluged by the need to make decisions about raising Bobby, how much should or could he know. They could lose custody in the wink of a bat's eye."

I pause, smile at the audience and then complete my mea culpa:

"I don't think that I'm suffering from the hostage syndrome when I say that my interest is no longer how *The Lull* should "work" for lesbians— now, I'm hooked on all these different readings and possible rewritings, generating more fragments beyond the fragments . . .

"Must lesbian culture always name itself? Must it be for a counterculture and about it? Why can't feminine desires be messy, nomadic, and anxious?

"Like all bad soap, neither my dilemma nor *The Lull Before the Storm* ever ends—we keep watching because there *is* a possibility that Dorothy, in the very next episode, may become a lesbian, leaving old George forever to that permanent baby-sitter, the TV.

"Will Dorothy have replaced the pleasures of the broom closet, cloth rack, and cupboard with the anxieties of the closet? Can she satisfy her yearning for sexual liberation and a wage increase? Will her prediliction for playing poker with her pals help her to place her cards on the table of unspoken desires? For the answer to these and other questions, stay tune to the next episode of *The Lull Before the Storm*. DREAM ON. . . ."

No Sex in the USSR

ANDREI PLAKHOV

translated by J. Jezioro

EDITOR'S NOTE: *Film critic and programmer Andrei Plakhov wrote this essay in 1991, before Gorbachev's downfall and the subsequent dissolution of the Soviet Union into separate sovereign states. What Plakhov describes, then, is a particular historical moment—between the heady days of perestroika and the more somber Yeltsin era. His references to the USSR may seem anachronistic, but this doesn't mean that Plakhov's observations have no relevance today. What he outlines is a process of change that is far from complete.*

"In the USSR there is no sex," said one of the participants of the Soviet-American television debate only three years ago. Or so thought, if not the majority, then a significant portion of Soviet men and women who had lived their entire lives in a country where a person was at best a cog in the state machine.

Today it is easy to identify a powerful sexual force—no matter how convoluted—bubbling up in the Soviet Union. In Moscow train stations and in underground (subway) crossings erotic postcards are sold, which, with each passing day, become more and more explicit. If as recently as a couple of years ago the militia could burst into a private apartment and throw into prison a person who was viewing, in the family circle, a videocassette recording of a completely innocent American film (it could be *The Godfather* or *The Last American Male*), then the very same militia is now opening video clubs with public screenings of erotic films. Komsomol—the organization of Communist youth, intended to coordinate the fostering of highly moral spirits in the young—has become another sponsor of a semilegal video business accessible to all. Trying to prove that they are still somehow necessary, the Komsomol functionaries are turning to "cultural activities." In video halls opened by these functionaries, Soviet audiences, starved of erotica, may watch *Emmanuelle* and other "masterpieces" of erotic film about which they had previously heard only damnation in the media.

All people who have experienced a taste of militarized totalitarianism are acquainted, as well, with its aftertaste: suppression of sexual freedom. To this end, religious precepts, political doctrines, national traditions, and state-familial moral codes were widely exploited. However, as soon as the dictatorship falls, the erotic energy explodes from underground, and produces an explosion shaking all the foundations. It was so in Germany after the collapse of the Kaiser's rule, and again after Hitler, in Italy after Mussolini, as it was in Spain after Franco. Not long ago in China, the death penalty for the distribution of pornography was introduced and almost exactly the same for excessive sexual activity (in order to reduce the population growth). It is not difficult to predict, however, what will happen as soon as the autocratic power of taboo and prohibition weakens.

In the Soviet Union this process is especially dramatic. After all, it is an entire empire, formed from ethnic regions culturally alien to one another; here Slavs neighbor the Baltic peoples, Turks, the Mongols. Christianity and Islam are only two of the main religions opposing one another, always battling for influence in this region. At the present time, also, the cultural inspiration of the Baltics and Galitsia (in western Ukraine), which gravitate towards Europe, are often completely opposite to those of the Central Asian peoples aligned with the Muslim world. In Uzbekistan, for example, as in India, the exposure of bare flesh is perceived as an infringement of the law of morality by the traditional mass of the population. Incidentally, one could come across approximately the same reaction in Russia not too long ago.

Three years ago the real shock to the Soviet people was *Little Vera*, which entered history as the first erotic film of the era of perestroika. There is, in fact, all of one erotic scene, quite modest, but "unorthodox": the heroine is straddled atop her partner. At approximately the same time, the Soviet censors were in a state of bewilderment as to how to release Ingrid Bergman's *Fanny and Alexander*. I heard one of the film censors complain, "I myself understand," he says, "that to cut Bergman's film would not be proper, and that the press [which by that time had become visibly more active] could come down on us, but what is one to do? There are three indecent scenes; the first [him atop her] which still could be shown; the second [her atop him] already somewhat too unseemly to be released; but the third is completely troublesome: the act from behind!"

The long-suffering guardians of that which is proper also attempted to censor the Japanese film *The Legend of Narayama*, which was awarded the Golden Palm at the Cannes Film Festival. How could they really present the audience with a scene of copulation with a dog?! It was necessary for the critics, including myself to write articles explaining to the public what constitutes an artistic concept in film, and why the author had need of such an extraordinary scene. Some were convinced, but some others continued to write indignant letters demanding the film be banned. This, too, is a fine tradition of Soviet society: censure from above and below simultaneously.

Local renters of movies may also step into the role of censor; in several cities the "seditious" scene was cut from *The Legend of Narayama* before the showing of the film and spliced back in afterwards.

Yet another recent scandal took place with the film *Extraordinary Incidents on a Regional Scale*, which evoked two waves of indignation. On one hand, the political, for the mafialike face of the Komsomol, the "educational" youth organization, was shown with a fair share of sarcasm and criticism. On the other hand, in order to discredit its hero morally, the authors of the film show how roughly he dominates his partner, right on the kitchen table and again—horror of horrors—from behind!

We'll stop at that, particularly since such conflicts lose their relevance when exposed to the light. The atmosphere of Soviet film, as with the whole of Soviet life, has changed strikingly in the last three years. You will see more or less explicit portrayals of sexual acts in practically any film. Here Soviet erotica is fairly specific and unidirectional. Most often it is combined with violence, human degradation, the wrenching inside out of the darker aspects of life. The society, being in the most serious crisis, and at the same time liberating itself from the power of censorship, has been pervaded with exhibitionism and masochism. The cinematographer, with sickening detail, fixes this state of affairs on film. If only a few years ago the typical heros of Soviet film were progressive workers and milkmaids, directors of factories and chairmen of collective farms, then today prostitutes, drug addicts, and the heads of mafia gangs have taken their places. It is already possible to see in Soviet films such specific scenes of erotica as sodomy and necrophilia in a morgue. It's only difficult to encounter people pleasurably involved in a love of mutual attraction.

This is nothing remarkable. There has never been any developed erotic culture in Russia, and the erotic line in literature is weak. Tradition prescribed aestheticism, the primacy of the soul above the flesh. More often, erotic motifs sounded in the subtext, imparting an accent of suppressed sensuality to the novels of Dostoevsky and Turgenev, to the music of Tchaikovsky, and to the films of Eisenstein and Tarkovsky. When erotica was legalized, and everyone who was not too lazy began to exploit it, there came about something forced, devoid of anything natural and light. It's difficult one fine day to become free—one has to be born free.

Intolerance: Concealed Homoerotica

For the most part I have so far discussed only heterosexual relations. Many inhabitants of the Soviet Union learned of the fact that homosexuality exists only thanks to perestroika. The others who knew considered it either a bourgeois remnant, a mental illness, or a serious crime. And this is not just someone's private misconception: the Soviet Union heads the list of those countries where, until now, the love of one man for another is punished as a capital offence. Some connect this legislation, which appeared in the thirties, with the caprice of Stalin, who harbored a deep hostility towards homosexual relations. André Gide had the opportunity to become convinced of the latter when he visited Moscow. At first he was enthusiastic about the Soviet Union, but soon reconsidered his attitude. Others believe that Stalin's policy towards homosexuality was influenced by Gorky, who could not come to terms with the homosexual tenor of his own son's character.

As a rule, the law against homosexuals exists only on paper, but it is remembered—most often out of political considerations—when it is necessary to dispose of one or another contrary intellectual. Some poets and theater directors became victims of the law, serving several years in prison. One of the most scandalous cases of the seventies was the trial of Sergei Paradzhanov. He was tried according to several articles of the constitution, among which were provisions against speculation in old religious icons, and homosexuality. In reality, they could not forgive him for the one sole sin: complete disregard for all authority.[1] Paradzhanov emerged from prison ill and broken. He lived another ten years, shot two films, went to the West for the first time, and in the summer of 1990 died of lung cancer.

Homosexual motifs have never been explicit in Soviet cinema, precisely since many prominent directors, beginning with Eisenstein, concealed their own homosexual predilections. Owing to this, the tragedies characteristic of the late nineteenth and early twentieth centuries (Tchaikovsky, Oscar Wilde) took on a new twist in the Soviet era. It is well known that the leading figures of Russian culture in the first two decades, such as the poet Esenin and the director-innovator of theater Vsevolod Meyerhold, gave homosexuality its due. Entire homoerotic literary-artistic groups and salons of those years are well known. However, in the thirties all of this went underground, subjugated to the official ideology with its cult of state and family and its point of view of man as soldier and slave. In order for the ideology to work, it had to be shrouded in the cloak of mythology. And it is precisely here that the internal contradiction of a totalitarian sociocultural structure is revealed: it cannot accept erotica as an expression of individuality, one distinct from others; nor can it get along without eroticism as the most powerful means of subliminal suggestion.

It goes without saying that in Stalin's era nothing was spoken directly about sex, of homo- or heterosexual variants. The ideals of destroying bourgeois morals, celebrations of free love, and pursuing group relations, which many first-generation Bolsheviks had professed, have long since been drowned in the atmosphere of a totalitarian society. However, it does have its sex symbols, as did the German period of Nazism. The handsome, sporty man of the people, who today builds and plows in sweaty labor, but who tomorrow will arise armed, a soldier, is one of these images. "Healthy spirit in a healthy body"—a euphemistic formula of an exaggerated sexuality, captured in a multitude of posters and in the paintings and sculptures of Socialist Realism. The overblown play of muscles, the surging vitality of youth, the erotic self-sufficiency of these images (which are remarkably reminiscent of Tom of Finland's earlier drawings) leave no doubt about their concealed homosexual nature.

Returning now to film, we find those same concealed homosexual motifs in the most outstanding films of the era of Socialist Realism, in mass media productions, and in later works of the Krushchev and Brezhnev eras. It's sufficient to recall in Eisenstein's *Ivan the Terrible*, the remarkably colorful scene of "The Dance of the Oprichniks," which is similar to the "Nights of the Long Knives" episode in Visconti's *Death of the Gods*. In the majority of his movies, Eisenstein's hypererotic designs and theoretical infatuation with the theories of Freud speak of an obsession with homoerotica which was painstakingly concealed and suppressed. Admiration for the male body, its musculature, and the physical expression of masculinity gradually yields to a preference for male characters with opposite characteristics: tender, delicate, wounded. This is connected to the overall change in policy of Soviet film, from militant patriotism and a global collective concept to the humanization of individual characters. This then can be linked to the atmosphere of the short Krushchevian thaw. The most important film in this vein is *Ivan's Childhood*, by Andrei Tarkovski (1963), in which the the physical and spiritual nature of adolescence resists the brutal dictates of war.

In the seventies and eighties homosexuality became a much more widespread phenomenon in a society where a departure into private life remained the only alternative to stagnation. However, from the point of view of homosexuality, one will not see any reflection of this process in the films of those years. Should you happen to, it would be very peculiarly reflected through metaphor and allegory.

In Iliya Averbakh's film, *Foreign Letters*, for example, an intelligent and lonely teacher expresses a desire verging upon homoeroticism towards a vulgar and spiritless female pupil. This is not surprising: when the spirit has had intercourse only with culture, the flesh longs for something much simpler and nonartificial. No matter what they were talking about, be it modernity, the history of the nineteenth century, or the last war, whether they were devoted to rural life or the problems of intellectuals, the hallmark traits of the Soviet "prestige" cinema of the seventies and the first half of the eighties were, in general, hysterical outbursts of emotion, nervous ecstasy, and an erotic substructure of spiritual outpourings.

Author-directors and screenwriters were usually oblivious to the homosexuality encoded in the structure of many Soviet films. The clearest example is the entire series of films cooperatively made by the screenwriter Aleksandr Mindaze and the director Vadim Abdrashitov. In these films, devoted to the severe social and moral conflicts in Soviet life, there is no hint of anything other than the traditional heterosexual union between man and woman. However, there is always a same-sex pair of characters connected by sadomasochistic relations in which antagonism and mutual desire become equally obvious. They may be women, as were the judged and accused in *A Word for the Defense*, or men—investigator and journalist (*The Train Stopped*), a youthful offender and his victim (*The Hunt for Foxes*), or the mafialike functionary and his protegé-servant (*The Servant*). In each of these couples is simultaneously encoded both sexual intolerance and social "supplementation," the need of one for the other. In a society built upon the erasure of human individuality, the distinctions between the sexes (in relation to their roles) are also worn away. Sadomasochistic social relations are, in a metaphorical sense, homosexual. Thus, it is not erotic conflicts which disclose their social nature, but rather, the other way around.

In Search of Lost Homosexuality

This idea is brought to the surface and subjected to an ironic analysis in the film *The Difficult Male Game*. The main scene in the film is the rape in a subway car of one man by another, to the complete indifference of the other passengers. In this way the concepts of social violence and suppression of the individual are expressed. This was impossible in the official Soviet cinema, at least until quite recently. But the film which we are talking about belongs to the so-called Parallel Cinema, which came into existence in the early eighties in the form of amateur theater. The leaders of the Parallel Cinema, the brothers Igor and Gleb Aleinikov, made many films which, to a great extent, are concerned with ironic reflections on the erotic. In the film *Tractors*, for example, the mythology of Stalinist homoeroticism is sharply ridiculed. The tractor and its driver have become ingrained in folklore as a symbol of male sexuality. And the irony in this film is not directed towards women, but to the state concept of masculinity.

Another director of the Parallel Cinema, Boris Yukhananov, shot the film *Crazy Prince Fassbinder*, a true masterpiece of intellectual satire. The main character is a provincial and a film fanatic, crazy about Fassbinder, who, throughout the course of the entire film, reads a half-schizophrenic lecture about him. Playing the role of the character is Evgeny Chorba, himself a fixture in the cinematographic and bohemian life of Moscow. Deftly used in the plot of the film is the well-known fact that among enlightened film followers who have been watching Western films there are many homosexuals. In the course of things, Chorba parodies the subject matter of Fassbinder, the ridiculousness of Soviet life, and even himself. His exaggerated fluidity of movement forces one to recall the hero-lovers of silent movies and, in the final scene, reaches the point of apogee. Chorba attempts to penetrate the anus of his partner, who is a bearded midget, with the help of . . . a drill.

Regardless of the parody of the situation, the film gradually turns tragic. Chorba, it seems, is completely transformed into and becomes Fassbinder. The only thing left to complain about is that this study, flawless in its psychoanalytic sketching, exists only on videotape.

The emergence into legal existance of the authors of Parallel Cinema (they now attend international festivals and publish their own magazine) attests to great progress. Soviet society finds itself in search of a lost homosexuality, true and open. Not long ago—the summer of 1990—the first issue of the homosexual magazine, *Anti-Aids*, began to publish materials clarifying to their widespread readership that homosexuality is a normal psychological and sociological phenomenon, accepted as such throughout the civilized world. An Association of Sexual Minorities has been created in the Soviet Union and published an appeal to President Gorbachev, demanding that he repeal the law that allows persecution of homosexuals. Soviet poets are taking part in international gay festivals. Many Soviet rock groups openly build their stage image on the concepts of androgyny and homosexuality.

This, however, does not at all signify that ignorance and intolerance have come to an end. Even now, owing to AIDS, articles appear in the press accusing homosexuals of the dissemination of this disease, although, it has been irrefutably established that the lack of sanitation in state hospitals and the shortage of disposable needles and condoms are the main sources of the epidemic. Outrageous incidents of mass AIDS infection of nursing children in maternity hospitals are causing distress across the whole country. However it is easier to put the blame on the "cursed pederasts."

This ridiculous and harmful attitude towards homosexuals is pushing its way into the cinema as well. In the documentary video *Of Risk Groups* social indignation is addressed at prostitutes and drug addicts; but the authors approach the problem of homosexuals with especially unethical methods. A waning, mentally ill man, clothed in a woman's dress, is filmed by a hidden camera, which creates an impression in the audiences' minds that all homosexuals are like him—and moreover, that they are a breeding ground for AIDS.

It is possible to ascertain how the public will react when the epidemic reaches a menacing dimension (according to forecasts, in the middle of the nineties), if only by the results of a public opinion poll released not long ago.

About one-third of those surveyed considered that homosexuals should be eliminated; approximately the same number said that they should be isolated; only the remaining third had an attitude of tolerance. One can find "comfort" in the fact that there is almost the same degree of intolerance towards prostitutes, drug addicts, and the mentally ill. As far as those with AIDS are concerned, only about half the population believes that it is necessary to provide them with medical assistance.

Despite such bigotry, the attempt to retrieve our lost homosexuality continues, and extraordinarily intensively. To some degree it is reflected in the orientation of the artistic cinema, sometimes superficially, as, for example, in the film *Bespredel* (*Without Limits*), where sensation was counted upon—the depiction of homosexual violence in prisons. But there are also attempts at a more in-depth treatment of the world of homoerotica.

Here I should mention first of all the films of the Leningrad director Aleksandr Sokurov. Filmed before perestroika, all his films were banned. The presence of homoerotica was one of the motives for their prohibition In the movie, *A Sorrowful Lack of Feeling*, a filming of George Bernard Shaw's play *Heartbreak House*, lesbian relations were shown quite openly, ones only hinted at in Shaw's work. In *Patience, Work* Sokurov introduces a scene of an athletic dance on ice of two men, a dance filled with eroticism. The aesthetic of the male body is a main theme in Sokurov's film *Days of the Eclipse*, also produced before perestroika. The friendship of two lonely young men is openly eroticized. The director does not hide his admiration for the beautiful, athletic body of the hero nor his longing for an unrealized love. This film, saturated with various types of intellectual and social motifs, produces an unusually strong emotional impression, above all else thanks to the exertion of male flesh, which stretches out towards its likeness. This outreach is no less powerful than emotional outbursts of the soul. In Sokurov's next film, *Save the Keep*, a loose adaptation of Flaubert's *Madame Bovary*, emphasis is placed upon the democratic power of the flesh, while the depiction of male characters is clearly and intentionally aestheticized.

The aforementioned are generally characteristic of the new era of Soviet cinema, even in those films where homoerotica is not present as such. For instance, that same *Little Vera* demonstrates an increased interest in the male body, which reveals itself to the cinematographers with a new quality: the body of a person who is becoming free.

It goes without saying that in this respect no one reached the level of Paradzhanov, the Soviet Warhol, and simultaneously, our Pasolini. Having positioned his films on the verge of lofty symbolism and kitsch, he was the unsurpassed master of collage and of ornamental, picturesque compositions, reminiscent of oriental rugs. But he was not drawn to life, carnal images, and personae. In his last film, *The Legend of the Fortress of Suram* and

Ashi-Kerib, the figures of hero-youths became the center of exquisite erotic compositions. One can only guess how Paradzhanov's talent would have developed if he had lived his life in a society without prohibition and persecution.

By Paradzhanov's time Soviet cinema had already reached deeper into the historical and cultural aspects of homoerotica. In the film of the young Leningrad director Valerii Ogorodnikov *The Paper Eyes of Prishvin*, amongst the symbolic images of Stalinist mythology subjected to critical analysis crops up the lampooned figure of Eisenstein. His exaggerated homosexuality in written into the context of time as a hidden yet unavoidable component. In discussions about the nature of Stalinism, the film even expresses the hypothesis that anal erotica was the underlying cause of all Stalinist mythology. For example, the Moscow subway, the former showy signboard of the Stalinist epoch is, in Ogorodnikov's proposed interpretation, a huge anus, a black hole swallowing up human vitality.

In a word, the filmmaker in the Soviet Union today attempts to experience the feeling of, and give sense to, much of that which exists in his subconscious, but, having been brought to the surface by the events of history, now uncovers new thoughts, new perspectives.

Note

1. Comparatively recently, Paradzhanov was asked in a television interview how he felt about Gorbachev. "Wonderful," replied the director, inimitable in his wit. "He has such lovely legs."

Pictures of Sickness:

Stuart Marshall's *Bright Eyes*

MARTHA GEVER

AUTHOR'S NOTE: This article was originally written in 1987. Therefore, the history of media attention to the AIDS epidemic and portrayals of people living with AIDS is somewhat outdated. Sadly, little has changed in the past six years that would recommend a revision of my assessment of the irresponsibility of the mass media regarding AIDS. Nor during that interlude have I altered my conclusion that *Bright Eyes* stands out as one of the most intelligent responses to the inadequate, frequently homophobic, public representations concerning AIDS.

FEMALE DOCTOR: "Are some symptoms easier to see than others?"
MALE DOCTOR: "Yes, I think that they are."
FEMALE DOCTOR: "Which symptoms do you think are the most easily seen?"
MALE DOCTOR: "Those that we recognize, those that are familiar to us, those that we've seen before."
FEMALE DOCTOR: "Are they always self-evident?"
MALE DOCTOR: "Sometimes a symptom is invisible, which means that it must be aggressively hunted out. Sometimes it is visible and we do not see it. . . ."

Bright Eyes, Part One

It isn't necessary to read every word published or to watch television regularly to know that mass-media coverage of AIDS usually takes the form of news of "medical breakthroughs" and government pronouncements, statistics offered by "experts," or discussions of the "social impact" of the epidemic (for the latter, projections of health care costs and the economic effect on the insurance industry are common). The only notable exception is coverage of celebrities with AIDS, beginning with Rock Hudson. Aside from news reporting, television's attention to AIDS is generally limited to "social problem" programs. Whether documentary or dramatic in format, these latter are usually described as sensitive, poignant, or tragic—adjectives that indicate not the seriousness of AIDS but rather the presumptions such programs carry in the first place. It is, of course, predictable that television producers and programmers would rely on conventional forms to publicize a major health crisis. The containment of knowledge about AIDS within familiar structures functions as reassurance for those worried about a "disease" that seems out of control.

Each news story, investigative report, panel discussion, talk show, or "realistic" drama about AIDS circulated by the mass media contributes to the shape of the narrative by which the epidemic is made comprehensible to "the public." And the impetus of this narrative is fear—a generalized fear that is alternately incited and allayed, again and again. (Picking up a newspaper, I read the headline, "AIDS Virus: Always Fatal?" The article proposes no answer to this question. In the meantime a TV newscaster promises, "Tonight at eleven: a new vaccine against the AIDS virus that scientists are ready to test.") Although scenarios painted with fear and propagated by the mass media are common devices used by public officials to promote support for their policies, which depend on such sentiments as a xenophobia and anticommunism, the manipulation of the fear of AIDS is of another order.[1] Unlike the typical crises proclaimed in the media—the "Middle East crisis," "the Sandinistas' threat to our national security," or, on the domestic front, the "drug crisis"—the AIDS crisis is not the invention of policymakers. Indeed, it is the *absence* of public policy concerning AIDS that has determined responses to the epidemic and has left the mass media to its own devices.[2] And what the mass media has produced reveals its complicity in constructing the very fears it presumes judiciously to mediate. From the beginning, when it was announced that AIDS was a syndrome that primarily affected gay men, the full machinery of homophobia—a particular sexual fear characterized by denial—went into action.

Almost every social crisis induced or supported by the mass media— teenage pregnancy or the disintegration of the family, for example—relies at least in part on a moral argument. But the battleground upon which the "war on AIDS"[3] is waged is morality itself. In the US, morality has become the rallying cry for conservatives, who berate the media for undermining the established order of patriarchy and capitalism and accuse the public affairs departments of television stations and networks of being incorrigibly liberal and amoral.[4] But the reticence concerning sexual matters evident in reporting on AIDS confirms that in news, as in entertainment, the television industry adheres to restricted, normalizing standards of morality, even when advocating tolerance of those whose "sexual orientation" is "different." That the decision to permit advertising condoms on TV was, and still is, considered morally questionable by many industry executives, whose business nevertheless depends on sexual come-ons to sell other products, reveals both the limits and the contradictions of their liberal postures. Even the national Public Broadcasting Service (PBS), which pretends to take greater risks in programming, has taken up the topic of AIDS only gingerly.[5]

PBS first broached the subject in a 1985 broadcast of an intensely homophobic, racist, and inflammatory documentary in their *Frontline* series. Purportedly a profile of a man with AIDS, Fabian Bridges, *AIDS: A Public Inquiry* portrayed an unemployed black, gay protagonist as a dangerous criminal irresponsibly roaming the country and engaging in sex with unsuspecting victims. The *Frontline* producers tracked the man down, pretended to befriend him in order to elicit personal information, then turned him in to the health authorities after they got their footage. As one of the first prime-time productions about AIDS in the US, with the imprimatur of public television further validated by documentary veracity, the program confirmed the most irrational, rabid fears of the promiscuous homosexual threatening public health.

Subsequently, PBS aired a segment of the science series *Nova* devoted to AIDS, featuring a pantheon of scientists and computerized animations of viruses and blood cells. The discussion focused on the methods being used to develop drugs that might alleviate, if not cure, AIDS and the likelihood of a vaccine against the HIV virus. Nothing was said, however, about the US government's reluctance to fund such research, to speed treatment drugs through the FDA approval process, or their insistence on the cruel use of double-blind testing procedures for people with a fatal disease. The drug featured in the program was AZT, the only drug to have achieved government approval; again *Nova* failed to raise the relevant questions about the relationship between the FDA and Burroughs-Wellcome, AZT's manufacturer: Why was this highly toxic drug rushed through the process when no others were? Why was the company allowed to charge up to thirteen thousand dollars per year for each patient? Why were ninety-eight percent of the patients in the studies conducted by the government's designated AIDS Treatment Evaluation Units being given AZT, even after this drug was available on the market?

In 1986 PBS aired *The A.I.D.S. Show*, a documentary by Peter Adair and Robert Epstein, based on a gay theater review staged by San Francisco's Theatre Rhinoceros. Because the theater production and the tape feature a number of gay characters—men with AIDS, their lovers and friends—this broadcast represented a departure from the commercial networks' offerings, which only show visibly debilitated, pathetically ill gay men and other PWAs. *The A.I.D.S. Show*'s emphasis on coping with death, however, replaces homophobic responses to AIDS with exemplary tales of personal suffering and strength.

At last, in the fall of 1987, with great fanfare, and with warnings to parents that they might want to exercise "discretion," PBS broadcast a special program, entitled *AIDS: Changing the Rules*, on safe-sex practices for heterosexuals. Introduced with the punning promise of "straight talk" on AIDS, the program is exactly the opposite. It begins with the assumption

that gay people have already learned about safe sex (from PBS?) and repeatedly asserts that "heterosexuals haven't really been at risk until now," with
no apparent awareness of the smugness and naiveté of this insupportable
statement. Because the program's agenda only includes advice for those
deemed respectable, responsible citizens—that is, straight adults—the fluidity of sexual desire is not even considered a possibility. Fear of sex determines
even "straight talk" about it: When Rubén Blades demonstrates the proper
use of a condom by putting one on a banana—"I sure wish there were an
easier way of showing you this"—he explains coyly, "Leave a little slack at
the end, you know, for what 'comes' [wink] later." And when Beverly
Johnson speaks with obvious embarrassment about oral sex, she says,
"When a man goes down on a woman, there's some danger, especially if a
woman is menstruating. Unfortunately there's not much you can do to
protect yourself." It is really possible that the makers of a safe-sex video are
unaware of the availability of dental dams to provide just such protection?

   And that, to date, is as much as PBS has been willing or has dared to
show, despite the fact that AIDS had been known to be a major public health
problem in the US for *over six years.*

In traveling from the known world to the unknown world, the seeker of truth will encounter
many strange phenomena as yet unclassified by science, and upon his shoulders rests the
responsibility of discovering order within this chaos. The light of scientific knowledge must be
brought to play upon the twilight world of nature and the exotic species which inhabit its dark
corners. Our guiding law must be the classification and categorization of all that is yet unknown,
in order that the truth of human society be thrown sharply into relief.

                                                              —*Bright Eyes,* Part Two

Until my first viewing of Stuart Marshall's videotape *Bright Eyes,* I had
intentionally avoided much of the mass-media coverage of AIDS, whether
that of the lurid tabloid press or of respectable public television. Like most
people, I am prone to anxiety about illness that no amount of scientific
explanation can ease. And what I saw on television or read in the mass
press either attempted precisely that—to pacify me with scientific data—or
conveyed a picture of collective panic manifesting itself in overt, vicious
homophobia, leaving me with feelings of both outrage and depression, and
affirming my impulse to steer clear. Nor have I revised my assessment of
what the mass media will allow in its coverage of AIDS. But my willful
avoidance was mitigated by Marshall's tape, not simply because it offers an
intelligent political and historical analysis of the underpinnings of the current
discourse on AIDS, but because the tape was conceived to contest the homophobia that has permeated the dominant media's representation of AIDS.

   Bright Eyes was produced for Britain's Channel Four, a commercial broadcast channel founded in 1979 by an act of Parliament with provisions

for funding and programming innovative television.[6] Marshall's video was broadcast in December 1984 in *The Eleventh Hour* series, a showcase for independent work whose title refers to its late-night time slot. Despite the fact that it received high ratings and repeated requests for a rebroadcast, Channel Four has thus far refused. Nevertheless, Channel Four has subsequently acquired and broadcast other work on AIDS, including the US production *Chuck Solomon: Coming of Age,* made by San Francisco filmmakers Marc Huestis and Wendy Dallas and turned down by PBS. After seeing the results of PBS's policies regarding programs on AIDS (as well as other topics deemed controversial), it seemed reasonable to assume that PBS will never show *Bright Eyes,* or any other work that offers a serious critique of the association of AIDS and homosexuality. Thus far, Marshall's tape has been shown in this country only at closed-circuit screenings,[7] although the conditions of its original exhibition, as well as the source of production funds for *Bright Eyes,* place the tape within the boundaries of the mass media.

Marshall's consciousness of the terms operating in this arena becomes obvious in the first few minutes of *Bright Eyes.* The tape opens with the desultory exchange quoted here as the opening epigraph. The two doctors' conversation about diagnostic dilemmas is repeatedly interrupted by shots of an approaching ambulance—the sort of images that might appear in *St. Elsewhere*—and culminates in close-ups of an orderly wheeling a patient on a gurney through a hospital corridor and shouting, "Stand back! This man has AIDS! He's highly infectious! Stand back!" Staged with a high-pitched tension common to television drama, the lines are convincing—until the action stops abruptly and the words "Moral Panic Productions Presents" appear, followed by the program's title superimposed on a freeze-frame close-up of the faces of two anxious hospital workers wearing surgical masks. The orderly's fallacious statement is thus accentuated, and Marshall replaces the familiar but terrible specter of viral contagion with a reference to the infectious appeal of dramatic clichés.

When the action resumes, the hospital setting has disappeared, the tone of emergency evaporated. After a rapid montage of newspaper headlines composed of phrases such as "The Gay Plague," "Sex Killer Bug," and "Gay Bug," together with photos from a tabloid spread topped by a banner that reads "Pictures that Reveal the Disturbing Truth of AIDS Sickness," one of the doctors from the previous segment reappears, now dressed as a late nineteenth-century gentleman. As his speech indicates, he acts the part of another doctor, this time reading an article on the advantages of photography for medical study published in an 1893 issue of the British medical journal *The Lancet.*

In these short sequences, Marshall reveals his method. The rapid cuts from realistic melodrama to still images to the cool recitation of a historical text typify the disjunctive technique used throughout. This functions to reframe and examine the meanings of myriad pictures signifying sickness and deviance and, in the process, to demonstrate the historical construction of both. Three historical moments provide the basic structure of the three-part tape: the late nineteenth-century consolidation of scientific authority in rationalizing, classifying, and regulating social subjects; the Third Reich's conscription of eugenic theories to justify policies of persecution and genocide of members of undesirable social groups; and the present, in which the effects of definitions of sexual pathology are again evident in the general complacency about the cruel, dehumanizing treatment of people with AIDS. The movement of the tape, however, never follows the uninterrupted course of a simple chronological progression or logical academic argument. Rather, present and past mingle, mediated by television artifice, which is likewise the object of analysis.

The tape's title derives from one such telling instance of historical reverberation. Marshall intercuts an illustrated text from a late nineteenth-century sociological treatise with two photos of PWA Kenny Ramsaur from a spread in the British tabloid *Sunday People*. These latter are the photographs— "before and after"—said to "reveal the disturbing truth about AIDS sickness" by showing "what the gay plague did to handsome Kenny." An off-screen voice reads excerpts from Havelock Ellis's *The Criminal*, detailing characteristics attributed to certain criminal types, including "sexual offenders," accompanied by caricatures and photographic studies from the same book. As Ellis is quoted saying, "In those guilty of sexual offences [Cesare] Lombroso finds the eyes nearly always bright," the image cuts to a close-up of Ramsaur's eyes in the "before AIDS" photo; the camera then pans to the caption: "Handsome Kenny: His bright eyes show no hint of the agony to come." On the sound track, Ellis's words continue: " . . . the voice either rough or cracked; the face generally delicate, except in the development of the jaws, and the eyelids and lips swollen." The photo of a healthy Ramsaur reappears and the camera pans again, stopping when the second photo of Ramsaur, his face swollen, fills the screen. Ellis again: "Occasionally they are humpbacked or otherwise deformed."

Marshall's presentation of the photos of Ramsaur in *Sunday People* demonstrates the continuation of a tradition where deviance—or nature's presumed punishment for it—is revealed as visible physical "deformity." The movement is easy, says an off-screen voice, since, "for more than a hundred years homosexuality has been described as a disease." Then, another picture from *The Criminal,* a photograph captioned "A Group of Perverts." Thus introduced, the young men posed together for this illustration become examples of the category of sexual offenders, a legal term employed by jurists and

Bright Eyes, Part I, Stuart Marshall

social scientists in the nineteenth century to describe, collectively, prostitutes, rapists, and homosexuals. Today, the classification "sexual offender" remains on the books, but now the three previously related types are legally separated. Prostitution remains an illegal (or state-regulated), although selectively prosecuted occupation;[8] rape is treated as a violent crime; and the offense of homosexuality is more a target for social disapprobation than grounds for imprisonment or internment in mental hospitals.[9] This latter observation may, however, soon be reversed, given intensified demands for mandatory HIV testing, contact tracing, and even tattooing or quarantining of HIV antibody positive individuals, many of whom are likely to be gay men. The persistence of attempts to link homosexuality and criminality are also confirmed in statements by homophobic politicians such as Jesse Helms and William Dannemeyer, and pundits such as Nat Hentoff and Pete Hamill writing in the *Village Voice*.[10]

All such proposals and policies lean heavily on medical science, which performs an ideological function similar to that of Western legal discourse, conflating homosexuality, deviance, perversion, and sexual pathology with one another and with abnormality. Representations that claim to reproduce reality are used by doctors and lawyers alike to identify and classify physical phenomena, thus isolating the components that constitute disease—either

Bright Eyes, Part I, Stuart Marshall

individual or social—in the form of visible evidence. As Marshall demonstrates in the first section of *Bright Eyes,* the images of illness produced and reproduced within the larger project of empirical, instrumental science function as concrete proof. The utility of photography in this regard, precociously argued by the doctor-author of the *Lancet* text quoted at the outset of *Bright Eyes,* established the camera as an instrument of presumed objectivity.[11] Marshall tracks one of the historical ramifications of this concept in part two of the tape.

Again in reenactment, photographs and books fuel a bonfire in a fictionalized newsreel of the Nazis' destruction of the Institute for Sexual Science in Berlin in 1933. A woman's voice relates a first-person account of the event to the institute's founder, Magnus Hirschfeld, who is shown as the sole spectator in a theater in Paris where the pseudo-newsreel plays on the screen. At intervals, Hirschfeld narrates, with no apparent emotion, the political history of the homosexual rights movement in Germany, dating back to 1897—including his efforts to enlist support from the medical and psychological professions in affirming the legitimacy of homosexuality—and the various attacks he and his allies endured. Marshall renders the facts of Nazi brutality at a distance—in past tense—as projected images of burning photographs and books, a symbolic act of annihilation that stands for the systematic extermination of gay men during the Third Reich (lesbians were not routinely arrested for sexual crimes, since lesbianism was not acknowledged in German law).[12]

Central to this narrative is Hirschfeld's passionate faith in photographic and scientific objectivity—the institute's collection of material on anatomy and sexual theories and practices numbered some twelve thousand books and thirty-five thousand photographs—and the corresponding passion of the Nazis' manic hatred, mobilized as a eugenic purge of the German population. The scientific credo of the Enlightenment, to which Hirshfeld ardently subscribed and which he regarded as the foundation of a rational, tolerant society, was easily conscripted by Heinrich Himmler and the SS to provide them with ideological ammunition for their murderous campaign against gay men.[13]

In the scene following the Hirschfeld story, a young man in Vienna is summoned to Gestapo headquarters, where he is shown a snapshot of himself and a friend, with an affectionate inscription on the back. The photograph is presented as evidence of his "unnatural" desires, sufficient proof to condemn him to a Nazi work camp. The horrifying details of gay men's experiences in these camps are reported, once again, retrospectively. The actor who played the sentenced man is now shown as a passenger in a car traveling on the autobahn in contemporary Germany. He has not aged, as the rules of historical realism would dictate, but nevertheless gives a first-person account of the conditions in the camps, where gay men were simultaneously starved and worked to death, or shot by SS guards who forced them to attempt escape. While he summarizes aspects of the little known and rarely acknowledged history of the Nazi persecutions of homosexuals, the woman driving the car periodically asks questions and interjects an equally disturbing story of two lesbians imprisoned and tortured by the SS. As an epilogue to this history lesson, Marshall contrasts shots of the overgrown, abandoned Nuremberg stadium, famous site of Nazi spectacles, with glimpses of the prosaic but well-maintained granite bridges traversing the autobahn. The male actor draws attention to what would otherwise pass unnoticed: built by prisoners in the Nazi work camps, the labor required to quarry, transport, and place the blocks for those bridges resulted in thousands of deaths.

The enactment of the inquest conducted by a Gestapo doctor, which concludes with the stunned young man signing a prepared confession, is performed in an understated and cinematically spare style that is consistently used in the tape. Instead of exploiting the conventional television techniques that render rhetorical constructions invisible (the fast-paced editing, multiple camera angles, and portentious music demonstrated in *Bright Eyes'* opening

Bright Eyes, Part II, Stuart Marshall

sequence and then abandoned), Marshall prolongs shots and silences, intercuts printed texts, and frustrates identification by not revealing off-screen
speakers and by casting the same actors in different roles. For example, the
actor who plays the condemned gay man and the former concentration camp
inmate in this second part of the tape also played the modern doctor in the
opening sequence and the nineteenth-century physician-author immediately
following. In the tape's third part, he will play first a television talk-show
host, then an undercover cop in a vignette demonstrating British police
practices used to entrap gay men for soliciting.[14]

The effect of these devices is that Marshall's analysis of the conflation of
truth with photographic imagery is extended to television's own forms of
veristic representation. At the beginning of the tape's third section, broadcast
journalism's role in shaping perceptions of AIDS is underscored in a sketch
in which a TV crew prepares for an interview with a man with AIDS. A
belligerent audio technician afraid of "catching" AIDS refuses to place a
microphone around the neck of the talk-show guest, who realizes that his
only option is to speak to the interviewer on an off-stage telephone—in other
words, to be invisible. Although enacted according to the rules of realist
drama, the characters and their situation seem too exaggerated to be credible.

But Marshall anticipates this response and answers it with a close-up of a newspaper item about just such an event that occurred on a TV program called *A.M. San Francisco*.

Bright Eyes's third and final part consists mostly of a series of interviews with people whose work involves AIDS—John Weber, a doctor and AIDS researcher; Richard Wells, a nursing advisor who coauthored guidelines for the care of people with AIDS; Tony Whitehead, chairperson of the Terrence Higgins Trust, Britain's first AIDS education and service organization—as well as Nick Billingham of the Campaign for Homosexual Equality, and Linda Semple, manager of Gay's the Word bookstore in London. Never cross-cut, this sequence of interviews moves from Weber's calm commentary on misunderstandings about AIDS to broader, though related cultural and political issues discussed by Billingham and Semple. Each speaker is shot from a single angle and edited sparingly. Though an interviewer's voice occasionally intercedes, the interviewer himself never appears. The absence of cutaways is somewhat unconventional, but otherwise this section of the tape conforms to recognizable television documentary form, or so it would seem if this material were divorced from everything that precedes it. But what these people say—together with the speech by People with AIDS Coalition cofounder Michael Callen at the tape's conclusion—has everything to do with what has come before. When Semple describes a raid by British customs officials on her bookstore and the subsequent confiscation of all imported materials, including those on AIDS, the interviewer asks, "Do you know what will happen to the confiscated books?" "They'll be burned," she replies, "Books that are confiscated are always burned."

The discussions with all six subjects abound with current examples of the relationship between forms of representation and ideas of deviance examined earlier. Weber, Wells, and Whitehead all confirm the influence of the mass media on public responses to AIDS, citing instances in which sensationalizing reports in the media created waves of paranoia and resulted in surges of telephone inquiries from people who believed, incorrectly, that they had contracted AIDS and therefore suffered morbid anxieties. Whitehead notes that, to the mass media, a gay person with AIDS is "not a story," and that gay people are seen as the cause or perpetrators of AIDS, whereas straight people with AIDS are frequently portrayed as innocent victims.

Callen's statement, a recitation of his testimony before a New York State legislative committee in 1983, serves as a counterpoint to the representations of disease in the first section of the tape. His passionate, detailed, and well-argued description of the experiences of PWAs ends with an eloquent (though now outdated) account of knowledge about AIDS and the responsibilities of medical and government institutions, not only in preventing AIDS but toward those who have been diagnosed with AIDS and ARC. Here, at last, a man with AIDS speaks for himself. But even here speech and image are not presented as unmediated, transparent truth. Although his address was originally conceived for a public forum, Callen appears in *Bright Eyes* against the background of an unpopulated, bucolic London garden. The scene is not constructed to feign spontaneity, and no effort is made to disguise the fact that Callen is reading a text. The camera remains fixed, and the edits are few, although at each edit the camera moves several steps closer. The emotional strength of Callen's testimony consists not in pathos but in his direct, careful, unapologetic language and delivery, which contradict all concepts of an object of medical curiosity or a pitiable victim of disease.

I went to see this National Health psychiatrist. . . . I was quite taken aback when he said something which didn't seem to have anything to do with me whatsoever, which was, "When you are older you will start hanging around public toilets. Do you want this?" I was totally shocked. I thought, "What's he talking about? He's nuts."

—*Bright Eyes,* Part One

I've strayed from the subject of fear—specifically, homophobia and its relationship to disease. This is in part because fear is *not* invoked in *Bright Eyes.* On the contrary, analysis of the pathology of fear and its manipulation are fundamental to the tape. Instead of counseling the imagined audience to correct irrational fears by following the advice of designated experts—the favored "solution" in the mass media's approach to AIDS—*Bright Eyes* encourages a recognition of fear's results—hatred of and discrimination against those classified as abnormal and therefore degenerate or dangerous or both—and the complicity of systems of expertise in establishing the authority of such categories in the first place.

Having reviewed the structure of Marshall's analysis of representations of disease and deviance, I want now to retrace my steps in order to discuss the less overt emotional content of the tape, which contradicts and exposes the insidious and oppressive links between mechanisms of identification and the narrative gambit of provoking anxiety and then providing psychic satisfaction through its resolution. For example, by thwarting identification with actors and thus abjuring a central tactic of emotional manipulation, Marshall dissociates the language of anxiety from the personal attributes and actions of characters, and shows it to exist instead on the plane of political relations. The final scene of part one, in which the speech quoted above appears, makes this clear.

The sequence of pictures of "abnormal" individuals—Ellis's "criminals" juxtaposed with the *Sunday People* photos of Ramsaur—immediately precedes an obviously contrived interview with a man whose face is obscured in shadow, the sort of disguise used in television interviews to conceal the identities of informants or criminals fearful of discovery. An apparently middle-aged man tells about coming out when he was eighteen years old— of an early memory of his mother's denigrating comment about a gay man in a TV drama, his father's dismay when his son tells him he loves a man, his visit to a psychiatrist who offers to cure him, and his recognition that he doesn't want to be cured because he is happy. He recalls telling the psychiatrist that he made the decision to refuse treatment because he understood, "The problem's not mine; it's my father's." In the annals of gay social history, similar accounts have often been reproduced as stories of courage in the face of oppressive scientific attitudes toward homosexuality, which often condoned torture in the name of therapy (the man accurately notes that the prescribed treatment for homosexuality twenty years ago was electric shock "therapy"). The scene works as an addendum to the cross-cutting of nineteenth-century taxonomies of unnatural bodies with present-day depictions of sick homosexuals. The ambiguous lighting not only invokes television styles used to ensure anonymity, but also suggests a correlation with other texts in the tape, especially one spoken as a commentary on a nineteenth-century painting, Sir Luke Fildes's *The Doctor*:

> A Victorian country doctor sits in the darkness of a worker's cottage trying to get a picture of a sick child's condition. . . . Night has begun to fall and he has angled the shade of the oil lamp to see more clearly. Light and dark, doctors and disease. The beam of lamplight pierces the darkness of the cottage, and the doctor's gaze pierces the darkness of her illness. . . . Someone else, possibly the child's father, is also watching from a dark corner, but, unlike the sick child, this person is not the object of medical surveillance, and so the beam of lamplight is not angled in his direction and he barely becomes a picture.

"Light and dark, doctors and disease." This elliptical sentence establishes the axes along which the discourse of homosexuality travels. Occurring at the approximate center of the tape's first part, the sentence refers to an earlier observation concerning the mass media's reportage on gay subjects. This activity, Marshall notes, often entails a visit to a "shadowy back street bar" and is couched in expressions like the "smoky gloom" of such hideaways, emblematic of the "twilight world" of gay culture. Such reports are reminiscent of those written by explorers of foreign lands, addressed to readers of the same class, race, and culture as the writer—in this case, those who have never frequented gay bars. Analogously, the man hovering in the shadows of the Fildes canvas, outside the doctor's lamplight, remains mysterious and vaguely ominous.

The light/dark dichotomy is recapitulated in the opening scene of part two, which consists of a parody of nineteenth-century empiricist prose, earnestly but ironically recited by a black actor. Appearing among the potted palms and stuffed peacocks of a room decorated in the orientalist style, speaking in a deadpan manner that downplays the text's racist overtones, the actor outlines the scientific excuse for imperialism: the "classification and categorization of all that is unknown," bringing "the light of scientific knowledge . . . to play upon the twilight world of nature and the exotic species which inhabit its dark corners."

In the sequence prior to the interview with the obscured gay man, there is a short interlude consisting of a few uncaptioned portraits of men. A voice-over considers the effects of being designated an object of "the light of scientific knowledge," or, alternately, of voluntarily emerging from the shadows:

> Every image of a gay man is in danger of becoming two pictures of a homosexual. When his image is just a depiction of a man, then he remains an individual. When he is identified as a homosexual, then he becomes a member of an exotic species and a case history of a pathological sickness.

The half-lit face of the gay man recounting his own history similarly presents two pictures, but not the same two: a picture of an unidentified man— neither exotic specimen nor visible case history—and the shadowy figure that troubles the image of heterosexual normality by refusing to "become a picture." But he also becomes a nearly literal representation of those "denizens of the twilight world of homosexuality," thereby placing himself on the negative side of the hierarchical terms of Enlightenment ideology— associations of light with order and dark with chaos, light with civilization and dark with nature. His ambiguous presence and the content of the interview represent a complex of historical conditions and relations. He is a man who was able to follow his own desires despite his parents' disapproval, but he did so within a set of predetermined social coordinates that relegate him to a shadowy existence. Nevertheless, he raises the question of who is really "nuts"—the "pervert," the doctor offering a "cure," or the father—and thus his story carries radical social meaning.

The positivist equation of visibility—pictures—with truth is disrupted by this man's refusal to accept an identity defined as abnormal, as is the assertion of the political neutrality of representations. Magnus Hirschfield assembled his photographic archive in the same positivist spirit as Cesare Lombroso and Havelock Ellis, collecting photographic records to establish the visibility—and thus the viability—of a social group, what Hirschfeld called an intermediate or third sex. Although it was not his belief in rational science that made him a target of the Nazis, but rather his untiring political organizing on behalf of full civil rights for gay men and lesbians (as well as for all women and for illegitimate children), Hirschfeld misunderstood the ideological malleability of representations, their uses in systems of thought, systems of social ordering. It is that malleability of meaning that Marshall makes evident.

A detail of the concluding interviews in the third part of the tape, where Marshall appears to abandon the complex constructions of the previous sections, also implies a subtle but important comparison involving the ideological function of images. Each speaker is captioned, labeled with superimposed words indicating each one's name and occupation and/or place of work. These bits of information appear to be nothing more than the standard means of identification used in television or film documentaries, but here they must also be considered in relation to the labels applied to the only other captioned pictures in the tape: the photographed deviants: "a moral imbecile," "an hysteric," "an intermediate type," and the "group of perverts." The labels accompanying these photographs indicate their subjects' status as unsocialized, abnormal people whose bodies are made to exhibit symptoms of degeneracy. The textual information provided about the people who speak in part three is, by contrast, specific to each subject; the categories of identification are associated with social integration.

The nameless and practically faceless gay man at the end of part one serves as a kind of mediator between these two groups. His speech indicates his understanding of his father's homophobia and his doctor's normalizing mission. But his anonymity bespeaks the impossibility, if he is *seen* as representative, of escaping the tyranny of being classified as a homosexual.[15] By the time Weber, Wells, and the others appear, Marshall has reversed the question of identity, away from abnormal, perhaps exotic, and disruptive sexual identities toward the self-identification of gay men and lesbians who understand the mechanisms of oppressive power and work to defeat them. Callen's speech extends this contradiction to people with AIDS, refuting the stereotype of AIDS "victim" Kenny Ramsaur, the grotesque product of insidious viruses and unnatural sexual practices, whose portrait is meant to serve as an icon of moral decay.

When the reigning ideology is subjected to scrutiny, as it is in *Bright Eyes,* the emotional constructions that it engenders and feeds upon lose their force. The photos of Kenny Ramsaur, for example, inspire neither horror nor pity, nor can they any longer be seen as proof of this man's inherent decadence. They signify instead only a rhetorical ploy devised by *Sunday People*'s editors. Probably naively, these media workers follow the dictates of scientific theology, taking pictures to "reveal . . . truth" about "sick homosexuals," in the tradition of the scientific objectivity that they claim to uphold. For science, and for those who subscribe to its power, AIDS represents social chaos that only rationalization can put in order. But those systems of rationalization are already in place, complete with their mania for classification and categorization and their ideological utility for opportunistic politicians, as well as for the mass media that makes those politicians authoritative public figures.

I do not wish to prescribe *Bright Eyes,* or any single work or action, as *the* sobering antidote to the effects of the institutions and instruments of social control. Nor will the tape be found "inspirational" in the sense of those works that attempt to counter stereotypes with stories of heroic role models. But the means Marshall employs to expose the relationships between the mass media, scientific systems of classification, and definitions of pathology suggest an important direction for sexual politics, a politics articulated in *Bright Eyes* by various representatives of gay institutions. These are gay men and lesbians who have initiated programs for AIDS education and advocacy for PWAs, who guarantee the availability of literature on gay subjects, and who promote political awareness about and organize resistance to official discrimination and antigay violence. Their participation in *Bright Eyes,* separately and collectively, does not constitute a plea for social acceptance, but rather purposes an outspoken, unequivocal assertion of the processes of self-identification that Marshall recognizes and represents. As their various contributions demonstrate, these identities are neither abstract, absolute, nor limited to individual integrity, but shaped through active engagement in social relations. Just as AIDS has sanctioned expressions of homophobia and revived supposedly outmoded methods for controlling sexuality, the conflation of AIDS with homosexuality has clarified political positions for many gay men and lesbians. And just as AIDS has confirmed and even escalated the hostility of the mass media toward lesbians and gay men, an extended critique of the mass media has become central to gay political work. *Bright Eyes* is a part of that work.

Notes

1. When early reports of AIDS in the US linked the syndrome with Haitian immigrants, however, the mass-media presentation of this information was redolent with the racism characteristic of our immigration policies.

2. As has been well-documented in the gay press, the mainstream press and television practically ignored AIDS for several years after the syndrome was first discovered in the US, and there is continuing censorship of news critical of the inertia of government and medical institutions—again regularly reported in the gay press.

3. President Reagan and most of his appointed officials has repeatedly delayed and at times obstructed funding measures for research, medical care, and social services for PWAs since the epidemic began. At the same time, however, the Reagan Administration adopted the rhetoric of warfare in issuing announcements about its concern for public health. In spite of this fact, continuing in the tradition of activism in the US, some AIDS activists

also favor military metaphors, conflating militarism with militancy and, unfortunately, reinforcing the war-mongering mentality that pervades our culture. Other AIDS activists, however, have criticized the use of military analogies. For example, Maxine Wolfe, a member of ACT UP, spoke out eloquently against the horrifying analogy in a proposed Human Rights Campaign Fund petition that would have called for a "Manhattan Project on AIDS." The petition ultimately called for an "emergency life-saving project."

4. The most prominent to hold this position have been Presidents Nixon and Reagan and their henchmen. But its most consistent proponent in the mid-eighties was *New York Times* television critic John Corry, who repeatedly insinuated this line into his regular reviews of political programs on network and public television. In a booklet published by the right-wing Media Institute, Corry outlines his critique of what he calls "the dominant culture," ruled by left-leaning journalists, lamenting, "The old consensus morality has disappeared. Once it was understood that the United States was generally right and its enemies generally wrong" (John Corry, *TV News and the Dominant Culture* [Washington, D.C.: The Media institute, 1986] p. 25).

5. The public television system is composed of autonomous stations, however, and some of these—notably KQED in San Francisco and WNET and WNYC in New York City—have regularly aired, and sometimes produced, programs on AIDS.

6. Though the grass on the other side of the Atlantic might seem greener, Channel Four has not always honored its obligations to gay audiences. They refused to air Caroline Sheldon's film *17 Rooms; or, What Do Lesbians Do in Bed?* which had been slated for a 1986 gay and lesbian series. Their reluctance in this case had nothing to do with what the film shows—in fact, nothing explicitly sexual—but rather with anticipated objections to its title.

7. In 1987 *Bright Eyes* was included in exhibitions at the New Museum of Contemporary Art, the Museum of Modern Art, and the Kitchen in New York City; and in the programs of the San Francisco Lesbian and Gay Film Festival, the Los Angeles Lesbian and Gay Film and Video Festival, and the American Film Institute's National Video Festival in Los Angeles.

8. It is no accident that, in the mass-media commentary on AIDS, the figure of the prostitute serves as the emblem of the pernicious female carrier of AIDS, the embodiment of threat to heterosexual men who are not IV drug users.

9. The 1986 Supreme Court ruling in *Bowers v. Hardwick,* upholding state laws prohibiting sodomy, however, appears to signal a reversal in the trend away from criminalizing homosexual acts that had prevailed in the late seventies and early eighties in the US.

10. Helms's and Dannemeyer's antigay bigotry is legion, and their statements and actions concerning AIDS surprised no one. Hentoff and Hamill, on the other hand, published their opinions in one of the most widely read liberal publications in the country. Hamill's proposal that the law treat seropositive individuals who transmit the virus to others as murderers is only quantitatively more insidious than the positions held by Herntoff, who advocates the scientifically dubious practice of mandatory HIV testing and persistently differentiates between the "innocent" and "guilty victims" of AIDS. At the same time, Hentoff, the self-proclaimed champion of civil rights, seems utterly unconcerned with the persecution of those deemed "guilty" of AIDS, all gay men and black and Latino IV drug users. See Pete Hamill, "The Secret Sharers," *Village Voice* (June 23, 1987) p. 10; and Nat Hentoff, "AIDS: A Failure of Intelligence," *Village Voice* (June 23, 1987), p. 34; "The New Priesthood of Death," *Village Voice* (June 30, 1987) p. 35; "Playing Russian Roulette with AIDS," *Village Voice* (July 17, 1987) p. 37; and "The AIDS Debate: A

Breakthrough," *Village Voice* (November 17, 1987) p. 38. Hentoff directly aligned himself with such moral conservatives in the Reagan Administration as Secretary of Education William Bennett and Presidential Assistant Gary Bower in calling for mandatory testing.

11. For a sustained discussion of instrumental uses of photography, see Allan Sekula, "The Body and the Archive," *October,* no. 39 (Winter, 1986), pp. 3–64.

12. For many years the history of Nazi persecutions of gay men was regularly ignored in literature about the Third Reich. One helpful corrective is Richard Plant, *The Pink Triangle: The Nazi War Against Homosexuals* (New York: Henry Holt and Company, 1986). Much of the material Marshall relates in this regard is also chronicled in Plant's book.

13. In his study of contemporary debates concerning sexuality and their precedents in the nineteenth century, Jeffrey Weeks quotes Hirschfeld: "I believe in Science, and I am convinced that Science, and above all the natural Sciences, must bring to mankind, not only truth, but with truth, Justice, Liberty and Peace" (quoted in Jeffrey Weeks, *Sexuality and Its Discontents: Meanings, Myths and Modern Sexualities* [London: Routledge and Kegan Paul, 1985] p. 71).

14. This is a device Marshall rigorously employs in his earlier tapes that deal with characterization and the construction of representations, such as *The Love Show* and *A Question of Three Sets of Characteristics,* both 1980.

15. Similarly, Adrienne Rich objects to the word *lesbianism,* because, she writes, it "has a clinical and limiting ring." See her influential essay "Compulsory Heterosexuality and Lesbian Existence," *Signs,* vol. 5, no. 4 (1980). Gay male writers such as Simon Watney have similarly insisted on the word *gay* rather than *homosexual* in order to counteract the oppressive medical connotations of the latter term.

Ecce Homo: On Making Personal Gay Cinema

JERRY TARTAGLIA

Around the beginning of 1989 I was thinking a lot about the way in which gay sex was being monitored by the medical authorities in San Francisco. The image of the prison guard in Genet's *Un Chant d'amour* kept reappearing in my mind. The guard's ever-watchful eye observed the men engaged in solo sex and interpersonal fantasies in much the same way as the eyes of the authorities were watching us.

I realized that I was making another film, which I tentatively call *A Song of Love,* after Genet. My journal writings from that period are excerpted here with the hope that they might shed light on the development of the politics expressed in the images and text of *Ecce Homo.* To some extent, these journal writings are the "scripts" or "film treatments" of my work. The labor of my cinema is as much connected to the writing process, in the case of *Ecce Homo,* and to the static image-making process, in the case of *Final Solutions,* as it is a shooting/editing process.

Those who might be seeking a literal interpretation of my work, steeped in political jargon, organizational rhetoric, or socially correct syntax are apt to be disappointed by my daily writings, which have served as the creative foundation for my films over the years. Mine is a cinema of the dreamworld, peopled with images and sounds "interplaying," with multiple meanings and frequent references to films, music, or poetry, all meant to help the viewer free-associate with the work. Rationalist discourses offer little help in this process; emotional openness, sensitive observation, and analogic thinking are more suitable tools for understanding my work.

On the other side, however, those who might hope to slip into the apolitical state of aesthetics which Auden described as "enraptured apathy" will receive no support from me or my work. While I honor and respect the truth, beauty, goodness, and justice of the individual human being, I cannot, in the Age of Warhol, accept the validity of the artist-as-hero/ine. I hope my cinema is a cinema of liberation. Of whatever freedom my films might speak, they are empty statements unless the work stirs in the viewer the sense of our mutual longing for freedom and the collective need for liberation and justice.

For me, in the end, an artist can at best try to point the viewer toward the processes of liberation which, by nature, begin in the mind. So long as one is fettered by culturally constructed self-identity, one cannot be free to plumb the depths of "gay spirit" or gay psychosexual human experience. Under such circumstances, an outwardly directed act of revolution is doomed to remain a prison rebellion which will be quelled by other, more corrupt prisoners—as Genet well knew.

The aim of my cinema is to begin to explore glimpses of the gay "window on the world" which doesn't fit neatly into an assimilationist framework. I rejoin myself to the human experience through personal gay cinema, and I invite the viewer to do the same.

February—March 1989
ECCE HOMO

A Song of Love—an optically printed piece—use super 8, all-male films and images from Genet film—color wratten gel filters and B & W.

. . .

Two possible directions in which we might go in the age of AIDS: decadence or eroticism.

. . .

Overturn traditional antisexual complaints about porn imagery: no story, no human feeling, boring sexuality, repetition, no memorable faces or actions. Use four images in optical printer. Use these and other devices: zoom in on one frame of Genet, expose extreme granularity, switch from four to two frames, use superimposition, show sprocket holes, suggest the materiality of the film itself.

. . .

The cop in the Genet film represents the sex police. They are the new antisex bigots who use AIDS to eliminate sexuality from gay experience.

The sex police say that sex-negative attitudes are best.
The sex police preach anti-body rhetoric and uphold hetero monogamy as the only model for sexuality.
The sex police condemn nonmonogamous gay sex as inherently pornographic, and pornography as inherently wrong.
The sex police are body-negative and anti-body.

Gay iconography is inherently pornographic to the sex police.
Homosexuality has become a sexless abstraction in the anti-body model of behavior.

. . .

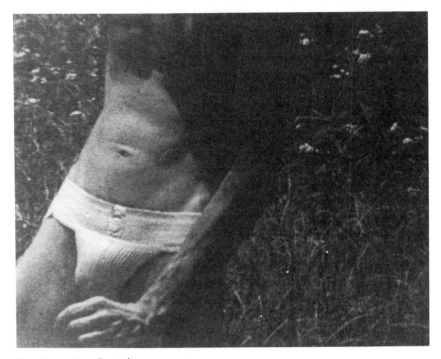

Ecce Homo, Jerry Tartaglia

Challenge the audience to cross the boundary between the viewing of a sexual (queer) icon, and *experiencing* the voyeuristic process. Make them do the thing itself!

Behold men—behold man—ecce homo—there's a title—the words with which the accused man was presented to his accusers.

REPRESENTATION VERSUS EXPERIENCE

Masturbation has even come under criticism in AIDS care circles. It's as if we're being told that we don't even have the right to have our desire.

In porno, the expression on a face can become frozen in the sexual fantasy—use the printer to achieve this.

Porn crosses the boundary between present visual pleasure and future procurable desire.

. . .

Make no mistake; the goal of the sex police is to permanently force all people, gay, straight, and bisexual, to conform to one and only one standard of sexual behavior. Married, procreative heterosexuality. The antisexual attitudes which are sweeping the country are targeting queers first. We are simply the first ones to be cited. The sex police are watching everyone.

. . .

I'm trying to understand the form for the images in the rushes from *Ecce Homo*. The film is an attempt to show the queer and his queer sexuality. To show the true harmlessness of pleasure. The Genet material is about repression and voyeurism; watching other peoples' desire. When we view the cop in *Un Chant d'amour*, or when we view the imagery in *Ecce Homo*, we are drawn into the same role of voyeur.

. . .

I think it is appropriate to allude to Genet in *Ecce Homo* because of the history of *Un Chant d'amour* in New York. It was for the showing of Genet and of Jack Smith's *Flaming Creatures* that Jonas Mekas was arrested. The police in 1963 insisted that Genet was pornographic.

It is the judgment which underpins the voyeur's role. *Ecce Homo* challenges the viewer to watch without judgment, for the moment we decide that the images are "porn," in that moment we become voyeurs, as much as the cop in Genet's film.

MANIFESTO

Ridiculous Theater, Scourge of Human Folly
by
CHARLES LUDLAM

Aim: To get beyond nihilism by revaluing combat.

Axioms to a theater for ridicule:

1. You are a living mockery of your own ideals. If not, you have set your ideals too low.
2. The things one takes seriously are one's weaknesses.
3. Just as many people who claim a belief in God disprove it with their every act, so too there are those whose every deed, though they say there is no God, is an act of faith.
4. Evolution is a conscious process.
5. Bathos is that which is intended to be sorrowful but because of the extremity of its expression becomes comic. Pathos is that which is meant to be comic but because of the extremity of its expression becomes sorrowful. Some things which seem to be opposites are actually different degrees of the same thing.
6. The comic hero thrives by his vices. The tragic hero is destroyed by his virtue. Moral paradox is the crux of the drama.
7. The theater is a humble materialist enterprise which seeks to produce riches of the imagination, not the other way around. The theater is an event and not an object. Theater workers need not blush and conceal their desperate struggle to pay the landlords their rents. Theater without the stink of art.

Instructions for use:
This is farce not Sunday school. Illustrate hedonistic calculus. Test out a dangerous idea, a theme that threatens to destroy one's whole value system. Treat the material in a madly farcical manner without losing the seriousness of the theme. Show how paradoxes arrest the mind. Scare yourself a bit along the way.
© Estate of Charles Ludlam

The AIDS Crisis Is Ridiculous

GREGG BORDOWITZ

In memory of Craig Owens

> *The only thing that is different from one time to another is what is seen and what is seen depends upon how everybody is doing everything. This makes the thing we are looking at very different and this makes what those who describe it make of it, it makes a composition, it confuses, it shows, it is, it looks, it likes it as it is, and this makes what is seen as it is seen. Nothing changes from generation to generation except the thing seen and that makes a composition.*
>
> Gertrude Stein[1]

A Fantasy about a Father

Charles Ludlam died of pneumonia on Friday, May 29, 1987, at St. Vincent's Hospital in New York City at about 1 A.M. just after his longtime lover Everett Quinton had left his bedside. He had recently been diagnosed with AIDS, and his death stunned our community, which is still struggling daily with the devastation of AIDS. My relation to Ludlam and his theater is particular to the historical circumstances of the AIDS crisis. I never met him, and I never saw him perform. When he died, I became part of a local, collective remembrance of this almost mythic, gay figure. I recently attended the opening night of the Ridiculous Theater Company's newest production of *Camille,* on my birthday. Everett Quinton performed in the role that Ludlam made famous. I could not resist viewing the final scene as about Ludlam's death and Quinton's mourning.

> [H]e was not, as has wrongly been assumed by the daily press, an avant-garde artist in the least; he was the reviver and purifier of a thousand traditions that had fallen into corruption, banality, and disrepute. He reinvented the burlesque tradition, the vaudeville and silent-film tradition of physical comedy, the tradition of playwrighting as an ongoing conversation with a faithful audience, the tradition of repertory acting.[2]

I know some details of Ludlam's life and career only through reading obituaries, yet I have a fantasy: I am having dinner with Charles Ludlam in a West Village restaurant, telling him about the article I am writing about AIDS-activist video. He seems intrigued, but actually he is humoring me. He thinks I'm a cute kid, and he's interested in getting into my pants. I'd let him. This is a fantasy about lineage. I desire a link with Ludlam, a link with the past, a place in history. There must be some continuity between our lives, and if not our lives, the history and the forces that have shaped them.

> When Ludlam turned, in Camille, to his maid in a boudoir in Paris and said (in that ruminating pathetic tone), "Throw another faggot on the fire!" whole ages of repression went up in shrieks. "There are no faggots in the house Madame," the maid replied respectfully. And Ludlam—rising on one arm on the chaise lounge to look directly out at the audience with that affable expression—would say "What? No faggots in the house?"
> There were lots of faggots in the house, of course—bronzed, muscular habitues of gyms, muscles, and mustaches—and if everything Ludlam did was ironic, a double entendre of sorts, so were their lives.[3]

In my fantasy I want Ludlam to fuck me without a condom. I'd receive his cum as a gift. Searching for a model, I wish for a legacy—the love and approval of a father. I want to achieve his stature. In my fantasy, Ludlam's greatness can be passed on to me through his semen. A condom would thwart this transference. This is a fantasy about immortality; that something exists greater than ourselves, shared between us—our community, for example.

> Excess was Charles Ludlams's point of departure, his first gift. He knew that what was attainable in reality was always within theater's reach. Castration, gender flops, defloration, psychotic episodes, and curtain-chewing were not only possible but commonplace at the Ridiculous Theater. Harder than imagining Ludlam—outsized, operatic, a force of theater and life—in a truly tragic role is knowing that we will never again see him waggle a dildo across the footlights or cock an eyebrow and stage lisp "I love my makeup tonight."[4]

My fantasy raises a number of issues regarding AIDS and HIV transmission. I am well aware of the implications of this fantasy. I am HIV antibody positive, and I was infected through unprotected sexual intercourse. Today I use condoms to protect myself from any number of infections that can threaten my already-compromised immune system. Yet I still dream about unsafe sex. When I tested HIV antibody positive in the spring of 1988, at twenty-four years old, I no longer felt part of my generation of gay men. I felt like a member of a past generation. My fantasy reveals that, unconsciously, I think that AIDS is the legacy I have inherited from the previous generation of gay men. It is difficult not to blame past lovers for my HIV infection, regardless of the fact that I know that no one is to blame—my lovers or myself. It has been equally difficult not to understand my HIV infection as a punishment, regardless of my sex radicalism. The hardest thing I have had to accept is that there is no reason that explains AIDS. There are historical, material conditions that create a situation of crisis, but there is no reason why some people die, why some get sick, why I am infected. There is no reason, but there is meaning. My experiences are filled with meaning. They're filled with pain, irony, and hope.[5]

Thus, I am motivated to establish a comparative relation between Ludlam's theater project and the growing body of video work to which I have contributed. This relation is somewhat implausible. Ludlam intended to make people laugh, but the intention of AIDS-activist video is to make people angry. The Ridiculous Theater is studiedly apolitical, while most AIDS-activist video work is propagandistic. Yet, I can conceive of a relation with Ludlam within what can be described as a psycho-geographic proximity. We exist in the same place at different times. Remember Gertrude Stein's words, "Nothing changes from generation to generation except the thing seen and that makes a composition." Consider that "the thing seen" is the AIDS epidemic.

Queer Structures of Feeling

There are countercultural strategies that belong specifically to queers. A queer structure of feeling shapes cultural work produced by queers. In the words of Raymond Williams, who coined the term, a structure of feeling is "the hypothesis of a mode of social formation, explicit and recognizable in specific kinds of art, which is distinguishable from other social and semantic formations by its articulations of presence."[6]

Within the relation between two factors, a queer structure of feeling is formed. These two factors are: how heterosexist oppression attempts to contain queer sexualities, and how queers fight oppression by forming communities. Thus, a queer structure of feeling can be described as an articulation of presence forged through resistance to heterosexist society. Cultural work can be considered within a queer structure of feeling if self-identified queers produce the work, if these producers identify the work as queer, if queers claim the work has significance to queers, if the work is censored or criticized for being queer. A particular work is queer if it is viewed as queer, either by queers or bigots.

A queer structure of feeling is a set of cultural strategies of survival for queers. It is marked by an appreciation for the ridiculous, and it values masquerade. Mockery is its form; posing is its strategy. These general terms describe a continuity in the structure that traverses a number of generations.

From generation to generation the emphasis of the structure shifts and new articulations surface to define the current moment. Some of the defining characteristics remain present in new articulations, establishing continuities in form.

The AIDS epidemic precipitated a crisis affecting the actual conditions of existence of many artists—many of them gay. Thus, many lesbian and gay artists took ideas current in the art world—appropriation, situationist strategies, institutional critique—and applied them to the struggle to wrest control of the public discussion on AIDS from right-wing fanatics who proposed homophobic and racist policies like quarantine. AIDS media activists also steal methods from dominant culture to make work that is meaningful to the communities affected by AIDS. Additionally, these activists deploy strategies that have been used effectively by lesbians and gay men to fight invisibility. These strategies are what ridiculous theater and AIDS-activist video share in common.

Material Conditions

These are among the material conditions that currently inform a queer structure of feeling. Queers use the limited amount of resources available to produce their work. Ludlam considers the material conditions of production:

> The theater is a humble materialist enterprise which seeks to produce riches of the imagination, not the other way around. The theater is an event not an object. Theater workers need not blush and conceal their desperate struggle to pay and landlords' rents. Theater without the stink of art.

Without access to substantial resources, AIDS video activists have organized around principles similar to those underlying Ludlam's seventh axiom. It is recognized that video "is not an object, but an event," because its production is part of a larger effort to organize increasing numbers of people to take action. Video "without the stink of art" is television. We are not primarily concerned with video as a form. The production of activist video is primarily concerned with audience and distribution. Many people who make video do not have access to airtime or broadcast-quality equipment. Despite the lack of access to substantial resources, AIDS activists make television which is radically different from the network television industry, where the only motivation is profit.

Among many AIDS video activists, video production is viewed as a collaborative effort, recognizing that material conditions dictate the form of production. Video production is a means to end government inaction on AIDS. This agenda compels activists to put work in as many places and in as many forms as possible. AIDS activist video is produced in a dialogue with the social movement to end government inaction. The documentation of protests is one form of direct action; distributions of these tapes are demonstrations.

Video Ridiculous

There are elements of the aesthetics of ridiculous theater to be found in current AIDS-activist video production, but there are no direct correlations. Current queer video practices draw upon the history of queer theater of the seventies, adding to it the political agendas of AIDS activism and lesbian and gay liberation as they are presently articulated and understood. In this way a new queer structure of feeling is articulated. The following considers aspects of the ridiculous that can be located in some AIDS activist videos. Each of the videos discussed here exemplifies different aspects of the current queer structure of feeling.

Stiff Sheets (1989), by John Goss, presents a video record of a theatrical performance by AIDS activists. From January 21 to 28, 1989, ACT UP (AIDS Coalition to Unleash Power) Los Angeles staged a continual vigil at LA County/University of Southern California Medical Center to protest the government's lethally slow response to AIDS. The protestors demanded the immediate creation of AIDS services and facilities. On the sixth evening of the vigil, an anonymous collective of gay artists, using the pseudonym Stiff Sheets, presented a fashion show to entertain the demonstrators.

The master of ceremonies started the show with "a little polite disclaimer," stating, "This fashion show is brought to you in the worst taste imaginable, and you are the most sensitized of audiences imaginable. So, if you are offended we are too." This is significant for two reasons. First, it aligns the performance within the history of queer theater—particularly ridiculous theater—by acknowledging its intentions to mine the depths of bad taste. Additionally, it acknowledges a specific audience of AIDS activists who will appreciate the humor in a particular way.

The performance acknowledged both the rage of the activists and some of the most morbid aspects of living with AIDS. For example, in a scene featuring "active sportswear," a model walks down the runway wearing a sweatshirt and sweatpants. The MC announces that the creation is titled "night sweats—more than a fashion, it's a condition; more than a style, it's a symptom." Another outfit presented was an ankle-length pink triangle with the slogan "Silence=Death" printed along the bottom. "When the epidemic started getting out of hand and no other gay organization responded to the great fashion needs required, we made the transition from checkbook activism and took to the streets," comments the MC. The irony here depends upon stereotypical views of gay men as stylish, or as drag queens, coupled with an awareness that a pink triangle accompanied by the Silence=Death logo *is* a fashion statement about the AIDS epidemic. The outfit, then, underscores the strategic role of style for AIDS activists.

A third ensemble modelled in the tape reveals changes in queer structures of feeling concerned with gay male sexuality. During the "bridal finale" two contrasting examples are presented. Last decade's look appears as a model dressed in a tattered bridal gown decorated with clumps of hardened sperm. Carrying wilted flowers, the old queen drags her tired ass down the aisle to make way for the chic and fabulous safe-sex bride of the eighties. Dressed in a white gown tightly bound with Saran wrap, this eager girl wears leather underwear, and she is prepared to have safe sex, "enabling her to stay alive for the divorce."

DiAna's Hair Ego, AIDS Info Up Front (1990), by Ellen Spiro, describes the efforts of the South Carolina AIDS Education Network (SCAEN)—a grassroots organization based in the salon, DiAna's Hair Ego. Here, the shop's owner, beautician DiAna DiAna, provides education about AIDS to all her clients. Printed matter and condoms are made available on shelves displaying beauty products; educational tapes are screened on a television monitor in the salon. The situation depicted in *DiAna's Hair Ego* is implicitly theatrical, a quality further emphasized by Spiro's documentation. Various shots of the beauty shop are recorded with a wide-angle lens, giving it the appearance of a fishbowl and suggesting that this site of community activism can be viewed microcosmically as a model for what AIDS education should be—a grassroots effort designed by a community in its own interests. And Spiro's camera direction is very theatrical at times. She wasn't intimidated by the mirrors in the beauty shop and didn't shy away from images that show her reflection in the shop's mirrors.

Spiro's incorporation of the activity of documentation in the tape echoes SCAEN's use of performance for AIDS education. DiAna is shown making presentations about AIDS at local conferences and directing others in role-playing exercises designed to address the complex issues of negotiating safer sex. Spiro also includes footage shot by DiAna of local schoolchildren asking questions about AIDS: "Can you get it from mosquitos?" "Why isn't a cure found?" "Do more blacks get AIDS than whites?" Employing a multitude of devices that complement SCAEN's efforts, *DiAna's Hair Ego* demonstrates the nexus of theater, video, and AIDS activism.

Bob Huff's *Rockville Is Burning* (1989), perhaps the most successful hybrid of ridiculous theater and video activism to date, is based on a performance about an AIDS-activist takeover of a network television news program. The performance included the use of video within the structure of the play, and both the performance and the videotaped material are set against

Diana Diana discusing her AIDS education methods in *Diana's Hair Ego,* Ellen Spiro

the background of the ACT UP/ACT NOW nonviolent takeover of the Food and Drug Administration (FDA) headquarters in Rockville, Maryland on October 11, 1988. This theater piece was the product of collaboration between Bob Huff and an ACT UP affinity group, Wave Three. Theater became one of their activities when they were invited to present a work at La Mama, ETC in Manhattan.

In the opening scene, an effeminate, implied closet-case director coaches a newscaster about the tone he should affect when presenting the news that AIDS activists have occupied the FDA building. He convinces the newscaster to agree to be more sympathetic to the protesters, explaining that the enormous, and increasing, number of people with AIDS and HIV "represents significant demographics." However, on the air the newscaster adopts a sensational tone and refers to the AIDS activists as "a group of homosexual protestors," a cliché common in the broadcast industry that has contributed to the misperception that AIDS is a "gay disease."

In the middle of the newscaster's presentation of the FDA action, three "AIDS terrorists" in white lab coats burst onto the set, announcing that they have taken control. Supposedly, other "AIDS terrorists" have control of the network's satellite transponder, enabling them to interrupt the news to receive transmissions from around the country. These segments consist of interviews Huff had previously recorded, with members of Wave Three playing different "AIDS victims"—an IV drug user, a mother, a person with AIDS, a hemophiliac, a child—each enacted as a drag performance.

This dramatized reworking of mass media representations in *Rockville Is Burning,* seen from an activist's perspective, fulfills many fantasies. Videotaping himself in his newscaster persona, superimposed on images of the actual action at the FDA, Huff reports a riot. Archival images of people rioting and buildings burning are likewise presented as live footage from the FDA action. This projection of riots, armed takeovers, and even assassinations represents the frustration of AIDS activists faced with the slow response of government institutions to the epidemic. It also represents the ongoing debates about the options open to the AIDS-activist movement; until now AIDS activists have relied upon nonviolent direct action to achieve their ends. Huff's tape pushes the boundaries of the continuing discussion concerning tactics in ways reminiscent of ridiculous theater. As Ludlam advises, "Test out a dangerous idea, a theme which threatens to destroy one's whole value system," and "Treat the material in a madly farcical manner without losing the seriousness of the theme."

Sorrow

For Ludlam, sorrow is at the center of drama:

> *Bathos is that which is intended to be sorrowful but because of the extremity of the expression becomes comic. Pathos is that which is meant to be comic but because of the extremity of its expression becomes sorrowful. Some things which seem to be opposites are actually different degrees of the same thing.*

But there is nothing intrinsically sorrowful about being queer. Oppression causes the sorrow in the lives of queers, and queers have developed a rich culture filled with joy in the face of sorrow. In particular, many AIDS media activists have organized into collectives, sharing resources to produce work vital to the interests of the communities affected by AIDS. I am a founding member of two AIDS video collectives: the Testing the Limits Collective, formed in 1987 to document emerging forms of AIDS activism and which produced a videotape of the same name; and DIVA TV (Damned Interfering Video Activists), an affinity group of ACT UP that documents actions and provides countersurveillance against police brutality at demonstrations. This loosely organized collective of approximately thirty members has produced three tapes thus far—*Target City Hall, Pride,* and *Like a Prayer* (all 1989).

Both collectives use democratic forms, such as consensus decision-making. The goals of both collectives are to quickly produce tapes that can be used by AIDS-activist direct action groups as organizing tools.

The processes employed by these collectives are significantly different from those found in the repertory theater. The Ridiculous Theatrical Company was a small ensemble, under Ludlam's direction, committed to changing the history of theater. During the AIDS crisis there is no sense that one can afford to work for years with a small group of people developing a set of ideas. And, although AIDS-activist collectives have their share of divas, they are leaderless. They function with an extreme sense of urgency. A number of collective members in DIVA have died from AIDS and many people, in both video groups, have lost numerous friends and lovers. Many AIDS activists are sick or HIV-infected. It is not possible for these groups to conceive of working relationships that aren't focused on well-defined, pragmatic goals that can be achieved in relatively short periods of time.

The production of *Target City Hall* addressed this imperative in its design as a work comprised of sections, each produced by a different group with different levels of experience. The tape documented ACT UP's efforts to take over City Hall in New York in the late winter of 1989, in order to call attention to the collapse of the city's health care system. A music video section introduces the documentary. Another section, produced by the late Costa Pappas, draws upon conventions of direct cinema and cinema verité. The third section was made by a group of lesbians who adopted the name LAPIT (Lesbian Activists Producing Innovative Television) and whose contribution uses images from commercial TV news broadcasts juxtaposed with interviews, performances, rap, and activist-produced protest footage. Interspersed between these segments, the collective's editing committee added scenes, shot on black-and-white super 8 film, of AIDS activists getting arrested at City Hall, which resembles archival footage of civil rights protests or demonstrations against US involvement in Vietnam. A full inventory of the conventions and tropes used in *Target City Hall* reflects the conflicting feelings of desperation and hopefulness that inform a queer structure of feeling, as well as a willingness to try any approach that will achieve a desired effect. This was true for Ludlam, and it is also true for many queer videomakers producing work about AIDS: "The theater absurd believes in nothing, the theater ridiculous believes in everything."[7]

The queer theft of straight culture must not be viewed merely as oppositional. Ridiculous theater, too, "is not a comment (nostalgic, ironic, adoring, or patronizing) on mass culture but it borrows from and imitates mass culture as fellow product of the popular imagination."[8] It is possible to feel both admiration and contempt for dominant culture, and queers may easily have contradictory feelings about the culture that ignores and ridicules us.

We are not acknowledged, nor are we invited to participate in this culture, but we comprise part of its audience. In his careful, studied use of material stolen from dominant culture—movies, plays, television, magazines, newspapers—Ludlam revealed a fascination with dominant culture. Similarly, videomakers resort to the stuff that has fascinated us all our television-watching lives. According to Ludlam, the aim of ridiculous theater is "to get beyond nihilism by revaluing combat." For AIDS activists, in order "to get beyond nihilism" one must overcome cynicism about one's role in historical change. By "revaluing combat" one assumes responsibility toward change, recognizing one's stake in dominant culture along the way.

Where Ludlam offers "instructions for use" of his manifesto, he counsels, "This is farce not Sunday school." This thought is useful when considering AIDS activists' efforts to criticize religious institutions as documented in the DIVA production *Like a Prayer*. The video chronicles the Stop the Church demonstration organized by ACT UP New York and WHAM! (Women's Health Action Movement) at St. Patrick's Cathedral on September 10, 1989, to protest the Catholic Church's—specifically Cardinal John O'Conner's—opposition to women's right to choose abortion and everybody's right to use condoms.

In this work, we find an overt overlap between Ludlam's theater practice and AIDS activism in Operation Ridiculous, a WHAM! affinity group whose name and actions parody Operation Rescue, the right-wing antichoice group that blocks women's access to abortion clinics. The DIVA tape shows members of Operation Rescue holding pictures of fetuses and carrying rubber models of fetuses at different stages of development. In parallel sequences, the Operation Ridiculous group arrives at the demonstration in clown suits holding dolls dressed as "clown babies" and screeching, "Save the babies! Save our clown babies." The affinity group intervenes wherever members of Operation Rescue gather to disrupt the protest at St. Patrick's.

As these images appear on screen, members of Operation Ridiculous proclaim:

> It's ridiculous that Operation Rescue, a predominantly white group, preaches carrying all pregnancies to term while there are over thirty thousand babies waiting to be adopted, the majority of whom are babies of color.
>
> It's ridiculous that the Catholic Church actively blocks safe sex and birth control education in the schools. Teenagers are exceptionally active. They're getting pregnant, and there has been a forty-percent rise in teenage AIDS cases.
>
> It's ridiculous that dialogue on reproductive rights has been limited to abortion when real issues like the lack of prenatal, neonatal, and gynecological care are virtually ignored.

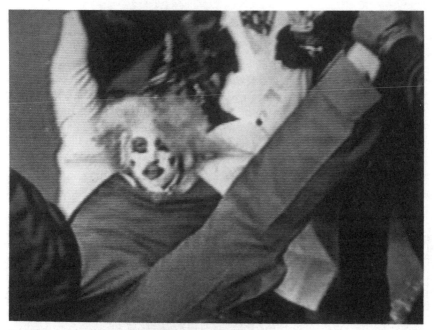

Operation Ridiculous at the WHAM!/ACT UP demonstration at St. Patrick's Cathedral, documented in *Like a Prayer,* DIVA TV

It's ridiculous that the Catholic Church preaches brotherly love yet promotes antigay and antilesbian violence by calling homosexuality a sin.

In *Like a Prayer,* Operation Ridiculous exhibits a keen sense of the ridiculous, combined with a sophisticated understanding of strategies of direct action, bringing to mind Ludlam's axiom:

> *Just as many people who claim a belief in God disprove it with their very act, so to there are those whose every deed, though they say there is no God, is an act of faith.*

Sex and Virtue

Ludlam describes religious paradox as a means to question all moral order: "Illustrate hedonistic calculus." The performers of ridiculous theater have been described as "erotic beings intent on self-affirmation."[9] Several AIDS-activist videos begin with the same premise.

In *Keep Your Laws Off My Body* (1989), by Zoe Leonard and Catherine Saalfield, images of two lesbians having sex are juxtaposed with shots of uniformed police officers at an ACT UP demonstration. More romantic than ridiculous, the slow pans caressing the women's flesh reveal that this material was shot by the two women. Stiff, overdressed, stuffy, and nervous, the lines of uniformed cops stare in one direction; sometimes they look directly into the camera. The alternating presence and absence of the lesbian lovers and the legion of law enforcement officers in the same frame creates a nervous tension. It's frightening to see the imposing figures of the police present at the scene of lesbian lust. It's funny to see the dumbfounded police lined up like toy soldiers when confronted with lesbian desire.

A stylistically very different tape, *Safer Sex Slut* (1988), by Carol Leigh, features Leigh, aka Scarlot Harlot, dressed in a black bathing suit, leopard skin jacket, dog collar, and a strand of pearls, performing a music video— a Janis Joplin-style anthem extolling the virtues of safe sex:

> I won't become disease infected/Me I'll be so well protected/I always pay my income tax/I eat granola for my snack/I don't make fun of lumber jacks/Or mess with sheep that have anthrax/Safe sex/At the movies, in a car/In a bathroom, at a bar/Safe Sex.

By proposing a preposterous criteria to judge goodness and safety, this song renders the whole notion of a safe *sexuality* ridiculous, while boldly promoting the notion of practicing safe *sex*. At the same time, *Safe Sex Slut* employs humor to diffuse feelings of resentment that accompany condom use. Leigh proclaims, "The bedroom is the last frontier. Condoms leave a souvenir." Behind this song is the belief that there is no moral to be learned from AIDS.

The comic hero thrives by his vices. The tragic hero is destroyed by his virtue. Moral paradox is the crux of the drama.

In *Safe Sex Slut*, Leigh becomes the comic hero who survives by her vices. Her preoccupation with safety motivates her pursuit of pleasure. The two lesbians in *Keep Your Laws Off My Body* are heros threatened because of their virtue. Moral paradox shapes the lives of queers: we are gay-bashed for living our lives honestly; we survive by celebrating the virtues for which we are despised.

Self-Mockery

The things one takes seriously are one's weaknesses.

Yet another axiom in Ludlam's manifesto can be revisited in terms of a new, queer structure of feeling, reread in relation to AIDS-activist documentaries that only cast activists in heroic light. A video that integrates performance and documentary, *Marta: Portrait of a Teenage Activist* (1990), by Mathew Ebert and Ryan Landry, exhibits the importance of this approach. Similar to Huff's *Rockville Is Burning,* and John Greyson's documentary on the sixth International AIDS Conference, *The World Is Sick (Sic)* (1989), the tape was shot during actual events—in this case, an ACT UP protest at the Centers for Disease Control in Atlanta. Dressed in very convincing parochial schoolgirl drag, Landry plays an overzealous, approval-seeking new member of ACT UP named Marta. Ebert taped the action, which was organized to protest the CDC's refusal to recognize lesbians as an epidemiological category in relation to AIDS, as well as to demonstrate against Georgia's sodomy laws, upheld in the famous *Bowers v. Hardwick* Supreme Court decision. Ebert also conducted interviews with AIDS activists about Marta, using actual events to stage a fictional story that comments on the social dynamic of activism. Despite her annoying eagerness to please everyone, all the activists interviewed were fond of Marta.

The name Marta must have been carefully chosen to bring to mind the word martyr. She is an overachiever—distributing hundreds of flyers advertising the upcoming actions under the doors of rooms at a motel occupied solely by activists who are there to attend the action. Marta holds her own protests. She demonstrates outside a theater in Atlanta presenting the movie *Peter Pan.* Underneath the marquee Marta screams into a bullhorn, "Why can't Peter Pan be played by a real fairy!? Shame! Shame! Stop Cathy Rigby! Stop *Peter Pan*! Now!"

> *You are a living mockery of your own ideals. If not, you have set your ideals too low.*

This Ludlam axiom expresses cynicism coupled with faith. Although it is true that queers are not martyrs by definition, the end many of us seek to achieve—liberation—is righteous. In *Marta* the profound sense of uncertainty that queer activists experience is presented as an important factor to be considered alongside the reasons that compel us to take action. Thus, the tape conforms the aims of ridiculous theater to the agenda of AIDS activism.

Landry and Ebert's insightful parody of the social behavior of activists, although witty and accurate in many respects, raises issues of sexism within queer structures of feeling. Although, Landry's performance works as successful gender-fuck, why are issues of uncertainty played out solely through the actions of a female character? A similar question can be posed about *The World Is Sick (Sic).* In that work, too, the main character is an inept woman played by a man in drag. In my experience, many women activists are seasoned organizers, and many are lesbians. They are not dizzy martyrs, nor are they uncertain about their political motives and beliefs. At the same time, both tapes exhibit a significant absence—uncertain, anxious, gay men.

It is not the drag performances per se that suggest sexism. In the practice of ridiculous theater the drag queen "poses the problem of psychosexual identity: to what extent male and female conduct, masculinity and femininity, are social role identities, cultural artifacts, what they are, might be, should be—how valid these roles are, how natural."[10] In these two examples, the drag performances share these aims; however, they function to the exclusion of male characters working through the fears and ambivalences we all have toward engaging in political actions. In both videos, this absence becomes manifest as a displacement of all negative feelings onto the female protagonists.

Ridiculous versus Lyrical

In contrast, uncertainties and insecurities produced by the AIDS crisis constitute the fabric of Tom Kalin's *They Are Lost to Vision Altogether* (1988). No conclusion can be drawn from the tape, yet it produces powerful emotional effects—sadness and an almost overwhelming sense of loss. Fragments of many different texts—visual and aural, stolen from movies and television—as well as original images produced by Kalin are interwoven in ways that produce confusion. Material from the nightly news collides with images from porn; dialogue from Hollywood films underscores archival footage. Rapid editing and music propel the viewer from one section to another. The structure of this tape has much in common with a play written by Ludlam, who described ridiculous theater as "a bundle of series of intensive image explosions."[11] Like Ludlam, Kalin refuses a claim to original authorship, but in one respect his tape differs markedly from ridiculous theater. Its power rests in the evocative material Kalin has collaged, and it relies on the sentimentality of the images. *They Are Lost to Vision Altogether* is lyrical; ridiculous theater is never lyrical.

The lyrical, elegic qualities of Kalin's tape express feelings of loss and absence many of us experience as the cumulative effect of many deaths from AIDS. We watch what is all around us turn into memory. We talk about an ever-increasing number of people in the past tense. We experience nostalgia for events that happened, not years ago, but months ago, weeks ago, because we miss people who participated in these events and died shortly after. To watch videos about AIDS activism produced two or three years ago, those of us who have been involved in the movement must be prepared to encounter the faces of at least twenty people who are now dead. Many of us are in a perpetual state of mourning.

This was not so, merely ten, fifteen, twenty years ago. A very different worldview reigned when Ludlam conceived his theater. Ridiculous theater

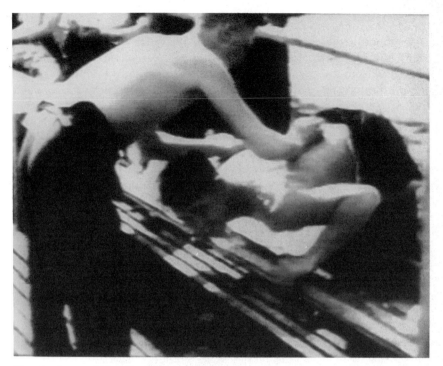

They Are Lost to Vision Altogether, Tom Kalin

represented a radical attempt, calculated to call into question the dominant moral order constitutive of the dominant social order—to reveal our socially formed identities to be characterological lies. In the words of Stefan Brecht, it "approaches the effects if not the status of a popular revolutionary art."[12] Ridiculous theater "considers established and recognized conventions of its medium as part of the culture's technique for artists and costumers to escape authentic actuality, and therefore would allow the artist to employ them only in a destructive manner—i.e., destroying the effect of tranquilized impersonality—hence insists on sabotage—of effects—at all points."[13]

Ridiculous theater questioned notions of sincerity, authenticity, and truth. AIDS activists also need to question sincerity, authenticity, and truth, but, unlike ridiculous theater, AIDS activist videos cannot sabotage all emotional effects. Ultimately we die, and the US government does nothing. The situation is obscene. It's ridiculous. The effect provokes laughter—the kind of laughter that forces tears and hurts the stomach, laughter filled with rage. For Ludlam, "What was funny was evident: the ridiculous obscenity of the human race."[14]

Evolution is a conscious process.

Throughout the development of this article I have felt I am writing polemically against death, a ridiculous endeavor. But a reasonable expectation can be derived from this preposterous refusal to accept death: I refuse to accept the death of certain ideas and certain practices. The recent deaths of such great artists as Ludlam, Jack Smith, and Ethyl Eichelberger pose a challenge to all of us who accepted the death of the author as a condition of cultural criticism. Ludlam's work was the product of a particular culture—gay culture, which is, in turn, the cumulative result of work done by and for a particular group of people, gay people—at a particular time in a particular place. His work is not lost with his death. Rather, the contributions of a figure like Ludlam can be measured by the different manifestations of his ideas in culture over time. The ridiculous is a tendency within queer structures of feeling, and its resonances are perceptible in the most recent emergence of queer art in all forms. And the ridiculous will continue to appear in different forms, despite the many deaths of those who have struggled to keep a queer culture of dissent alive.

Notes

1. Gertrude Stein, "Composition as Explanation," in Carl Van Vechten, ed., *Selected Writings* (New York: Random House, 1962) p. 516.

2. Michael Feingold, "The Great Continuum," *Village Voice* (June 9, 1987) p. 88.

3. Andrew Holleran, "New York Notebook: Tragic Drag," *Christopher Street*, no. 113 (July 1987) p. 12.

4. Guy Trebay, "The Gift of Excess," *Village Voice* (June 9, 1987) p. 98.

5. I would like to thank Peter Bowen, Jeff Nunokawa, Michael Perelman, and Daniel Wolfe for discussing this fantasy with me and for helping me to understand it.

6. Raymond Williams, *Marxism and Literature* (Oxford/New York: Oxford University Press, 1977) p. 135.

7. Richard Elovich tells me that he saw this statement on a poster advertising a Ridiculous production in the seventies.

8. Stefan Brecht, *Queer Theater* (London/New York: Methuen, 1978) p. 48.

9. Ibid., p. 38.

10. Ibid., p. 54.

11. Ibid., p. 44.

12. Ibid., p. 48.

13. Ibid., p. 83.

14. Ibid., p. 83.

Making the Most of Your Backyard: The Story of an Ideal Beauty

KAYCYILA BROOKE

Many a maid holds dreams to be deceptive.
All wonderful; but without bearing in the world we know.
Other women, I have known say dreams can prophesy
The good the bad, the things that come.
Else it is said,
What we have is here and now and it be the truth to know.
The rest is but an opiate to keep things as they are in this world of woe.
Then what are dreams?
Some say that dreams our darkest truths unfold.
Others say the dreamer in a tale
Is oft the mark of a story badly told.
An easy ploy without finesse or subtlety.,
A childish game to lead the reader to another reality.
But I fear this is a story I must tell,
(As roughly hewn as it may be),
For it is the dream that makes this scenery
No other design for rendering its nature has arisen.

'Twas spring and balmy in this southern clime
And I like any woman like me,
Grew tired one night after the sun had set.
Although my weary eyes would droop,
The television kept projecting Ted Turner's stable
Of girls who loose their glasses
Whilst gaining wedding rings and lots of other things.
Matrimony seems a poor exchange for vision lost...
But even so, the transformation of these lovelorn lasses to loved ones,
(The sentiment of realizing the dream they didn't know they dreamt of),
Was making my face all moist and dewy.

As the music swelled and
I heard my lover calling me to her side,
I drifted off into a reverie so strange and twisted
That I know not what to make of it.

Making the most of your back yard
The story behind an ideal beauty

II. The viewer comes to a garden.

Panel (top): THIS WAS A PLACE OF INCOMPARABLE SYMMETRY. THE DESIGNS OF THE WALKWAYS WERE SO WELL DEFINED. I MARVELED AT HOW NEATLY THE GRASS LEFT OFF AND THE PATH BEGAN. "THE EDGES" MY LOVE ONCE TOLD ME "ARE IMPORTANT TO ALIGN." SHE TOLD ME THAT TO MAKE OUR VIEWPOINT CLEAR THE HORIZONS SHOULD NOT TWIST AND FLEX BUT BE FOUND TWO THIRDS FROM THE BOTTOM OF THE PICTURE PLANE.

III. The viewer spies the "Rose"

Speech bubble (1): WE WATER. IT GROWS. I MOW. I EDGE. IT GROWS. WE WATER.

Panel (3): I REALIZED THAT ONE BLOOMED MORE VITALLY THAN THE REST. METHOUGHTS HER BEAUTY THE GREATEST SEEN. WAIT, THIS WAS NO ROSE WITHIN THE GARDEN WALL. LET'S LEAVE ALLEGORY TO IT'S OWN TIME. IT WAS A MAIDEN THAT I SPIED.

Speech bubble (2): "ONE THIRD FROM THE TOP?" I ASKED, AS I WAS TRYING TO GET IT STRAIGHT. "EITHER OR", SHE SAID, IN THIS THERE WAS GREAT FLEXIBILITY. IT SEEMED THAT FROM WHERE I STOOD I WAS THE CENTER OF THE UNIVERSE. ALL NATURE LAID OUT PERFECTLY BEFORE ME. WHILST I WANDERED IN MY PHILOSOPHIZING ABOUT ART AND BEAUTY, MY EYE RETURNED TO ANOTHER SOMETHING NOT YET SAID. THERE WERE ROSES IN THIS GARDEN AND THE PROMISE OF SUCH LOVELINESS, BADE ME LOOK A LITTLE CLOSER.

Panel (4): AND 'TWAS THIS BEAUTY AN INVESTIGATION DID INSPIRE. SHE SEEMED OF ME QUITE UNAWARE. I DECIDED TO APPROACH SURREPTITIOUSLY. TO SEE AND SEE SOME MORE MY PLEASURE WAS. I SAW NO CHARM IN BEING SEEN.

Speech bubble: ALL THESE ORDERED HARMONIES ARE BORING ME. YOU TAKE THINGS FROM OTHER RACES AND PLANT THEM IN A FOREIGN SOIL AND WHEN YOUR MASTER PLAN HAS QUIETED THE THREAT OF INSURRECTION THEIR CULTURE BECOMES FASHION. EACH ONE IN ITS SEPARATE BED MAKES YOUR BACKYARD A TIDY PLACE.

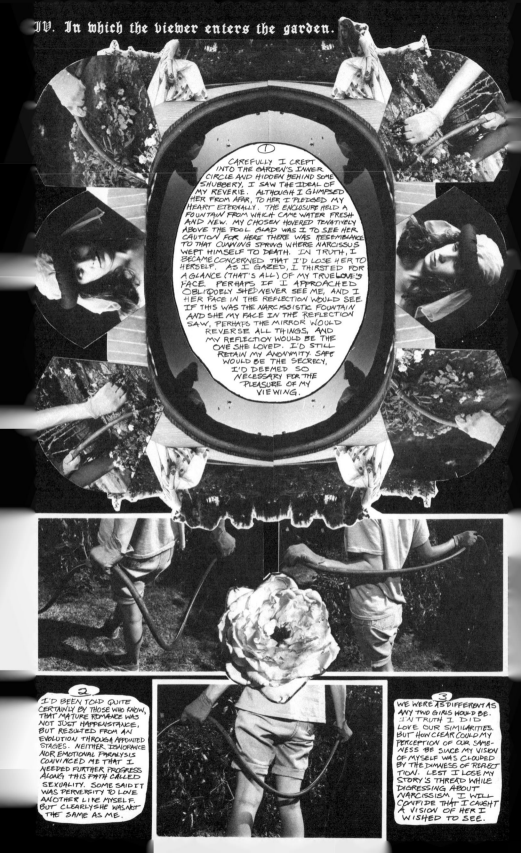

①

CAREFULLY I CREPT INTO THE GARDEN'S INNER CIRCLE AND HIDDEN BEHIND SOME SHUBBERY, I SAW THE IDEAL OF MY REVERIE. ALTHOUGH I GLIMPSED HER FROM AFAR, TO HER I PLEDGED MY HEART ETERNALLY. THE ENCLOSURE HELD A FOUNTAIN FROM WHICH CAME WATER FRESH AND NEW. MY CHOSEN HOVERED TENATIVELY ABOVE THE POOL GLAD WAS I TO SEE HER CAUTION FOR HERE THERE WAS RESEMBLANCE TO THAT CURVING SPRING WHERE NARCISSUS WEPT HIMSELF TO DEATH. IN TRUTH, I BECAME CONCERNED THAT I'D LOSE HER TO HERSELF. AS I GAZED, I THIRSTED FOR A GLANCE (THAT'S ALL) OF MY TRUE LOVE'S FACE. PERHAPS IF I APPROACHED OBLIQUELY SHE'D NEVER SEE ME, AND I HER FACE IN THE REFLECTION WOULD SEE. IF THIS WAS THE NARCISSISTIC FOUNTAIN AND SHE MY FACE IN THE REFLECTION SAW, PERHAPS THE MIRROR WOULD REVERSE ALL THINGS, AND MY REFLECTION WOULD BE THE ONE SHE LOVED. I'D STILL RETAIN MY ANONYMITY. SAFE WOULD BE THE SECRECY, I'D DEEMED SO NECESSARY FOR THE PLEASURE OF MY VIEWING.

②

I'D BEEN TOLD QUITE CERTAINLY BY THOSE WHO KNOW, THAT MATURE ROMANCE WAS NOT JUST HAPPENSTANCE, BUT RESULTED FROM AN EVOLUTION THROUGH APPOINTED STAGES. NEITHER IGNORANCE NOR EMOTIONAL PARALYSIS CONVINCED ME THAT I NEEDED FURTHER PROGRESS ALONG THIS PATH CALLED SEXUALITY. SOME SAID IT WAS PERVERSITY TO LOVE ANOTHER LIKE MYSELF. BUT CLEARLY SHE WASN'T THE SAME AS ME.

③

WE WERE AS DIFFERENT AS ANY TWO GIRLS WOULD BE. IN TRUTH I DID LOVE OUR SIMILARITIES. BUT HOW CLEAR COULD MY PERCEPTION OF OUR SAMENESS BE SINCE MY VISION OF MYSELF WAS CLOUDED BY THE DIMNESS OF REFLECTION. LEST I LOSE MY STORY'S THREAD WHILE DIGRESSING ABOUT NARCISSISM, I WILL CONFIDE THAT I CAUGHT A VISION OF HER I WISHED TO SEE.

1
I COULD SEE SHE REALIZED SHE WASN'T ALONE. I KNEW THAT MY INTRUSION ON HER PRIVACY EVIDENCED THE SELF CENTEREDNESS OF MY DESIRE. ALTHOUGH I WISHED HER TOTAL HAPPINESS I WAS HELPLESS AGAINST MY OWN ACQUISITIVENESS.

2
SHE WOULD HAVE DUG ME OUT AS IF I WERE A COMMON WEED. BUT LIKE A WEED MY ROOTS WERE DEEP AND 'NER WOULD I QUIT THIS FERTILE SOIL. MY LOVE FOR HER WOULD NEVER WAIN.

3
I REALIZED THIS AGITATION DISTURBED MY LOVE'S MEDITATION AND DECIDED TO RETREAT A BIT. BELIEVING THAT LOOKING WOULD MY PLEASURE BE I WATCHED IN AWE AS HER BEAUTY WAS REVEALED TO ME. IT SEEMED SHE WAS THE ONE DESCRIBED BY GILBERT OF HOYT, "THE BREASTS ARE MOST PLEASING WHEN THEY ARE OF MODERATE SIZE AND EMINENCE." THOUGH I WAS SEDUCED BY THIS IDEAL OF BEAUTY, I BEGAN TO WONDER WHAT WOULD BECOME OF ME?

I LIKE TO SEE A WOMAN USING TOOLS!

4
MY BREASTS WERE DIFFERENT THAN THE PICTURE OF THE PLEASING SIZE. IF SHE WERE PERFECT AND I WERE NOT, WHAT WOULD BECOME OF US. IF SHE RETURNED MY GAZE AND FOUND ME LACKING? SOMETHING IN MY EXPERIENCE WAS NOT MATCHING WITH THE PLEASURE THEORIES. PERHAPS THIS ONE WAY IDOLATRY WAS NOT ALL IT WAS CRACKED UP TO BE.

WHO ARE YOU LOOKING AT? IF YOU DIG DOWN DEEP, YOU'LL FIND THAT NONE OF THIS HAS ANYTHING TO DO WITH ME. FOLLOWING AT THESE SAFE DISTANCES IS COWARDLY. YOU KNOW, YOU DON'T LOOK SO BAD YOUR SELF.

VIII. In which the viewer accepts the maiden's voice and shuts up already.

Birth of a Notion:

Towards Black Gay and Lesbian Imagery in Film and Video

MICHELLE PARKERSON

In mainstream media, gay men and lesbians of color are either woefully present or predictably absent. The litany of black gay and lesbian characters in Hollywood films and network television reads like its own form of blackface.

They range from the burly, black "bulldagger" as whorehouse madam in the 1933 film, *The Emperor Jones* (starring Paul Robeson) to the predatory lesbian vamp in Spike Lee's 1983 *She's Gotta Have It;* from Eddie Murphy's ultra-camp Miss Thing hairdresser on NBC's *Saturday Night Live* to the snap! queen duo on Fox TV's *In Living Color.*

These relentless stereotypes are part of a continuum of silence, mockery, and denial surrounding lesbians and gay men within our own African American community—a community that is, of course, one of the largest consumers of Hollywood and network entertainment. With no other screen alternatives, audiences believe this is who we are.

In reducing our lives and complexity to caricature, such program formulas, capitalizing on homophobia and racism, produce big profits for mainstream media. The constricted images of black gays and lesbians are the same appropriated to all non-whites in film and video: enemies, entertainment, or exotica.

Recently, a new generation of gay and lesbian filmmakers of color has begun to produce imagery countering this invisibility and social stigma. These filmmakers are using media to reverse decades of misrepresentation, replacing negative myths with whole and humane depictions. The films and videos currently being produced *by* black gays and lesbians *about* black gays and lesbians—this birth of a notion—represent the opening of a dialogue, overdue and unflinching. From the United Kingdom, witness Isaac Julien's lush cinematic meditation *Looking for Langston,* and here in the US, Marlon Riggs's *Tongues Untied.* Both feature the incisive poetry of Essex Hemphill and the music of Blackberri. These groundbreaking, black, gay directors expand the discourse on race and homoerotic desire in their current works:

Julien's ebullient *Young Soul Rebels* and Riggs's video shorts, *Affirmations* and *Anthem.*

Among younger generations of black gay men and lesbians, the films and videos of Dawn Suggs, Thomas Harris, Sylvia Rhue, Cheryl Dunye, Jacqueline Woodson, Jack Waters, Aarin Burch, Jocelyn Taylor, and Yvonne Welbon are emerging. Their works challenge the boundaries of experimental, autobiographical, and documentary genres. They offer innovative production styles in presenting visions of being "in the life." These productions are also changing the complexion of AIDS media—exploring the devastation and celebrating the courage of a community disproportionately ravaged by the epidemic. These film and videomakers are the first wave of a developing black gay and lesbian film movement. Now a legacy begins. . . .

Several other films by white producers and directors have investigated black gay life—from Shirley Clarke's 1967 experimental study of a black hustler, *Portrait of Jason,* to the Greta Schiller and Andrea Weiss documentary, *Tiny and Ruby: Hell-Divin' Women.* This 1987 film highlights the lesbian flamboyance of Tiny Davis, former trumpeter extraordinaire for the International Sweethearts of Rhythm jazz band and is narrated by African American lesbian poet Cheryl Clarke. More recently, Jennie Livingston's remarkable, controversial, 1990 documentary, *Paris Is Burning,* explores the world of vogueing balls created by young black and Latino street queens in New York City.

As the body of black gay and lesbian films expands, a wellspring of critical analysis and theoretical study has concurrently evolved—validating this birth of a notion. Scholars in lesbian/gay studies, film theorists, and cultural activists have proclaimed, in articles and new publications, the significance of this first wave of black gay and lesbian media (particularly the works of Riggs and Julien) in illuminating the transgressive territory of identity and gay representation. Many of these critics are themselves black gay men and lesbians. In the UK are filmmaker Pratibha Parmar and critics Kobena Mercer and Stuart Hall. In the US the writings of Marlon Riggs, Thomas Harris, Essex Hemphill, and bell hooks (who is not gay) have been influential and provocative.

Indicative of the growing visibility and accessibility of gay film, a recent media conference in New York was solely dedicated to investigating the concept of queer aesthetics unique to lesbian and gay imagery. The most compelling and contentious moments of that 1989 "How Do I Look?" conference were stimulated by discussions of race and representation in the works of Isaac Julien and other black gay artists, as well as white gay artists— such as Robert Mapplethorpe—who were perceived as commodifying black male sexuality.

In tandem with increased production has been an upsurge in the marketing of black gay and lesbian films and videos. Among those distributors who have been particularly responsive to the influx of work by African American lesbians and gays are Women Make Movies (the largest distributor of feminist media with a longstanding focus on lesbian issues), Third World Newsreel (targeting the new wave of films and videos by gays and lesbians of color), and Frameline (a lesbian and gay arts organization which supports the distribution and exhibition of films and videos).

In the 1980s and early nineties, Hollywood negotiated easy heterosexist niches for homosexuality on the silver screen, allowing for the commercial success and mainstream acceptance of films such as *Personal Best* (1982), *Desert Hearts* (1985), and *Longtime Companion* (1990). These were palatable categorizations reducing gay experience to lifestyle comedies, sexual preference soaps, and AIDS dramas.

Then, at the top of nineties came three films which complicated the issue of homosexuality with affirmations of blackness and differences of race politics. These films imposed diversity upon the lily-white, largely male stereotype of gay experience.

The censorship surrounding the controversial PBS broadcast of *Tongues Untied* brought to public attention the realities and intersection of race and sexuality. *Looking for Langston,* flagrantly breaking the complicity of silence surrounding the homosexuality of black poet-icon Langston Hughes, swiftly drew condemnation from many in the straight black community, and a lawsuit from the Hughes estate. *Paris Is Burning* emerged from subculture success on the gay and lesbian film festival circuit to become the US box-office surprise of 1990. All three programs garnered critical acclaim, awards, and enthusiastic international audiences. They catalyzed national debates about freedom of expression and brought to many their first awareness of a black gay community.

But where in the current flurry of black gay male visibility on screen are the black lesbian movies—our own "evidence of being"? The question that remains for us, as we turn the century, is not so much "How Do I Look?" but "Where Am I?" Lack of viable economic support, limited exhibition and distribution, and, indeed, a real and pervasive racist/sexist bias within our own gay and lesbian community all contribute to the marginalization of black lesbian productions.

Yet the short films and videos of Cheryl Dunye, Dawn Suggs, and Aarin Burch, among others (including my own 1987 film *Stormé: The Lady of the Jewel Box*), have reached the screen in the face of tremendous odds, against a rising reentrenchment of censorship. These black lesbian film and videomakers embody the cinematic tenet of persistence of vision.

The Audre Lorde Film Project, now nearing completion, is hopefully the seed of a trend toward full-length documentary and dramatic productions concerning black lesbian life and history. This documentary feature will engage the work and perspectives of the late African American feminist poet Audre Lorde, and the context of her life as a lesbian of color in America. Using Lorde's words and images as its core, the film is referenced with scenes of her literary and political activities, and commentary by her family members, contemporaries, students, and others affected by the emergence of an international, lesbian, feminist agenda among women of color.

The recent phenomenon of progressive black gay and lesbian imagery will not continue without growing numbers of openly gay and lesbian African American filmmakers committed to producing works that address ethnicity and sexuality as equally critical identities. Black gay and lesbian filmmakers face sexism and homophobia within the black independent cinema movement, as well as racism in the feminist film community and the whitewash pervasive in gay and lesbian media. Historically, we have been locked out of the Hollywood and television industries. But such challenges inspire me to make the movies that *Desert Hearts* and *She Must Be Seeing Things* are *not:* films that are lesbian-specific, but just as importantly, race-conscious.

As black filmmakers, how can we broaden gay and lesbian experience and imagery beyond "the celluloid closet"? How will we construct an ethnocentric, diverse nation of lovers? How will we undertake this birth of a notion?

Perhaps, twenty-four frames at a time.

Dark and Lovely Too: Black Gay Men in Independent Film

KOBENA MERCER

We are in the midst of a wildly creative upsurge in black queer cultural politics. Through political activism and new forms of cultural practice, we have created a community that has inspired a new sense of collective identity among lesbians and gay men across the black diaspora.

The recent work in film and video by Isaac Julien and Marlon Riggs emerges from and contributes to the movement and direction of these new developments. I will begin by framing Riggs's *Tongues Untied* and Julien's *Looking for Langston* in the specific context of black lesbian and gay cultural politics, in order to open up a discussion on questions of difference and identity in the general context of contemporary struggles around race, gender, and sexuality. In this sense, what is important about black lesbian and gay cultural politics is not simply that we have created a new sense of community among ourselves—although the importance of that cannot be emphasized enough—but that our struggles make it possible to arrive at a new perspective on political identity and imagined community at large.

To invoke a couple of well-worn metaphors, we have been involved in a process of "making ourselves visible" and "finding a voice." Through activism and political organization, from large-scale international conferences to small-scale consciousness-raising groups, black lesbians and gay men have come out of the margins into the center of political visibility. One need only point to the numerous service organizations created in response to the AIDS crisis—or more specifically the crisis of indifference and neglect in the official public health policies of countries such as Britain and the United States—to recognize that our lives are at the center of contemporary politics. Such activity has created a base for collective empowerment. If I think about my own involvement in a small collective of gay men of African, Asian, and Caribbean descent which formed in London in the early eighties, what was so empowering was precisely the feeling of belonging which arose out of the transformation from "I" to "we."

It was through the process of coming together—communifying, as it were, that we transformed experiences previously lived as individual, privatized, and even pathologized problems into the basis for a sense of collective agency. This sense of agency enabled us to formulate an agenda around our experiences of racism in the white gay community and issues of homophobia in black communities. I think I can generalize here to the extent that the agenda of black lesbian and gay struggles over the past decade has been shaped and defined by this duality, by the necessity of working on at least two fronts at all times, and by the difficulty of constantly negotiating our relationship to the different communities to which we equally belong.

For this reason, rather than conceptualize our politics in terms of "double" or "triple" oppression, it should be seen as a hybridized form of political and cultural practice. By this I mean that precisely because of our lived experiences of discrimination in and exclusion from the white gay and lesbian community, and of discrimination in and exclusions from the black community, we locate ourselves in the spaces *between* different communities—at the intersections of power relations determined by race, class, gender, and sexuality. What follows from this is a recognition of the interdependence of different political communities, not completely closed off from each other or each hermetically sealed like a segregated bantustan but interlocking in contradictory relations over which we struggle. If you agree with this view, then it has important implications for the way we conceptualize the politics of identity.

We habitually think of identity in mutually exclusive terms, based on the either/or logic of binary oppositions. As black lesbians and gay men we are often asked, and sometimes ask ourselves: Which is more important to my identity, my blackness or my sexuality? Once the question of identity is reduced to this either/or dichotomy, we can see how ridiculous and unhelpful it is; as black lesbians and gay men we cannot separate the different aspects of our identities precisely because we value both our blackness and our homosexuality. It is this contrast between both/and against either/or that is at stake in the problem of "identity politics"—in the pejorative sense of the term.

We are all familiar with the right-on rhetoric of "race, class, and gender," so often repeated like a mantra to signify one's acknowledgment of the diversity of social identities at play in contemporary politics. What is wrong with the "race, class, gender" mantra is that it encourages the reductive notion that there is a hierarchy of oppressions and thus a hierarchy of "doubly" or "triply" oppressed identities. What often occurs when different communities try to come together is a tendency to use our differences as a means of competition and closure in order to assert who is more oppressed than whom. In this way, difference becomes the basis of divisiveness, encouraging group closure in the competition for resources, rather than the recognition of the interdependence of our various communities. This is because identity is assumed to be an essential category, fixed once and for all by the community to which one belongs—a view which ignores the fact that we very rarely ever belong exclusively to one homogeneous and monolithic community and that, for most of us, everyday life is a matter of passing through, travelling between, and negotiating a plurality of different spaces. Black lesbians and gay men are not exempt from the worst aspects of such categorical identity politics. But precisely because of our hybrid legacy, drawing on the best aspects of our dual inheritance from both black struggles and lesbian and gay struggles of the sixties and seventies, we might arrive at a better appreciation of the politics of identity which begins with the recognition of difference and diversity.

Let me put it like this: the literary work of writers such as Audre Lorde, Joseph Beam, Essex Hemphill, Cheryl Clarke, and Assoto Saint—to name only a few—has been absolutely essential to the process of finding a voice and creating community. Through their stories we have transformed ourselves from objects of oppression into subjects and agents busy making history in our own right. Such narratives have been indispensible to the formation of our identity. As Stuart Hall has put it, "Identities are the names we give to the different ways we are positioned by, and position ourselves within, the narratives of the past."[1] But what we find in their work is not the expression of one singular, uniform, homogeneous, black lesbian or gay male identity that is at all times identical to itself. Rather we find stories that narrate our differences and the multiplicity of experiences lived by black lesbians and gay men. We find that black lesbians and gay men do not all speak in one voice. To me, this suggests the recognition of the possibility of unity-in-diversity, and implies a skeptical disposition towards categorical identity politics. Such work suggests that we give up the search for a purified ideal type or a positive role model of political correctness, because it teaches us to value our own multiple differences as the very stuff of which our queer diasporic identities are made.

Insofar as these issues inform the interventions that Isaac Julien and Marlon Riggs have made in independent film, it is important to situate their work in relation to the question of identity. Namely, that identities are not found in nature but historically constructed in culture—or to put it another way, *identity is not what you are so much as what you do.* Black queer cultural politics has not expressed an essential identity that was always already there waiting to be discovered, but has actively invented a multitude of identities through a variety of activities and practices, whether organizing workshops and fund-raising parties, lobbying and mobilizing around official policies, writing poems, publishing magazines, taking photographs, or making films.

Finding a Voice: Independent Cinema and Black Representation

Tongues Untied and *Looking for Langston* share a number of similarities: both are the "first" black independent productions to openly address black homosexuality, because prior to now such issues have been avoided or omitted from black independent cinema; both tell our stories of the experience of dual exclusion, being silenced and being hidden from history. And, taking all this into account, both have won similarly enthusiastic responses from various audiences around the world, and have received numerous awards and prizes.

At the same time, these two works could not be more different in style and approach. Whereas *Tongues* foregrounds autobiographical voices that speak from the lived experiences of black gay men in the here and now, and emphasizes the immediacy, direct address, and in-your-face realism associated with video, *Langston* speaks to black gay experience by tracking the enigmatic sexual identity of one of the most cherished icons of black cultural history, Langston Hughes, whose presence is evoked through music, poetry, and archival film to create a dreamlike space of poetic reverie, historically framed by images of the Harlem Renaissance of the 1920s. To put it crudely, the contrast in aesthetic strategies turns on the difference between a video which embodies the values of documentary realism and a film which self-consciously places itself in the art cinema tradition.

Rather than play one off against the other, I want to use these differences to underline my point about the plurality and diversity of identities among black gay men. From this perspective we can recognize the way in which both Julien and Riggs participate in a similar cultural and political project that concerns the struggle to find a voice in the language of cinema, which, up to now, has treated the black gay subject as merely an absence, or present only as an object of someone else's imagination. In this sense, Julien and Riggs deepen and extend the critical project of black independent cinema: to find a place from which to speak as a black subject in a discourse which has either erased and omitted the black subject, or represented the black subject only through the mechanism of the stereotype, fixed and frozen as an object of someone else's fears and fantasies. However, between them, the two works also challenge and disrupt certain assumptions within black independent cinema itself, and in this way their strategies bring to light an important paradox about race and representation which parallels the problem of identity in political discourse.

Both Julien and Riggs are independent practitioners, which is to say that the conditions of production in which they work are distinct from the conditions that obtain in the commercial film industry, in which production, distribution, and exhibition are monopolized by private corporations, mostly centered in Hollywood. Yet, as James Snead has pointed out, the term independent is something of a misnomer, since such practitioners are highly dependent on the role of public sector institutions, not only in the funding of production, but in terms of the subsequent distribution and exhibition of films regarded as "noncommercial."[2]

Indeed, public funding is a key condition enabling both works. *Tongues* was financed by a range of grants from various foundations and institutions, including a Western States Regional Fellowship from the National Endowment for the Arts, and *Langston* was funded principally by the British Film Institute and Channel Four Television, both of which have an official mandate and responsibility to support work from and about social constituencies underrepresented in film and television.

Although such public sector institutions have shaped, influenced, and sometimes curtailed the renewal of black independent film in the 1980s, there are salient national differences in the conditions of independent practice. Whereas Julien's film is a Sankofa production and emerges from a context in which collective methods have flourished in the British workshop sector, which includes Black Audio Film Collective, Ceddo, Retake, and other groups, mostly in London,[3] Riggs directs his own independent production company, based in Oakland and works on an individual basis, as do most black practitioners in the United States—from Julie Dash and Haile Gerima to Charles Burnett and Michelle Parkerson—where the independent sector is more dispersed.

It is significant, however, that, at the point of exhibition, both *Tongues* and *Langston* have been shown twice on public television, on PBS in the United States and on Channel Four in Britain. This is significant, not simply in making the works accessible to a broader range of audiences, but in terms of the responsibility of public television—as opposed to commercial cinema—to represent the underrepresented. This can be seen as the locus of a particular problem in the politics of representation that all minority practitioners encounter, namely, that representation does not simply denote a practice of depiction but also has the connotation of a practice of delegation, in which the minority practitioner is often positioned in the role of a representative who speaks for the entire constituency from which he or she comes. Elsewhere, I have discussed this problematic as the "burden of representation" which black artists and filmmakers have had to negotiate once they gain access to the apparatus of representation.[4]

In a situation where the right to representation is rationed and regulated, so that minorities experience restricted access to the means of representation, there is often an assumption on the part of funding institutions and an expectation on the part of audiences that they should "speak for" their particular community. This is felt and lived as a real dilemma for artists and practitioners themselves, as Martina Attille, formerly of the Sankofa Collective, put it in relation to the making of *The Passion of Rememberance* in 1986:

> There was this sense of urgency to say it all, or at least to signal as much as we could in one film. Sometimes we can't afford to hold anything back for another time, another conversation or another film. That is the reality of our experience—sometimes we only get the one chance to make ourselves heard.[5]

What has emerged in the "new wave" of black independent film during the eighties, particularly in the British context, is the awareness of the impossibility of carrying this burden without being crushed by it. It is impossible for any one individual to speak as a representative for an entire community without risking the violent reductionism which repeats the stereotypical view within the majority culture that minority communities are homogeneous, unitary, and monolithic because their members are all the same. It is impossible for any one black person to claim the right to speak for the diversity of identities and experiences within black society without the risk that such diversity will be simplified and reduced to what is seen as typical, a process which thereby reproduces and replicates the logic of the racist stereotype that all black people are, essentially, the same.

Julien and Riggs both recognize these pitfalls in racial representation, and what is remarkable is that through entirely different aesthetic strategies they enact a film practice which refuses to carry the burden of representation, instead opening it up to displace the assumptions and expectations contained within it. To examine how they do this I want to focus first on the articulation of multiple voices in *Tongues Untied* and then turn to the gaze and looking relations as articulated in *Looking for Langston*.

Dialogic Voicing in Documentary Realism

One of the adjectives most frequently invoked in response to *Tongues Untied,* especially among black gay men, is "real": we value the film for its "realness." A cursory historical overview of black independent cinema would reveal the prevalence of a certain realist aesthetic, which must be understood as one of the privileged modes through which black filmmakers have sought to contest those versions of reality inscribed in the racist discourses of the dominant film culture. As a counterdiscourse, the imperative of such a realist aesthetic in black film, whether documentary or drama, is to "tell it like it is." What is at issue in the oppositional or critical role of black independent cinema is the ability to articulate a counterdiscourse based on an alternative version of reality inscribed in the voices and viewpoints of black social actors.

Tongues is congruent with the tradition of documentary realism in black film culture, as it foregrounds a range of autobiographical voices that dramatize the power of witness and testimony. Through the authority of their own experiences, black gay men come to voice as primary definers of reality. As Riggs has said in a recent interview:

> We live in a society in which truth is often defined by your reflection on the screen. . . . But you don't really live and you're not really somebody until you're somehow reflected there on the tube or in the theatre. . . . What films like *Tongues Untied* do, especially for people who have had no images of themselves out there to see, is give them a visible and visual representation of their lives.[6]

In this sense, the "realness" of the work concerns the desires and expectations of a black gay audience who decode it. But in terms of the aesthetic strategy in which it is encoded, such "realness" is an effect of the consistent use of direct address, whereby in place of the anonymous, impersonal, third-person narrator which tends to characterize the documentary genre,

Tongues Untied, Marlon Riggs

individuals tell their stories directly to the camera, creating the space for an interpersonal dialogue that is simultaneously confessional, affirmative, and confrontational. Its "realness" consists not simply of the accuracy or veracity of its depiction of the experiences of African American gay men—through poetry, rap, drama, dance, and music—but through this dialogic mode of address which brings the spectator into a direct relationship with the stories and experiences that find their voices.

Of the four cinematic values associated with documentary realism—transparency, immediacy, authority, and authenticity—*Tongues* seems to emphasize the latter through Riggs's presence, as he tells his life story, which serves as a thread connecting the multiple components of the video: from the poems performed by Essex Hemphill, Steve Langley, and Allan Miller, and the scenes in which the homophobic voices of a black preacher, an activist, and various black entertainers conspire to silence, ridicule, and intimidate, to the eroticism of a tender embrace between two lovers, and scenes showing rallies and Gay Pride marches. The emphasis on authenticity, honesty, and truth-to-experience through personal disclosure is underlined by Riggs's visual presence at the beginning, where he appears nude: a gesture of exposure not only suggesting the vulnerability of revealing one's own life through one's story but also establishing the framework of personal disclosure that guides the work as a whole.

It is precisely the achievement of *Tongues Untied* that its realism foregrounds such authenticity without recourse to the master codes of the documentary genre, in which the function of the impersonal voice-of-God narrator seeks to resolve all questions raised, tie up all loose ends, and explain everything as the narrative inexorably moves towards the movement of closure. *Tongues* displaces this function entirely: there is no unifying voice-over, nor indeed any single voice privileged in a position of mastery, explanation, or resolution. In terms of his own presence, Riggs does not speak as a representative whose individual story is supposed to speak for every black gay man; rather, he speaks as one voice among others, each of which articulates different experiences and identities. He does not seek to typify some unitary and homogeneous essence called "the black, gay, male experience" by presenting his story as the only story or the whole story; rather, he speaks from the specificity of his own experience, which, because of the presence of other voices and stories, is not generalized or typified as such.

This kind of dialogic voicing assumes crucial importance for a number of reasons. First, by contrast, it highlights the degree to which black independent cinema has often inadvertently replicated the problem of exclusion by reproducing the monologic voicing of the master codes of documentary realism, in order to authorize its own counternarratives. Furthermore, because he does not privilege any one voice as the source of authority, Riggs highlights the degree to which those voices in black cinema that claim implicitly to be representative, and to speak for the entire black race, very often tend to be only the voices of black men, whose heroic and heterosexist accents often exclude the voices of black women and black gay men. In this sense, *Tongues* can be said to challenge the heterosexual presumption that so often characterizes the documentary realist aesthetic in black cinema.

To contextualize this issue, one might point to the dual role of Spike Lee as director and narrative character in *Do the Right Thing,* where he is positioned, along with the other main young black male protagonists, as the embodiment of the Bedford-Stuyvesant community itself, pitched into antagonism with white society across the battle lines of race and ethnicity. By making the implicit claim to speak for the condition of young black men in the urban US (in terms of both the narrative structure and the marketing of the film), Lee seems to replicate the all-too-familiar stereotype of the "angry black man" consumed with rage about the politics of race and racism on the streets, to the exclusion of any other politics, such as his sexual politics between the sheets.

The second reason why the dialogic voicing of *Tongues* is important has to do with its awareness of the multidimensional character of the political. In this sense its "realness" has to do with the acknowledgment that real life is contradictory—"home is a place of truth, not peace," as Riggs comments at one point. In the autobiographical sequence, as he narrates his first kiss and being bussed to a nearly all-white school in the South, Riggs's narrative presence is framed by the concatenation of abusive epithets—"punk," "motherfuckin' coon," "homo," "nigger go home"—spat out at rhythmic intervals that underline the interplay of racism and homophobia, experienced at one and the same time. It is this awareness of a dialectic in the politics of race and sexuality that is maintained throughout the work by virtue of its dialogic strategy. *Tongues* does not seek to reduce, simplify, or resolve the lived experience of real antagonism but is constantly vigilant to the complex effects of contradiction—particularly as these enter into the interior space of our own relations with each other, our intimacy, and our aversion.

If the work refuses facile notions of "internalized oppression," it equally rejects the reductive tendency of the current discourse of endangered species in which black men are seen as victims and nothing but victims. Such questions concerning the contradictions through which black masculinity is lived are forcefully raised, but rather than provide the false security of easy answers, the strategy of direct address brings the viewer and audience into the dialogue as active participants who share an equal responsibility in the search for answers. By invoking a certain answerability on the part of the audience, what the film gives is not a neat resolution to the contradictions of the real, but a range of questions for the audience to take home.

If all this sounds terribly earnest, I should emphasize that the irreverent humor of *Tongues Untied* is absolutely crucial to the subversive force of its dialogic strategy. More to the point, the element of playfulness and parody, like the aesthetics of dialogic voicing, is thoroughly embedded in the oral tradition of African American cultural expression. As the Lavender Light quartet pleads in the tape, "Hey, boy, can you come out tonight?" *Tongues* shows that its tongue is firmly in cheek in this appropriation of black pop acappella from the doo-wop tradition of the fifties. Like the freaky-deke ritual on the killing floor of the dance halls of the thirties, the Oaktown ensemble engaged in the electric slide and the beautifully stylized boys caught vogueing in New York City underline the affirmative role of black expressive culture—and the contributions black gays have made to the renewal of its expressive edge. As elements of black queer subcultural ritual, such dance forms enact a performative body politics, in which the black body is a site both of misery, oppression, and exploitation, as well as of resistance, transcendence, and ecstacy.

Moreover, considering the dialectic of appropriation as a constitutive feature of diasporan culture—in the case of vogueing, for instance, how black gays appropriate the poses of white female models in glossy fashion magazines to create a stylized dance form, are then appropriated in turn by white performers such as Malcolm McLaren and Madonna—*Tongues Untied* performs a doubly critical role in its affirmation of black gay pleasures. On the one hand, by reinserting black gay subcultural style into the expressive context of the African American cultural tradition as a whole, it refutes the premise that gayness is a "white thing." On the other, by recontextualizing such styles in the lived experience of black gay men, it brings to light the extent to which our pleasures may be misappropriated by white audiences, who are nevertheless fascinated and perhaps even, in some sense, envious of them. Let's face it, who wouldn't want to be a member of the Institute of Snap!thology? "Don't mess with a snap diva!" If you want the politically correct party line, please stay at home and dial 1-900-Race-Class-Gender instead.

Looking Relations: Allegories of Identity and Desire

In turning to Isaac Julien's *Looking for Langston*, I want to develop the theme of appropriation as a figure in diaspora culture. This is important, not simply because of the stylish way in which he film appropriates art cinema conventions, but more fundamentally because it is impossible to understand the formation of black British identities, gay or otherwise, without a recognition of the way in which different signs have been appropriated and rearticulated to construct new forms of political identity and imagined community in this specific context.

Here I would emphasize "imagined" in Benedict Anderson's term "imagined community,"[7] because without the notion of a collective historical imagination, how could we understand why a black British filmmaker whose parents migrated to London from St. Lucia would chose to make a film about a black American writer from Kansas City?

If one thinks about the naming of the black subject in postwar Britain, it becomes necessary to reiterate the theoretical view that subjectivity is indeed socially constructed in language. What we see are not simply different names used to designate the same community but the historical becoming of such a political community in and through a struggle over the signifiers of racial discourse. The displacement of the proper name—from "colored immigrants" in the 1950s, to "ethnic minorities" in the sixties, and to "black communities" in the seventies and eighties—vividly underlines the point that social identities are not just there in nature but are actively constructed in culture. Of course, this did not just happen in the realm of language alone, since a whole range of nondiscursive practices have constituted Black Britain as a domain of social and political antagonism. Nevertheless, it is crucial to acknowledge the material effects of symbolic and imaginary relations.

For over four hundred years in Western culture, the sign /black/ had nothing but negative connotations, to say the least. However, we have also seen that the signifying chain in which it was equated with negative values was not totally closed or fixed. In the US context during the 1960s, the term /black/ was disarticulated out of the negative chain of equivalence in racist discourse, and rearticulated into an alternative chain of equivalences as a sign of empowerment, indicated by the shift from Negro to Black. In Britain during the 1980s something similar happened, inspired and influenced by the black American example, as blackness was disarticulated out of one discursive system and rearticulated into another, where it became a sign of solidarity among Asian, African, and Caribbean peoples, and functioned as a term of a politically chosen identity rather than a genetically ascribed one. The cultural politics of the black diaspora thus highlights a deconstructive process in which the central signifiers of racist ideology, based on the binary opposition of white/not-white, were rearticulated to produce a new set of connotations in one and the same sign.

It is an awareness of the multi-accentual character of the sign that informs the critical project of black British workshops, such as Sankofa and Black Audio Film Collective. And this awareness is not merely the result of an engagement with difficult poststructuralist theories, but something achieved through a practice of trial and error and open-ended experimentation inscribed in their productions, such as *Territories* (1984) and *Handsworth*

Songs (1986). *Looking for Langston* continues the critique of racial representation signalled by those earlier works, but deepens and complicates it by
extending it into the domain of fantasy. I would argue that the film is not a
documentary search for the "truth" about Langston Hughes's ambiguous
sexual identity so much as an investigation into the psychic reality of fantasy
as that domain of subjectivity in which our desires and identifications are
shaped. The film is as much a meditation on the psychic reality of the political
unconscious—which concerns the imaginary and symbolic conduits of the
diaspora, through which black Britons have sought to symbolize our political
dreams and desires in part through identifications with black America and
black Americans—as it is a poetic meditation on the psychic and social
relations that circumscribe our lives as black gay men.

This double reading is suggested by the ambiguous sense of time and place
evoked by the montage of music, poetry, and archival imagery across the
film's monochrome texture and stylized art direction. Characters inhabit the
fictional milieu of a twenties speakeasy, where tuxedoed couples dance and
drink champagne, celebrating hedonistic pleasure in defiance of the hostile
world outside. It is this outside that intrudes at the end of the film when
thugs and police raid the club only to find that its denizens have disappeared,
while eighties house music plays on the soundtrack almost like a music video.
The multilayered texture evoked by the ambiguity of past and present,
outside and inside, fact and fantasy, thus allows more than one reading
about what the film is looking for. I want to focus on only two possibilities:
an archeology of black modernism and an allegory of black gay male desire.

Langston Hughes is remembered as the key poet of the Harlem Renaissance and has come to be revered as a father figure of black literature, yet
in the process of becoming such an icon, the complexity of his life and the
complexity of the Harlem Renaissance itself has been subject to selective
erasure and repression by the gatekeepers and custodians of "the colored
museum." Hughes is remembered as a populist, public figure, but the enigma
of his private life—his sexuality—is seen as something better left unaddressed
in most biographies, an implicit gesture of denial which buries and represses
the fact that the Harlem Renaissance was as gay as it was black, and that
many of its key figures—Claude McKay, Alain Locke, Countee Cullen,
Wallace Thurman, and Bruce Nugent—were known to be queer, one way
or another. *Looking for Langston* engages with and enters into this area of
enigma and ambiguity, not in order to arrive at an unequivocal answer
embodied in factual evidence, but to explore the ways in which various facets
of black cultural life are subject to psychic and social repression, from within
as well as without.

As an archeological inquiry, the film excavates what has been hidden from
history, not only the fluidity of sexual identities within the black cultural

Looking for Langston, Isaac Julien

expression of that period, but the intertwining of black culture and Euro-American modernism. Just as official histories of modernism tend to erase and selectively repress the work of black artists, official versions of the Harlem Renaissance narrative tend to avoid the sexual politics of the "jazz era." Yet the film suggests that it was precisely the imbrication of race and sexuality that underpinned the expressive and aesthetic values of the cultural practices of that time—from Picasso's *Demoiselles d'Avignon* to Josephine Baker, for instance. But *Looking for Langston* is not a history lesson: the point of archeology is not to research history for its own sake but to search for answers to contemporary dilemmas, in this case the need to historicize the hybrid domain of black British cultural production in the eighties and nineties.

The film looks for Langston, but what we find is Isaac. Not so much in an autobiographical sense, but in terms of a self-reflexive awareness of the multiple influences that inform his artistic choices and methods. The desire to unravel the hidden histories of the Harlem Renaissance serves as an emblem for an inventory of the diverse textual resources which have informed the renascence and renewal of black artistic and cultural practices in contemporary Britain. From this perspective, one might describe the film as a visual equivalent of a dialogue with the different cultural traditions from which Isaac Julien has invented his own artistic identity as a black gay auteur.

This view is suggested by the promiscuous intertextuality which the film sets in motion. Alongside visual quotations from Jean Cocteau, Kenneth Anger, and Jean Genet, the voices of James Baldwin, Bruce Nugent, Toni Morrison, and Amiri Baraka combine to emphasize the dialogic and hybridized character of the text. In this "stereophonic space," in Barthes's phrase, Julien acknowledges the importance of the Euro-American avant garde as much as the importance of black American literature as textual resources which black British artists have used in the process of finding their own voices. It is significant, therefore, that the film articulates theory and practice not in terms of didactic prescription but in terms of enacting an translation of cultural studies into cultural politics. This reflexive enactment of cultural theory is implicit in the role played by Stuart Hall in the film, who performs the voice-over narration, as his presence suggests that the intellectual practice associated with British cultural studies now informs Julien's filmic practice as a black gay auteur.

There is another aspect to this intertextuality that concerns what the film is looking for in the more literal sense. Its languid, dreamlike texture seduces the eye and its avowed homoeroticism solicits the gaze. Issues of voyeurism, fetishism, and scopophilic obsession arise across its sensual depiction of beautiful black male bodies. But the film does not simply indulge the pleasure in looking; it radically problematizes such pleasure by questioning the racial positions of the subject/object dichotomy associated with the dialectic of seeing and being seen.

Here the key motif is the direct look, whereby the black subject looks back (whether as auteur or character) and thus turns around the question of who has the right to look in order to ask the audience who or what *they* are looking for. This motif appeared in Julien's first film made with the Sankofa Collective, *Territories,* in the context of a confrontational, and somewhat didactic, inquiry into the objectification and fetishization of black culture as framed by the white gaze. In *Langston,* however, by virtue of the seductive and invitational direction of the textual strategy, he achieves a more penetrating insight into the structures of racial and sexual fantasy, precisely by setting a trap for the gaze and by the provocative incitement of our wish to look.

It is significant that the ghost of Robert Mapplethorpe is present in this staging of the look. This occurs not so much in the scene in which a white male character leisurely leafs through *The Black Book*—while Essex Hemphill reads one of his poems pinpointing the reinscription of racism in white gay culture—but in terms of a set of aesthetic conventions, such as fragmentation and chiaroscuro lighting, which the film employs to punctuate its incitement of our pleasure in looking. In this way, Julien's strategy of promiscuous intertextuality appropriates a range of visual tropes associated with white artists like Mapplethorpe to lay bare the way in which race determines the flow of power relations through the gaze in complex and ambivalent ways.

Hence, in one key scene an exchange of looks takes place between the actor who may be interpreted as "Langston" (Ben Ellison) and his mythic object of desire, a black man named "Beauty" (Matthew Baidoo). This provokes a hostile, competitive glare from Beauty's white male partner (John Wilson), who makes a grand gesture of drinking more champagne. As he turns away to face the bar, Langston drifts into a daydream. In this sequence, Bruce Nugent's poem "Lillies and Jade" is read, over images that portray the Langston character searching for his lost object of desire in a field of poppies. At the end of his reverie, Langston imagines himself coupled with Beauty, their bodies entwined on a bed as if they have just made love. It is important to recognize that this coupling takes place in fantasy, because it underlines the loss of access to the object of desire as being the very source of fantasy itself. Moreover, it shows how race enters into the vocabulary of desire: as the object of both the black and the white man's gaze, Beauty acts as the signifier of desire as his desirability is enhanced precisely by the eroticized rivalry between their two looks.

It is here that the trope of visual fetishism found in Mapplethorpe's photographs makes a striking and subversive return, in close-up sequences set in the nightclub, intercut with Langston's daydream. From Langston's point of view, the camera lovingly lingers on the sensuous mouth of the actor portraying Beauty, with the rest of his face cast in shadow, like an iris shot in the silent movies. But, as in Mapplethorpe's images, the strong emphasis on chiaroscuro lighting invests the fetishized fragment, or body part, with a compelling erotogenic residue. The "thick lips" of the Negro are hypervalorized as the iconic emblem of Beauty's impossible desirability. In other words, Julien takes the risk of replicating the racial stereotype of the thick-lipped negro precisely to reposition the black subject as the desiring subject, not the alienated object, of the look. Like the image of the two men entwined on the bed, which recalls the homoerotic photographs of George Platt Lynes, yet also critiques them, it is only by intervening in and against the logic of fetishization in racial representation that Julien is able to open up the ambivalence of the psychic and social relations—of identification, object-choice, envy, and exclusion—inscribed in the brief relay of looks between the three men. Of each of these, I would draw attention to envy— wanting the object possessed by the Other—not only because it informs the kind of scopic obsession that Mapplethorpe works upon, suggesting that the white subject sees blackness as an enviable quality, but because as Julien recodes it, turning the fetish inside out, he points to the way that intraracial relations among black men themselves also entail feelings of rivalry and envy at the very basis of our identifications with each other.

I have focussed on this particular moment because it strikes me that there are important formal similarities between Julien's strategy of working in and against the logic of racial fetishism and that of Nigerian-British gay photographer Rotimi Fani-Kayode, whose work is also inflected by a dialogic engagement with problems raised in Mapplethorpe. In contrast to the isolation effect in Mapplethorpe's work, whereby only one black male nude appears in the field of vision—a device that encourages a fantasy of mastery—in Kayode's work, such as *Technique of Ecstasy,* black men's bodies are coupled and contextualized to evoke an eroticism that seems to slip out of the implied power relations associated with the interracial subject/object dichotomy. Kayode creates an Afrocentric homoerotica precisely and perversely by appropriating conventions associated with the Eurocentric history of the fine art nude.

What Julien and Kayode share in common is not so much the fact that they are both black gay male artists, but that as artists they both use an intertextual strategy of appropriation and rearticulation in order to signify upon, and thus critique, the dominant regime of racial and sexual representation but without negating, denying, or disavowing the reality of the fantasies that give rise to such representations. Rather, by virtue of working in and against the master codes that regulate and govern the stereotypical, they begin to unravel what takes place at the borderlines between the psychic and the social, between fantasy and history.

In this brief discussion of *Looking for Langston* I have emphasized the formal dimension of its aesthetic strategy in order to draw attention to its enunciation of an allegory of desire, which is the source of its emotional resonance, not just for black gay men but for others in the audience as well. Although it is not the only available theory of desire, psychoanalysis suggests that desire is always about loss: our search for pleasure, the search for a significant other, is about the attempt to recover a state of fusion, wholeness, or nonseparation, which can never be fully retrieved. In so far as this lost object of desire can never really be found, the search for pleasure inevitably entails frustration, privation, and despair.

The achievement of *Looking for Langston* lies precisely in the way it shows how desire and despair run together, and thus how desire always entails rituals of mourning for what is lost and cannot be recovered. There is a sense of mourning, not just for Langston, buried in the past under the repressive weight of homophobic and ethnocentric narratives, but mourning for friends, lovers, and others lost to AIDS here and now, in the present. There is mourning, but not melancholia: as Langston himself says at the end of the film, "Why should I be blue? I've been blue all night through." Just like the multiple allusions of the term "blue," the textual strategy of the film as a whole creates an evocative "structure of feeling," in Raymond Williams's

The poster for *Looking for Lanston* appears in a scene in *Tongues Untied*

sense, that speaks not only to black gay men—although I can think of no other film which has laid bare our desire and despair in quite the way that it has—but to any desiring subject who has experienced the blues.

I want to conclude with a brief discussion of the issue of authorship, because the work of Marlon Riggs and Isaac Julien urges us to rethink questions of identity and agency that many thought were dead and buried with the poststructuralist argument concerning the "death of the author." That these are among the first cinematic texts authored by black gay men means that it really *does* matter who is speaking. We can all live without the return of Romantic notions of creative genius, which always placed the author at the center of the text—resembling the godlike figure of the "universal intellectual" who thought he had an answer for everything—but we need to revise the notion that the author is simply an empty, abstract function of cultural discourse through whom various ideologies speak.

The welcomed development of postmodernism that accompanied the collapse of the grand narratives and the decentering of universal Man was that it revealed that the subject who had monopolized the microphone in public culture—by claiming to speak for humanity as a whole, while denying that right of representation to anyone who was not white, not male, not middle-class, and not Western—was nothing but a minority himself. If postmodern-ism simply means that the era of modernism is past, then hurrah! The pluralization and diversification of public space, where a variety of subjects find their voice and assert their right to speak, has only just begun. As black gay artists, "specific intellectuals" who speak from the specificity of their experience, Riggs and Julien, like other black lesbian and gay artists, have actively contributed to the cultural and political terrain of postmodernism.

Precisely because their work is so important, we should do more than merely celebrate. Above all, we should be deeply skeptical of a certain assumption embedded in categorical identity politics that would argue that these films are of aesthetic and political value *because* their authors are black gay men. Throughout this paper I have drawn attention to the formal strategies in *Tongues Untied* and *Looking for Langston* because I want to resist the conflation between artistic value and authorial identity that so often arises in debates on emerging artists. The problem here is not simply that bad works get celebrated alongside good ones but that constructive criticism is inhibited by the fear of being seen to be politically incorrect: if it is assumed that a black film is necessarily good because a black person made it, any criticism of the film is likely to be read as an attack on the very person who made it rather than on the film that was made.

Analogously, we are familiar with that rhetorical strategy of categorical identity politics in which a statement is prefaced by the adjectives that describe one's identity—for example, "As a black gay man, I feel angry about my place in the world." The statement may be entirely valid, but, because it is embedded in my identity, it preempts the possibility of critical dialogue, because your disagreement might be interpreted not as a comment on what I say, but as a criticism of who I am. So, in relation to *Tongues Untied* and *Looking for Langston,* I would adopt an anticelebration position, because I want to emphasize that these rich, provocative, and important works do indeed "make a difference" not because of who or what the filmmakers are, but because of what they do, and above all because of the freaky way they do it.

Notes

1. Stuart Hall, "Cultural Identity and Cinematic Representation," *Framework*, no. 36 (1989) pp. 68–81; reprinted in Jonathan Rutherford, ed., *Identity: Community, Culture, Difference* (London: Lawrence and Wishart, 1990) p. 225.

2. James Snead, "Black Independent Film: Britain and America," in Kobena Mercer, ed.,

Black Film/British Cinema, ICA Document 7, (London: Institute of Contemporary Arts, 1988) p. 47.

3. Sankofa Film and Video Collective comprises Isaac Julien, Maureen Blackwood, Nadine Marsh Edwards, and Robert Crusz. It was formed in 1984 in London with the aims of developing an independent black film culture in the areas of production, exhibition, and audience discussions. Under the aegis of the ACTT Workshop Declaration, the Collective has been funded from a variety of sources, including the Greater London Council, the British Film Institute and Channel Four. For background information on their work, and that of the Black Audio Film Collective, see interviews in Coco Fusco, ed., *Young, British and Black,* (Buffalo: Contemporary Hallwalls Arts Center, 1988).

4. See Kobena Mercer and Isaac Julien, "De Margin and De Centre," introduction to *Screen* vol. 29 no. 4 (Autumn, 1988) pp. 2–10, and Kobena Mercer, "Black Art and the Burden of Representation," *Third Text,* no. 10 (Spring, 1990) pp. 61–78.

5. Martina Attille in Jim Pines, "The Passion of Remembrance: Background and Interview with Sankofa," *Framework,* no. 32/33 (1986) p. 101.

6. Marlon Riggs in Ron Simmons, "Tongues Untied: An Interview with Marlon Riggs," *Black Film Review,* vol. 5, no. 3 (1989); reprinted in Essex Hemphill, ed., *Brother to Brother: New Writing by Black Gay Men,* (Boston: Alyson, 1991) p. 191.

7. See Benedict Anderson, *Imagined Communities: Reflections on the Origin and Spread of Nationalism* (London: Verso, 1983).

Fassbinder, Franz, Fox, Elvira, Erwin, Armin, and All the Others

DOUGLAS CRIMP

for Joseph Jacobs

1. The Subject

The story narrated by *In a Year of Thirteen Moons,* that of the last five days in the life of a despairing transsexual, is nearly submerged in textual excess. The explicit presence of text as text, often recited by the actors in a detached voice, as if reading directly from the script; the plurality of textual sources and styles—vernacular, literary, philosophical; the disjunction of text from image: this textual overdetermination constantly threatens to disrupt the narrative. Yet it is precisely this logorrhea which structures the film, gives it its particular, odd appeal. That, and the brilliant performance by Volker Spengler as the character Erwin/Elvira.

As *October* prepared its special issue on Fassbinder, *In a Year of Thirteen Moons* became its focus, with the film's script as its central document. Fassbinder's representative in Germany responded to our request to publish the script with the following sentence: "Es freut uns, dass Sie *In a Year of Thirteen Moons* publizieren wollen; als ein sehr persönlicher Film ist dies geradezu ein Schlüssel zu Fassbinder's gesamten Werk." "Because this is a very personal film, it is actually a key to Fassbinder's entire oeuvre." I remembered similar phrases about this special subjective nature of *Thirteen Moons* from the reviews that had appeared when the film was released in New York. This babbling of the Doxa—"Public Opinion, the mind of the majority, petit bourgeois Consensus, the Voice of Nature, the Violence of Prejudice"—kept nagging at me: "Fassbinder at his most personal," "Fassbinder assumes total artistic control," "Fassbinder's immediate response to the loss of his lover." Thus, Wilhelm Roth, in his annotated filmography of Fassbinder:

> Fassbinder worked on the film from July 28 to August 28, 1978, a few months after the suicide of his friend Armin Meier, who appeared with

Elvira Weshaupt (Volker Spengler) in a cafe restroom, *In a Year of Thirteen Moons* (*In einem Jahr mit 13 Monden*), Rainer Werner Fassbinder

him in *Germany in Autumn*. Fassbinder not only wrote the script and directed, but was responsible for the sets and editing, and did the camerawork himself for the first time. Never before had he taken a film so fully into his own hands; hardly any other film is so much tied up with his life.

A film about a transsexual, whose narrative I had experienced as constructed in a complex relation to a series of texts, is also understood to be Fassbinder's most personal work, the film most tied to his life. (Of course, the same has been said of Fassbinder's television adaptation of Alfred Döblin's *Berlin Alexanderplatz*. Wolfram Schütte: "What story is Fassbinder finally telling us? The story of himself.")

2. A Trilogy for Armin Meier

In 1974 Fassbinder made *Fox and His Friends,* a schematic melodrama in which a working-class homosexual is taken up by a group of middle-class gays, is systematically exploited and humiliated by his lover, and finally commits suicide. Fassbinder plays the title role in the film, which is dedicated to his lover, Armin Meier, "and all the others." Roth: "*Fox* stimulates speculation as to interpretation. For the first time in five years, Fassbinder again plays a leading role, the most extensive so far in his films. It seems to me that Fassbinder wants to depict here, in a distanced way, his experiences with German cultural life."

Three years later Fassbinder made a segment of *Germany in Autumn*, a collaborative effort in response to the recent political events: the kidnapping and murder of Hans-Martin Schleyer, the Mogadishu hijacking, and the "suicides" in Stammheim of three members of the Baader-Meinhof group. In Fassbinder's thirty-minute sequence, he and Meier constantly quarrel, their relationship evidently a shambles as a result of Fassbinder's overworking (he is at work on *Berlin Alexanderplatz*), his despair and paranoia about the political conditions of contemporary Germany (the *Berufsverbot* legislation had just been passed), and his inability to communicate any of this to Meier due to irreconcilable differences between the two. Meier, a working-class man who had been a butcher, voices standard clichés about terrorism and authority, which literally makes Fassbinder sick and causes him several times to throw Meier out of the apartment.

The following year Fassbinder made *In a Year of Thirteen Moons*, in which a transsexual (who had been a butcher) is berated and left by her lover, fails to find sympathy from her friends, and commits suicide.

3. Another Trilogy

To write on oneself may seem a pretentious idea; but it is also a simple idea: simple as the idea of suicide.

—Roland Barthes by Roland Barthes

When Roland Barthes died a month after he was hit by a laundry van, Alexander Cockburn published a snide obituary in *The Village Voice*. Knowing of Barthes's despair over his mother's recent death, Cockburn suggested that Barthes's own death had been a kind of suicide, a lack of the will to live as a result of that extreme attachment to the mother that is said to be a condition of homosexuality. This innuendo has continued ever since (Michael Starenko: "Did Barthes throw himself under that laundry van?"), finding its confirmation in certain passages of *Camera Lucida*, Barthes's final and "most personal" book. But the suggestion of suicide extends beyond Barthes's loss of the will to live, to encompass a loss of faith in his work. The last three books, *Roland Barthes by Roland Barthes*, *A Lover's Discourse*, *Camera Lucida*—Tzvetan Todorov has designated them an "egoist" trilogy—are taken as a volte-face, a repudiation of Barthes's "position" against the authorial voice, the voice of an irreducible subjectivity. With *Camera Lucida* especially, Barthes is said to have renounced writing for autobiography, to have discovered his own "mortal voice" in the construction of a "more humane discourse" (J. Gerald Kennedy: "*La chambre clair* marks a fundamental break with his past writings").

4. To Abjure—Another Trilogy

Each voice might appear authentic if we heard it in isolation; together, each stamps the others with the sign of borrowing (if not of theft).
    —Tzvetan Todorov, "The Last Barthes"

The horror is this: it is Barthes's death that allows him to come into being, to become an essence. This is what he recognized as deathlike in photography: " . . . for what society makes of my photograph, what it reads there, I do not know (in any case, there are so many readings of the same face); but when I discover myself in the product of this operation, what I see is that I have become Total-Image, which is to say, Death in person; others—the Other—do not dispossess me of myself, they turn me, ferociously, into an object, they put me at their mercy, at their disposal, classified in a file, ready for the subtlest deceptions. . . ."

Unlike Balzac, who felt the spectral layers of his essence being peeled away one by one with each photograph taken of him, Barthes feels his essence under construction—"I am neither subject nor object but a subject who feels he is becoming an object: I then experience a micro-version of death (of parenthesis): I am truly becoming a specter." It is the integration of his being which is death, which converts Barthes into a specter, self-present to himself. Kennedy: "In this last book, he has become the faithful witness of his own being." This tendentious reading of Barthes converts his meditation upon how a metaphysics comes to be instituted through the sentiment attendant upon death into a plea for the truth of that sentiment. And this is then taken as the *definitive* Barthes.

Camera Lucida is not a prophesy of Barthes's death (a banal mysticism), but a recognition that mortality consists, whenever and however death comes, of no longer being able to set paradox against the Doxa, no longer being able to assume another voice, to abjure an earlier pose or fiction. *Camera Lucida* might have been taken as a cautionary tale; instead it has been taken as "a memorable emblem of being, a reconciliation between the writing self and the 'I' of writing" (Kennedy).

Barthes relished the drift, the constant movement of the writer, likening it to the game of hand over hand. He traces this drift in his own career in the "autobiography":

Let us follow this trajectory once again. At the work's source, the opacity of social relations, a false Nature; the first impulse, the first shock, then, is to demystify (*Mythologies*); then when the demystification is immobilized in repetition, it must be displaced; semiological *science* (then postu-lated) tries to stir, to vivify, to arm the mythological gesture, the pose, by endowing it with a method; this science is encumbered in its turn with a whole repertoire of images: the goal of a semiological science is replaced by the (often very grim) science of the semiologists; hence, one must sever oneself from that, must introduce into this rational image-repertoire the texture of desire, the claims of the body: this, then, is the Text, the theory of the Text. But the Text risks paralysis: it repeats itself, counterfeits itself in lusterless texts, testimonies to a demand for readers, not for a desire to please: the Text tends to degenerate into prattle (*Babel*). Where to go next? That is where I am now.

The "now" is 1975, two years prior to his appointment to the Chair of Literary Semiology at the Collège de France. No wonder that he took the opportunity of his inaugural address to comment upon the irony of this appointment to a professorship of something he no longer professed—and to speak once again of the necessity to abjure, this time in relation to the work of another who had suffered posthumous integration (after a violent death in which he is said to have been complicit—the fate of a homosexual of his tastes):

It is precisely because it persists that writing is forced to shift ground. For power seizes upon the pleasure of writing as it seizes upon all pleasure, to manipulate it and to make of it a product that is gregarious, nonperverse, in the same way that it seizes upon the genetic product of love's pleasure, to turn it into soldiers and fighters to its own advantage. *To shift ground,* then, can mean: to go where you are not expected, or, more radically, to *abjure* what you have written (but not necessarily what you have thought), when gregarious power uses and subjugates it. Pasolini was thus led to "abjure" (as he said) his *Trilogy of Life* films because he realized that power was making use of them—yet without regretting the fact that he wrote them in the first place. "I believe," he said in a text published posthumously, "that *before* action we must never in any case fear annex-ation by power and its culture. We must behave as if this dangerous eventuality did not exist. . . . But I also believe that *afterwards* we must be able to realize how much we may have been used by power. And then, if our sincerity or our necessity has been controlled or manipulated, I believe we must have the courage to abjure."

The death that Barthes foresaw in his mother's death—his own—was his final annexation and integration, an end to the drift of writing. He recorded this recognition in *Camera Lucida.* How ironic, then, that this very same book should be the occasion for gregarious power to manipulate Barthes's writing into a product that is nonperverse, to unify it immediately into an oeuvre. Susan Sontag: "The voice was always singular." "Much of what

Barthes wrote now appears autobiographical." "Inevitably, Barthes's work had to end in autobiography." The most accidental of deaths—crossing a street—determined the end of Barthes's work. Yet gregarious power reads it as inevitable, essential. Starenko: "The temptation to turn *Camera Lucida* into a kind of testament has been almost irresistible." *Camera Lucida*—the book which parts company with all Barthes's other books; the book which constitutes and retrospectively humanizes Barthes's oeuvre.

5. An Oeuvre

I am isolating three films by Fassbinder and letting them stand for his oeuvre, but only in order to ask in what ways that unity might be constituted. The three can be bound together by this "biographeme": Fassbinder's lover Armin Meier. But also by the repetition (and variation) of a particular scene involving the characters that we take to represent Armin Meier.

Two scenes precede Franz's suicide at the end of *Fox and His Friends*. In the first, Franz (Fox) returns to the apartment he had bought for himself and his lover Eugen, only to find that the locks have been changed. He rings the

Franz (Fassbinder) and his bourgeois lover Eugen (Peter Chatel) in their apartment, *Fox and His Friends (Faustrecht der Freiheit)*

bell and the door is opened by Philip, Eugen's former lover, who tells Franz that the apartment now belongs to Eugen. Franz screams: "It's *my* apartment, paid for with *my* money." But, as one more step on the way toward his total destruction at the hands of Eugen's scheming family, Franz had signed his apartment over to the family business so that it could be put up as security for a loan. The next scene shows Franz at his alcoholic sister's place, to which Eugen has sent his belongings. After insisting that Franz repay her for the delivery charge, she, too, throws Franz out, only to regret it and plead with him to return, but too late.

In the opening of Fassbinder's sequence of *Germany in Autumn*, Fassbinder returns to his Munich apartment a day earlier than expected. Finding Armin still in bed, he berates him for his slovenly life. Armin: "How could I know you'd arrive today?" As they begin to fight about the Mogadishu hijacking, Fassbinder loses his temper and orders Armin out of his apartment. Armin: "It's *our* apartment." Fassbinder: "*My* apartment." Armin prepares to leave, saying as he does that it's for good.

At the beginning of *In a Year of Thirteen Moons*, Elvira returns to her apartment after being beat up by a group of hustlers. Her lover Christoph has unexpectedly returned and shows surprise at seeing Elvira in her degraded state. Elvira: "How was I supposed to know that today you'd . . .?" During the ensuing fight, Christoph reproaches Elvira for her worthless life and orders her to stop screaming. Elvira: "This is my apartment, Christoph, my apartment, you know, and I'll do whatever I want here." Christoph: "So, it's your apartment?" Elvira: "Yes, my apartment, mine, mine, mine!" Christoph packs his belongings, preparing to leave, this time for good. Elvira, regretting her words, pleads with him to stay, but too late.

Through these repetitions, a possible theme of this oeuvre we have constructed for Fassbinder: the catastrophic effect of property relations on lovers (for if we can constitute an oeuvre, then we can discover its thematic unities). Thus, an exchange from *Gay Left*: Bob Cant: "Fassbinder's *Fox* is a film about the corruptive nature of capitalism. The fact that the main characters are gay men does of course make it interesting for gay men but it is not primarily a film which attempts to Deal With The Problem of Homosexuality." And, "Relationships are more than just a matter of good individuals and bad individuals—they are a clear reflection of the economic structure of a society and are no doubt intended here to be seen as an allegory of such." Andrew Britton replies: "A clear, honest, coherent portrayal of the ways in which gay relationships are repressed, perverted, curtailed in bourgeois-capitalist society might be . . . admirable. This is *not* what *Fox* is. Its version of homosexuality degrades us all, and should be roundly denounced."

Fassbinder: "I think it's incidental that the story happens among gays."

In taking these three films, which explicitly show a homosexual milieu, as representative of Fassbinder's work, I have already imposed on his oeuvre the necessity of conforming to a biographical fact: Fassbinder's homosexuality. And having isolated this biographical fact as essential, as determinant, it is then possible to proceed to a more specific thematics of the oeuvre, thus continuing to move in the wrong direction.

6. The Essential Biographeme: Homosexuality

Can one assume that you use camouflage in your films, that homosexual relationships are disguised as heterosexual relationships? I'm thinking of Fear Eats the Soul.
FASSBINDER: No, that's what the good Marcel Proust did with his thing— with the boys and the girls. That's not the case with me.
And it's not true even for The Bitter Tears of Petra von Kant?
FASSBINDER: They are two women, and that's what they're supposed to be.
But you dedicated the film "to him who became Marlene."
FASSBINDER: Surely one can dedicate a film to someone.

Yes, but isn't that a hint?

The question camouflaged in the foregoing is: is he "out" in his work? A filmmaker who is gay evidently has only two choices: either he makes films which are not about homosexuality, in which case a disguised homosexuality will be the inevitable result—*Who's Afraid of Virginia Woolf?*—or he makes films about homosexuality, in which case he necessarily presents his *version* of homosexuality. Homosexuality, it seems cannot merely be there; if there, it has to be in the foreground. No matter what the film's official pretext, the subject is "coming out." Richard Dyer: "There is nothing attractive about the situation or the character [in *Germany in Autumn*]—yet it is moving in a way different from the compassion displayed/provoked in the earlier films. Partly, no doubt, this is because one recognizes Fassbinder as Fassbinder, and this makes the sequence the most unambiguous coming out in his work. Coming out is always a difficult and moving occurrence. . . ."
But it is moving only to the extent that we have already assumed the essential nature of the author's homosexuality. Then the unambiguous act of self-revelation can be understood to free the subject to speak what he has always wanted to say. Such bids for freedom are usually seen as courageous. Sontag: "A brave meditation on the personal, on the self, is at the center of [Barthes's] late writings and seminars. Much of Barthes's work, especially the last three books, with their poignant themes of loss, constitute a candid defense of his sensuality (as well as his sexuality)—his flavor, his way of tasting the world." Anything short of this candor must presumably be subter-

fuge, an elaborate ruse of writing masking the inability simply to *come out with it.* The complex strategies of the text reduced thus to reticence and mystification. Kennedy: "In one sense this [consideration of the haiku in a late seminar] was a typical bit of mystification: as we see in *Roland Barthes* and *A Lover's Discourse,* he was driven to self-revelation yet curiously unable to bare his heart except in formal, oblique ways."

7. The Subterfuge of Writing

Barthes's textual ploys—erudition, method, theory; classification, citation, fragmentation; digression, ellipsis, parenthesis—these are employed against what he called the terrorism of discourse. In opposition to the languages of authority, their instrumentality an effect of their directness and transparency, Barthes sought unwarranted languages—for example, the lover's discourse—"spoken, perhaps, by thousands of subjects (who knows?), but warranted by no one." What is this discourse? How does it proceed? "The lover, in fact, cannot keep his mind from racing, taking new measures and plotting against himself. His discourse exists only in outbursts of language, which occur at the whim of the trivial, of aleatory circumstances." These outbursts are called figures, and placed under headings arranged alphabetically. They disrupt the inexorable flow of discourse with what Barthes labels the *Argumentum:* " 'exposition, account, summary, plot outline, invented narrative'; I should add: instrument of distancing, signboard à la Brecht." *A Lover's Discourse* adds another kind of Brechtian signboard, as well— the small-type marginal notes of reference to "ordinary reading . . . insistent readings . . . occasional readings . . . conversations with friends": Pasolini, *The Marriage of Figaro,* Balzac, La Rochefoucauld, *Pelléas,* Diderot, double bind, Proust, Hölderlin, Freud, *Bouvard and Pécuchet,* Zen, Sartre, Greek, D.F., *Symposium,* etymology, Mme de Sévigné, Gide, Schönberg, haiku. . . . A quick leafing through the text produces this list. One reference, however, appears incessantly: *Werther.* Barthes's book constantly returns to Goethe's, as if to a manual; *A Lover's Discourse* is written through *Werther.*

And what becomes of these ploys in *Camera Lucida?* The *Argumentum* is still present, but simply as the traditional table of contents corresponding to the numbered textual fragments. And these now run together smoothly, under the guise of a return to a more traditional narrative. Kennedy: "By its form alone, this work signals a difference, a basic realignment of writer and subject. Surprisingly, the discussion unfolds not through whimsically arranged fragments but through a sustained, cumulative reflection on the nature of photography."

And yet, is photography the object of Barthes's narrative? Is this where its directness and transparency lead us? The photography critics agree that *Camera Lucida* is *not* about photography, at least not in any instrumental sense. Starenko: "For both [Sam] Varnedoe and [Andy] Grundberg the verdict seems to be that *Camera Lucida*, contrary to its subtitle [*Reflections on Photography*], is really about something other than photography— Barthes himself, Proust's epic novel, or death. Any reader of *Camera Lucida* could easily add to the list: the ontology of photography, semiotics, writing (*écriture*), Lacanian psychoanalysis, desire, the death of a beloved, Barthes's mother, homosexuality, the soul, phenomenology, immortality. . . . Whichever term one chooses will determine what the book is 'about'." For his part, Starenko chooses sentiment: "This, to answer the original question, is what *Camera Lucida* is 'about'."

And who is this " 'I' writing," now realigned with his subject? Is it not another's voice that speaks through Barthes, or through which Barthes speaks? Is this not the voice of Proust: "One day, quite some time ago, I happened on a photograph . . ." and "Now, one November evening shortly after my mother's death, I was going through some photographs"?

The narrative machine of *Camera Lucida* may operate smoothly, but we are still left to conjecture about who operates it and where it leads. For if *A Lover's Discourse* is produced through a concatenation of narratives, *Camera Lucida's* single narrative produces a concatenation of objects.

8. The Concatenation of Narratives

The first time I saw *In a Year of Thirteen Moons*, I saw a print in which the episodes had been spliced together out of sequence. I know that this has forever stamped my sense of the film as *essentially* fragmentary. After having read the script and subsequently seen the film again, this time with its sequences in the right order, I realized that its more or less self-contained episodes do follow a certain narrative logic. That logic pertains to the film's narrative present. But a number of past-tense narratives jostle this logic: Elvira's story of her life with Christoph, told to Zora at the slaughterhouse; Sister Gudrun's story of Erwin's childhood, told to Elvira and Zora at the cloister; the cancer victim's story of Saitz, told to Elvira as she is about to enter Saitz's office building; Elvira's interview with Hauer, played as a voiceover during the film's final sequence. And these are interspersed with other narratives, more obliquely connected to Elvira's last days: Soul Frieda's dream, Zora's fairy tale, the suicide's recitation of Schopenhauer, Hauer's fable. Even within these, other narratives: the final monologue of Goethe's *Torquato Tasso* in Elvira's story at the slaughterhouse; the Dean Martin/ Jerry Lewis musical number from *You're Never Too Young* mimicked by

Saitz and his lackies; the changing video images as Zora flips television channels after telling her fairy tale—an interview with Fassbinder, news footage of Pinochet, Chabrol's *Le Boucher.*

The present tense of the narrative then came to seem like nothing other than the space within which the past narratives could be declaimed. As I was thinking about this narrative form, I read this, from *A Lover's Discourse:*

> As Narrative (Novel, Passion), love is a story which is accomplished, in the sacred sense of the word: it is a *program* which must be completed. For me, on the contrary, this story has *already taken place;* for what is event is exclusively the delight of which I have been the object and whose aftereffects I repeat (and fail to achieve). Enamoration is a *drama,* if we restore to this word the archaic meaning Nietzsche gave it: "Ancient drama envisioned great declamatory scenes which excluded action (action took place *before* or *behind* the stage)." Amorous seduction (a pure hypnotic moment) takes place *before* discourse and *behind* the proscenium of consciousness: the amorous "event" is of a hieratic order: it is my own local legend, my little sacred history that I declaim to myself, and this declamation of a *fait accompli* (frozen, embalmed, removed from any *praxis*) is the lover's discourse.

NIETZSCHE: *The Case of Wagner.*

But more than simply providing the space of the various narratives' agglomeration, *In a Year of Thirteen Moons*'s present-tense story depends upon what is disclosed in the past tense for its intelligibility; and this intelligibility is retrospective. At the film's end, we hear the interview given to Hauer by Elvira, the publication of which causes Irene's fear and her extraction of Elvira's promise to go to Saitz for mercy. Seeing Saitz again pushes Elvira toward her final despairing act, which occurs as we hear her say, on tape: "He didn't even care. That hurt me a lot. Maybe what I did was right, I don't know, I can't say. . . ." Elvira is referring to her earlier suicide attempt when she had returned from Casablanca a woman, only to be rejected by Saitz anyway. As the final scene fades out, Elvira's voice-over continues, explaining how she was saved from her suicide.

Not only does the narrative momentum of *In a Year of Thirteen Moons* build inevitably toward this final suicide, but suicide everywhere pervades the film: a central meditation on suicide—from *The World as Will and Representation*—is spoken by one character after another:

> Soul Frieda: That outward manifestation which I call my body, I am also conscious of in a completely different way, as my will. Or, my body is the objectivization of my will. Or, as my body is a figment of my imagination, it is thus merely my will.

Elvira visis Anton Seitz at his office

. . .

Sister Gudrun [holding a copy of Schopenhauer]: God can't be that cruel; if so there would be no God.

. . .

Bum: We can say that the world itself is one's worldview. To understand suicide only as the negation of the will to live, as an act of negation, is to completely misunderstand it. Far from being a negation of the will, this phenomenon is a strong affirmation of the will, since this negation means a denial of the joys, not the sorrows of life. The suicide desires life, but is just dissatisfied with the conditions under which life has come to him. He in no way, therefore, gives up the will to live; rather he merely renounces life, and destroys the outward appearance it has for him.
Elvira: I think you'd better do it now.

9. Suicide and Biography

Madame Bovary, c'est moi.
  —Flaubert

Der Biberkopf, das bin ich.
  —Fassbinder

I guess the film In a Year of Thirteen Moons *was a direct reaction to the suicide of your friend Armin Meier. To what extent was the movie an existential necessity for you?*

Fassbinder: I felt the necessity to do something. There were basically three possibilities. One was to go to Paraguay and become a farmer. I don't know why Paraguay; it just came to me. It might sound like coquetry now but at the time it wasn't that at all; it was real to me. Another possibility was to stop being interested in what was happening around me. That would have been like a mental illness. The third possibility was to make a film—certainly the easiest for me. It's perfectly logical that that's what I did. What's important for me is that I managed to make a film that doesn't simply translate my emotions about the suicide, my pain and despair about the fact that lots of things went wrong in our relationship. Of course I made a film which takes its impulse from Armin, but—this I wouldn't have been able to do before—it extends far beyond that impulse. It tells much more than what I could have told about Armin, and that, for me, was a decision for life.

In a Year of Thirteen Moons opens with a barely visible scene in which several male hustlers cruise along a bank of the Main at dawn. On the sound track is the adagio movement of Mahler's Fifth Symphony (also used at the opening—again at dawn—of Visconti's *Death in Venice*). A rolling title, the film's epigraph, suggests that what we are about to see is a story of fate, governed by natural forces:

> Every seventh year is a year of the moon. Certain people, whose existence is influenced mainly by their emotions, suffer from intense depressions in these moon years. This is also true to a lesser degree of years with thirteen new moons. And when a moon year is also a year with thirteen new moons, it often results in inevitable personal catastrophes. . . . One of these is the year 1978 [the year of Armin's suicide; the year of Elvira's suicide]. . . .

As the day begins to brighten, Elvira (dressed as a man) is introduced; she slips a hustler some money, initiating the first in a series of encounters of the last five days of her life. Fassbinder: "The film *In a Year of Thirteen Moons* describes a person's encounters during the last five days of his life, and attempts to determine—through these encounters—whether this one person's decision not to carry on beyond this last day, the fifth, should be rejected, at least understood, or maybe even found acceptable."

What are these encounters through which such a determination might be made? They are—again—the means by which we will encounter Elvira's biography. Fassbinder has published an extended narrative of the life of Erwin/Elvira Weishaupt under the simple title "A Biography." It begins, as biographies do, with the story of the mother, Anita Weishaupt, who bore Erwin illegitimately while her husband was a prisoner of war. This is the story we hear told by Sister Gudrun (played by Fassbinder's own mother, Liselotte Elder/Lilo Pempeit), although in less detail. Indeed, this biography, the central text of *In a Year of Thirteen Moons,* never appears in its entirety; like suicide, "A Biography" simply pervades the film.

In a note preceding his story of Elvira, Fassbinder attributes the biography not this time to the forces of nature but to their opposite, to the city of Frankfurt, "a place whose particular structure virtually provokes biographies like this one—or at least doesn't make them seem particularly unusual." Another such story is *Berlin Alexanderplatz,* Döblin's novel of 1929, written in a montage technique which "allows the city of Berlin to speak in a thousand voices." It is the story of Franz Biberkopf (the full name of the central character of *Fox*—Fox der sprechender Kopf), which Fassbinder read as an adolescent: "It helped me to admit my tormenting fear, which almost crippled me, the fear of acknowledging my homosexual desires, of realizing my repressed needs. . . ."

When he later reread the novel, he recognized that he *was* Franz Biberkopf: "An enormous part of myself, my attitudes, my reactions, so many things that I had considered all my own, were none other than those described by Döblin." Quoting these phrases, Wolfram Schütte is dismayed: "A second-hand life, dictated by literature: an 'I' invented by someone else."

10. The Soul

ZORA: You know, Elvira was a very beautiful woman the first year after the operation.
SOUL FRIEDA: Cancer?
ZORA: No, no disease. She just had everything down there cut off.
SOUL FRIEDA: So? That's not the reason she's unhappy. She was probably always a woman in her soul.
ZORA: No, that's just it. She just did it. And she didn't even have a good reason, like, because of her soul, or something. I don't think she was even gay. Isn't that right, baby? You weren't even gay when you went to Casablanca.

This conversation rehearses the clichés of transsexualism: its denial of homosexual desire, its determination by an essential identity—to make the body conform to the soul. But Elvira's identity, like Fassbinder's, is arbitrarily imposed from without, in her case the result of an offhand remark by Saitz: "It would be really nice if you were a girl." The terrifying arbitrariness of such an act as Elvira's trip to Casablanca is what a faith in the soul, in human essence, would abolish.

According to Kennedy, Barthes, too, had a conversion experience in Casablanca, one which would ultimately lead to his "rediscovery of the soul." This "mortality crisis" was related by Barthes in one of his late seminars:

Barthes recalled how one afternoon he had visited a waterfall [a favorite site near Casablanca] with a few of his graduate students, but feeling increasingly detached and depressed, he returned alone to his apartment and there experienced a powerful consciousness of his impending death. The encounter with this "physical presence" lasted several hours, and afterward Barthes felt a remorse about his career, perceiving an absolute rupture between his emotional life and mental life.

The direction the seminar took from this relating of the "incident in Casablanca" to a discussion of the "poetics of the haiku" caused Kennedy's accusation of Barthes's evasiveness, of his failure to express his real need to recenter himself, to integrate his emotional with his mental life. But with the writing of *Camera Lucida,* it seems, the evasion disappeared, and Barthes "finally arrived at a concept of a soul in defiance of his own theory of the subject." "*La chambre claire* reflects a centering of consciousness in the use of a single voice, a consistent perspective, through which Barthes expresses concerns which are rigorously personal." "The voice *belongs* to Barthes and the story is self-evidently his own."

Sontag agrees: "His voice became more and more personal, more full of grain, as he called it." But, of course, precisely the reverse: the grain of the voice, as Barthes described it, is not the personal but its opposite, all that is individual without being personal. It is the (material) body, not the soul. To explain what he means by the voice's grain, Barthes describes the Russian church bass:

> The voice is not personal: it expresses nothing of the cantor, of his soul; it is not original (all Russian cantors have roughly the same voice), and at the same time it is individual: it has us hear a body which has no civil identity, no "personality," but which is nevertheless a separate body. . . . The "grain" is that: the materiality of the body speaking its mother tongue; perhaps the letter, almost certainly *signifiance.*
>
> . . .
>
> . . . the whole of musical pedagogy teaches not the culture of the "grain" of the voice but the emotive modes of its delivery—the myth of respiration. How many singing teachers have we not heard prophesying that the art of vocal music rested entirely on the mastery, the correct discipline of breathing! The breath is the *pneuma,* the soul swelling or breaking, and any exclusive art of breathing is likely to be a secretly mystical art (a mysticism levelled down to the measure of the long-playing record). The lung, a stupid organ . . . , swells but gets no erection; it is in the throat, place where the phonic metal hardens and is segmented, in the mask that *signifiance* explodes, bringing not the soul but *jouissance.*

Not content with merely opposing the body to the soul, Barthes resorts to this image of fellatio. Should we then suppose that his mother's death forced him to repudiate this as well? that the body's pleasures, impersonal as they are, were forsaken for more "rigorously personal concerns"? The voice of *Camera Lucida* as returning to an unproblematic notion of human essence, as a book which is "purposive and referential," as constituting a "work rather than a text," and as possessing an "end beyond the play of words— the rediscovery of a soul" (Kennedy)—this view would deny, precisely, *significance:* the indeterminacy, the arbitrariness, the erotics of the signifier, the disappearance of the subject in the text.

11. The Dedication

What follows the dedication (i.e., the work itself) has little relation to this dedication. The object I give is no longer tautological (I give you what I give you), it is interpretable; it has meaning (meanings) greatly in excess of its address; though I write your name on my work, it is for "them" that it has been written (the others, the readers).
—Roland Barthes, *A Lover's Discourse*

Much has been made of Barthes's dedication of *Camera Lucida* "in homage to *L'Imaginaire* by Jean-Paul Sartre." Dana Polan: "It is not surprising that *Camera Lucida* is dedicated to the Sartre of *L'Imaginaire,* for Barthes's narrative of his personal involvement duplicates the agon of the existential individual central to Sartre's early work." Sontag: "While a quarrel with Sartre's view of literature lies at the heart of his first book, *Writing Degree Zero* (Sartre is never mentioned by name), an agreement with Sartre's view of the imagination, and its obsessional energies, surfaces in Barthes's last book, *Camera Lucida* (written 'in homage' to the early Sartre, the author of *L'Imaginaire*)." In fact, Sartre is mentioned by name repeatedly in *Writing Degree Zero,* a book for which Sontag wrote the introduction to the first American edition; though she claims to have known Barthes "personally," she can hardly claim to have read him carefully.

There is no question but that Barthes has turned to those philosophical problems which engaged Sartre in his early work on the phenomenology of the image, but to say that *Camera Lucida* represents anything so simple as a duplication of, or direct agreement with *The Psychology of Imagination* is precisely the kind of reductive view that Barthes's book resists. Indeed, given Barthes's argument for the necessity to abjure, it may well be that he has returned to Sartre in order to counter the reverse but equally reductive view that Barthes's work stands in simple opposition to Sartre's. Barthes returns to the early Sartre, to "classical phenomenology, the kind I had known in my adolescence (and there has not been any other since)," through returning to photography; for the photograph raises for Barthes "questions which derive from a 'stupid' or simple metaphysics (it is the answers which are complicated): probably the true metaphysics." But these questions cannot be identical with those of *The Psychology of Imagination* since Barthes sees them as posed precisely because the photograph is unlike any other kind of image: "It is precisely because Photography is an anthropologically new object that it must escape, it seems to me, usual discussions of the image." Sartre, on the other hand, makes no distinction at all for the photograph: "Mental images, caricatures, photos are so many species of the same genus, and from now on we can attempt to ascertain what it is they have in common." In this attempt Sartre moves from image type to image type, ultimately arriving at his object: the mental image of his friend Peter. But at every step along this route, if the image of Peter has meaning it is because Sartre himself has "the intention that animates it": "If I see Peter by means of the photo, *it is because I put him there.*" Barthes takes up this notion only to complicate it, to render this intentionality fundamentally ambivalent: "Suddenly a specific photograph reaches me; it animates me, and I animate it. So that is how I must name the attraction which makes it exist: an *animation.* The photograph is in no way animated (I do not believe in 'lifelike' photographs), but it animates me: this is what creates every adventure." What had been for Sartre the simple "I animate it," has become for Barthes the far more problematic "It animates me, and I animate it." To reduce these to an equivalence is not to grant Barthes his individuality but to abolish it.

The specific photographic adventure to which the second half of *Camera Lucida* is devoted is Barthes's attempt to rediscover his mother, to find the image that would assurage his grief. This search for the essence of his mother in an image reenacts Sartre's search for the image of Peter—that is, its strategy is this textual doubling—except that Barthes's quest is couched in private terms. This is not, however, in order "to fill the scene of the text with my individuality; but on the contrary, to offer, to extend this individuality to a science of the subject."

12. The Voices in the Text

(for in order to speak one must seek support from other texts)
—*Roland Barthes by Roland Barthes*

Roland Barthes, *Camera Lucida*, trans. Richard Howard (New York: Hill and Wang, 1981).

——, "The Grain of the Voice," in *Image-Music-Text*, trans. Stephen Heath (New York: Hill and Wang, 1977) pp. 179–189.

——, "Lecture in Inauguration of the Chair of Literary Semiology, Collège de France," trans. Richard Howard, *October*, no. 8 (Spring, 1979), pp. 3–16.

——, *A Lover's Discourse: Fragments*, trans. Richard Howard (New York: Hill and Wang, 1978).

————, *Roland Barthes by Roland Barthes,* trans. Richard Howard (New York: Hill and Wang, 1977).

Andrew Britton, "Foxed," *Gay Left,* no. 3; repr. *Jump Cut,* no. 16 (November, 1977), pp. 22–23.

Bob Cant, "Fassbinder's *Fox,*" *Gay Left,* no. 2; repr. *Jump Cut,* no. 16 (November, 1977), p. 22.

Richard Dyer, "Reading Fassbinder's Sexual Politics," in Tony Rayns, ed., *Fassbinder* (London: British Film Institute, 1980) pp. 54–64.

Rainer Werner Fassbinder, "In einem Jahr mit dreizehn Monden: Exposé zu einem Spielfilm," *S!A!U!,* no. 2 (1978), pp. 52–59.

J. Gerald Kennedy, "Roland Barthes, Autobiography, and the End of Writing," *The Georgia Review,* vol. 35, no. 2 (Summer, 1981), pp. 381–398.

Wolfgang Limmer, *Rainer Werner Fassbinder, Filmemacher* (a collection of interviews), (Hamburg: Spiegel-Verlag, 1981).

Dana Polan, "Roland Barthes and the Moving Image," *October,* no. 18 (Fall, 1981), pp. 41–46.

Wilhelm Roth, "Annotated Filmography," in *Fassbinder,* trans. Ruth McCormick (New York: Tanam Press, 1981).

Jean-Paul Sartre, *The Psychology of Imagination* (Secaucus, N.J.: Citadel Press, 1972).

Wolfram Schütte, "Franz, Mieze, Reinhold, Death and the Devil: Fassbinder's *Berlin Alexanderplatz,*" in *Fassbinder,* trans. Ruth McCormick (New York: Tanam Press, 1981).

Susan Sontag, "Writing Itself: On Roland Barthes," *The New Yorker* (April 26, 1982), pp. 122–141.

Michael Starenko, "Roland Barthes: The Heresy of Sentiment," *Afterimage,* vol. 9, no. 4 (November, 1981), pp. 6–7.

Tzvetan Todorov, "The Last Barthes," trans. Richard Howard, *Critical Inquiry,* vol. 7, no. 3 (Spring, 1981), pp. 449–454.

Madame X of the China Seas

PATRICIA WHITE

> *Madame X, a harsh, pitiless beauty, the cruel, uncrowned ruler of the*
> *China Seas, launched an appeal to all women willing to exchange an*
> *everyday existence of almost unbearable boredom, though safe and easy,*
> *for a world of uncertainty and danger, but also full of love and adventure.*

These are the first words of Ulrike Ottinger's lesbian pirate film, *Madame*
X: An Absolute Ruler, before the credits, spoken over the exquisite image
of the junk *Orlando*'s figurehead, exact replica of the pirate queen (both
played by coproducer and costume designer Tabea Blumenschein), shot
against a deep-blue sky. The promise sounds much like that of cinema itself—
the guarantee of pleasure is the beautiful, cruel woman. Here, however,
that woman speaks this contradictory, gender-specific appeal. Feminism's
promise to transform our everyday existence, too, is contradictory; it does
not engage "all women" in the same way or with the same agenda. Ottinger's
film, in taking up the appeals of both cinema and feminism, both "collective
fantasies," both "public spheres," addresses the spectator not only as *female*
(a claim Teresa de Lauretis makes for women's films such as *Born in Flames*
and *Jeanne Dielman*),[1] but also, I will try to demonstrate, as *marginal*.

Such a spectator might be willing to agree with one of the film's characters:
"This is something—this is *extreme*—the *Outlaw*—the *Misfits*—This is what
I was looking for!" exclaims Betty Brillo.[2] The excess encapsulated by her
remark is not foreign to Ottinger's cinema, is indeed its defining characteristic. Her films feature elaborate costumes, painterly shot composition, anti-
realist performances, and eclectic and abundant musical and sound quotations. Ottinger manipulates a visual and aural collage technique drawing on
sources from the Shangri-La's to Yma Sumac, Gustave Moreau to Man Ray,
Oscar Wilde to Virginia Woolf, to produce a feminist surrealism, or what
might be called queer cinema. However, I wish to go beyond the notion that
Ottinger's style appeals to a marginal audience through some subcultural
sensibility or gay aesthetics. Rather, Madame X's invocation to her crew
and the test of the fool Belcampo's gender identity function to foreground
the *construction* of the film's address.

Teresa de Lauretis has recommended that we "re-think women's cinema and aesthetic forms . . . in terms of address—who is making films for whom, who is looking and speaking, how, where, and to whom," in the context of her claim that "feminism has not only invented new strategies or created new texts, but more importantly it has conceived a new social subject, women: as speakers, readers, spectators, users and makers of cultural forms, shapers of cultural processes."[3] *Madame X: An Absolute Ruler* was produced within and in reference to the current wave of feminism. It dramatizes the relation of women as social subjects to woman as supported and produced by the cinematic apparatus. As yet another remake of the Hollywood *Madame X,* it acknowledges a long history of female spectatorship. The pirate genre provides the context for a feminist adventure in which social gender roles are transformed by role-playing and inversion, thematized as both sexual inversion and carnival. Ottinger's citations and disruptions of classical cinematic codes take women's visual pleasure, even fetishism, for granted, displacing the presumably masculine spectator. And, as I shall attempt to demonstrate through an analysis of the love scene, the film also reworks the relation of woman as image to the apparatus. Lesbianism foregrounds the difference of women from woman, insisting on spectatorial desire as well as identification. My final brief discussion of feminist film theory suggests that the impasse regarding female spectatorship is related to the blind spot of lesbianism.

The China Seas upon which the junk *Orlando* sails is a thinly disguised Lake Constance, where Ottinger shot the film in 1977. It was funded by ZDF, German television, and the low budget is at least partially responsible for the innovative sound mixing. Ottinger continued to use post-sync sound, however, on her next, better-funded feature, *Bildnis einer Trinkerin (Ticket of No Return,* 1979). Many of the actresses in *Madame X* worked with Ottinger in later films, and filmmakers Cynthia Beatt and Yvonne Rainer appear in the film. Criticized or ignored upon its release, Ottinger's first feature has a cult following and is beginning to be critically reevaluated.[4]

The film's first movement is the collection of a motley crew of women from "various nations and all walks of life" who join Madame X (mistress of "satanic sea art") and her faithful servant Hoi-Sin on board the *Orlando.* The voice-over introduces each exemplary character, who receives the following message, delivered in German or English, often via an actual communication system (newspaper, analysis session, car telephone): 'Chinese Orlando—stop—to all women—stop—offer world—stop—full of gold—stop—love—stop—adventure at sea—stop—call Chinese Orlando—call Chinese Orlando—stop."[5] The telegram stops insist on the danger of the proposition, the prohibition of the wish. Yet each character "makes her decision and her judgment in a flash" and sets off for the ship. The community (of women) is constructed by the look of astonishment on the face of each woman when she reaches the ship. We are refused the reverse shot; the first image of the next woman in the chain stands in its place. The crew are summoned by a call "to all women," but their consent implies something like Monique Wittig's definition of homosexuality: "the desire for something else that is not connoted. This desire is resistance to the norm."[6]

Each character is representative, overdetermined by costumes, names, activities, props, and music. Flora Tannenbaum, German forestry expert and Goethe admirer, is seen breakfasting outdoors dressed in hunter's green. A dachshund delivers the *Frankfurter Allgemeine* in which she reads Madame X's message; she shoulders her rifle and marches off to military music. Blow-up, an Italian cover girl, instructs her chauffeur to change direction as Satie's *La Diva de l'empire* plays on the sound track. Betty Brillo is disenchanted by "all that American Hausfrauen-dream" and Noa-Noa, a native of Tai-Pi, has been rejected by her husband for infringing a taboo. Australian bush pilot Omega Centauri would rather be an astronaut; Josephine de Collage, international artist on roller skates, is "bored to death by the academic cultural round"; and psychology graduate Carla Freud-Goldmund arrives at the ship in a rickshaw pulled by her Chinese analysand, as a heart beats on the sound track.

So the characters are not realistic. Nor are they allegorical. They serve as so many figures in a mise-en-scène of female bodies which work through specific possibilities and scenarios of desire within the background fantasy of the pirate ship, the women's movement, lesbian utopia. Seduction, jealousy, and mutiny culminate in the successive deaths of all but one, the "primitive" Noa-Noa. Madame X herself survives, as does Belcampo, the hermaphroditic manicurist whom the crew rescue en route.

The classical fool aboard the Ship of Fools, Belcampo is subjected to a personality test, the object of which is the determination of his/her gender. "The decision—a man—would doubtless have meant being thrown overboard." But Belcampo passes the test by jamming the apparatus. (To Carla Freud-Goldmund's questions Belcampo replies with flash-forwards, flashbacks, and false fragments of the film. The sequence ends with aggression against the analyst, to the crew's cheers.) Then the women direct their course to the pleasure yacht *Holliday,* at the hands of whose unsubtle crew Belcampo had suffered exactly that threatened fate. The women "massacre" Lady Divine and the other pleasure-seekers on board the yacht to the sound track of a B horror flick and divide the spoils.

In the film's final sequence, the crew of the *Orlando* is reassembled onshore not by an explicit invocation but by the ritual of carnival. The women are resurrected, via costume change, as new versions of their former personae. The sadistic Carla Freud-Goldmund returns as a bike dyke in leather; Hoi-

Madame X of the China Seas, Ulrike Ottinger

Sin, who had finally committed ritual suicide, comes back as the femme, *Leader of the Pack* on the sound track. The imperialist Flora Tannenbaum now wears blackface and jailbird stripes and sweeps the sidewalks. "All the discontent within them was unified into one overriding power and they set sail one day with a favorable wind behind."

The staging of regeneration is, on one level, resonant of Woolf's *Orlando,* in which the eponymous hero/ine is both transsexual and transhistorical. A flashback presents the director herself as Madame X's lost lover Orlando, narcissistically reading Woolf's novel—the inscription of the author as "Wunschbild der Vergangenheit" ("ideal of the past," to use Ottinger's term). On another level, the film's ending points to an indefinite number of possible re-visions. Put another way, *Madame X* recommends not the "destruction of pleasure as a radical weapon" as Laura Mulvey proposed in 1975,[7] but the radical reconstruction of a number of possible cinematic pleasures for women. Teresa de Lauretis suggests:

> Cinema could be made to re-present the play of contradictory percepts and meanings usually elided in representation, and so to enact the contradictions of women as social subjects, to perform the terms of the specific division of the female subject in language, in imaging, in the social.[8]

It is within such a problematic that I would like to situate Ottinger's film as an exemplary remake. For not only does it simultaneously embrace and reject the terms of the cinematic production of femininity, it does so in reference to a specific Hollywood text—or rather set of texts, for *Madame X,* the melodrama of the unknown mother, was filmed in six Hollywood versions, spanning from the silent screen to the made-for-TV movie. She was played by Dorothy Donnelly (1916), Pauline Frederick (1920), Ruth Chatterton (1929), Gladys George (1937), Lana Turner (1966), and Tuesday Weld (1981). Feminist film theory has rhetorically proclaimed the historical absence of "woman *as* woman" from Hollywood cinema (and even from cinema audiences). "Madame X" can be seen as a synecdoche for the critical proposition of woman's absence from history, while insisting on her (almost uncanny) return. Ottinger articulates the contradictions of this representation with the social field of feminism, and "meanings usually elided in representation" are central to this lesbian remake of what must already be considered a fetish text.

But it is not so much the maternal melodrama as the frame of the pirate film which allows Ottinger's *Madame X* to rewrite gender within genre. The film is not merely an *inversion* of a dominant genre (although inversion may be its theme), for it enacts not "women on top"[9] but a homosocial world (including male homosexuality, represented by Belcampo and the Russian sailor he rescues). Women's exile is both utopian premise and cause for rebellion. From real Chinese women pirates pictured in the screenplay, to *Anne of the Indies* and *La Fiancée du pirate,* two key texts in early feminist film culture;[10] from classical camp like *The Pirate* and *China Seas* to gay films such as Anger's *Fireworks,* Fassbinder's *Querelle,* Shroeter's *Weisse Reise,* and Ottinger's own short *Infatuation of the Blue Sailors,* the implication of ships and sexual identity has a connotatively rich cultural and cinematic lineage.

The freaks on board the *Orlando* (Ottinger takes up the theme in her 1981 feature *Freak Orlando*), whose photos are snapped by Lady Divine aboard her spectator-ship the *Holliday,* have affinities with the Ship of Fools as well as with Hollywood. Ottinger sums up her method: "I use traditional cinema's clichés for my own purposes."[11] The pirate captain's prosthesis becomes the remarkable studded leather glove through which Madame X "speaks." Her dismembered right hand functions as a joke on castration, circulates in Belcampo's antics and is reembodied later in the film. The conventional parrot appears here as a character, although a mute one.

The film cites Hollywood conventions, yet ignores the construction of narrative space by dialogue and classical editing. This selective appropriation extends to the choice of genre. Critics have seen the strong generic expectations attached to certain films as enabling ideological rupture. Ottinger goes this critical claim one better, actually bringing to life signifiers of femininity repressed in the classical tradition (notably the ship's figurehead) with resounding implications for narrativity, closure, and identification. The refusal of dialogue emphasizes women's oppression, while the film incorporates quotations from Hollywood films, by synchronizing snatches of music and sound effects with characters' gestures and with larger fragments of the film.

Discussing *Madame X's* reception, Ottinger commented: "Some women have accused me of sexism and leather fetishism. I do not see it this way. I do not think women should now turn into grey mice."[12] The question of what women *should* turn into touches on the theme of metamorphosis in the film as well as on de Lauretis's assertion that "women's cinema has been engaged in the transformation of vision."[13] Laura Mulvey's claim that "women . . . cannot view the decline of the traditional film form with anything much more than sentimental regret"[14] is the only gaze specifically allocated to women in her classic essay. Drawing on classical cinema, Ottinger's *Madame X* exploits the radical potential of this sentimental regret, thereby taking up Claire Johnston's challenge: "in order to counter our objectification in the cinema, our collective fantasies must be released: women's cinema must embody the working through of desire: such an objective demands the use of the entertainment film."[15]

Character positions within the film are used to establish not only the geography of the junk, but also narrative space itself. Madame X's point of view is established as a high-angle shot. Hoi-Sin is depicted in the background to the side of her mistress; in close-up she looks left. The figurehead is shot in low-angle profile. Noa-Noa takes up the figurehead's position twice, gesturing and pointing towards Belcampo's raft and later towards the yacht. Her identification with the figurehead is one indication of how "woman" as guarantor of cinema is distributed across a number of positions in this film, with its plethora of female characters, each connoting, in her own way, to-be-looked-at-ness.

Taking up these already established character positions, the film's love scene makes use of conventional filmic construction to represent the unrepresentable. The following analysis will help to demonstrate how the cinematic apparatus is made strange in order to "embody the working through of desire."

The women find Madame X's gaze intolerable and draw lots to determine who will attempt to appease her. Noa-Noa loses (wins?). Here is the shot breakdown of the seduction:

1   Madame X, wearing a huge hat decorated with mirrors, in low-angle, medium close-up (the same as an earlier shot which denotes her unapproachability); a lion on sound track.

2   Noa-Noa in high-angle, long shot, wearing "ritual headdress"; arranges and dances within a circle of leeks; drum music.

3   Madame X as in shot 1, glove drawn back defensively silent.

4   Noa-Noa as in shot 2; drums beat faster.

5   Jump cut to Noa-Noa, long shot, bearing tray of "exotic fruits" climbs steps towards camera; plucked strings and percussion instruments.

6   Hoi-Sin in close-up, shielded behind mast; looks left; percussion continues.

7   Noa-Noa creeps up to Madame X's feet in medium shot; camera reframes to include Madame X's face; she thrusts her glove several times at Noa-Noa, who cowers but timidly persists, standing to offer Madame X a cauliflower; the movements of the glove are accompanied by roars, grunts and growls; no music.

8   Hoi-Sin as in shot 6; raises her eyebrows as growls become more frequent, softer.

9   Madame X and Noa-Noa as in shot 7; Madame X accepts a bunch of bananas from Noa-Noa and sits at her side; camera reframes as Noa-Noa makes more offerings; silent until end of shot, Polynesian music fades in.

Madame X of the China Seas, Ulrike Ottinger

10   Hoi-Sin as in shot 8; narrows eyes, pinches lips, does an exaggerated double take; music continues.

11   Madame X's extended silver-heeled foot, medium shot; camera tilts up her leg; she pulls Noa-Noa toward her by her shell necklace; camera reframes to include their faces; they caress each other tentatively; camera tilts down to Noa-Noa's hand on Madame X's leg; music continues.

12   Hoi-Sin as in shot 10; blinks, rolls eyes, and looks away; music continues.

13   Madame X and Noa-Noa as in shot 11; Madame X runs her studded glove through Noa-Noa's hair, they continue to caress each other awkwardly; loud purring, music continues.

14   Hoi-Sin as in shot 12; looks down sadly; music continues.

15   Madame X and Noa-Noa as in shot 13, camera moves to frame Madame X's pump and Noa-Noa's bare feet as Noa-Noa runs her hand down Madame X's leg; music fades, loud purring.

16   Madame X framed against sky as in shot 1, claps once; no music.

With the exception of the jump cut in shot 5, the editing is classical. And although the mast logically obstructs Hoi-Sin's gaze at the lovers, the point of view construction is naturalistic in effect. The scene takes place in pantomime; the decisive action occurs on the sound track as the roars and growls dubbed to Madame X's thrusts and parries are tamed to the purring of a kitten. The mixing of musical themes in Hollywood romance is parodied. Noa-Noa's charms are associated here and, during her subsequent flirtation with Blow-up, with Polynesian music; and purring returns as the couple's theme. Exaggerated makeup and mugging, absurd fetishes (the long, thin chains Noa-Noa wears from her waist to her wrists, vegetables, and purring), contrasts between hat and headdress, leather and grass skirt, and replacement of explicitness by the eroticism of texture and sound combine as hilarious musical comedy reworked to suit a love triangle among women. The humor of the offscreen growls which pique our curiosity as we watch the watcher, as well as adherence to the one-foot-on-the-ground rule, suggest the pleasurable effects of Hollywood censorship. The refusal of the kiss (denied Belcampo and the sailor as well) simulates suspense, yet goes further to indicate the ultimate incompatibility of the apparatus with the representation of homosexuality.

The crew, said to represent women from all walks of life, are actually highly coded cinematic stereotypes. A consideration of Noa-Noa as "woman of color," or of the exoticism of Hoi-Sin, Madame X, and the venture itself, must attend to this insistence on the stereotype. Noa-Noa is the object of desire in this love story. She is presented as spectacle differently from the others. Her breasts are bare and her dance is performed for Madame X's gaze. Her primitivism is emphasized by her interest in the pirate queen's metallic ornaments and by her selection of a huge tortoise in the division of the booty from the *Holliday*. She expresses herself entirely through pantomime.

Structurally, too, Noa-Noa is set off from the other women; drawing last in the otherwise silent lottery scene, her timid approach is accompanied by music. She is the last to join the crew, approaching the ship alone in her canoe. Like Belcampo, she comes from the sea. Most importantly, she survives the journey, and with Madame X and Belcampo assembles the resurrected crew at the end. Her privileged position is assumed at the expense of Hoi-Sin, who was "in place" at the beginning of the journey. It is suggested that the women encoded as non-white survive one cycle of the Ship of Fools' passage as Madame X's servant/lover. Hoi-Sin is an ordinary crew member in the next round. Perhaps next time the character in blackface will take Noa-Noa's place?

Thus relations of domination are explicitly thematized and erotically invested. Madame X as "oriental despot" is more powerful than Hoi-Sin as Chinese cook. Ottinger's orientalism is at the same time Germanic, an appropriation of the (generally male homosexual) traditions of aestheticism and decadence for lesbian representation, and a provocative masquerade. She allows the feminine, the ornate, and the East to be aligned, impenetrable, and parodic, yet pleasurably textured. The "primitive" represented by Noa-Noa deploys a different set of imperialist codes. Her specificity, in contrast to the relative interchangeablity of the other women, can also be understood in terms of the production of difference within other, more conventionally narrative, lesbian texts.[16] Noa-Noa is the film's major concession to narrativity itself. With the exception of the victimized Russian sailor whose similar position as object of desire should not be overlooked, the entire cast is coded feminine. Noa-Noa, however, is the "girl."

Because Blow-up is presented as a spectacle of Hollywood femininity, coded "cultural" in contrast to Noa-Noa as "natural" beauty, the romance between the blond, glamorous diva and the "exotic" is in some sense transgressive. Blow-up will later direct her third attempt at mutiny against the ship's figurehead, displacing the struggle with the terms of her imaging from the heroine to the image-making machine, reciprocally made in woman's image. Blow-up trips a mechanism and is strangled by the *imago*; her body is taken up in the arms of Omega Centauri who, quite literally, longs for the stars. In turn, Omega is killed for having discovered the switch that animates the figurehead, exposing the apparatus.

Madame X's identification with this animated figurehead puts cinema on the side of women's self-presentation; the apparatus does not merely secure an image of woman as not-man. An exact replica of Madame X, the figurehead fits the image, produces the illusion perfectly. The image (woman) animates the mechanized, or enchanted, leather-clad female body which stands in for the apparatus (the title of the film appears across the first image of the figurehead). For the figurehead itself is given an image of woman "made to speak," reciting "Gold, Liebe, Abenteuer" when Madame X wishes to give "convincing proof of her absolute power and authority." It is both the pirate queen's narcissistic projection (the double à la Dorian Gray, a figure Ottinger later returned to in *The Image of Dorian Gray in the Yellow Press*, 1984), and a fantasmatic representation of her omnipotence which crushes Blow-up's rebellion.

Yet the fact that the figurehead in turn produces Madame X in its own image prevents any simple reading of women's reappropriation of the means of representing woman. Madame X's robotic movements and mechanical sounds indicate that she is not altogether human: her severed hand is restored like a spare part. The synchronization of sound effects associates her body with the register of sound mixing. One in particular refers unmistakably to the MGM lion, whose roar authorized the unfolding of decades of Hollywood stories. Finally, Madame X's gaze is one of the major organizing principles of the film.

The figurehead is the conventional female emblem of piracy, and of sailing in general, gendering the ship itself. It is significant to *Madame X's* narrative structure that the translation from male genre to female utopia maintains this marking of the journey. On the one hand the film's moral can be read off, as Ottinger suggests in interviews, as the inability of the women's movement to do away with figureheads of power: on the other, power itself is granted the various affirmative connotations it has within contemporary lesbian feminism. As an antidote to "Mister X," the anonymous yet coherent "invisible guest" of classical cinema, Madame X herself is split between the conditions of production of her femininity. The pirate queen is caught between her projected image (the figurehead) and the film which takes her name. She is no more than a *figurehead* of absolute authority, for Madame brings the X into an uneasy relation with patriarchal naming.

> In saying that a film whose visual and symbolic space is organized in this manner *addresses its spectator as a woman,* regardless of the gender of its viewers, I mean that the film defines all points of identification (with character, image, camera) as female, feminine or feminist. However, this is not as simple or self-evident a notion as the established film-theoretical view of cinematic identification, namely, that identification with the look is masculine and identification with the image is feminine. It is not self-evident precisely because such a view . . . is now accepted: that the camera

Madame X of the China Seas, Ulrike Ottinger

(technology), the look (voyeurism), and the scopic drive itself partake of the phallic and thus somehow are entities or figures of a masculine nature.[17]

What might indeed be self-evident in this context is that any elaboration of *lesbian* spectatorship must displace the "established film-theoretical view." Ottinger's text allows us to do this in the direction of de Lauretis's re-vision.

The figure of Belcampo offers a condensation of the film's address to the marginal subject. For if the crew respond "naturally" *as women* to Madame X's call (recognizing themselves in the address and their desire in the promise), the interpellation of Belcampo, as unnatural "woman," is more problematic. Classically, the fool's discourse frustrates sexual identification. In the personality test sequence, two discursive models are opposed: psychoanalysis and its imposition of order (represented by Carla Freud-Goldmund, who administers the test), and carnival as ritualized disorder. Psychoanalysis's negotiation of sexual difference is staged, and Belcampo negotiates for his/her life on the stakes of femininity itself. It is important to realize, however, that Belcampo's sexual indeterminacy is not posited at some post-gendered answer to patriarchal oppression. Belcampo is accepted as a "woman" by the onlooking crew at the end of the sequence; moreover, the question of his/her suitability to the enterprise is resolved by their approval. Belcampo's case attempts to make sense of the non-sense of gender. S/he makes explicit the film's trope of female impersonation that might be considered germane to lesbian identity. Finally, "his" romance with the Russian sailor, whom "he" rescues and attempts to shield from Madame X's wrath, introduces yet another "invert" trajectory to the lesbian narrative, hinting at the alliance between gay men and lesbians which Ottinger's representational strategies reflect.

The test sequence opposes a "realistic" mise-en-scène, in which Carla quizzes Belcampo and times his/her answers with a stopwatch, to extra-diegetic images and sounds which Belcampo enunciates. A third space is represented by the reaction shots of the other characters which dominate the end of the sequence.

Belcampo's first answer, given as flashback, is in response to the question: "Are you an important personality?" We see the exact *reverse* of the shot immediately preceding Belcampo's rescue, where the women were represented as "eating" a meal prepared by Hoi-Sin with a close-up of a large fish violently attacked by chopsticks, as seagulls screeched on the sound track. This time the fish is reconstituted. The jangle of a tambourine marks the beginning of this shot, which is followed by a detail of Carla clicking her stopwatch. Belcampo's carnival defies the linear unfolding of the film and the logic of question and answer, fleshing out the film's fantasy of regeneration as enacted in the final scene. The trick shot foregrounds the apparatus. Attempting inversion among the inverts, Belcampo draws Madame X herself into his/her discourse, breaking down the established hierarchy, if only momentarily. Carla asks if Belcampo feels strongly attracted to members of his/her own sex: s/he is literally unable to comprehend the question. Carla repeats it and we see, instead of Belcampo, Madame X throwing back her head with a resounding lip-synched laugh. Our understanding of the question coincides with hers in the only appropriate answer—defiant but affirmative laughter. As Blow-up and Betty Brillo caress each other in the following shot, gazing seductively at the camera, Carla asks in voice-over: "Have you always wanted to be a woman?" Although her question seems to decide the very issue the test is designed to resolve, assuming the you addressed is not already a woman, the connoted desire for "resistance to the norm" (implying both the advantages of being a woman and the option of refusing to become woman) is unmistakable here as in the film as a whole.

Three questions bear directly on spectatorship. Carla asks Belcampo, "Do you see around you things, or creatures of fable, that others do not see?" The response is an image of Madame X, as if standing in for the film, a fabulous hallucination. Later in the sequence Belcampo is asked whether s/he enjoys adventure stories. This prompts Belcampo to transgress the spatial boundary set up even in this transgressive sequence. S/he leaves the analytic space for the outside world (the diegetic spectators' realm) and takes Omega Centauri's water pistol, returning to squirt the analyst. We are reminded of Mulvey's description: "In contrast to woman as icon, the active male figure . . . demands a three-dimensional space. . . . He is a figure in a landscape."[18] The conventions of spectatorship again inform Carla's last question: "Do you like to see love scenes at the movies?" At this point both Carla and Belcampo lose discursive agency (Carla's mouth is taped shut) and we see a rapid montage of the crew participating in general disorder. On the sound track Betty Brillo sings the words from her opening speech as the film's romantic theme: "Jesus, Babyfolks! This is *extreme. . . .*" The preferred response to Carla's question is "*this* is what I was looking for!"

Mary Russo, in her article on carnival (of) theory, cautions: "In liminal states . . . temporary loss of boundaries tends to redefine social frames, and such topsy-turvy or time-out is inevitably set right and on course."[19] Within the social frame of Madame X's absolute authority, however, setting right and on course means continuing the women's journey with the figurehead in the bow. Having rescued the damsel in distress, the women direct the junk "south-south-west" (the figurehead mouths the words) to revenge "her" injustice. Carnival is recovered for the marginal. Belcampo's sexual difference is not a simple critique of the rigidity of gender, but serves to shift the terms of its elaboration within the course of the lesbian adventure tale.

Here is the film's invocation once more:

> Madame X, a harsh, pitiless beauty, the cruel uncrowned ruler of the China Seas, launched an appeal to all women willing to exchange an everyday existence of almost unbearable boredom, though safe and easy, for a world of uncertainty and danger, but also full of love and adventure.

To what degree does *Madame X* the film offer to spectators the booty promised by Madame X to all willing women? Isn't there a contradiction in the fact that a film which purports to call on all women is excessively long, "boring," has no synchronous dialogue, too many heroines and a hero in drag? One can certainly refuse to take part in what Ottinger has described as the film's initiation stories; one might regard "a comedy about the women's movement" as unfunny.[20] As an all-too-willing spectator, I believe I have struck gold.

Feminist film theory has argued that if "cinematic codes create a gaze, a world, and an object, thereby producing an illusion cut to the measure of desire,"[21] female spectators pledge themselves at their own risk, for very uncertain pleasures. *Madame X,* which posits a female gaze ("Madame X's gaze was so fearsome that the women trembled"), a female world (of playfully evoked erotic domination and submission), and a female object (like mainstream cinema, Ottinger's film attaches desire to women's gaze at woman), is a dangerous enterprise. Love is certainly on offer at the movies, is even considered a specific (albeit masochistic) appeal to the women in the audience. Yet love is tied into a very precise ideological project concerned with endlessly reproducing the heterosexual couple. Women enjoy adventure films surreptitiously, wearing, to quote another of Mulvey's tailor-made metaphors, "borrowed transvestite clothes."[22] Both assumptions—the impossibility of the female spectator's desire on the one hand; her trans-sex identification on the other, have left lesbians in the dark.

In her 1981 "Afterthoughts" Laura Mulvey returned to "Visual Pleasure and Narrative Cinema" to face up to the female spectator. Narrative cinema was reevaluated in the light of the author's "own love of Hollywood melodrama,"[23] but visual pleasure remained unaddressed. Mary Ann Doane would write that same year: "One assumption behind the positing of a female spectator (that is, one who does not assume a masculine position with respect to the reflected image of her own body) is that it is no longer necessary to invest the look with desire in quite the same way."[24] Assuming that it is necessary to posit the female spectator differently, I would like to redress this disavowal of female fetishism through a brief discussion of the implications of the figure of the transvestite.[25]

Mulvey describes her earlier position: "at the time, I was interested in the . . . 'masculinization' of the spectator position regardless of the actual sex (or possible deviance) of any real live moviegoer."[26] Lesbianism, although nowhere mentioned explicitly, would seem to coincide so exactly with "masculinization" in these arguments as to constitute an *impossible* deviance. In any case, it is *not* deviance but actual sex to which Mulvey returns in the figure of the transvestite. She writes: "as desire is given cultural materiality in a text, for women (from childhood onwards) transsex identification is a *habit* that very easily becomes *second Nature.* However, this Nature does not sit easily and shifts restlessly in its borrowed transvestite clothes."[27] This nature, secondary or not (as indeed the little girl's heterosexuality can be said to be *second* nature in the Freudian account upon which Mulvey draws), sounds suspiciously essentialist. For why must *transvestite* clothes be borrowed? This process would be more accurately described as masquerade, a metaphor Doane opposes to transvestism in her essay "Film and the Masquerade."[28] It is the question of desire which leaves her restless with Mulvey's use of the term.

Doane argues that "the transvestite wears clothes which signify a different sexuality, a sexuality which, for the woman, allows a mastery over the image and the very possibility of attaching the gaze to desire."[29] Yet the different sexuality in question is evidently not homosexuality. In fact, the very possibility of *any* desire of one's own is eradicated by the next sentence: "Clothes make the man, as they say." Doane dismisses this supposedly facile "masculinization": "sexual mobility would seem to be a distinguishing feature of femininity in its cultural construction. Hence, transvestism would be fully recuperable." Lesbians must take issue with this assumption of mobility which, if true at all, has only been made possible by feminist mobilization. Transvestism, unlike the masquerade, is not a psychoanalytic concept. Nor does this use of the term imply the social practice of transvestism, which clearly does not make the man. The "metaphor" seems to be a thinly veiled reference to an impossible, reprehensible, or at best recuperable deviance on the part of the female spectator. Masquerade is to be considered as less "recuperable [than] transvestism precisely because it constitutes an acknowledgment that it is femininity itself which is constructed as mask—as the decorative layer which conceals a non-identity."[30] But the false opposition between masquerade and transvestism impoverishes even the "straight" story, discovering a new essential femininity in the non-identity behind the mask, defined as nothing more than a screen for male desire.

Masquerade (as "hyperbolization of the accountrements of femininity"[31]) and symptomatic transvestism are of course not irrelevant to the consideration of women and cinema. Nor to Ottinger's film, which draws on the genre loosely termed spectacle, for example, de Mille's *Madam Satan,* in which a costume party aboard a blimp ends in disaster. These figures for spectatorship beg the question of the real live moviegoer and her visual pleasure. As Ottinger's characters "lay aside their petticoats to try their luck at new trouser roles,"[32] they become figures of spectatorial desire. And if Belcampo (who is of course not an hermaphrodite, but a male transvestite) permits transsex identification in "his" adventure story, deviance is made explicit.

Doane writes, "It is quite tempting to foreclose entirely the possibility of female spectatorship. . . ."[33] I would suggest that we succumb to other temptations. We can continue to gaze with sentimental regret at the classical Hollywood construction of femininity without becoming grey mice. My reading of *Madame X: An Absolute Ruler* argues that the film's address displaces two assumptions—that feminism finds its audience "naturally," and that the female spectator is destined to miss the boat. Gold, love, and adventure lie just beyond the horizon.

Notes

1. See Teresa de Lauretis, "Aesthetic and Feminist Theory: Rethinking Women's Cinema," *New German Critique* 34 (Winter, 1985) pp. 154–175.

2. Ulrike Ottinger's screenplay, *Madame X: Eine Absolute Herrscherin* (Basel/Frankfurt: Stroemfeld/Roter Stern, 1979) contains not only narration of this kind, but a mass of material, both written and visual, relating to the film.

3. Teresa de Lauretis, p. 163.

4. Marc Silberman, "Surreal Images: Interview with Ulrike Ottinger," *Jump Cut* 29 (1984) p. 56. See also, Miriam Hansen, "Visual Pleasure, Fetishism and the Problem of Feminine/Feminist Discourse: Ulrike Ottinger's *Ticket of No Return*," *New German Critique* 31 (Winter, 1984) pp. 95–108.

5. The voice-over remains unidentified; the call is delivered by Yvonne Rainer. Due to lack of space, I am unable to discuss the number and kinds of relationships the film posits between the woman's body and the woman's voice, without, however, granting her speech. See Kaja Silverman, "Dis-Embodying the Female Voice," in Mary Ann Doanne et al., eds., *Revision: Essays in Feminist Film Criticism*, American Film Institute Monograph Series 3 (Frederick, MD; University Publications of America, 1984) pp. 131–149.

6. Monique Wittig, "Paradigm," in George Stambolian and Elaine Marks, eds., *Homosexualities and French Literature* (Ithaca: Cornell University Press, 1979) p. 114.

7. Laura Mulvey, "Visual Pleasure and Narrative Cinema," *Screen*, vol. 16, no. 3, (Autumn, 1975) p. 7.

8. Teresa de Lauretis, *Alice Doesn't: Feminism, Semiotics, Cinema* (Bloomington: Indiana University Press, 1984) p. 69.

9. See Natalie Zemon-Davis, "Women on Top," in her *Society and Culture in Early Modern France* (Stanford: Stanford University Press, 1986) pp. 124–152.

10. See Claire Johnston, "Femininity and the Masquerade: *Anne of the Indies*," in Claire Johnston and Paul Willemen, eds., *Jacques Tourneur* (London: British Film Institute, 1975) pp. 36–44. "It is hardly surprising that [Tourneur] should have chosen a pirate film aimed at children's audiences to represent such an extraordinary masquerade, for children's literature is rich in bisexual phantasy," pp. 37–8.

11. Marc Silberman, p. 56.

12. Roswitha Mueller, "Interview with Ulrike Ottinger," *Discourse* 4 (Winter, 1981/1982) p. 120. Ottinger's sentiments are shared by Kaja Silverman, who suggests that "the sartorial reticence of North American feminism . . . is the symptom of what might almost be called 'The Great Feminine Renunciation' in "Fragments of a Fashionable Discourse," in Tania Modleski, ed., *Studies in Entertainment* (Bloomington: Indiana University Press, 1987) p. 149.

13. Teresa de Lauretis, "Aesthetic and Feminist Theory," p. 159.

14. Laura Mulvey, p. 18.

15. Claire Johnston, "Women's Cinema as Counter Cinema," in Claire Johnston, ed., *Notes on Women's Cinema* (London: SEFT, 1975) p. 28.

16. Butch/femme or marked differences in age and experience structure lesbian films from *Daughters of Darkness* to *The Bitter Tears of Petra von Kant.* Jackie Stacey's "Desperately Seeking Difference," *Screen* (Winter, 1987) vol. 28 no. 1, pp. 48–61, discusses the narrative implications of one woman's identification with and desire for another in *All About Eve* and *Desperately Seeking Susan.*

17. Teresa de Lauretis, "Aesthetic and Feminist Theory," p. 161.

18. Laura Mulvey, pp. 12–13.

19. Mary Russo, "Female Grotesques: Carnival and Theory," in Teresa de Lauretis, ed., *Feminist Studies/Critical Studies* (Bloomington: Indiana University Press, 1986) p. 215.

20. Roswitha Mueller, "Interview with Ulrike Ottinger," p. 121. "This, if you wish, is also my feminist point of view, the freedom for women to go out and experience on their own. This freedom, of course, also includes the possibility to fail. These ideas are contained in the notion of adventure, the freedom to try out things, and the freedom to fail."

21. Laura Mulvey, pp. 12–13.

22. Laura Mulvey, "Afterthoughts on 'Visual Pleasure and Narrative Cinema' Inspired by *Duel in the Sun." Framework* 15/16/17 (1981) p. 15.

23. Ibid., p. 12.

24. Mary Ann Doane, "*Caught* and *Rebecca:* The Inscription of Femininity as Absence," *Enclitic,* vol. 5 no. 2/vol. 6 no. 1 (Fall, 1981/Spring, 1982) p. 76.

25. Miriam Hansen has also discussed this choice of metaphor; see her "Pleasure, Ambivalence, Identification: Valentino and Female Spectatorship," *Cinema Journal,* vol. 25 no. 4 (Summer, 1986) p. 8. Jackie Stacey, op. cit., addresses a similar omission in feminist film theory: "While this issue [of the woman spectator's pleasure] has hardly been addressed, the specifically homosexual pleasures of female spectatorship have been ignored completely," p. 48.

26. Laura Mulvey, "Afterthoughts," p. 12.

27. Ibid., p. 13.

28. Mary Ann Doane, "Film and the Masquerade: Theorizing the Female Spectator," *Screen* (September-October, 1982) vol. 23 no. 3-4, pp. 74-87.

29. Ibid., p. 81.

30. Ibid., p. 82.

31. Ibid.

32. *Hosenrollen.* See Ulrike Ottinger, *Madame X: Eine Absolute Herrscherin,* p. 4.

33. Mary Ann Doane, "Film and the Masquerade," p. 87.

My Affair with Pasolini

JOHN DI STEFANO

While everyone was asleep that scorching afternoon, I went walking through the deserted streets. I was heading for a lonely bridge over the river which for some days had been my favorite goal, holding some unknown allure. Upon reaching it I leaned on the parapet and looked down. I remained there for some time then raised my head, and, looking around, noticed a detail that had previously escaped me: along the street bordering the river, but quite secluded, stood an old urinal surrounded by a sheet of rusted iron. This structure was new to me, since in the village from which I came, there was nothing of the sort. Approaching, I entered, and saw a slab of yellowed marble, wet from the continual dripping of water. There was a sharp, persistent stench of ammonia. Very excited, and as though on the point of committing something forbidden, I was about to urinate in that place that up until now had been foreign to me. Suddenly, I heard voices approaching. Two men were speaking, and they were already inside as I was about to run away; I could no longer get away and remained there, in the middle, between the two men, against the marble slab, bowing my head, waiting for them to leave.

When later I was alone again by the river's edge, I realized that I was completely overcome by a new, intoxicating, spasmodic palpitation. My modesty had recieved a shock so violent and unexpected that even that pleasure that I had just discovered, different from anything else I had previously experienced, seemed to reclothe itself in somewhat more compelling attractions. I was unable to decifer them then though. I was simply thrown into the midst of their violence. But the fiercely logical thoughts of a child began to connect themselves in line with a practical and interested order. By now I was seeking a way to again obtain for myself that offense to my boyish modesty. As was natural for me, a plan immediately formed in my mind on which the temptations and curiosities of that different adult atmosphere, imbued with sin, had been impressed: I would pretend to be looking at the river as usual, and as soon as someone stopped at the urinal, I would go in too. I devoted the first deserted and burning hours of the noonday to plotting my course from that urinal to another similar one that I had discovered near the Market. As I stood before the sultry slabs I often heard the buzz of bluebottles, of horseflies, or of some stray wasp.

(1948-1949)

Accattone (1961): Franco Citti (Accattone) and his partners-in-crime just before the crime that leads to Accattone's death. This film was the first film in the history of Italian cinema to get an "18 years and over" rating. It was considered "vulgar" in it's representation of the sub-proletariate, causing the Italian Parliament to take an unpresidented vote to censor it. Pasolini was assaulted during a riot in the theatre on it's openning night.

The rules by which we live: Sex and friendship don't have much to do with each other. To take desire cast it away and at the same time exaggerate the desire or ugliness in us so we can express it. To be honest with a person that I want to lick the feet, but to not care. Exaggerate pain because the government wants me to ignore what I feel. Never break up a friendship when a friend knifes you in the back.

Salò (o Le 120 Giornate di Sodoma) (1975):
Two fascist guards dance together in the final
scene. A poignant portrayal of the decline of
fascism in Italy at the end of World War II,
this film was banned in most countries on
grounds ranging from indecency and
pornography to politcal subversion. This was
Pasolini's last film before his untimely death.

Teorema (1968): Terrence Stamp
(The Visitor) and Andrès José Cruz
(Pietro) undress before going
to bed. A film that was widely
condemned and considered
scandalous because of it's
depiction of a (sexually) decadent
bourgeois-upper class.

I saw Pier Paolo for
the first time through
a store window in
New York's Little Italy.
We cruised each other
through the glass.
It was 1966 and
Pasolini's was on his
first (and only) trip to
North America.
When we were in bed
later on I told him that
I too was Italian;
he wouldn't believe me.

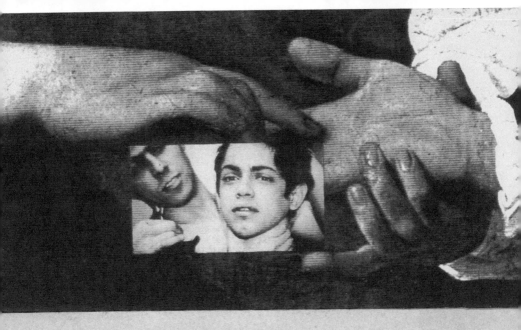

"... *my inditements* have been institutionalized and have become part of mainstream contemporary Italian culture, Italian history. I've been anthologized; my writings and films have been carefully reinterpreted, revised. The eros in my work has been either ignored or aesthetisized. The beauty has been gutted-out or else it has been turned ugly. Synthesized, compacted, edited, decontextualized, deconstructed, it has all become part of other people's discourses and rhetoric, becoming abstracted. Why has my essay "The church, the penis and the vagina" been forgotten for so many years? Why haven't my essays "Homosexuality" and "Jail and the fraternity of homosexual love" been translated? Why has so much of my work been supressed ... not to mention the pieces I've written on abortion, extra-marital sex, terrorism, fascism and anti-fascism, etc. Why didn't the people at the Museum of Modern Art call a spade a spade (a fag a fag) when they elevated me to the status of a "Modern('s) Master" with their (not my) travelling film retrospective? It is becoming apparent why I have been reconstructed into a white-washed (anti-)hero. The lines on my face are being softened by revisionist historians of (homophobic) bourgeois sensibilities. This is my real murder, my real condemnation. This is my real sacrifice. My life flashes before my eyes ...

"(I would've been 69 this year) and I'd have lived through over half a century of perhaps the most violent changes in Italian and world history. I was born in '22, the year Mussoloni came to power. My father was a fascist by convention. I remember his black shirt. I witnessed the downfall of fascism after the War which took away the life of my only brother. I participated in the rise of communism, in reaction to the atrocities, amoung them the death of my brother and the brainwashing of my father. It was an attempt at washing away the violence of those black shirts, those black years. Soon though, the Partito Communista Italiano expelled me from it's ranks for alleged "perverse actions" of which I was aquitted undeniably in court. My sexuality was a threat to their attempt at assimilation. I was naive then ... But I've seen something even more terrifying: I've seen the machine of mediocrity woo away an entire nation with the promise of security and a heavenly afterlife; the Democratic Christian Party guarenteeing prosperity to the working class, offering them the promise of rising into the ever swelling ranks of the bourgeoisie. I've witnessed the mass-production of FIATs, appliances, designer clothes, gourmet foods, smiles and stars. The decline of culture bartered in exchange ofor a bit-part in a CineCittà film or a gig in a foto-romanzo. The bourgeoisie and it's moralism are the real evil.

Friendship, not
ove, is sacred and so must encompass violence. Work is every-
hing.

"I've been part of the counter-culture as it has been defined by the dominant-culture.
I've tried to create a space where open discussions of taboos, sexual and other, could take place.
I was told endless times by every faction of the Left with whom I aligned myself during the years,
to down-play these forums and to think of the greater struggle of the nation for now . . .
everything would later fall into place. How could I be so egotistical when there were more
important and pressing things to fight for? '. . . the collective, the collective. . . we Italians are
excessively social beings. . . after all homosexuality doesn't really exist in Italy. No, Pier Paolo,
you're suffering from an unresolved psychological trauma regarding your parents. You're a
true Italian, a poet; focus your energies towards more noble matters, toward the people,
the nation, La Patria. . . '

"I've heard it all. I've been disregarded, misinterpreted, and when I resisted,
mocked, humiliated and vilified. I was brought into courthouses all across Italy on various
charges during these years, all fuelled by an incessant homophobia. (I was aquitted everytime.)
The media lynched me year after year and had a fieldtrip with my courtdates, the constructed
scandals around my private life, the censorship of my films and novels, my newspaper columns,
essays, public speeches, all acts of violence against me . . . and with all this, created the image
of a monster to the public. I was a genious perhaps, but also a pervert, a corrupter of youth,
a subversive, a homosexual; thus I was dispensible. Does this shed light on that night in 1975,
when I was killed? And why did the courts never fully complete thier investigation into
the cause of my death (read: assasination) even after repeated formal requests
by their own constituents? Get Real!

"The italian slang for faggot is 'finocchio', the italian word for fennel. Why?
In the Middle-ages when homosexuals were burned at the stake, f
ennel was thrown on the remains. The fennel had an almost miraculous quality
of halting the unbearable stench of the charred flesh.

I've become both the object of loathing, as well as it's appeasment.

Often the sexually charged scenes in many of Pasolini's films were really repressions of his own homosexual desire, cloaked in what seemed to him to be the only viably acceptable currency: heterosexuality, often in the guise of comradery between men. Thus, gay male sexual desire was interupted or denied altogether. Where Pasolini's gaze may have been driven by gay desire, his actions were driven by self-loathing. While asserting an image of defiance to the order of italian *machismo*, he was somehow complicit with it's logic. In order for his unacceptable desire to be tolerated it had to be somehow meshed with this logic; it had to be conflated with political ideology. To be taken seriously in Italy, one must align oneself religiously to the ideology of a political party. He chose early on to align himself with the Left. His dedication to communist ideals helped displace the shock of his homosexuality to his contemporaries. It became the alibi for his desire, and may partly explain his obsession with the subproletariate, and specifically with subproletarian men. Pier Paolo aligned himself with the plight of this class socio-politically, but his position was inevitably directed by his sexual desire - a desire that also tried to deflect guilt from the power he wielded as a member of the *literati*. Ideologically, his patriarchal benevolence, his altruistic interest in the boys of the *borgata* gave him the only possible access to desire that he could accept ethically. This is exemplary of the hypocrisy on which the italian intelligentsia is often founded - the hand that contributes to sexism, racism and homophobia Of this hypocrisy, Pasolini was guilty. As visible as he was in the public sphere as a gay man, he was not as radical as perhaps he wanted to be. For what he expressed, there was an equal amount left unvoiced. Pasolini was torn, his conviction diluted. He was still invisible.

These "repressions" in Pasolin's films mirrored the compromised marxist adoption of bourgeois restraint in Italy - the betrayal of his true desire: the desire to see two men happy together on screen (and in *his* own life). He chose the security of patriarchal logic to present his desire to a society that didn't want to hear. He adopted as a model the institutionalized myth of the Freudian homosexual-victim manifested in the unresolved Oedipal complex. He went as far as making a film about the Oedipal myth, which lacked any significant reference to (his) homosexuality. He had a morbid love for his mother, and a quite predictable hatred of his father -

the man you desired the most and who you could never allow yourself to love, but had wished to possess; the man you wanted to fuck hard and violently and by whom you wanted to be fucked passionately; the man whose cock you wanted to suck as if it were a milk-giving nipple; the man who you wished would ejaculate all over your chest and whose cum would envelope you. Why did we never see this on the screen? Why did we never read this in your books? Why did we have to wait years for it to be said by someone else? Why did you deem the only acceptable way for your sexual desire to be expressed was when it was with a hustler whose services you had to pay for, in a field at night, or in an alley, in your car, on an empty soccerfield in Ostia . . . I read once were you paid ten (or more?) neapolitan youths to jerk-off in a circle around you while performing fellatio on several of them. Was this the real scene you wanted to shoot for one of your films? You've been accused of worse, why didn't you show italians that they are homos too and that it could mean something different; that it didn't have to be about power and marginality. You were not the only one. (I am not the only one.)

It has been said that you were sexy in your radicalism and vitality (Laura Betti sure fell for it!). It has been said that it turned your facial features into beacons. I have been told that you were very sensual when you talked of politics, when you got angry, livid, and raised your cocky eyebrow. It has been whispered in my ear that your sexiness was persuasive in particular when you spoke of revolution and desire, when you tried to re-write it. (I could believe in that.) Some say you filled a void that no person since has quite been able to fill. Some have told me that they were not afraid to look to you; they were no longer ashamed.

Bedtime Stories

The ways we talk about sex occupy at least two thousand and one nights, and the ways we represent (and understand) our social and sexual desires are even more plentiful. The narratives of our pleasures are as complex and convoluted as the ways we speak them. These articles all proceed from the notion that the social and the sexual are inextricable. Deocampo's personal polemic of coming out as a fag and filmmaker under fire is echoed in different ways through every other contribution, finding a full menu of expressions, from the wistful to the furious, from the romantic to the melancholic. Within this contested field, it's clear that no image can simply "represent our desires." Instead, each one must be voraciously interrogated, along with being voluptuously consumed.

Desiring Conquest

LAWRENCE CHUA

NOTE: Three recent commercial gay-themed features from Thailand, and a video performance piece from Hong Kong, together served as the trigger for this text. The films are: *The Last Song* and *Anguished Love*, by Pisan Akkaraseni, and *I Am a Man*, by M. L. Panthewanop Thewakul. The latter is a sort of remake of the 1970 Hollywood sort of classic *Boys in the Band*. The video/performance *Rooms of Desire* was by Joseph Lau.

I. "How many Eurasians does it take to screw in a light bulb?"

Payl:

"Where's your bit of rice?" I wasn't supposed to be walking into the women's bathroom and they were clearly surprised when they saw me. My boyfriend was sitting on the sink, his milky cheeks flushed. The woman who posed the question regarded her drink for a full moment before slurring, "I'm so glad you're white and polished and not all brown and fried." It triggered the expected laughter. I smiled, so everyone else wouldn't perceive me as overly sensitive to these kind of things, and walked away. At home my boyfriend asked me to urinate on him, and all the while I stood over this man, drenching him, I couldn't help but wonder if this wasn't inspired by some misplaced need to apologize.

Virapong:

His body in recline is formed by one brush stroke of gold ink. An orchestration of ligament rendered to give the appearance of ease. He has a boxer's face with a flattened nose and dim, petty eyes. His most lucrative feature, though, is his foot-long cock, as thick as my wrist. I can't stop thinking about him. I've already travelled twice around the world on his cheeks, imagined the universe spread over his skin, his mouth covering me like a cloud. I push my nose into the back of his neck where the hair is shaved to velour. There are exactly two hairs growing from his armpit, which smells of sweat and cheap soap. The first night I watched him play with the revolving doors at a nightclub. Later, he buys me a rose, puts his hand up to my ear as if to tell me a secret, but kisses me instead. The next week, he slips a silver ring on my finger. I like the way he gets all possessive around

Poster for *The Last Song*, Pisan Akkaraseni

other guys and calls me his little monster, even though we're the same height, the same age, the same skin color. I live with his family now, and early in the morning, we fool around in the basement before his father wakes up. I still get restless when he leaves me at night to go to work. It's becoming quite apparent that he adores being the whore with the hard-on of gold, but he's becoming more selective in who he allows to regard him. They don't let white men into the places where he works. That kind of lust is entertained elsewhere.

Jerry:

I let him take my hand, wiggle his thumb in my palm. We exchange drinks and I smoke half a cigarette from between his thick fingers. He puts my head on his chest. His cool skin is thumping underneath his shirt. His family just came here from the capital and he's lonely. He wants to travel. I hear him tell our friend he wants someone to take care of him, to pay the fare as far as Singapore. I hear him say this, but he doesn't specify the gender. He never brings it up when he drives by at 5 A.M. to take me for a spin on the beach, where, in the glow of predawn, we talk, kiss, and grope distractedly, each too tired to fulfill what we've started. He has tiny nipples that taste like starfish. I like the feel of his broad tongue in my mouth. I avoid his eyes, looking instead at his sticky, manicured hair. If I don't leave tomorrow, I'll call you, I promise.

Joe:

You make me nervous. I've been wanting your bones for nearly a year, since I first saw you next to that Harvard chink with a profile like Bart Simpson. Now, sitting next to you, I can barely speak. There is some gap between us I can't bridge. Solidarity is the moment our heads touch the back of the couch at the same time and I can see the light growth of hair dusting your cheekbones. I'm thinking of your inner thigh rubbing against my lips, of the pattern the hairs might form growing down there. I'm wondering how you taste and I want to tell you that I think I love you, but instead it comes out as "I love your shirt," or maybe, in a more intimate moment, "I love the way you smell." I sense that your own desire is defined more by a sense of fair play. You've become bored, like me, of the specifics of vanilla charm we grew up with, but you still haven't made the leap between conscience and consciousness. Call me when you've worked it out.

II. "Let's get together, drink white man's piss and overthrow China."
—graffiti in Causeway Bay, Hong Kong, 1991

Jardine Pacific:

As late as 1991, leading Hong Kong companies like Jardine Pacific and the Hong Kong Bank were testing potential employees for what one newspaper called "the killer AIDS virus" to protect themselves against huge medical claims. A spokeswoman for Hutchinson Whampoa, whose subsidiaries include Watson's and Park 'n' Shop, said such tests were "for the health of the staff. After all it is infectious. Any healthy person would not like to catch it. There is a psychological effect if you know someone working next to you has AIDS."[1]

Hong Kong public service announcements about AIDS:
Every opportunity has been taken in the mass media to portray AIDS as a direct result of "illegitimate" desire. Car doors slamming on potential pickups, two men walking hand in hand into a void, a pyramid construction bearing the characters: "The more sexual partners you have, the greater your risk of becoming infected with the AIDS virus." Only recently have condoms been seen in these television spots. One opens on a satisfied vacationer unwinding on a plane, looking at Polaroids he's taken of brown-skinned women. "Where's Steve?" asks one voice. "On vacation," says the other. "He's quite the ladies' man." "I wouldn't muck about with all this AIDS around." On cue, the commercial cuts to Steve convalescing in a hospital bed.

A prominent Hong Kong "gay rights activist" and author:
Pimply, insecure, but well intentioned, he autographs a copy of his book on the history of homosexuality in China and whispers through a smile that he hopes the American author who purloined large chapters of his book "gets AIDS."

Sodomy:
Hong Kong repealed its antisodomy laws in the late 1980s, thereby "decriminalizing" homosexuality.

The guy who couldn't hold my stare at the Yin/Yang (a queer bar in Hong Kong):

Joseph Lau's performance *Room of Desire:*
The performance text reads, in part—"Desire leads to despair . . . Despair leads to destruction.
Desire kills discipline . . . Discipline kills desire.
However you look at it, desire is simultaneously fulfilling and disastrous.

Joseph Lau is absorbed in his fulfillment.
Joseph Lau is trapped in his despair. . . ."

The boy on TV:
He says he was the laughing stock of his class. "Everybody ridiculed me because I was so sissy."

The boy on the bed:
In his underwear, lying very still.

A boy enters the room:
He looks at the man lying in bed, then looks at the mirror. He begins to search as if he has lost something. He looks at yellowing photographs on an antiseptic table that looks like an "affordable" copy of a Philippe Starck original.

The policeman, the doctor, the lawyer, the thief, the exhibitionist:
They all file past the bed for a piece of something.

A woman's nightgown:
The boy on the bed tries it on.

Room of Desire:
As in the space for desire that is somewhere between "B & D" and "tickling" on the fetish shelves. See "Konerak Sintasamphone. . . ."

The boy on the bed:
The body that is simultaneously engraved in the economy of pleasure and the economy of discourse, domination, and power.

The boy on the bed:
He misplaces his innocence when he, a victim, articulates desire.

Passive:
The position of discourse here is missionary. The characters in *Room of Desire*, except for the talking heads on the television monitor, function in a kind of non-life. In many ways, *Room of Desire*'s inability to interrogate the victim paradigm is characteristic of the simultaneously privileged and colonized gaze of Hong Kong image-makers. The next step in Lau's troubling equation is that of desire and death.

III. "Don't call me Oriental because I'm Teochew. Call me Oriental because I lie like a rug."

Location:
Thailand is one of the only nations in the Third World that has never been colonized outright by a European power. That is not to suggest, however, that the country has been insulated from the era of imperialism. During the nineteenth century, it was compelled to sign unequal treaties with foreign countries. Foreign capital embarked on industrial enterprise over one hundred and twenty years ago, bringing the Thai proletariat into being.[2] There is an astute, if unspoken, understanding of cultural self-determination that is evidenced in events like the banning of *The King and I* for its inaccurate representation of the monarchy, or the removal of the English writer's books that referred to the "Cheshire cat grins" of the Thai people.

Rehabilitating desire:
Few countries outside Africa face the problems Thailand does in confronting AIDS. Surveys show that four percent of men going for treatment at government-run clinics have tested HIV-positive. In some provinces, particularly in the rural north, the figure is as high as eighteen percent. In 1987, only one percent of drug addicts in Bangkok tested HIV-positive. Three years later, the proportion rose to more than fifty percent. This year, the Prime Minister's Office estimates about four hundred thousand people with positive status. Fifteen percent of army recruits from the Chiang Mai region are HIV-positive. The government has moved from a position of ignoring the problem to attacking those directly affected by it. Last year, the Ministry of Public Health drafted a law that would allow health officials to test anyone it considered suspect, against their will if necessary. Those who would not

Poster for *Anguished Love*, Pisan Akkaraseni

cooperate would be sequestered in specially built centers for up to one hundred eighty days. Five and a half million dollars was approved as the budget for building one of these camps in the northern province of Lampang, far from water sources, populated areas, and, needless to say, tourist attractions. The site used to be a leper colony.[3]

The sex industry in Thailand:
   The coup d'état which ousted popularly elected Chatichai Choonhavan as Prime Minister has promised to curb the country's legendary sex industry, even though it is a substantial source of foreign income.

The International Labor Organization in Geneva on the sex industry in Thailand:
   "The migration gave them an earning power which was simply astounding relative to normal rural budgets. A couple of years of work would enable the family to build a house of a size and quality which few people in the countryside could hope to achieve in the earnings of a lifetime. . . . They were engaging in an entrepreneurial move designed to sustain the family units of a rural economy. . . . Our survey clearly showed that the girls felt they were making a perfectly rational decision within the context of their particular social and economic structure."

The sex industry in Thailand:
   Phaitoon Manchai of the Foundation for Children estimates there are eight hundred thousand children and one million two hundred thousand adults working as prostitutes in Thailand. In the years following the Gulf War, which uprooted Thai labor in the Arab world, the figures are likely to increase.[4]

Tolerance:
   It's a word that permeates any portrait of queer identities in Thailand, identities that are more complex than the standard Euro-American paradigms. The distinction between heterosexuality and homosexuality is more tenuous. "It's not bad to be gay, it's just better if you weren't."[5] Tolerance is largely about negotiating exclusion and incorporation. The gay bourgeoisie have developed a significant business community that embraces bars, brothels, and discos. The first sight after clearing customs in Bangkok is the full-color Ciba transparency beckoning visitors to Pattaya's world-famous

transvestite cabaret. Some of the country's most revered historical figures have been gay. There are several gay actors and pop singers. Mainstream films acknowledge a gay audience, albeit an unruly one. Buddhist morality, resisting the missionary thrust, has never lent itself to the same historical malignance towards homosexuality as Christianity, Judaism, or Islam. The government has never adopted repressive tactics against queers as such, but gay Thai men face instead subtle negation and a lack of social awareness of gay and lesbian issues. Identity is an element of a fragile economy.

Varayut Milintajinda:
  One of the country's leading gay actors. He tells the magazine *Midway,* "Everybody loves good people. So be good people. Do some good work for society, and society will accept our life-styles."

Forms of address:
  "Oh, that one," Toi says when he sees the video I'm carrying. He rolls his eyes. In those uncomfortably lucid moments when I do not feel like throwing myself in front of a speeding taxi after I have broken up for the fifth (but not final) time with the same person, I notice there are a lot of European, Australian, and American tourists who congregate in specific parts of Bangkok, Asian and African tourists in other parts. Every time I see a tourist, most fixed with the vacuous look of game-show hosts, I can't help but think they're here for some kind of uncomplicated social intercourse denied them at home. It is as "uncomplicated" as any discourse that flies in a holding pattern of relativeness. It is a relationship of commerce unburdened by economy. It is an intercourse to which I do not have access. The Patpong prostitute is not a Brechtian metaphor. The queens in *I Am a Man* are and are not the same tragic royalty of *The Boys in the Band. The Last Song* is and is not about the limited life span of the average Pattaya drag queen.

M. L. Panthewanop Thewakul's *I am a Man.*
"I am a man":
  Mohd, the airplane pilot, announces this after he exchanges his uniform for makeup, a witch's hat, and the loud attire of a psycho-coquette.

"I":
  The "I" is the feminine reference.

Tonight:
Mohd is hostessing a birthday party for his friend Toi.

Nat:
The flamboyant jewelry salesman. He attended prestigious Chulalongkorn University, but couldn't find a job after graduation, so he has to work as a flamboyant jewelry salesman. Nat tells Mohd that he doesn't want to blame his failure on his parents.

Failure:
For Nat this is inextricably linked to his sexuality.

Dang:
His professional name is Ung Ahn, but all his sisters call him Dang. His husband is named Luk. In the beginning of the film, Dang is "interviewing" a potential model for his business, but the interview consists mostly of Dang mauling the boy.

Luk:
He is a reservoir of dignity. He encounters Nat in the opening of the film, when he goes to buy a ring for his wife. Nat thinks the wife is a woman and is immediately disinterested in Luk.

Today:
Luk says, "Do you know what day is today?" Dang says, "It's Toi's birthday." Luk slips a ring on Dang's finger. It's their anniversary and Dang has forgotten.

Em:
The pockmarked drag queen who discovers her kept boy with a woman ("a real woman"). He has a loud mouth and a big nose. He rents a boy from a bar on Patpong for the party.

Anh:

Mr. Machismo, a schoolteacher from Chiangmai. A "real man" according to Mohd, who went to school with him. He leaves his wife up north, dons his cowboy hat and heads down to Bangkok. He is having a crisis of identity, and he nurses it in the airport bar, throwing back shots of whisky. Anh tries to make two phone calls from the bar. The first doesn't connect; the second is to Mohd, whom he hasn't seen in years.

Faggot:

On his way to Mohd's house, Anh stops to help what appears to be a young woman whose car has broken down. He calls Mohd to say he won't be coming after all. Then the woman, who could really be a man, says there's nothing wrong with the car and makes some kind of sexual innuendo towards Anh, who responds by calling her a faggot.

Feelings:

Mohd cautions his guests not to show their real feelings because Anh is a real man.

Taigaree/Bang a whore:

When Anh and Mohd were in college up north, they went off one night to visit prostitutes, as is the custom between upper classmen, but Mohd stays outside on the street to smoke a cigarette.

A costume party:

Everyone is in drag when Anh shows up unexpectedly. It's an uncomfortable moment, but they explain it to him by saying it's a costume party and by overcompensating with aggressive displays of masculine behavior. Only Em refuses to participate in this form of charade, saying, "I am proud of my femininity."

Luk and Anh:

Anh bonds with Luk because they're both teachers and because they're the only ones at the party who aren't wearing dresses. Anh thinks Luk is straight because he's dressed like Marlon Brando in *The Wild Ones*.

Bird:
A college chum of Mohd and Anh. Bird initiated Mohd but harbored secret desires for Anh. When he finally confessed his love to Anh, he was repelled. Mohd thinks Anh is in Bangkok to find Bird.

The thunderstorm, the telephone, the doorbell, the bevy of transvestites on the soccer field:
Interventions. The thunder peals at dramatic moments, like when Anh finally attacks Em and rips off his wig. The telephone introduces Anh, then erases the anxiety of his arrival. The doorbell keeps on ringing at Toi's birthday party, but it's never Toi. Only the peal of thunder signals Toi's arrival.

Toi:
The wise old queen.

The telephone game:
The game the rictus of beauty queens play. You get one point for dialing the number of the person you love the most, another point if they pick up the phone, a third point if you say, "I love you."

Em:
Loves this dentist. The dentist doesn't love Em.

Nat:
Remembers being initiated in a poolside shower stall, but while he says the other guy led him in, we see Nat leading the other man in, confusing the object of desire and the issue of power. Nat tries to call the man, but has a nervous breakdown after he dials the number.

Luk:
He loves Dang. "I told the truth," he says to Anh, who is shocked because he never considered this choice; because he never considered the possibility of a man expressing passionate affection for another man. "I left my wife, I left my children, because I love Dang. Nobody wants to be born queer. I

married as a test of my masculinity. I loved my wife, she loved me, but in the end I lied to myself."

Dang:

He loves Luk, but says that he believes in variety. He loves freedom. "Don't make me promise," he says. "Promises are what end a relationship."

Anh:

Mohd insists Anh left his wife to resurrect the relationship he ended with Bird, but Anh is lost somewhere in thought. Finally, he picks up the phone, dials a number, and says, "Anh loves you." His wife is on the other end.

Toi:

With a teenage prostitute on his arm, he admonishes the dejected Mohd, "You created the game to tear everyone apart, and you are the loser." His advice to Mohd is to love himself and to love someone else, whether it's a man or a woman. But even saying this, we realize that Mohd can never love anyone.

Anh and Mohd:

Anh's projected innocence is a provocation to Mohd. Mohd is both intimidated by Mohd's obliviousness to his desire—which he perceives as masculinity—and ashamed of his own desire. He becomes incensed when Anh won't own up to what Mohd believes is his sexual destiny.

Camp/tragedy:

The queens in *I Am a Man* are busy. They are mediating the spaces between queer suffering and queer carnival, between queer desire and queer denial. Between queer this and queer that. The gulf between those who can afford to be camp full-time and those who can only practice it part-time seems implicit in the relationships between the men in *I Am a Man*.

Konerak Sintasamphone and the idea of opposites attracting:

Orientalphilia is a model of Otherness that inverts the repressed dread projected onto the Other in displays of Orientalphobia. For instance, contrast the Thailand of travel guides, a country of endless sun, mindless fun, and congenial bodies, with the Thailand in the mind of John Cardinale, the former Peace Corps volunteer who murdered Ly Yung Cheung, a pregnant garment worker, by pushing her in front of an incoming Manhattan subway train. As the No. 6 ran over the woman, he was heard to say, "Now we're even."[6] Based on his time in Thailand, he told the court by way of an excuse, he had developed a fear of Asian peoples. Or the relationship in the mind of Joseph T. Gabrish, the Milwaukee policeman who told the press, "There was just nothing that stood out, or we would have seen it," after he returned naked and bleeding fourteen-year-old Konerak Sintasamphone to blond mass-murderer Jeffrey Dahmer.[7]

Malaysia and malaria:
A lot of people in the schools I went to in America got these two words mixed up also.

Two films by Pisan Akkaraseni:

The Last Song:
Somying, the transvestite cabaret performer working in Pattaya, sings this before he blows his brains out on stage after cutting off his hair and clothes. It's a beautiful moment.

Boonthaum:
His name means "long stalk." He comes from a poor family up north. He and Somying become lovers, but the relationship ends when he leaves Somying for Au, the lover of Phrao, the lesbian chanteuse and Somying's best friend.

Tragedy:
Boonthaum watches the spectacle, horrified, and tries to intercede, but it's too late.

Sticky rice and fish sauce:
Boonthaum is cute in a way that the privileged look at the disenfranchised. When he asks the waitress at a Pattaya restaurant for sticky rice and fish sauce, everyone at the table teases him, but they are clearly enamored with

his back-country ways. Boonthaum is an interloper in the house of grace. Grace being a reprieve from disempowerment. Grace being the ability to articulate. In a sense, Boonthaum's initial desire for Somying is a fantasy of pressing up against the sexual Other. Somying's desire for Boonthaum could be a need to rub against an economic Other.

Boonthaum and Somying:
  Their affiliation mirrors the relationship between the economically and sexually oppressed, a need to identify with each Other, to ignore the differences because of the commonality of their experiences, to collapse these different identities into one convenient anthropological Other. It is a game played out between different kinds of privilege and alienation: gender, sexuality, class. Also, an affirmation of queer role-playing predicated along the lines of heterosexual power.

Anguished Love:
  Somying's brother Somnuek hunts down Boonthaum to avenge his death, but they wind up falling in love with each other. In the end, Boonthaum retreats to a monastery where he is ordained, and Somnuek pays obeisance to him on the steps of the wiharn.

Thanks to Oi Siripon Butranon, Boonlert Setthamongkol, Dome Sukwong, Benjamin Liu, Hilton Als, and Norman Wang.

Notes

1. "Screened Out Due to AIDS?" *South China Morning Post* (January 10, 1991) p. 17.

2. *Sammakkee Soorb,* Thailand, 1977.

3. "AIDS Homes In," *The Economist* (February 4, 1989) p. 37; "AIDS? What AIDS?" *The Economist* (March 24, 1990) p. 36; "The New Lepers," *The Economist* (September 15, 1990) p. 44; "Poor Man's Plague," *The Economist* (September 21, 1991) p. 21.

4. "Poor Man's Plague."

5. "Behind the Bars," *OG* (Spring 1990) p. 22.

6. David Bird, "Teacher Seized in IRT Slaying Faced Job Loss," *The New York Times* (March 2, 1984) p. 6.

7. "Officer Defends Giving Boy Back to Dahmer," *The New York Times* (August 26, 1991).

When Difference Is (More Than) Skin Deep

B. RUBY RICH

The love that dares not speak its name has a new name with an old sound: race. Imagine the context in which this article was conceived: the year was 1991, the place New York, the time summer. *Jungle Fever* was playing in the movie theaters and *How I Became Hettie Jones* was just out in paperback. This article was hanging out in the corner, waiting to be written. The economy, even then, was getting worse and worse, the R-word of recession spoken louder and louder, and race was the boiling point, the valve on the pressure cooker that kept blowing up and hitting the ceiling (Bensonhurst, Central Park, Atlantic Beach, St. John's).

Horror after horror, year after year, continuing, escalating, as the eighties gave way to the nineties. Race and (hetero) sex. Miscegenation. I mention these particular New York City cases (and not the more recent episodes of Crown Heights riots or the Julio Rivera murder in Jackson Heights or, for that matter, the Rodney King verdict and the Los Angeles rebellions) because every one of these New York four involved some ignition of cross-race sexuality, as understated as the unearned suspicion of a date, as overstated as gang rape.[1]

The politics of race are more present than ever, but relations between the races seem to be the worst in many years, maybe in my/your lifetime. Races collide! But more often, they don't. Separatism, self-determination, and old-fashioned segregation—both enforced and elected—have made social spheres more and more uniracial. This at the same time that the banner of "multiculturalism" is hoisted atop the heap, a Band-Aid atop a gaping wound. The indisputable phenomenon of race-merging, the realness of multiracial identities like the melting pot's boosters never foresaw, have had little impact on the demagogic return to racial purity as a last-ditch ideological maneuver. Nationalisms and communities of origin are upheld and revived as sources of identity, even as a new mixed-race generation (products of a more optimistic time) search for places to fit, or for new subject positions entirely.[2]

The queer nations are not exempt from various forms of racism that have come to fruition in the eighties and nineties. But race is different for lesbians and gay men, and I suspect has been for quite some time, shifting about in terms of what *kind* of difference over the decades. Just as class long ago defined one trope of gay male practice ("rough trade") and age another ("chicken hawk"), so race in its most superficial aspects gave rise to a variety of tags for gay men in recent times (the "safari hunter," the "rice queen"), names used subculturally, some as ironic celebration, others to assert authority over and against the white men who came to call, seeking the Other. The approaches differ by gender in the queer universe, as Jackie Goldsby has noted: "Dykes politicize race, gay men eroticize it. . . ."[3] Among white lesbians, sure enough, it tended to be a different story: lots of lip service to "antiracism," a tokenistic inclusion on the Rolodex of life, an often-genuine ideological engagement derived from feminist politics . . . but, in general, same-race socializing (and, minus the sexual adventuring of the gay male world, usually same-race sex) and a womyn's community style drawn far too much from white WASP culture.

Among African American and Latina lesbians, there was a determined staking out of identity and territory, beginning with landmark anthologies like *Home Girls: A Black Feminist Anthology, All the Women Are White, All the Blacks Are Men, But Some of Us Are Brave,* and *This Bridge Called My Back* and the subsequent writings of Jewelle Gomez, Gloria Anzaldúa, Cherríe Moraga, Cheryl Clarke, Barbara Smith, and many others, all preceded of course by the mother of them/us all, Audre Lorde. In general, their subject was race identity, lesbian identity, and what you get when your very being combines the two. With the exception of Audre Lorde's *Zami,* the dissonance of crossing the two was usually not a focus of concern.[4]

The fact that something was falling between the cracks of the various discourses first began to occur to me as I was working on an earlier piece treating feminist sexuality in general during the eighties, a time of struggle that I like to call "the sex wars."[5] It seemed to me that the sexual practices which were at the heart of the controversies tearing lesbian communities apart, for both right and wrong reasons—top/bottom and butch/femme— were clearly attempts to introduce "difference" into same-sex couplings as a strategy for maintaining eros. As such, the roles made perfect sense at the level of strategy despite the arguments raised at the level of ideology.

What about race, though? In this article, I presume to argue that queers have the potential for a different *relationship* to race, and to racism, because of the very nature of same-sex desires and sexual practices. I'm arguing here for potential, not guarantee; hypothetical, provisional, but nonetheless, distinctively possible. In my own life and the lives I've observed over several decades, it has been apparent that many lesbian couples cross race lines for reasons in keeping with the other strategies just outlined: to create a union based on difference, replacing the gender difference of hetero coupling with a racial difference that counterbalances sameness at the level of gender identity. Much attention has been paid, and rightly so, to the pernicious effects of racism at institutional and interpersonal levels, but very little attention to the still-surviving attractions that cut across race differences to fuse the self and the other into unions. Sometimes, it seems as though the debates only feel safe at the level of ideology or political action, at the level of coalition or theory, demonstration or representation, but not at the intimate personal level of relationships, in the flesh, the heart, close to the bone. Searching for citations to anchor these thoughts, I find it difficult to locate texts that postdate the end of the integration fantasy of the sixties, back when crossing race lines was briefly considered as radical as crossing the property lines of sex in marriage for "free love" alliances; in general, the seventies tried to ignore race, the eighties to embrace it (for oneself) or problematize it (for others), but rarely to cross it.[6]

Much of my life as a lesbian has been negotiated across racial and cultural divides, drawn always by the attractions of cultures that were far more intact and infused with richer histories than my own family's assimilationist amnesia could afford. Desire for me has been inextricably linked to differences, at first from positions of inevitable ignorance and fascination, eventually from more evolved positions of knowledge and recognition. The mirror phase never appealed: sameness times two was not sexy, nor was there ever a burning need to see myself reflected back to me by its double. Instead, it was difference that held the magnetic charge, one that was not always easy or automatic, but a challenge to be met and an ongoing series of negotiations to be contracted, with pleasures always paid in return.

Paradoxically, this very difference can become a new route back to the self, since nothing any longer is self-evident. The tangle of individual versus cultural, the dissection of that place where personality leaves off and social construction begins, where imagined stereotypes merge into actual habits or disappear into erroneous projections is one that must be confronted only when lovers of different races, cultures, religions, or classes face the political in the personal. It is there that desire must be wrestled into the light of day. It's a high-wire act without a net, as each partner seeks to move beyond empathy into a kind of identification, without falling into the limbo of cultural transvestite.

Is it, then, only because my own life as a lesbian in the nineties is defined across cultures, between Mexican and Jew, that I seek meaning in the cross-race paradigm? Factor in another presence, too: my now-familial relationship to children who construct themselves according to yet another set of differences, part Mexican, part ethnic European, searching out others whose identities are fused into similar alchemies of once-distinct national elements.

Is it a search for their present, their futures? Certainly autobiography can never be ignored, nor taken for granted, nor presumed innocent . . . and yet, I know that race provides a fulcrum in queer couples far beyond my own personal Exhibit A, for race is always a factor between or among people, a source of identification as well as differentiation, even (especially?) if it is never mentioned.

Race occupies the place vacated by gender. The non-sameness of color, language, or culture is a marker of difference in relationships otherwise defined by the sameness of gender. Race is a constructed presence of same-gender couples, one which allows a sorting out of identities that can avoid both the essentialism of prescribed racial expectations and the artificiality of entirely self-constructed paradigms. The possibility exists, then, for a kind of negotiation of identities not found elsewhere, of what Kobena Mercer, writing about "the gaze" as seen in Robert Mapplethorpe's portraits of black men, has called an "element of reversibility." Analyzing the relationship between subject and object in these photographs, he observes that:

> The gaze certainly involves an element of erotic objectification, but like a point-of-view shot in gay male pornography, it is reversible. The gendered hierarchy of seeing/being seen is not so rigidly coded in homoerotic representations, since sexual sameness liquidates the associative opposition between active subject and passive object.[7]

Queers who cross race into a union that no longer fits either neighborhood comfortably may well find that there are different issues at stake than those considered in the Hettie Jones memoir or the Spike Lee film Sometimes, it's a question of racial difference itself seeming to call lesbianism into existence as a necessary explanation. For example, art historian Linda Nochlin once pointed out just such a mechanism in nineteenth-century French orientalist painting, wherein "the conjunction of black and white, or dark and light female bodies, whether naked or in the guise of mistress and maidservant, traditionally signified lesbianism," even in the absence of any overt gestures to sustain such an interpretation.[8] Inversely, the presence of lesbianism can itself suggest the crossing of races, even when no such thing is going on. In her recent study of the construction of homosexuality in *Jet* magazine in the 1950s, Alycee J. Lane discovered that the interviewer and editor created a clear white presence in a profile of two black lesbians (implying that the rejection of black men implicit in the women's choosing of each other was, by default, an alliance with white men, who were thus prominently inserted—via photos of their lawyer and minister, and fairly gratuitous commentary on each).[9]

I've been struck, in reading the literature that constitutes the chronicles of the sex wars, by the narrow range of attention given to the many ways women choose to structure difference in lesbian couples. The ever so visible solutions of cross-class, mother-daughter, fat-thin, and always, above all, cross-racial attraction, which could be seen in any bar or block of queerdom, were virtually ignored—despite the popular complaints of "lesbian bed death" caused by overmerging, by the dissolving of self into (too like) other. Here, the more equal power relations possible in (though certainly not guaranteed by) queerness could be martialed to alter the dynamics of queer coupling. And, indeed, friends at Gay Pride parades in recent years have reported seeing far more race-crossed couples, especially among the young, than anywhere in the heterosexual population.

In general, queer films didn't play out on this particular territory. In the mid-eighties, though, something changed, and three feature films emerged, stylistically experimental and thematically visionary, two by women, one by a man, all dealing with cross-race interactions—with radically different outcomes. Lizzie Borden made *Born in Flames* in 1983. Gus Van Sant made *Mala Noche* in 1986. Sheila McLaughlin made *She Must Be Seeing Things* in 1987. Together, these three films can be seen in retrospect as the starting points toward a cinematic examination of cross-race dynamics for lesbians and gay men.

Lizzie Borden's *Born in Flames* (1983) marked a key stage in what I am taking to be a collective discourse about race and (homo)sexuality in the land of independent film. It combined documentary and fiction into a utopian vision of black and white women loving and working together, fighting a common enemy (patriarchy, the state). Rather than assume the inherent unity of a documentary like *Word Is Out* or the problematized symbiosis of *Mala Noche,* Borden's *Born in Flames* staked out its terrain of unity on the basis of difference, whereby a posse of white girls and a posse of black girls unite for the benefit of their revolutionary goals (and their leaders' personal benefit, complete with a shower scene).

But what happened? When the film showed in a conference at the University of Milwaukee in April 1985, a number of black women in attendance attacked it. Charges and countercharges of racism and homophobia were exchanged. When, two months later, the film was the subject of a roundtable at the Society for Cinema Studies conference in New York, a second volley of attacks was levelled, this time on technical and aesthetic grounds. While impossible to prove, it's nevertheless likely that the mix of lesbianism and cross-race alliances in the film was explosive and was the catalyst to these impassioned reactions. The film's in-your-face style, pre-hip-hop but nevertheless street-smart, mixing modes like a DJ on a turntable, ensured a "hot" presentation . . . and a hot response.

With no knowledge of Borden's working process nor autobiography, academics could see the film as, variously, naive or cooptive. Borden made

Honey at the mic of pirate station Radio Phoenix, *Born in Flames,* Lizzie Borden

the film in a quasi-collective process, working collaboratively with a large and evolving group of black and white women and men. The African American cinematographer Al Santana was one of the cameramen credited; long-time activist and all-around troublemaker Flo Kennedy was a starring player. The center of the film, however, at both a narrative and iconic level, was Honey—Borden's companion at the time, the leader of Radio Phoenix within the film, the African American woman whose face beamed out at the public from the posters plastered all over lower Manhattan and everywhere else the film eventually showed. It was Honey who, for a time, accompanied Borden to festival screenings, who had lived the life of the mean streets in Williamsburg, had once acted with the Split Britches company, and composed the title song. These details, of course, are extra-filmic and therefore not a part of the discourse of textual analysis. However much biography and working process may bear upon a particular film, film theory has not yet found a way to incorporate the kinds of materials that routinely provide the popular press with its movie coverage.

Still, given the nature of filmmaking in an auteurist era, the film's creator was Borden in all the credits, and the film must be seen as a reflection of that authorship, that is, a white perspective. In interviews at the time, Borden spoke of her efforts to get the film seen by audiences beyond those usually constituting the art film market, and, indeed, at least in New York, it managed to play a range of alternative circuits and attract an audience that consistently crossed racial (and generational) lines. Since then, in addition to its cult popularity with audiences, the film has gathered significant critical stature.[10] Seen from the vantage point of the nineties, *Born in Flames* seems innocent, even utopian, in its vision of cross-race communication and alliance, as well as its enactment of guerrilla politics.

What is equally striking today is the extent to which its political subsumes the place of its personal, such that the film pictures its characters as political agents but never as subjective subjects. In terms of my investigation here of race as a constitutive factor within homosexuality, then, the film has little to say. Race is problematized in collective and political terms, with the aforementioned transgressive shower scene between a white and black woman constituted as a seemingly uncomplicated act, private rather than public, safe in the realm of "natural" sexuality (however "unnatural" it might have appeared at the point of reception by the film's actual viewers).

The release of Gus Van Sant's *Mala Noche* was a breakthrough in the opposite direction of the personal, laying bare the more-than-subcultural, less-than-subliminal fascination that its white hero has for the dark-skinned Mexican boys who arrive in Portland's tenderloin district looking for a break. Though the film doesn't ever break through to any real sense of the actual subjectivity (or economics) driving these objects of the protagonist's lust, it does go further than anything since Rainer Werner Fassbinder's *Fox and His Friends* in taking the viewer deep into the particular magnetic field governing people who reverse the usual same/different equation: matching genders but opting for different races (or classes).

Van Sant's hero is not unconscious of the contradictions of his own position, since he himself is a marginal member of Seattle society by virtue of his sexual identity and occupation within a community of immigrants, *braceros,* hustlers, and other societal outsiders. Yet the film makes it clear that his frustrated relationship with one young Mexican cannot escape the dynamic of colonial exploitation which the global grid of their meeting dictates. Such a perspective infuses the film's every frame with surplus meaning, as Van Sant exposes more than he may even have intended in the signature camerawork that comes to embody the subjectivity of the film's white protagonist, the filmmaker's alter ego.[11] This character can see his own desire in these young men, never their desires; he never questions the "why" of their presence in his native town, the "who" of their own subjectivities, outside the structuring gaze of his native interest. Finally, one young man's unexpected and unwarranted death indicts the hero, implicating his self-absorption with his own desires, illustrating with the finality of mortality that race is not a casual game, that it can be fatal. Van Sant can picture the tragic contradictions of his protagonist's position but has no language to alter it.

The importance of Van Sant's work is that it began an investigation into the subjectivity of cross-race desire—even if only from the one, predictably white, side—a theme which hadn't been taken up as a serious cinematic project before then. Certainly, there had been documentaries—*The Word Is Out, Before Stonewall*—which, in recuperating gay and lesbian history and identity, had included people of color (though, in the kind of trade-off that has too quickly become the terms of "multiculturalism," the people of color could be found in front of the camera but not behind, in either of these collectively-made projects). In such documentaries, the question of race was seen as a *component* of gay identity, rather than posing a challenge to the notion of gay *inclusivity* to which both films were dedicated, and in neither was the theme of cross-race attraction particularly explored.

The release of *She Must Be Seeing Things* in 1987 showed Sheila McLaughlin to be fusing some of the concerns of the Borden and Van Sant films in her portrait of a lesbian couple—one a blond filmmaker, one a Brazilian lawyer (played by an African American actress)—picking their way through a minefield of issues clearly occupying lesbian, feminist, and film communities at that moment. The film's central project concerned lesbian identity, as threatened on the one hand by heterosexual fantasy, on the other hand by jealous paranoia. The issues that were foregrounded by the film, especially concerning power relations and modes of domination between women, held a relevance for issues of race—but neither race nor the women's cross-race relationship was the main focus of the film. Their relationship was at stake, but not in those terms. McLaughlin herself acknowledged that race played a role in mise-en-scène more than narrative.

I don't think that racial difference is the most important difference between the two protagonists. For me the most important thing was that they be as different as possible and race is part of that . . . black actors want good roles in film and not to be cast simply for being black. Of course race is always an issue, but I personally felt an obligation and an interest in beginning to address that. For me it's a very difficult and important thing to do.[12]

The film tended to be received, and vocally so, by most feminist and lesbian audiences (generally overwhelmingly white) purely in terms of their own "hot spots" of unacceptable sexuality. Thus, the film's projection was stopped at one British screening when the local women-against-pornography crowd denounced it as an S-M movie, while other audiences rejected the film because it dared to portray a lesbian's heterosexual fantasies and temptations.[13] There was also an appreciative critical assessment of the film, and a pronounced positive reception at the level of audience (it played successfully at New York's Film Forum and elsewhere, nationally and internationally).[14]

Questions about race have never really had the chance to surface, amidst the greater attention paid to the film's contributions to gender construction, identity, and the nature of lesbian desire. Yet the film opens itself to just such a reading because (unlike Van Sant) McLaughlin does picture the subjectivity of the Other and (unlike Borden) does take politics right down to an intensely personal level: the political is personal in *She Must Be Seeing Things*. In some ways, the film was ahead of its time, taking on questions of race, lesbian role-playing, and S-M back when visual representations had not yet caught up with the literature and conference debates—and paying a price for its lead.

From the perspective of race, a central moment of the film occurs when the Brazilian protagonist, fearing heterosexual betrayal at the hands of her lover, goes for solace to an African American dyke buddy, who advises, "What did you expect? You knew she was heterosexual when you got involved with her." McLaughlin herself has reported the reaction of African American viewers in postscreening discussion: they've consistently corrected her on that line.[15] Such a character would have focused on race, not sexual identity. Rewrite: "What did you expect, getting involved with a white woman?" This imagined dialogue is central to a discussion of race precisely because of the centrality, in the original version, of sexual identification but not racial identification.[16] McLaughlin sees this particular exchange as a scripting error on her part, but it's equally symptomatic of the great difficulties faced by any filmmaker who attempts to cross the racial divide at a moment when there are few models to follow and innumerable mistakes to be made.

Because race isn't constructed as a subject by the film, the differences that might be expected to surface between the characters of the two lovers aren't delineated in terms of race. Precisely through her intention to imbue both characters with equal subjectivity, and to frame her fictions within the terms of the reigning debates in the New York lesbian communities, McLaughlin ended up reinscribing whiteness as the place of authority, the unnamed essence that's nonetheless palpably in charge. As did Van Sant. As did Borden (though her collaborative improvisational process gave her film a more heterogeneous authorship, even as her own authority exerted itself more prominently in the extra-filmic sphere of auteurist media attention).

These three films are important for their pioneering work in beginning to articulate a cinematic investigation of cross-race romance. The whiteness of their subject positions is thrown into relief by a recent exploration of the subject by writer Jackie Goldsby:

> I am in love with a white woman and have been partner with her for four years. We have carefully examined our motives for taking up with each other and can safely pronounce to any and all who ask that our attraction is "healthy" and that neither of us, me in particular, is succumbing to internalized racism. We say this, even to ourselves, even though we know differently: where, in the context of lesbian political discourse on race, can we acknowledge that our knowingly crossing boundaries of race and class *is* part of our desire for each other?[17]

If call and response can be posited as a form of audience reception, then Goldsby's thoughts might be taken as the beginning of a reply to the questions raised by these films, as queer communities begin to deal with the long-unspoken challenge she outlines.

More recently, other filmmakers have begun to contribute works that engage in these discourses around cross-race interaction on the erotic front. Joy Chamberlain's *Nocturne* brings to the foreground, more than any other recent film, the pitfalls into which queer white filmmakers can fall in creating characters drawn from other races or cultures. In this fantasy drama, a repressed bourgeois woman returns home after her mother's death, only to be intruded upon by two young, punked-up, working-class women (one white, one black) who decide to have their way with her, much to her eventual pleasure. The story seems meant as a fable about class and sex, with obvious Lawrentian overtones. The casting of the black woman, however, shifts gears in the direction, first, of incoherence (as the narrative segues from the playful romance between the two young women to their encounter with their host) and then of a dreadful coherence (as the black woman is put increasingly into a position of subservience through the domination game of the two white women).

Chamberlain's casting demonstrates the limits of any "color-blind" approach to cinema or lesbian relations. Her exploration of class and transgressive sexuality ends up reinscribing the worst sort of racial stereotypes, with the black character ordered about, infantilized, marginalized, and finally scapegoated, all in the name of liberation (of the repressed white woman, that is). It's tempting to see the film's failures as those of the script itself, or of the difficulty inherent in this kind of allegorical fiction, wherein ambiguity and symbology tend to condense meaning in complex and unpredictable fashions.[18] However, it's equally clear that the real failure here is one of racial position: for a white woman to take up such charged areas, without adequate extra-filmic grounding in race politics, is to invite precisely the dangers etched into the screen by *Nocturne.*

Lesbian subjectivities are certainly in need of examination from the perspective of race. Ideally, however, the construction of such fictional characters should be the culmination of a filmmaker's work and thinking about race, not the beginning. In the second half of the eighties, white feminist filmmakers began to respond to the debates about racism and "white solipsism" that had gained in force and authority throughout the decade. For white filmmakers who took such principles to heart, the move into fiction became a way to engage the debates at a deep level. Every solution, though, uncovers another layer of problems, and this one has been no exception. Particularly for filmmakers whose lives are largely uniracial, there is a danger in attempting such a strategy of representation within cinema, without a broader sphere of political experience or action to help situate such work. In *Privilege,* for example, Yvonne Rainer tried to work through her own ambivalences and feelings of responsibility regarding cross-race representation, but ended up inciting equally ambivalent responses: Michele Wallace took her to task for her representation of blackness, while the trade journal *Variety* collapsed the film's levels and mistook the "Yvonne Washington" character (the African American filmmaker-within-the-film, played by Novella Nelson) for Rainer herself, and reviewed *Privilege* as a film by an African American director.[19]

How much more difficult, then, are the representations of lesbian sexuality by white filmmakers essaying this same task of cross-race representation within lesbian erotic narratives; indeed, they have tended to reinforce rather than rupture stereotypes. When Cindy Patton showed *Current Flow,* a lesbian "safe sex" videotape by Jean Carlomusto, at the How Do I Look? conference in New York in 1989, there was considerable discussion, both formally and informally, of the tape's depiction of the African American character as that favorite stock image—the stud—servicing her white lover with unfailing, unflagging sexual energy.[20] Similarly, Suzie Bright's popular show of lesbian porn fails to examine pornography's heritage of racial stereotyping, simply celebrating all manifestations of sexuality as inherently liberatory, failing to move beyond a basic First Amendment stance to critique the inscription of the body into an articulated set of meanings and values with a racial hierarchy. However, sex anxieties tend to overwhelm racial concerns in many of the responses to Bright's show: debates have tended to focus on the existing sex battle lines (censorship, S-M, homophobia, repression) and, once again, predictably and depressingly, race stereotyping as a subject is once again deferred.[21] Isaac Julien's response to *Current Flow* is emblematic here: "In trying to visualize safe sex or sexual desire, the creation of porn tapes is a minefield in terms of trying to grapple with the different dichotomies constructed around racial difference."[22]

In general, such concerns were forestalled by the overall invisibility of cross-race portrayals in gay or lesbian cinema of any kind. To be sure, there were exceptions, such as Sally Potter's *Gold Diggers,* in which the character played by black actress Colette Lafonte rides into a ballroom on a horse and spirits Julie Christie away on horseback. The general absence of cross-race work in the 1980s, moreover, is true not only for works by white filmmakers, but also for the works of documentary and fiction by women of color. Not that there weren't women of color making films: ever since the seventies, when feminist filmmaking had taken an almost entirely white route through documentary into the start of fiction filmmaking, there had been a constant coming-of-age of women of color—Asian American, Latina, Chicana, Afri-

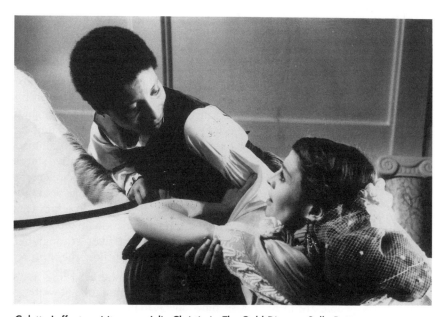

Colette Laffonte spirits away Julie Christie in *The Gold Diggers,* Sally Potter can American—as makers of their own images, and producers of films and videotapes that finally began to embody the diversity of experiences and subjectivities that "art" ought to embody.

Not surprisingly, however, the last thing that interested most of these filmmakers was the inscription of white women into their work, which usually dealt more urgently with the identity and issues (history, family, art, labor) important to women of color themselves, whether in documentary or dramatic modes. A few films by women of color do deal with heterosexual cross-race sexuality, though: not surprisingly, the subject is suffused with negative vibes, inevitable given the male/female dynamics of power and the history of that power's abuse across race. In Julie Dash's *Illusions,* for example, which treats the subject of a passing woman in a Hollywood studio during wartime, and her bond to a young darker-skinned woman singer, a major subplot is her sexual harassment by a nasty white army officer. Tracey Moffat's *Nice Colored Girls* foregrounds cross-race interactions but refuses victimization by reversing the power of point-of-view: her camera follows young aboriginal women on a night on the town, during which their financial exploitation of a lecherous Australian drunk is shown to be scant recompense for the colonial and neocolonial exploitation, and sexual exoticization, of their peoples by the British.[23]

Some filmmakers began to touch on the lives of lesbians of color or the subject of cross-race courting. By the eighties, Michelle Parkerson in the US, Pratibha Parmar in the UK, and Midi Onodera in Canada had begun their cinematic investigations of lesbians of color, whether training the camera on themselves or (more often) others. In *Flesh and Paper,* Parmar's portrait of Suniti Namjoshi, there's even a staged formal scene in which the Indian poet and her white English lover read their poetry in the lush sanctity of a pseudo-pleasure dome. While race is present, then, as a sign of demarcation within the couple, it's more of a structured absence within the film's narrative than an examined presence, as the subject of investigation is really Namjoshi herself. In *10 Cents a Dance (Parallax),* Onodera used race as an almost-comic element of lesbian sexuality, even including herself as tentative suitor in a date scene set in a sushi restaurant. In her autobiographical documentary *The Displaced View,* however, Onodera elided the subject of her sexuality in order to focus on questions of race and nationality. Once the film was done, she spoke of the difficulty she'd had, during production, in reconciling her identity as an Asian woman with her identity as a lesbian—though her very speaking of the contradiction began the process of healing the rupture.

> I become seriously concerned when I hear us talk of interracial love as though it is merely an aberration, suggesting that the natural roles of white and black people are to be, for all time, adversarial, and corrupt with cruelties and indignities."[24]

Isaac Julien's *Looking for Langston* marked a new advance in the cinematic treatment of cross-race eros, even as its historical reclamation of Langston Hughes provoked the homophobic antagonism of the Hughes estate. Julien's film is situated historically in the Harlem Renaissance, which takes him back not only to a time of intense self-definition in the African American cultural community, but also to a time of more fluid race-crossing among the bohemian intelligentsia that constituted its world. At the same time that Julien incorporates white men into his vision of a new black world, however, he's always interrogating their relatively benevolent or malevolent presence there: the terms of the interchange are always defined by the "beautiful black man" who holds stage center and has the last word.

Julien accepts the truths of identity politics as a necessary point of entry, yet constantly calls into question the limits of cultural nationalism. He catches the spin of racism in a glance, the scent of commerce in the come-on, but he still plays the scenes through, looking for the loopholes. He chips away at notions both of normative sexual identity and of race as a totalizing or unidimensional essence; his film crosses the borders of race and gender with the same passport, privileging neither over the other.

It's an elegantly rigorous vision, but one which was necessarily blurred by the mists of time. Julien's next film, *Young Soul Rebels,* made explicit what was only implicit in the earlier work: the force of attraction between black and white, despite the barriers. By opening up his cinematic universe to a variety of characters, Julien is here able to deconstruct the pleasures and pains—and the fatal dangers—of crossing racial borderlines, while still determinedly focusing upon the questions of black masculine identity central to his subject. Actually, the film is set in 1977, the year of the Queen's Silver Jubilee, which allows Julien to situate his narrative within the relative racial pluralism of the soul-boy scene in the discos of that era, while at the same time providing the frenzy of street scenes that seem to teeter constantly on the edge of race/class war.

The film's narrative concerns may range from police harassment to murder, from romance to music trends to politics, but nothing quite compares to the black-on-white bedroom scene between the Billibud and Caz characters. It's the sexiest moment in the film, and therefore the film's clear-cut (dramatic) climax, despite the (anticlimatic) action scenes that follow. Julien identifies the erotic power of difference, and uses it. But he doesn't minimize the conflicts. Caz disapproves of Billibud's naive white-punk politics, both he and Billibud are criticized at different points for hanging out with each other, and the clash of values is even reflected in Billibud's trouble in choosing the right music for getting it on. Julien knows that these tensions also explain the heat, and he's honest enough to show how.

For Marlon Riggs, the frontier between the races is less permeable.

Caz (Mo Sessay) and Billibud (Jason Durr) in *Young Soul Rebels,* Isaac Julien

Tongues Untied is not a celebration but a repudiation of cross-race bonding. Riggs places his images up front, with first-person address and larger-than-life immediacy, the language ricocheting off the screen as confidently as the figures who approach the camera. Employing an explicitly autobiographical framework, Riggs traces his own picaresque journey out of the Castro to Oakland, out of the traps of cross-race attraction (complete with a photo of an early white-boy lover) into the chosen community and self-realization spelled out by his controversial end-title: "Black men loving black men is *the* revolutionary act."

Is it inevitable that the issue of cross-race loving, then, ends up being raised off-screen? The premiere manifesto of cult-nat queerness, *Tongues Untied* has been widely exhibited and praised. In 1991 and 1992, the film's entry into the public television system resulted in its demonization, first by the powers of censorship of the religious right that led many local stations to cancel its broadcast, then by the campaign ambitions of presidential candidate Pat Buchanan, who marshalled scenes from the broadcast to use as an attack on gay and lesbian rights. The need to defend the film against reactionary forces has meant that another controversy, within the gay community, was set aside and forgotten. That controversy, played out in the pages of the *Gay Community News,* centered on the extra-filmic—specifically, on whether the filmmaker's own biography (that is, his longtime white boyfriend) contradicted the apparent message of the film. In a film full of the courage of coming out of the closet on the subject of queerness, it looked as though Riggs had stayed in the closet on the subject of race (as object of affection, not identity).[25]

The complexities of race/sex conjunctions ensured that the debates would be fractious. For example, one African American woman colleague argued to me that the film would have been rejected by the African American community it sought to reach if this fact of the filmmaker's having a white lover had been allowed to surface in the text of the film. Meanwhile, the *GCN* debate continued in the letters column and turned nationalist, revolving not around whether Riggs could have enlarged the autobiographical scope of the work to include his actual relationship, but rather on whether he had any right to speak with authority now that he'd been exposed.

Finally, Essex Hemphill tried to bring some sense to the pages of *GCN.* Acknowledging that he spoke from a position of contradiction, given his own preference for mating inside the race, Hemphill nevertheless offered the examples of Langston Hughes, James Baldwin, Lorraine Hansberry, Bayard Rustin, and Pat Parker, all black queers who had white lovers.[26]

> I want to court outside the race,
> outside the class, outside the attitudes—

but love is a dangerous word
in this small town.[27]

Richard Fung, the Canadian video artist, has undertaken journeys similar to those of both Onodera and Riggs, producing a body of work dedicated to unearthing his own identities and to furthering dialogue with those constitutive communities to which he finds he belongs. In *Chinese Characters*, Fung upped the ante by directly engaging the relationship of Asian gay men to commercial pornography (both as consumers of the product and as objects of consumption within the sex scenarios). A range of gay Asian men discuss their attractions, their sexual experiences across racial divides, and their conviction that mainstream Western society denies sexuality to the Asian man (particularly if Chinese). Because the tape included actual pornography along with its analysis, Fung managed to sexualize his "Chinese characters" for this audience and not just talk about its absence.

Fung points out that, in pornography, the Asian man as active protagonist (as opposed to fuckee) is so rare that one tape could actually be advertised: "Sum Yung Mahn makes history as the first Asian who fucks a non-Asian."[28] But Fung is cautionary regarding any solutions within the realm of pornography.

> The liberal response to racism is that we need to integrate everyone—people should all become coffee-colored, or everyone should have sex with everyone else. But such an agenda doesn't often account for the specificity of our desires. I have seen very little porn produced from such an integrationist mentality that actually affirms my desire. It's so easy to find my fantasies appropriated for the pleasures of a white viewer. In that sense, porn is most useful for revealing relationships of power.[29]

Indeed, porn was the inspiration but not the arena for an installation, "Those Fluttering Objects of Desire," conceived by Shu-Lea Cheang as a product of collaboration by women of color on the subject of sexuality and presented at Exit Art Gallery in New York in the spring of 1992. All the videotapes were made to be shown on small monitors in the gallery, which would play only when quarters were deposited by the visitor, and which could be switched from channel to channel with manual controls. The intent was to replicate the interactivity of a porn booth, subverting its usual function in favor of interrogating the intersection of sex and race. The tapes by and about lesbians crossing race lines make a particular contribution to the arena constituted by this article; in the use of the porn-booth apparatus as site of exhibition, they can be taken as participating in the construction of what Jennifer Terry has called "vengeful countersurveillance."[30]

Cheryl Dunye contributed *Vanilla Sex* to the installation, a tape which takes on the discourse of sex and economically reflects its theme in its title. Dunye zeroes in on racial difference within the mythical lesbian community by reinterpreting a stock phrase, enacting thereby what Terry had described as the "system of epistemic relay" that enforces the lesbian to negotiate and translate always "between the rules of the courtroom and the semiotics of the street" or between authoritative knowledge and experience."[31] Dunye recalls describing a panel discussion (authoritative knowledge) to her friends (experience): the white lesbians on the panel used "vanilla sex" to mean sex that wasn't S-M, but her black friends used the same term to refer to occasions of black women's sleeping with white women. The short tape manages to play out its images in time with the anecdote: the punch line is also the tape's finale. Renegotiation is left to the viewer.

Adrienne Jenik and J. Evan Dunlap collaborated on *What's the Difference Between a Yam and a Sweet Potato?* and took the installation instructions about sex to heart: Jenik and Dunlap are rollin' around in bed with their questions, their images alternately moving or frozen on the screen (via the still camera Cheang employed as a mechanism in all the tapes) as their voices question racial assumptions that both unite and divide them. Jenik and Dunlap felt that the very context of the installation—knowing they'd be one pair among sixteen women contributing—was liberatory: "It allowed us to focus on pleasure." Relieved of the burden of having to be *the* representative work about race and sex, they could play: with each other, with the subject, with the body and the color of its flesh, and even the simple (not so simple) names of the food that nourishes it. And play, as with sex itself, can steer a sure route through the shoals of race.

> For me, it's important that we begin to question the positioning of sexuality as the transcendental signifier. We must begin to engage in a self-reflexive racialized sexual space. I am very much interested in that space—that contradictory liberatory space where we can all be vulnerable and fully interrogate our race, gender, and class positions in order to fully claim our decolonized sexual subjectivities.[32]

The personal is political: the most tired phrase in the feminist language, and still true. For queers seeking to make work that deals with the explosive powers of race and cross-race alliances, the day is long and the work is never done. This article is the most preliminary of inquiries, intended hopefully to begin to ask the questions posed by identity in this multicultural moment. Equally preliminary is my notion that there's *something* about queers and race that has something new to tell us about how difference itself is constituted, and the functions it serves when gender isn't there to do the job.

Perhaps the dialogue surrounding cross-race alliances that broke off in the aftermath of integration's failure in the 1960s can be reengaged, wiser for the years and struggles that have intervened, redefined as a negotiation of differing and even conflicting identities, and not as the melting-pot myth of the first time around. The advantage of romance as a launching pad for political engagement is that it carries built-in optimism, just possibly enough to move ahead in these times of race-hatred and scapegoating. With lesbians and gay men, there's the chance for a kind of confidence, in the face of AIDS and cancer, hate-speech and bias crimes, that dares to stand up to mortality itself.

The desire for dialogues, representations, and theories of cross-race attraction is neither individual nor frivolous. *Young Soul Rebels* shows what happens when the attraction to the Other is allowed no other expression but violence; Jeffrey Dahmer showed another version.[33] The rate of violence against gay men and lesbians is rising inexorably, whether on the streets of Queens or on the Appalachian Trail. So is the rate of violence against people of color. The combination of race and sex can be inflammatory, as the Clarence Thomas hearings clearly proved, and the public's inability to provide any context or analysis for such an intersection invariably works against the integrity of people of color, women, and most of all, women of color. If they don't get you on the streets of Bensonhurst, try the US Senate or the Supreme Court.

The combination of queerness and racial difference, however, has its own volatility. Until we begin to understand the psychic components of cross-race desire, and to analyze the interstices of sexual attraction as well as repulsion on the basis of race, we risk a continuation of tragedies in the future. As the generations coming up continue to produce more and more mixed-race youngsters, full of identity crises of their own, the need for new frameworks that frankly acknowledge the indivisibility of complex identities is urgent. Nation time versus postmodernism? Nothing so binary. Rather, a call for a dialectics of racial and sexual intersection, a road map for the future of representation, a call for all the questions that must be sorted out before any answer can ever present itself.

The queer nations have important clues. Just as homosexuality was once touted as the ultimate challenge to the bourgeois patriarchal family (etc., etc., etc.) so today there may be an argument to be made about queerness, in its outsider guise, as a potential laboratory for the renegotiation of race relations, a place where oppressions can be not ranked in hierarchy but productively combined. The films and videotapes of the past decade discussed in this piece are the first, necessarily tentative, steps in that direction. As audience and critic and inescapable repository of lived experience, standing impatiently at the bus stop of my own subject position, waiting for a ride, I eagerly anticipate the arrival of the next conveyance.

Notes

1. In the Bensonhurst incident, a black youth's death was caused by the mistaken assumption that he was en route to a date with an Italian teenager coveted by one of his attackers; he was actually going to buy a car. In the St. John's case, a black woman law student who filed charges of gang rape against a group of white students found herself made into an object of slander, her life demeaned to win an acquittal for the defendants in an eerie prelude to the Anita Hill experience at the Clarence Thomas hearings, where once again public discourse would deny a black woman's claim to virtue.

2. See, for example: Andrew Parker, Mary Russo, Doris Sommer, and Patricia Yaeger, eds., *Nationalisms and Sexualities* (New York/London: Routledge, 1992).

3. Jackie Goldsby, "What It Means to Be Colored Me," *Outlook: National Gay and Lesbian Quarterly* no. 9 (Summer, 1990), p. 11.

4. An important exception is Audre Lorde's classic *Zami: A New Spelling of My Name* (Watertown, Mass.: Persephone Press, 1982). In this "biomythography," Lorde delves at length into the complexities of race and cross-race couples in the lesbian scene of the 1950s and 1960s, as viewed through the lens of her own life.

5. B. Ruby Rich, "Feminist Sexuality in the 80s," *Feminist Studies,* vol. 12 no. 3 (Fall, 1986), pp. 525–562.

6. Notable exceptions, which I don't consider here due to my emphasis on lower-budget, nontheatrical film and video, are the films based upon Hanif Kureshi's scripts: *My Beautiful Laundrette* and *Sammie and Rosie Get Laid.* They evoke the utopian liberation of an earlier period in their insistence on constituting communities of transgression that cut across racial and sexual identity to affirm mutual attractions. Undoubtedly *My Beautiful Laundrette* constituted a precedent for much of the work that followed, on both sides of the Atlantic.

7. Kobena Mercer, "Skin Head Sex Thing: Racial Difference and the Homoerotic Imaginary" in the Bad Object Choices, ed., *How Do I Look? Queer Film and Video* (Bay Press, 1991) p. 182. It is noteworthy that this entire area of cross-race eroticism is so little articulated and so emotionally complex that Mercer's text represents a radical resituation of his own position on Mapplethorpe as expressed in earlier work.

8. Linda Nochlin, "The Imaginary Orient," *Art in America* (May, 1983) p. 126.

9. Alycee J. Lane, "Hegemonies Within: *Jet* Magazine and Its Construction of 'the' Black Homosexual," panel presentation, Fifth Annual Lesbian and Gay Studies Conference, Rutgers University, November 2, 1991. Based on author's notes.

10. See, for example: Teresa de Lauretis, "Rethinking Women's Cinema: Aesthetics and Feminist Theory" in her *Technologies of Gender* (Bloomington: Indiana University Press, 1987).

11. The phrase "alter ego" should not be taken too literally. The film was actually based upon an autobiographical story by a Portland writer, which was adapted by Van Sant.

12. Alison Butler, "*She Must Be Seeing Things:* An Interview with Sheila McLaughlin," *Screen* vol. 28, no. 4 (Autumn, 1987) pp. 24–25, reprinted in this volume.

13. See Susan Ardill and Sue O'Sullivan, "Sex in the Summer of '88," *Feminist Review* no. 31 (Spring, 1989), pp. 126–134 for an account of the "notorious scandal" in which "a small minority of women" at the 1988 summer school called for an "outright ban" of the

film. See, also, Victoria Brownworth, "Dyke S/M Wars Rage in London," *Coming Up!* (October, 1988) pp. 14–15.

14. See, for example: Teresa de Lauretis, "Guerilla in the Midst: Women's Cinema in the '80s," *Screen* vol. 31 no. 1 (Spring, 1990) pp. 6–25.

15. Personal communication with the author.

16. The question of where authority rests for any such choice of statement or focus is a real one. Is it only because McLaughlin is white that this line is challenged? Does authority extend to the point of generalization, so-called essentialism, cultural nationalism? Would a filmmaker of color also be challenged on the construction of certain characters? No doubt—as responses to Isaac Julien's work have indicated. Crossing race is a dangerous act for everyone. See the discussion of the film that took place following the original presentation by Teresa De Lauretis of her "Film and the Visible" article, as recorded in the *How Do I Look?* anthology, pp. 264–276.

17. Goldsby, "What It Means to Be Colored Me," p. 11.

18. In fact, Chamberlain declared at the festival screening in New York that the script had originally not been written to include a black woman, but that she was committed to enlarging casting opportunities for women of color and therefore cast the part accordingly. It is this kind of "solution" that I find problematic. In the tighter, more manageable form of soap opera, however, Chamberlain had earlier done much better: the black character in *Domestic Bliss* (1984), her pilot for a never-produced television series, was interesting, lively, and credible.

19. See Michelle Wallace, "Multiculturalism and Oppositionality," *Afterimage* vol. 19 no. 3 (October, 1991) pp. 6–9.

20. For the discussion of the videotape and the issues raised by cross-race pornography, as debated by Gregg Bordowitz, Jean Carlomusto, Cindy Patton, Richard Fung, and others, see, again, *How Do I Look?*, pp. 51–63.

21. Goldsby, however, makes precisely this point (see above). Goldsby's article, along with other published and anecdotal accounts inform this analysis, since I haven't seen Bright's show.

22. From the same *How Do I Look?* discussion (see above), p. 62.

23. More recently, Camille Billops and James Hatch have produced *Finding Christa*. While the film is centrally concerned with the story of Billops's giving her child up for adoption and then finding herself once again in contact with her, years later, there is a substantial subplot relating the Billops-Hatch meeting and union as an early example of "integration" and as a controversial, though unacknowledged (as such) choice by both parties, as related by friends and families (loquaciously on Hatch's side, almost silently on Billops's).

24. Essex Hemphill, "Choice," *Gay Community News* (May 6–12, 199), pp. 9, 13.

25. See the review of *Tongues Untied* by Cary Alan Johnson in the *Gay Community News* of February 25–March 3, 1990, for example, in which he calls the film "deceptive" for concealing that Riggs has a white lover. See, too, Hemphill's response, "Choice," and the interview with Marlon Riggs, "Speaking Out About *Tongues Untied*," by Phil Harper, in a subsequent *GCN*. More recently, Hilton Als used the pages of the *Village Voice* to challenge Isaac Julien on his attraction to white men.

Unfortunately, Riggs himself has contributed to a drawing up of sides. In his interview in *Release Print* (Film Arts Foundation) of March, 1990, he harshly criticized Julien's film: "[A]ll the men are beautiful, by and large light-skinned, well-dressed, tuxedoed, refined. I wanted to avoid, as you say, that kind of entrapment, that sort of construction of another stereotype in the process of trying to break down a stereotype of black gay men and black gay experience. That often happens when groups who are on the outside try to win favor with the dominant culture, as well as to define themselves."

26. In his GCN piece, Hemphill admitted that "I have often said, among my closest friends, that I could never love a white man in America. I don't believe that I could endure the challenges interracial couples face solely for the prize of love." But he went on to advocate a laissez-faire attitude, citing Billie Holiday's song *Ain't Nobody's Business If I Do.*

27. This verse appears at the start of Hemphill's "Choice" in *GCN.*

28. Quoted by Fung from *International Wavelength News* 2, no. 1 (January, 1991).

29. Richard Fung's ad hoc response to commentary following his formal presentation published in *How Do I Look?,* p. 166.

30. Jennifer Terry, "Theorizing Deviant Historiography" in *Differences* vol. 3, no. 2 (Summer, 1991) p. 59. Terry actually is employing the term more specifically to characterize a process of historical research and retrieval, but it suggests itself so powerfully as a description of this work and its apparatus that I take the liberty of extending her words in this unintended direction.

31. Ibid., p. 70.

32. Lyle Ashton Harris, "Revenge of a Snow Queen" in *Out/Look,* no. 13 (Summer, 1991) pp. 8–9.

33. Dahmer is the Milwaukee serial killer who murdered young men whom he trapped in his apartment; most of his victims were black or Asian. The most notorious murder was that of a fourteen-year-old Laotian boy who escaped out to the street. Black women who witnessed the scene called the police; the white cops returned the boy to Dahmer, who then murdered him. There was an uproar in Milwaukee in the wake of the monstrous discovery of the crimes, focused on the racism of the police response: their lack of interest in the disappearance of youths of color followed by their ridicule of the accurate fears of the black woman who called 911, only to be laughed at.

Thanks for help along the way, at various stations of the cross, to: John Greyson, Martha Gever, Rosa Linda Fregoso, Isaac Julien, and, as ever, Lourdes Portillo.

India Postcard:
or Why I Make Work in a Racist, Homophobic Society

SUNIL GUPTA

In the canon of world cinema and video, and indeed the written word and other forms of visual representation, there has been a complete silence around the presence of the Indian gay man. One immediate problem of course is with definition. Gay is a word that does not appear to exist in the vernacular languages of India. The nearest one can come to is an idea approximating "homosexual relationships,"[1] aside from the usual terms of abuse referring to sodomy, and so on. Furthermore, writing from a British "South Asian" (a term usually truncated to "Asian") perspective about Indian cultural histories can present a problem with boundaries, as the subcontinent is now firmly broken up into separate nation states. Those of us who live in the West have had the particular experience of redefining and reappraising our cultural position. I, for example, was literally born Indian, became Canadian, moved to London, where I became an ethnic minority, then Asian, then black, and finally South Asian. I think I would like to return to being simply Indian and a gay man.

Cinema has been the mainstay of Indian popular culture for decades. Bombay musicals dominate regional output and reaffirm the popular mythologies of a secular state and a spoken language that is a hybrid of Hindi and Urdu. The division into India and Pakistan gave rise to a nationalistic drive to enforce each of the languages as the official language of the new state; however, in India this has met with stiff opposition. Although the country is linguistically divided, the strength of Bombay's commercial cinema continues unabated. Like Hollywood, it has developed it's own moral codes; no kissing was allowed but wanton sexuality was on display. No openly gay characters emerged but often what was left unsaid created its own unspoken meaning. A campness permeates a number of now-classic films, like *Pakeezah, Teesri Kasam,* and *Umrao Jaan.*

I made the *India Postcard* videotape[2] as a greeting not just from gay men in India to lesbians and gay men in Britain, but specifically also to South Asian lesbians and gay men. The format was a musical with two characters who never meet, except in their subconscious, in Delhi and Bombay. The opening song came from a noir film that describes the villainy of Bombay; the theme was "looking" and cruising, immortalized for us in the song "Chalte, chalte"[3] whose lyrics literally translate as "walking, I met someone," an event underscored by the whistle of a train, reminding us that

sexuality in India is not buried *that* deep under the skin. I felt that by using a cultural device like this I could get away from the explanatory problematizing of being a cultural minority within a sexual minority, and give some intrinsic pleasure to lesbians and gay men of South Asian origin here in Britain.

One of the most limiting aspects of trying to make work within a foreign dominant culture is constantly having to explain one's references. In short pieces, that means using up most of the duration of the film or tape simply explaining away what it's like to be a double minority with very little room left for pleasure or developing particular stories. After all, with an Indian population approaching eight hundred million the general questions can become seriously self-limiting, and in the nineties in Britain have acquired a sense of déjà vu.

For us South Asian migrants in the West the pitfalls of a nationalist emphasis on culture can mean that we fall between the cracks. In my view it's time we reasserted our right to be in the center, and demonstrate that as producers of an informed cultural output that forms the link, the basis, of global cultural exchange, we have a voice that goes in both directions. As an Indian gay man living in the West, I take pleasure in my heritage of Indian popular culture, whilst challenging the Eurocentric lesbian and gay world I live within; at the same time I feel that I have something to contribute to gay men in India as they struggle to assert their own positions.

Notes

1. In Hindi, the dominant language of the North, "sumlaingik sambandhan."
2. For Fulcrum and Abseil's *Out on Tuesday* series on Channel Four, 1989.
3. From the film *Pakeezah*.

Porno?

WIELAND SPECK

Turn on your television set these days and the whole world pours out convulsively at you like chocolate sauce onto an ice-cream cake. It seems as though any subject is permitted, and as a rule you eventually slip into a coma without realizing that there is one topic that is definitely taboo: our sex life. You can watch people killing, eating, conducting experiments on animals, blathering on about careers, waging war, cooking meringue—but fucking? Any fucking is merely implied. Only the most conservative, unimaginative, initial stages of the suggested sex act—and, of course, strictly according to the rules of the majority orientation, that is, heterosexual—are shown on TV.

In many cases this incongruence disturbs a homosexual's sense of harmony, and he will endeavor to round out the incomplete, deficient TV program by switching on his VCR. In an effort to save himself from the sins of omission of television and thus salvage his evening, he takes in, in immediate succession, all the suppressed sequences, all the scenes of sophisticated sexual contact that have obviously been edited out. TV programs received by antenna or cable thus make pornography on cassette an absolute necessity for a complex view of the world. Anyone who does not realize this simple fact is an ignorant fool.

Pornography is now part of daily life in the West, and at times even provides a model for our sexual behavior. Older men are often surprised these days by the competence of younger men who, though they have little actual sexual experience, have mastered techniques and skills, obviously picked up through close observation, that can drive their partners absolutely wild. Incontrovertible proof of the power of the media!

Porno!

What can I do, as a filmmaker, to help stem the AIDS crisis? In 1985 I went public with an idea for a series of safer-sex videos. Yet instead of being greeted with open arms, I had to spend four years scraping together the funding. Neither gay porn producers I approached in France and the US, nor condom manufacturers, nor a gay publishing house in Germany were interested in backing what was such an obviously timely project. PorNO was the reply from the people who make their money with porn and have an obvious interest in the survival of their clientele.

In 1988/89, I finally received some official state funding from the Deutsche AIDS-Hilfe (German AIDS Relief). It wasn't much compared with the government funding earmarked for TV information campaigns about AIDS aimed at the heterosexual community, but it was enough to make a start. I made six videos, with a total running time of sixty minutes, for far less than what a single regular, two-minute TV commercial must cost. As intended, these six videos are now being used successfully as shorts before main features on rental and retail video cassettes, and being screened for free in sex shops, gay bars and saunas, safer-sex workshops, and even at mainstream film festivals. This wide dissemination was possible because the content of the videos ranges from the amusing and educational to pure porn.

Any scandalous reaction at public screenings remained muted, with the sole exception of the video *Gay TV*, which features the well-known gay German writer Detlev Meyer moderating a show in which a number of young men roll condoms on and off (and demonstrate how to put a condom on your partner's penis using your mouth). This video was shown on a big screen in the lobby at the official opening of the main German-language Young Filmmakers Festival, the "Max Ophüls Preis." A delegation of filmmakers from Georgia, USSR, enjoying their new-found freedom to travel, took one look at what was happening on the screen—and decided that this wasn't what they understood by freedom. The upright Soviet citizens marched off together to complain bitterly to Oskar Lafontaine, the Premier of Saarland, the province where the festival was being held. Mr. Lafontaine, however, saw nothing to get worked up about.

Hard On

As a filmmaker I have always worked in feature films, and so I naturally began writing the scripts in this genre. Since I myself use condoms for anal sex, I was able to create characters that naturally used condoms without any of the problems raised by many of the people I spoke to during the four years I spent trying to get the financing together. I had all these problems, prejudices, and aversions drawn up in a nice, neat list, so I could easily check whether I was skirting around or neglected some reservation or other. Rather than threaten, order, or plead with viewers to use condoms, I wanted as much as possible to make a video that would seduce them into making condoms a natural part of sex.

It is important to note here that the safer-sex rules illustrated in the videos are based on the principle of *livability*. Sexual conduct that ensures ninety-eight percent protection against HIV transmission is therefore *not* recommended to viewers, contrary to the current position in France. There, fellatio, sperm on skin, and even mouth-to-mouth kissing are proscribed. In Holland, people are advised not to practice anal intercourse *as much as possible.*[1] What on earth is "as much as possible" supposed to mean in this context? I'd say that when in doubt people are simply going to disregard the rules and screw without a condom. A frequent result of this policy is that sexually active people find that the rules are too restrictive and complicated to follow, and the uncontrolled spread of HIV is thus given a further boost.

What doctors and AIDS-relief and public health officials in Germany consider to be sufficiently safe can be summarized as follows: (1) *Don't let yourself be fucked without a condom, and don't fuck someone else without one;* and (2) *Don't let anyone come in your mouth.* In the interests of solidarity, we would add, *and don't come in your partner's mouth.* Safer sex is thus reduced to two *livable* basic rules that many gay men observe because

Weiland Speck (left) on the set of *Safer Sex Promotion Videos*

they regard them as reasonable and practical. This position is much more effective overall, because a far higher proportion of men actually follow the rules.

Furthermore, doctors and sociologists agree that practices such as rimming and water sports, which safety fanatics categorize as absolutely forbidden, can give you all sorts of things, but that it would be very difficult to get HIV from them. Obviously, any infection is harmful to the immune system—the common cold is proof of that. This cannot, however, be the subject of a safer-sex video, which, in four to eight minutes, must sell fun, sex, love, and orgasms—with and despite condoms—to do justice to the main, fatal problem—the transmission of HIV.

Following a screening of my video *Mehr als nur einen—Don't Forget Your Lubricant*—in which two young men are seen having anal sex when their last condom breaks, so one of them takes both their cocks in one hand and brings himself and his partner to orgasm—a French doctor, visibly very upset, came up to me and shouted, "You're killing people!" I replied that in my opinion the murderers were the asexual safety fetishists who ran around preaching paper-tiger rules that hardly anyone was capable of living up to.

I tried to promote the use of condoms by showing that they can break, too. This goes back to one of the chief points of my above-mentioned list of problems. Men said to me, "Rubbers can break, so I don't use them." My video's answer to this, as the title indicates, is that we shouldn't engage in sex if we have only one condom with us, and that when properly lubricated, that is, with a greaseless, water-soluble lubricant, condoms break only very rarely.

Another argument went, "I can't get a condom on. I lose my erection." This problem is addressed in the video *Übung macht den Meister—Discover Your Rubber*. A young man buys some condoms in a supermarket and tries them out at home in the kitchen of his parent's apartment. My idea was that if he gets the hang of it by himself, then he'll definitely find it easier to get the thing on when he's with a partner. The style of this short has much in common with the refreshing dirty movies made in Northern Europe. Filmed in super 8 with a shaky hand and set in cheap hotel rooms, these films stand out as little gems in the imperialist avalanche of offerings from US studios. When a hot scene in one of these films seems to go on forever, I always get a kick out of letting my eyes wander to check out the background—the tacky flower arrangement, the underwear and porn magazines strewn about on the floor, the half-dressed cameraman who suddenly appears in the dressing-table mirror for a second as he does a clumsy pan shot. It's not just live, it's life.

During our filming, I eventually came to the realization that porn films are actually documentaries, and that the script must be handled with far more flexibility than I was used to. I therefore decided not to clean up the videos by editing out condom problems, but instead to show the whole procedure in its entirety. I think that for the time being we don't have any other choice than to accept condoms as a routine part of our sex life. If someone puts one on the wrong way round, he just takes it off and puts it on properly—I find that charming. And it's really quite exciting the way the young man finally pumps his seed into the condom's reservoir tip.

Questions

A number of questions were raised after a screening in Amsterdam: Isn't it racist to have a young black getting fucked by a white (*Mach Freunde mit Gummi*)? What was my purpose in having a "blond German" get reamed by dark-haired young men (*Mehr als nur einen* and PORNO 90)? Isn't it irresponsible to show group sex in a tea room, and why does the Turk only get himself serviced (*PORNO 90*)? Why didn't I show any fist-fucking or hard-core S-M?

I'm afraid my answers were not as political as my American questioner would have liked, since I had to admit that I had left the choice of passive and active roles up to the actors. I was reasonably happy about how the first film turned out, however, because I think that the stereotype of the super-potent black stud is even more racist. The hair color issue, on the other hand, had completely escaped my attention. As for the tea room sequence, I said that I wanted to promote the idea that it doesn't matter with whom, with how many and where one has sex, but that it must be done safely. Had I had the Turk do the fucking, I wouldn't have been comfortable with the distasteful cliché; and had he let himself be fucked, probably no one in Berlin would have believed it. The most difficult question to answer was the one about S-M: I promised to look for colleagues who would deal with this subject authentically on film. I just didn't feel capable of doing it myself, because of a lack of experience, libido, and so on—though at this point these are pretty weak arguments, I know.

In the course of casting and filming, we discovered that young men who had come out at the time of the safer-sex campaigns had very little difficulty in using condoms. Those who had the most problems were men who had fucked away freely between 1975 and 1985. They often had trouble over-coming the psychological hurdle of having to give up or abandon a sphere of freedom they had had to win. They felt competent sexually, but disliked using condoms and often had erection problems. As was to be expected, this was the age group with which we had the most trouble during filming. We always had to have one or two stand-ins ready just to keep to our shooting schedule. Yet their performance was very laudable when you consider that there is no gay porn industry in Germany and so no actors with professional experience. The casting, I must admit, was the most stressful part of the production (with the exception of finding the funding).

Equalizing

Another fact makes safer sex the only satisfactory form of sexuality for the 1990s: it makes us all equal again in bed (or wherever)—regardless of whether tested, untested, positive, negative, or ill. Safer sex helps protect those who are HIV-negative from getting the virus and those who are HIV-positive from the risk of yet more serious infection. It's time to abandon the absurd illusion that if you have a negative test result you can go on screwing as you did before AIDS as long as it's with someone who also has an HIV-negative certificate. HIV is not a sexually transmitted disease that can be controlled adequately by tests every three months. Once you have it, you have it for good. The repeatedly tested, one hundred percent monogamous couple may have the option of climbing into their UFO and launching themselves into orbit for the rest of their lives, but for the time being, for the rest of us the only alternatives to safer sex are self-sex and no sex at all.

Here is an example: The Thai government is now issuing HIV-negative passes to its sex industry workers, who show them to Western sex tourists to convince them that there is no danger in having unprotected sex with them. This is simply inviting catastrophe, since a person can be negative one day and positive the next—and, as everyone knows, you can say whatever you like on paper. And what is more commonplace than forged documents? People's responsibility for the transmission of HIV is thus being undermined, and the doors left wide open for the spread of the virus. Terrific!

Cinematic Perspectives

I think that in the future the sole viable option for gay and lesbian film work (the porn videos described here represent "only" a sideline of my feature film work) is to pool small national budgets into an international film fund. This is the only way we will be able to produce and market films that can capture the permanent place they have hitherto been denied in the media. Lesbians and gays make up about ten percent of the population, but our presence in the media amounts to less than one percent. A gay film comes onto the German market, for instance, about once every three years; people don't want to hear about us more often than that. Yet only by making a full range of diverse films will it be possible to paint a complex picture of our reality, and thus break out of the vicious circle of the exceptional, where every lesbian and gay film is now categorized, much to its disadvantage. Let this be a cry for help to international lesbian and gay producers!

Notes

1. AIDS activists in the Netherlands meanwhile, in 1991, changed their perspective to an attitude similar to the German one. In France there is movement as well.

Shortcomings:

Questions about Pornography as Pedagogy

RICHARD FUNG

The camera moves, hand-held, down a corridor lined with rooms. A handful of men dressed only in towels are chatting further down the hall. A white man passes, looking lasciviously into the lens. The camera peers into a room in which another man is sleeping on a cot, and then looks into the next doorway, where a white man, in his fifties, is seen reading a book. As he looks up, the frame cuts to a reverse shot of a young East Asian man in the doorway. A faint smile crosses his face as he moves on. The camera continues down the hall with the frame now cinematically identified with the point of view of the Asian man—the cruiser. The ensuing doorways reveal: a young black man in a leather harness, an East Asian man lying on his stomach who at first looks into the lens and then rapidly averts his glance, a young white man who mouths the word "no" while shaking his head, and finally, a South Asian man who smiles directly at the camera. Cross-cutting produces a mutual smile. The cruiser enters the room and the two men begin to kiss and caress. After a series of shots of the two men licking and fondling each other, there is a brief negotiation. The South Asian man puts a condom on the cruiser (in close-up) and then sits on his penis (in medium shot). The camera pans away to show a mirror reflection of the two men enjoying anal sex as text rolls up the screen:

Fuck safely,
use a condom!

The message is repeated in Tagalog, Hindi, Chinese, and Vietnamese.[1]

The videotape I've just described is *Steam Clean,* a three-and-a-half-minute piece I directed in 1990 for New York's Gay Men's Health Crisis, the largest grassroots service agency for AIDS and HIV-related issues in the United States. This tape is one of GMHC's "safer-sex shorts," a component of its educational program in fighting the spread of HIV in the lesbian and gay communities.

I met Jean Carlomusto and Gregg Bordowitz, video production coordinators for GMHC, in 1989, at a conference on gay and lesbian representation. Although I am based in Canada, they approached me to produce the "short" for Asians,[2] presumably because they knew and liked my work, but also because they could not locate an openly gay Asian videomaker in the United States who would undertake such a project. For my part, I was interested in producing the tape because it offered the chance to create sexual images of gay Asian men; images that represent them as sexual subjects in the process of realizing their desires; images that disrupt the various racial/sexual clichés about passivity, premature ejaculation, small dicks, and so on; images that challenge our almost total exclusion from the North American gay erotic imagination.

While *Steam Clean* was produced as one of the "shorts," it was completed several months after the other tapes, which had already been distributed together as a package. This compilation had been screened at a wide variety of venues, including workshops, bars, gay theaters, conferences, and film and video festivals. By the time I produced *Steam Clean* I had the benefit of having seen the "shorts" with different kinds of audiences, and I had developed my own thoughts about what worked for me in each of the individual pieces, as well as in the package as a whole.

Convincing people to practice safer sex by depicting it as pleasurable is a currently favoured AIDS prevention strategy of progressive public health educators, as well as lesbian and gay groups. However, this necessitates promoting the pleasure of sex in itself, and entails depicting sex in a more or less explicit way. These are always points of conflict with religious and

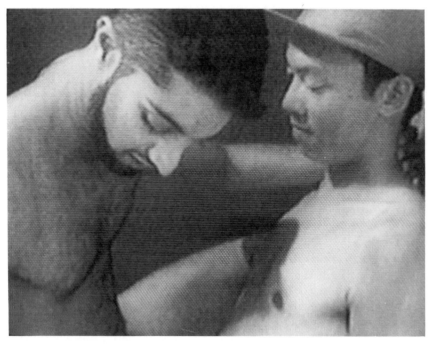

Steam Clean, Richard Fung

political conservatives, for whom the only acceptable approaches in inhibiting HIV transmission are sexual abstinence and (heterosexual) monogamy.

Given the struggle over the right to produce and disseminate sexually explicit safer sex materials,[3] I feel a knee-jerk reaction to rally behind the "safer-sex shorts"; to uphold their efficacy and to vindicate the progay, proporn lobby. *Steam Clean* has now been screened in several film and video festivals, and has been used in workshops and elsewhere. Feedback has been positive on its "hotness" and its usefulness in triggering discussion. However, I have increasingly begun to question the assumptions that shaped the tape's form and function. How do gay Asian men actually watch video porn? How do they derive pleasure from what they see? How does the inclusion of Asian actors affect the tape's reception by gay Asian spectators? Can the pleasure premise of porn coexist with the pedagogical? *Steam Clean*, the other "shorts," as well as a significant portion of safer-sex propaganda all rely on a set of interlocking assumptions about pedagogy and pornography that warrant continuing interrogation.

The Premise of Pornography

Jean Carlomusto and Gregg Bordowitz sum up the purpose of the safer-sex shorts as "getting the message out that you can have hot sex without placing yourself at risk for AIDS."[4] According to the GMHC's information sheet, *Safer Sex Porn: Format and Design,* each short is to be designed by a specific task group, which decides on the scenario, the characters, and the kinds of sex acts to be depicted: "The objective of this project is to come up with a number of culturally sensitive tapes addressing the needs of a number of communities regarding safer sex."[5] The sheet also uses "advertisements," "music videos," as well as "pornography," as references to the way the tapes should look—"extremely slick"—and interact with their viewers: "These 'shorts' must be conceived as consumable."

Apart from the obvious parameters of length and sexual explicitness, the shorts reveal other similarities of approach. For instance, most of the tapes use fictional narrative only minimally, to set up a scene for sex. In *Current Flow,* for example, a woman is masturbating with an electric vibrator when another woman pulls the plug. The intruder then lays out a "tool kit" of safer-sex aids, which the two try out on each other. In *Midnight Snack,* a man opens a fridge in a darkened kitchen. Suddenly, the lights go on and another man appears and begins to rim him, using a dental dam as a barrier. *Something Fierce, Law and Order,* and an untitled piece with voguers are even more minimalist. Of the five original "shorts," *Car Service* is the only tape that is based on a fairly developed scenario: A black businessman in a suit and with a briefcase takes a taxi. During the ride, furtive glances are exchanged between him and the chatty, black driver. When it is time to pay, the businessman finds that he is out of cash and has only condoms in his pocket. The driver accepts these, and the tape ends with the two men having sex in the back of the car. Supplementing the narrative, each "short" ends with a brief printed text on the screen, which reinforces the specific aspect of safer sex promoted in the tape. *Midnight Snack*, for example, closes with the instruction: "Use latex condoms. Cut condoms lengthwise to use for rimming."

Whereas the mode of address varies from tape to tape, all of the "shorts" incorporate very prominent music tracks, from club hits to Sinead O'Connor. The music is used to create a sense of sexual energy, but it also serves to constitute the tapes and their message as fashionable and "in the know" for the target audiences. The repositioning of the appropriated lyrics with the queer sexual imagery at times endows the tapes with a layer of wit and campy humor. Whenever I've seen *Current Flow* with an audience, for instance, women always respond to the O'Connor sound track with chuckles.

One of the most obvious aspects of the "shorts" as a group is the attention paid to race, and specifically, the consistent presence of people of color. *Car Service* features two black men, *Something Fierce* a single black man, and the entire cast in the vogueing tape is black. *Midnight Snack, Law and Order,* and *Current Flow* depict interracial sex with one black and one white actor. *Steam Clean* might also be said to portray interracial sex, since Indian and Chinese people are seen in this society as "racially" different, in spite of the fact that they are technically both Asian.

The frequent use of black and Asian actors, together with the common depiction of interracial coupling, sets this body of safer-sex propaganda apart from commercial porn. This perhaps reflects the proselytizing aspect of AIDS educational material aimed at high-risk populations, combined with greater sensitivity on the part of white AIDS educators to the politics of race and racism. Yet it is a mistake to think that the spectacle of queer miscegenation would only draw criticism from the racist right. At the How Do I Look? conference,[6] *Current Flow* became a subject of controversy because the black woman in the tape is the "top," reproducing, it was felt, the common stereotype of black hypersexuality. Carlomusto and Bordowitz denied any racist intention and stated that the black woman in the tape chose the role she would play. Carlomusto also pointed to the burden placed on a work when there is only one of its kind: "If this tape existed within a series of tapes about lesbian sexuality, there wouldn't be as much tension around this particular frame or that particular image."[7]

As producers, it is crucial to understand the discourses embedded in the depictions we fashion. It is our responsibility. At the same time, there is sometimes an unrealistic expectation that representations transcend, or even solve, problems that exist as social relations outside the text. The fact is that images of interracial sex cannot magically escape the burden of racism in the history of cinema, indeed in history itself. The possibilities for any portrayal of whites and people of color having sex are already overdetermined. If the black woman were the "passive" partner, or had there been a completely symmetrical reciprocity between the two women, the underlying problem would remain.

In producing *Steam Clean* this became very clear to me. As described above, the tape involves anal sex between a Chinese and an Indian man. I already knew that in depictions of sex between East Asian and white men, the Asian man was almost invariably the "bottom." I knew that this reproduced a stereotype that Asian men resented. I could not, therefore, portray the Chinese man as the "passive" partner in anal intercourse if I wanted East and Southeast Asian men—the target group—to get pleasure in the tape. But what about the other man? Was it less problematic to show a South Asian getting fucked because, as a group, they are rarely represented sexually in North America? And how did all of this relate to the privileging of penile pleasure and patriarchal assumptions about the superiority of penetration? In the end, I had the Chinese man penetrate, though I attempted to "equalize" the situation by having the Indian man sit on him, thereby asserting the pleasure of the anus.

I don't feel that my solution in any way resolved these crucial problems, because the fact of racism lies outside and beyond the tape, overdetermining the possibilities for maneuver within it. An option could have been to foreground the problem in a deconstructive manner; to produce a meta-pornography, a tape focusing on the workings and underpinnings of porn. I had already ventured such a strategy in an earlier video called *Chinese Characters* (1986). However, that tape didn't attempt to produce pornographic pleasure, but rather to analyze it. It seems difficult to reconcile deconstruction with eroticism in a single moment. In the context of a three-minute piece such a task strikes me as nearly impossible.

Talking Sex

What is peculiar to modern societies, in fact, is not that they consigned sex to a shadow existence, but that they dedicated themselves to speaking of it *ad infinitum,* while exploiting it as *the* secret.[8]

—Michel Foucault

Whenever I write or talk about sexuality, there is always the ghost of Michel Foucault, looking over my shoulder . . . laughing cynically. The project I embark on is inextricably tied up with what he identifies in sexual terms, as the two "modes of production of truth: procedures of confession, and scientific discursivity."[9] I talk with people about their sexual lives and I document, analyze, bringing together the confessional and the scientific.

In the first volume of *The History of Sexuality,* Foucault identifies the two historically predominant procedures for producing the "truth of sex."[10] On the one hand is the *scientia sexualis* of contemporary Western societies, and on the other, an *ars erotica* that developed in Asia, the Arab and Muslim societies, and Rome:

> In the erotic art, truth is drawn from pleasure itself, understood as practice and accumulated as experience; pleasure is not considered in relation to an absolute law of the permitted and the forbidden, nor by reference to a criterion of utility, but first and foremost in relation to itself; it is experienced as pleasure, evaluated in terms of its intensity, its specific quality, its duration, its reverberations in the body and soul.[11]

This passage, tinged with both romanticism and orientalism, warrants many qualifications. First, the circulation of an erotic art among a privileged sector of certain societies, or the use of sexual motif as religious practice, do not in themselves indicate an absence of sexual regulation, simply different regulations and taboos. Secondly, through continuous contact (including colonialism), the existence of two such mutually exclusive systems is no longer plausible. Finally, whatever the discourse and practice of sexualities may be in contemporary Asian societies, among diasporan Asian communities in North America, the legacy of an *ars erotica* has not resulted in a particularly candid or nonjudgmental discussion of sex.

I have been involved with the group Gay Asians Toronto (GAT) since its inception in 1980. One of the primary reasons for starting the group (as well as for its continuing survival), has, in fact, been talk. Not surprisingly, in both our formal (discussion groups) and informal (gossip) talk, constant themes are: sexual self-image in relation to the dominant representations of white masculinity; our desire (or lack of it) for other Asian men, white men, men of color; our absence from gay pornography; boyfriends. The sense of unburdening we feel—the pleasure of the talk—is precisely rooted in the "secret" nature of sex in North American (and Asian) society, and thus in our "confessing" it. Although there are profound differences—of class, language, culture, ethnicity, politics, and very importantly, (life-)style—the group offers a rare place where we can talk safely from roughly similar places at the intersection of race, gender, and sexual orientation.

To explore my investigation of porn and pedagogy, I interviewed three gay Asian men. Two are active members of GAT, and all are friends or acquaintances. Such a small and idiosyncratic sample precludes any claim to quantifiable findings, and I'm certainly not interested in constructing any uniform category of "gay Asian men." My purpose in these interviews was not to produce a Kinsey Report based on an "average" or "typical" gay Asian spectator, but rather, to see how porn figures in the actual life of *any* gay Asian viewer. Finally, as it was known that I directed *Steam Clean*, I didn't feel it possible for me to elicit candid discussion of the tape. It would have been as appropriate as writing a review of my own work. In any case, my interest lay in the men's reaction to the "shorts" in general, and not in generating a critique of the individual pieces. *Steam Clean* is certainly implicated in whatever criticism or questions I raise in this paper.

In choosing the men to interview, the principal criteria were that they be East or Southeast Asian (the target group for the tape), that they watch video porn to some extent, and that they would talk candidly with me. As a result, there is a certain similarity among the participants in terms of their age, class, educational background, and participation in the dominant gay male community. Further, while I had spoken about sex with these men before, the "scientific" purpose of these conversations shifted our relationship with each other—from friends to the roles of interviewer and subject—and hence our talk.

Ken is second-generation Chinese-Canadian. He grew up in rural Ontario where his family owns a restaurant. He is in his mid-twenties and has a degree in semiotics. He works as an arts administrator and lives in Chinatown. Frank is an engineer, born in Hong Kong. He works for the government and has a second job in a music store. He also packages music for fashion shows. He was, at the time of the interview, involved in campaigning for the New Democratic Party (Social Democrats) in the municipal elections. Li is also from Hong Kong. He supported himself through art school, and after working for two years in a yogurt store, he is now employed in a graphic design firm.

The men I interviewed watch porn only on an occasional basis. Frank owns about a dozen tapes, which he watches rarely because he does not particularly enjoy watching the same tape more than once. Neither of the others own any tapes, Ken because he is "too cheap" to purchase them, and Li because he lives in a rooming house and can only watch porn on the house VCR when his landlady and his heterosexual roommate are both out (both know he is gay, but his landlady does not approve of pornography). All three men rely on friends as a source of tapes since, until recently, censorship laws in Ontario have necessitated the communal sharing of out-of-province purchases.[12]

For all three men, porn is linked primarily to masturbation, though Frank has looked at videos while having sex with a partner and finds it particularly exciting, "like having sex in a car." All have watched tapes socially, with friends, during and after which no sex followed. Li also watches porn in gay bars and finds it exciting.[13] However, he tried not to be seen looking at it because he is afraid of being judged negatively by his peers: "This generation! I'm sure they do it at home, but when they get into a bar, they don't want people to think that they like porn. It's associated with sleaziness."

When looking at porn, Frank and Ken both rely heavily on the search functions of the VCR, which disrupts the narrative and allows the viewer to reconstruct the tape according to his taste.[14] Ken describes his viewing style as follows:

> I just zoom to the sex scenes. I zoom through all the stuff where there's no sex happening and I stop at the sex scene and watch for a bit to see if I think it's exciting. If it's not, I zoom to the next. Sometimes, I zoom through sex scenes too, 'cause I think they're too long . . . 'cause they're kind of boring to watch."

Ken also says that while he prefers written porn over video porn—because narratives build up slowly to sex—he dislikes most narrative in video, because "it's mostly so hokey." When watching tapes in repeat viewings, he simply zooms ahead to his favorite segments. Li, on the other hand, watches tapes right through, from beginning to end. Yet he rarely finishes them in one sitting, moving through each tape, section by section, over a period of time. Li prefers older tapes because they have more "story," as well as for the kind of men they feature. In fact, all three men express dissatisfaction with the "new" aesthetic in actors: in Ken's words, "clean, their pubic hair shaved, mostly blond and a lot younger."[15] The word used by all three to sum up the shortcomings of the "new" porn is "mechanical." Yet what the three men look for varies considerably.

All have various ways of negotiating the mode of spectatorship with the tapes they are watching. "Totally as a voyeur" is how Ken describes his viewing position. And here are two excerpts from Frank's interview:

> Looking at porn while having sex with someone, the other person can forget who you are and imagine you are the idol on the screen. They can forget about whatever shortcomings you have.

> If it's a hot scene with people I find attractive I would sometimes just watch it as an observer. There is an excitement of voyeurism, in terms of you seeing things that people do very privately, especially of people that you might never really meet in real life, and the kind of situation you might never get into in your real life.

Li's lack of identification with the tape—not imagining himself as part of the action—is a very conscious decision:

I made this point to myself a long time ago, before I looked at tapes. I always look at tapes purely as fantasy. I never associate tapes with reality. For me the two don't mix. I know it's not good for me to want more because I know it would never happen.

Fantasy is a common enough mode for viewing pornography. However, the unattainability of the (all-white) pornographic scenario in one's real life is often interpreted as having racial significance for Asian viewers. Men often say, "This couldn't happen to me because I'm Asian." Because the tapes that do include Asian men and white men are produced for a white audience, they don't offer productive avenues for sexual fantasy either.

All three men do in fact avoid racially mixed porn with Asian and white actors because of what they describe as its "offensive" or "stereotypical" quality regarding the Asian actors—they are always the "submissive" characters. However, this is not a statement regarding the extent to which they imagine themselves within the scenarios they are watching (identification in an active sense). It is more a question of how others might view them because of these stereotypical representations (identification in a passive sense). This also emphasizes that in many instances the men's relationship to what is occurring on the screen is distant and purely observational.

As for other options, Ken says that he would like access to all-Asian porn, but did not find the single Japanese tape he had seen exciting. It is the image of explicit sex that turns him on and the Japanese tape featured the "roving dot."[16] Similarly, Li says he only watches tapes with white or black men.

Conflicting Agendas?

What do the viewing habits and preferences of the three men interviewed suggest about the efficacy of the GMHC tapes? Two of the men—Ken and Frank—had in fact previously seen the "shorts," but in very different circumstances: Ken at the lesbian and gay film festival, and Frank at a "mixed" (gay and straight) nightclub in Montréal, where the tapes were screened in a video room away from, but accessible to, the main dance area.[17] Li had not seen the "shorts," but there were scenes of men using condoms in some of the porn that he watched.

In examining how the men read what they saw (and what they didn't see) in the "shorts," I want to begin by looking at how safer sex fits into their lives and their fantasies. Li has "come out" only since the mid- to late eighties; since the advent of safer sex. One of the main reasons he cites for his attraction to older porn tapes is their depiction of unsafe sex—something he has never done, but fantasizes about:

the idea of having unsafe sex and having people actually come without using a condom . . . I know that's not right to actually do it—but, with video you're only *watching* people do it, right?

Both Ken and Frank, on the other hand, had been "out" before the AIDS epidemic and express difficulty with actually practising safer sex, finding the condom disruptive to the flow of love making.

> KEN: It's really difficult to have safe sex with intimate partners. Safe sex with a stranger is easy. When sex is about intimacy a condom interrupts that meaning. This isn't addressed in the safe-sex propaganda.

GMHC guidelines state that the "shorts" should demonstrate that "safer sex is fantastic and explosively pleasurable." The five "shorts" show condoms as coming naturally to the men in the scenarios. Frank finds the unproblematized presentation of safer sex valuable in that they remind him that, if he keeps trying, condom use will eventually come naturally to him as well. Having the tapes, and other safer-sex informational material available and visible also creates a context that makes it easier for him to negotiate with his partners around condom use. At the same time, I believe that the attempt to transcend the distaste many men have of condom use—by simply showing it as pleasurable—could also have liabilities. Men such as Ken may feel inadequate or inferior because of their discomfort with using condoms. In *Steam Clean,* I attempted to address this problem by depicting at least a minimal negotiation around using the condom: in the middle of lovemaking one man leans over and whispers to the other, who then reaches for the condom.

Ken's overall assessment of the "shorts" is that he "didn't find them exciting." Although all of the tapes except the vogueing short contain depictions of at least one sexual act, Ken's memory of them is that "there wasn't any sex going on in them; it was all telling you." He adds that, as a body of work, "it doesn't disguise itself very well as porn." Frank similarly finds the tapes lacking in their ability to excite him:

> I don't find them sexy because they carry more of a medical or a social message than a pure porn film, where its purpose is different. There's a barrier there for people to really enjoy the safe sex because there's too much of a purpose to it. . . . They were something else trying to be porn.

This last sentence sums up my sense of what both Frank and Ken find lacking in the "shorts": that while they contain sexually explicit material and purport to be porn (the word is used by GMHC is reference to the "shorts") they do not look like the porn the men have seen and do not fulfill their sexual fantasies: because either the men, the narratives, the structure, or the aesthetic are "not right" according to their tastes. It is interesting to note here that in the structuring of the tapes around single pieces of music, they owe as much to music videos as to pornography. Yet no one I interviewed complained that the "shorts" were lacking in relation to their own expectations of that highly produced and competitive genre.

All three men claimed that they had sexual types or "favorites" in the porn tapes they watched. They all used the search function of the VCR to locate segments featuring their favorite actors and to pass over others. GMHC (and I in *Steam Clean*), on the other hand, have made a conscious effort to eroticize ordinary people, as opposed to relying on the conventions of age, beauty, and race described by Ken above. Whereas the men (and women) in the "shorts" all have "good" bodies, *Law and Order* is the only tape in which the actors embody the beefy look of commercial pornography. But while all the men interviewed expressed dissatisfaction with existing gay porn because it does not eroticize men who look like them, they find the men in the "shorts" lacking in comparison to commercial porn actors: in the case of *Steam Clean,* both race and body type break the rules. This reception is not as fickle as it might at first appear. For the tape to function well, two mechanisms are assumed. On the one hand, the Asian viewer must be asked to relate the message of the tape to his own experience and sexual practice. But the tape must also engage his libido, offering him the pleasure of pornography. However, people are not automatically attracted to others who look like them, and many gay Asian men are not interested in other Asians as sexual partners. For these men, the two criteria do not coincide. At the same time, everyone wants to be attractive to others. So it is important, even for them, that Asian features and bodies be shown as desirable. And since neither the commercial porn conventions nor our individual sexual tastes are monolithic and static, the eroticization of different types of men and women as seen in the shorts could be viewed as a positive change in our sexual environment.

The "cultural sensitivity" of the "shorts" assumes that, to reach out to and educate men of color, the tapes have to portray men of color. This goes hand in hand with the notion that in order to communicate with gay men, the tapes must speak in a language that they understand and like—namely porn. However, rather than work together, my conversations suggest that these two agendas actually point toward different strategies. "Trying to be porn," in Frank's words, means that the "shorts" open themselves up to be judged by the highly personalized criteria each individual viewer brings. So the tapes may fulfill their pedagogical function *in spite of* their pretense at being porn, rather than because of it. The mechanisms of producing pleasure and viewer interest, and the mechanisms of imparting information to that viewer, while mutually reliant, are not the same.

This is not to suggest that the "shorts" are failures in their pedagogical task, but rather, that the ways they work may be different from what has been assumed and intended. Neither does this mean that educators should give up the use of sexually explicit material for demonstrations of safer sex: explicitness seems to me a prerequisite for clear education, at the very least. However, if safer-sex educational material is going to attempt to disguise its pedagogical intention with a sugar coating of sex and pleasure, then it has to negotiate the conventions of porn with the impulse to depict a wider range of ethnicities, ages, and body types with more savvy.

The existing GMHC "shorts" fulfill a particular and significant function. But while it is instructive to analyze and assess how they operate, they don't carry the whole burden of safer-sex education. That task involves both the continued and expanded production of different types of safer-sex shorts, straight and gay, using a range of representational, pedagogic, and pornographic strategies. It also involves dialogue with the commercial porn industry, about the representation of both safer sex, and racial and ethnic difference.

I would like to thank Tim McCaskell, Kerri Sakamoto, Lisa McCaskell, Kari Dehli, and John Greyson for their generous comments and criticism.

Notes

1. In the Canadian version, preceding the English text there is a French slogan: Enculer en securite, Utiliser un condom!

2. Although Asia encompasses a wide variety of peoples, from Turks to Japanese, the term "Asian" is generally used in the United States (and to a lesser extent in Canada) to refer to East and Southeast Asians. In producing *Steam Clean,* I worked under the assumption that this was my primary target group.

3. See Jean Carlosmusto and Gregg Bordowitz, "Do It! Safer Sex Porn for Girls and Boys Comes of Age," Allan Klusacek and Ken Morrison, eds., *A Leap in the Dark* (Montréal; Vehicule Press, 1992) pp. 180–181.

4. Carlomusto and Bordowitz, p. 177.

5. The word "communities" here is used in racial, ethnic, linguistic, and sexual terms, and there is an attempt to make up for the significant gaps in safer-sex information available to groups not considered part of the mainstream of the gay communities. Because *Steam Clean* was not directly produced by GMHC, there was no task group, and I developed the scenario on my own.

6. See Bad Object Choices ,ed., *How Do I Look?* (Seattle: Bay Press, 1991) discussion, p. 62.

7. Bad Object Choices, p. 63.

8. Michel Foucault, *The History of Sexuality, Volume 1: An Introduction* (New York: Vintage Books, 1990) p. 35.

9. Foucault, p. 64.

10. Foucault, p. 57.

11. Foucault, p. 57.

12. As of the writing of this essay, pornography is still officially illegal in Canada. Canadian Customs continues to seize lesbian and gay materials, and the various provincial censor boards and police forces occasionally organize raids.

13. Porn is shown on monitors in some gay bars in Toronto. The monitor is usually placed above the counter or elsewhere, and alternates between football games, music videos, as well as the porn tapes. The tapes are edited to take out all "hard-core" images, that is, shots that depict any form of genital contact between actors. Since explicit sex acts constitute the majority of screen time in porn tapes, the resulting videos produce very discontinuous narratives.

14. Many of the "new" tapes rely more on display—the sheer spectacle of sex—than on constructing eroticism through narrative. However, most gay porn tapes are structured episodically, with perhaps a loose organizing scenario that functions as a context for the subnarratives.

15. Gay porn from the seventies and early eighties generally favored a more mature masculinity signified by the use of older models than those of today, mustaches, and visible body hair.

16. Due to censorship, Japanese tapes made for the internal market use different strategies to hide the genitals, including what would technically be described as a "circle wipe," which moves across the screen obscuring the actor's exposed loins. Otherwise, careful camera positioning and the inventive use of curtains, screens, and other objects serve to guard the offending articles from visibility.

17. Frank at first said that he had not seen the GMHC tapes. However, when he described the safer-sex tapes he had seen at the club, it was clear that it was the same material. This is the second account I have heard of the tapes being shown informally in Montréal (the other was at a large party). To my knowledge, in Toronto the tapes have only circulated formally at workshops and public screenings organized specifically to demonstrate safer sex.

She Must Be Seeing Things:
An Interview With Sheila McLaughlin

ALISON BUTLER

New feminist cinema has emerged under interesting but often difficult conditions. As well as the usual problems of entry for women into traditionally male-dominated cultural and industrial spheres, it has had to bear the additional burden of working alongside the paralyzing paradigms of a feminist cultural theory in which historical diagnoses have tended to harden into proscriptive dogma (for instance, that the gaze is inevitably voyeuristic, exploitative, and male, and that these terms are, to some extent, interchangeable. That fetishistic modes of producing meaning are absolutely unavailable to women, or at any rate, femininity, and so on . . .). Working within the confines of difference theory's binary structuration, feminist theory has become—for a time—gridlocked by its own conceptual topology. Recent work on fantasy (Elizabeth Cowie and others[1]) and nonphallic fetishism (Laleen Jayamanne) is beginning to show how this blockage might be dismantled, and to open new possibilities for a feminist cinema which is both visually pleasurable and politically radical (that is, which might recoup some of the "endless loss inherent in the 'tradition of the new' "[2]).

Sheila McLaughlin's first fiction feature (she codirected *Committed* with Lynne Tillman), *She Must Be Seeing Things,* is not a theory film, but it occupies a terrain in which the concerns of feminist theory are unavoidable. Narrating its story of a lesbian relationship troubled by intimations of heterosexuality, it progresses through fantasy scenarios which articulate the movement of women's desires across different discursive registers. As a narrative film, it of course makes use of the structuring binarisms to which narrative can always be resolved, but by playing with polar oppositions, reworking and recontextualizing them, it reminds us that social reality, unlike the classical narrative, is nonbinary and heterogeneous, and that a code is not the destiny of the history that mobilizes it but only the trace of the histories that precede it.

ALISON BUTLER: She Must Be Seeing Things *is one of the few films I've seen in this festival*[3] *which doesn't concentrate on the oppression of women by men, either in a personal sense, or socially and culturally under patriarchy. It's a lively, positive film which deals with the areas of some women's lives where questions of power and identity are open to negotiation to some extent. In this it's very different from your previous film,* Committed, *which dealt with the oppression of one woman, Frances Farmer, under various patriarchal institutions: the family, the Hollywood star system, the mental hospital. Does this change of emphasis in your work follow a shift—or a split—in North American feminist discourses away from histories of oppression and towards notions of empowerment?*

Sheila McLaughlin: I hope it represents a shift rather than a split. It's impossible to make a film that doesn't in any way relate to patriarchy and women's oppression, but what I wanted to do in this film was to foreground the relationship between the two women and then have that act in relation to male culture. I think it's positive because women have been talking about difference, sexuality, and desire for a very short time, and I think that during the sixties and seventies we came into danger of becoming our own police and being extremely moralistic and judgmental about what one can and can't do as a "feminist." With this film, I'm saying that there's more than one way to be a feminist, there's more than one feminism. I wanted to open up the notions and possibilities of what women can do, to try to confront and be iconoclastic towards what have become lesbian and feminist taboos. And hopefully by confronting them, to begin to break down the power that they have, to digest them somehow. I don't think this represents a split; I think it's just a more open way of thinking about women's sexuality. It's dealing with notions of power between women, and opening up questions of sado-masochism, bondage and so on. When Agatha goes to the sex store to look at dildos, it's not really clear how much the two women participate in that together; she doesn't buy the dildo, but not because she's against it, she just doesn't buy it right then, she may in the future, who knows? I was trying to deal openly with the ultimate lesbian horror, the fantasy of having sex with a man. Having that fantasy doesn't necessarily mean that you're not a lesbian or you're a bad woman, or anything like that. I think that fantasy is inescapable, so I wanted to raise issues around that and confront them.

The film explores erotic lesbian imagery, but it does so neither in terms of a narcissistic relation of sameness nor in terms of an otherness from or previousness to patriarchal power relations that some radical separatists have preferred to use. Instead it plays with the given positions of sexual difference theory, masculine and feminine, defined against each other. In other words, the film doesn't attempt to invent or discover a "new language of desire," but rearticulates and—I think—subverts the existing codes in the dominant culture. Why did you choose to work this way?

Heterosexuality is the dominant code of the society that we live in, and it defines and in a sense creates our own sexuality, whether we choose to participate as literally heterosexual or not. I think it's somehow inescapable, that we're inextricably bound up with that. We've gone through a long time of trying to deny that, and yet it's important, if we ever want to get beyond that stage, to find a "new language" or whatever you want to call it, to work through that in some sort of discourse before we can free ourselves from it, or figure out what our desire is or is about.

One new thing that's happened, at least in the North American lesbian scene, in the eighties—it started before, but now it's really started to come out—is the taking on again of butch-femme roles and playing with those, which was not approved of before. There was more of the "clone" look, and women were representing themselves to the world as each other, as like each other, looking the same. I think that it's a reestablishing of difference, which reestablishes a certain eroticism in relationships. Ruby Rich talks about this in her article "Feminism and Sexuality in the 1980s."[4] I think that taking on these roles is a way of subverting them, showing how fragile they really are. One of the reasons I cast the two women I did was that they really

Agatha (Sheila Dadney, left) and Jo (Lois Weaver) in *She Must Be Seeing Things*, Sheila McLaughlin

couldn't be more different from one another, even at the level of physical appearance. They use role-play to empower themselves in their own way rather than being victimized by it. I wanted to undermine the idea of women as narcissistic extensions of each other because I don't think that's true. That's not why women are together. Also, women have been thought of as having sex that's very "nice," you know, like "making nice," and it's very sweet and gentle, touchy-feely-kissy, and almost prepubescent or something, and that's not what happens between women. It's so often thought of that way, I think, because of the absence of the phallus, since sex is thought of as a phallic thing. I wanted to bring out the eroticism between them, particularly in the seduction scene, and the aggression in their sex, to show that the strong attraction, the eroticism that's there is not just "nice"; sex is to do with aggression.

With the two parallel dressing-up sequences, where Jo puts on the silk underwear that Agatha gives her, and later, when Agatha dresses as a man, in the sequence where she's following Jo because she suspects that Jo is sexually involved with a man, were you referring to notions of femininity (and masculinity) as masquerade?

It has to do with the butch-femme issues I was talking about. But when they dress as stereotypes, I wanted them to use their masquerades with a clear sense of irony. When Jo dresses in the baby-doll outfit, she allows for a stereotypical erotic response at the same time that her consciousness of that brings humor and irony to it. Similarly, Agatha dressing as a man masquerades as that which she is threatened by. In a way, she is using the disguise to do battle with the thing that she is disguised as. By representing herself in the image of the rival, she deflates it.

So the masquerade devices are used to suggest that gender roles, like clothes, can be put on and, by implication, taken off, so that they aren't assumed as biologically determined, but as social constructs which are subject to variation and open to transformation?

I agree that gender is a social construction, you're not born with it. But its social construction determines what the possibilities are that one is given in the world today. Redefining ourselves as androgynous is something we can't do, at least not at this point; it hasn't been created and it's a very difficult thing to create, if at all possible. But that doesn't mean that you're fixed simply as "masculine" or "feminine": it's important in the film when Jo says to Agatha, "Do you really want a cock?" and she says, "No. Yes. Maybe, sometimes, but I don't want to be a man." You can play with these ideas, but it doesn't necessarily mean that you want to be a man, and I think that's the danger that some women feel, that if you take on that role it implies something that it doesn't necessarily have to, and it doesn't; a dildo is something that you can take on and off as well as a role. You can use it

Jo contemplates her attraction to a male acquaintance (Ed Bowes)

as you like and then discard it. Similarly, Jo at times appears as a sex object, but that is also undermined by showing her in an active role, working on her film.

So you're really undermining notions of phallic power by playing with them and making a joke of them?

Yes, making fun of them. Like when Jo does her dance in her little baby-doll outfit, the camera starts off with a very "male" point of view, as she does this traditional sex-strip dance. But it's undermined by the music that she puts on. The image-sound tension makes it into a very weird thing that she's doing, and she makes it absolutely ridiculous. Agatha laughs at it, and when Jo puts her stockings on, there's a hole in one of them and her foot goes through it. When a "real" person does these things, they don't happen the way they're "supposed to." It makes a ridiculous scene of it, which is what I really wanted to do: I wanted to have the camera pan down her body and show her in this very stereotypical way and then make it ridiculous, constantly having things going on within the scene that would undermine that point of view and that stereotype and make fun of it.

One of the unusual things about the film is that it addresses the question of differences between women, rather than assuming a universal Female Subject. One of the most important differences between the two protagonists of the film is racial difference: Agatha is Brazilian and Jo is an "all-American" blond, the ultimate WASP. There differences give rise to a powerful mutual fascination. There's also a power dynamic working here: Agatha says that she wanted to possess Jo, but instead became possessed by her. I'm interested in whether you saw racial difference as an important issue, for example with regard to the distribution of roles and positionalities in the film. For example, Agatha seems quite "male-identified," and even says at one point that she identified with her father rather than falling in love with him, whereas Jo is almost a Marilyn Monroe type. Both self-representations are survival strategies, but there seems to me to be more necessity involved in Agatha's assumption of a mask and more play in Jo's masquerade, which relates directly to the different levels of access to power which white women and women of color usually get.

I don't think that racial difference is the most important difference between the two protagonists. For me the most important thing was that they be as different as possible and race is part of that. It is very difficult to represent a black/white relationship because the issue of race often dominates. Before I shot the film I considered reversing their roles and having Lois Weaver play Agatha and Sheila Dabney play Jo. As I was thinking about casting a black woman in that role, I tried to think of her in various different roles. It seemed to me that she could be positioned in many different ways, and, depending on one's point of view, all the roles could be read as racially problematic. If she had played Jo, she could have been stereotyped as the "sexy black bitch," for example. As Agatha, she can be read as male-identified or she can be read as a strong professional woman, a lawyer operating in the world successfully, politically committed, and doing something she has chosen to do. In the scene where she dresses as a man, what's important is not that she's a black dressing as a man, but that she's a woman dressing as a man, and that's appropriate as part of the narrative in the film. Also, black actors want good roles in film and not to be cast simply for being black. Of course race is always an issue, but I personally felt an obligation and an interest in beginning to address that. For me it's a very difficult and important thing to do.

The question of the visual is central to the film, signalled by the title, She Must Be Seeing Things, *and also by the fact that one of the protagonists is a filmmaker, and that the final resolution comes about when they're looking at her film on the editing table. This resolution is structured as a revision of the Oedipal scenario with a "happy ending," intercutting the sequence in the film-within-the-film where the young girl overlooks the couple in bed having sex, which is interrupted when a man rushed in a knifes the man in bed and the young girl rescues the woman, with images of Agatha, distraught and caught up in her own jealous and fearful fantasies about Jo. The use of reverse-shot here interpolates Agatha into the film-within-the-film. Could you explain a bit about your use of notions of fantasy in the film?*

One thing I wanted to do formally in the film, when I was thinking about how to deal with Agatha's fantasies, whatever "she must be seeing," was to make the images of what she "sees" extremely realistic. I didn't want to go into other cinematic modes, with strange or surrealistic things going on, because in fact those fantasies are extremely real, even more real than "real life." I wanted to make it ambiguous at certain points in the film whether things are or aren't happening. Similarly, I tried to weave the film-within-the-film in as well, to make it work within the "reality" of the contemporary story, to show how fantasy and "reality" are irrevocably linked in these two lives. There are two obsessions going on in the film: there's Agatha's obsession, and there's Jo's obsession with her film, and these come together in the end. Jo is unaware of what Agatha has been going through, but at the same time she's making a film that strongly relates Agatha's experiences, so there's some kind of unconscious synchronicity going on. The film that Jo's making brings these elements together in the end. It's ironic that what this produces can be seen as a different version of the Oedipal situation, where instead of the woman killing the mother in order to take her place, to be with the father, the man is killed and the woman runs away with the woman. So, yes, it becomes a sort of happy ending.

The film-within-the-film is generically very removed from the contemporary context which frames it. Based on the Thomas De Quincy story of a seventeenth-century nun who rebels against and runs away from the convent, it doesn't bear immediately on the situation of New York lesbians. Could you say a bit more about its function in the film?

When I first started making the film, that was the film I wanted to make. I was interested in the story of Catalina de Erauso, but then decided that I didn't want to make another period film about the life of one woman, and also, it would have been very expensive. There's a certain historical parallel between Catalina's necessitated male identification (she has to dress as a boy to protect herself outside the convent) and Agatha's, to less of an extent. The fact that Jo's making this film provides some resolution to the conflict between the two women at the level of fantasy and in the realist narrative. In the scene where Jo is directing and Agatha watching, Jo is completely in control of the situation: "Catalina" is being directed by her, and Agatha, in a sense, is also reacting with reference to the situation that Jo has set up. As Agatha witnesses the scene, she has the same reactions as those of the character whom Jo has created.

As a film about voyeurism and the fascination of one woman for another, She Must Be Seeing Things *is like the repressed fantasy of* Desperately Seeking Susan, *the film that some feminists wanted it to be. The voyeur-detective is becoming an increasingly common narrative figure in feminist film. To some extent, I think this has to do with the contradictions involved in being a feminist and loving the cinema, which, to date, has been largely made by, about, and for men. Do you think that a nonvoyeuristic women's cinema is possible?*

I think that's what cinema literally is, I mean the relationship between an audience and the images they're seeing on a screen makes it impossible for cinema to be nonvoyeuristic. That's what so much of it's about. As to whether the voyeuristic gaze can be anything but male, I don't know. What I wanted to do in the film was to make a voyeuristic female and constantly put her in the position of taking on the look.

Did you intend to identify the look of the woman spectator with the look of Agatha?

The film is told from Agatha's point of view—we know what's going on inside her head. In the strip scene the camera is behind her back, so we're in the same position that she is; there's an attempt to take on her point of view. I don't think that it can completely displace a male point of view, but by camera position, there's an attempt to introduce a certain question or conflict about who's looking.

Your film seems to belong to a small "school" of New York independent films, including those of Bette Gordon and Lizzie Borden, which deal with questions of desire and sexuality which haven't yet been addressed much within the women's movement. Instead of the soft-focus sentimentality of Lianna, *it refers to cross-dressing, butch-femme roles, and bondage. Although it doesn't depict sex explicitly, its frame of reference makes it a risky film to have made—what were you hoping to add to the feminist agenda that's important enough to justify taking such a risk?*

As I said before, there are a lot of taboos that many feminists still hold onto, and if we don't confront them, we're limiting the possibilities of understanding our own sexuality and desire. It was this representational space I was trying to open up. I'm not the only one who's doing this. Lois Weaver, who plays Jo in the film, is one of the founding members and an important director of WOW (Women One World), a lesbian theater company that works around these kind of issues and plays with them in a completely anarchic and outrageous fashion. This theater and publications like *On Our Backs* are important elements which have a strong impact on the lesbian community in New York City.

Have you had much feedback from men watching the film?

No, none at all. I literally just got it out of the lab and brought it straight here. This is the first screening. I have no idea what men are going to think, and that will be interesting in terms of distribution, because the people who make those decisions and have that power are mostly men, and I don't know that there's any way for them into the film.

Why did you choose to premiere the film at Créteil, given that quite a lot of women don't bring their films here first, because there isn't a market or a tradition of easy access to markets and distribution outside of the feminist distributors?

That's why I did it. Since I just finished it I haven't worked out any real distribution strategy quite yet. Having been at Créteil before, where there was very little marketing, I thought it would be a good chance to see how women reacted to it, to see how controversial it would be, whether anyone would go for my jugular, or whether they would enjoy it.

Has anyone really attacked the film?

I think that perhaps people were a bit shocked at first. As I expected, some gay women were disturbed by the role-playing and the heterosexual fantasy in the film. I was speaking to some women from England who said that they'd been talking to some other English women after the screening. They'd said "It was great, wasn't it?" and the other women answered, "No! God!" But it was said in a way that was like "what will people think?!"

Maybe that's because the women's movement in England has become rather polite, perhaps because of its fragility in the current political climate.

It's not too polite a film, so hopefully it will engage more discussion than not.

As a woman filmmaker working at the avant-garde edge of the American independent sector, is it difficult to get funding for projects?

Very, yes. It's especially difficult in America. I suppose the grass is always greener, but Europe seems better by comparison: you have much more government funding, television funding, and national film theaters where the stuff can get shown without the primary consideration being its commerciality. That doesn't exist so much in America. This film was funded by grants and German television, and I got just about everything I asked for. I know that won't ever happen again, and I don't know how I'll get funded. If I look for private funding, I don't know that they're going to want to fund someone who's made this film about a couple of dykes, with all this sex stuff and it's—you know—weird . . . it is very difficult.

Notes

1. Elizabeth Cowie, "Fantasia," *m/f* 9 (1984), pp. 71–104 and Donald Greig, "The Sexual Differentiation of the Hitchcock Text," *Screen* vol. 28 no. 1 (Winter, 1987) pp. 28–46.
2. Laura Mulvey, "Changes: Thoughts on Myth, Narrative and Historical Experience," *History Workshop*, no. 23 (Spring, 1987) p. 7.
3. The 1987 Créteil International Women's Film Festival.
4. B. Ruby Rich, "Feminism and Sexuality in the 1980s," *Feminist Studies* vol. 12 no. 3 (Fall, 1986).

Dessert Hearts

MANDY MERCK

When Joe Lorenzo discovers his fiancée Silver Dale and her friend Cay Rivers sharing a bath, he declares that the foam-covered duo look "like two desserts"—a remark which wasn't lost on the London critic Suzanne Moore. In her review for the Labour monthly *New Socialist,* she observed that *Desert Hearts* precisely "wants to have its cake and eat it—because all the men are so nice and understanding, because the women are just so gorgeous to look at, any challenge lesbianism might represent is underplayed."

The association of lesbianism and "challenge" in the cinema is hardly new—indeed British reviewers often dealt with *Desert Hearts* in these terms, praising it in some quarters for not "alienating" viewers, and damning it in others for the same reason. Yet the truly challenging lesbian film has proved notoriously elusive, beckoning faintly from cinema's remote past (the much-mythologized 1931 *Girls in Uniform*) or its imagined future. Thus, a review of *Desert Hearts* in the feminist magazine *Spare Rib* argued, "[A] film which attempts a broader exploration of issues around lesbian identity and contemporary lifestyles still remains to be made."

But while we can all imagine the genuinely progressive text, I sometimes think we are oddly less in touch with the current situation, in which the lesbian romance is becoming a conventional—and highly conventional-ized—narrative in the "art" cinema of Europe and North America. By "art" cinema I mean theatrical features which oppose the "international style" and subjects of Hollywood—films which have historically involved an emphasis on cultural specificity (of a nation or social group) and personal authorial "expression" (the director typically being designated as auteur). Such a definition could easily apply to certain US filmmakers working outside Hollywood (for example, the John Sayles of *Lianna,* but not the John Sayles of *Piranha*), and it is intended to. Historically, such a cinema has proposed itself as the exponent of a more realist representation of sex and sexuality than that afforded by the Hays-censored Hollywood of the thirties and later, or by the various formulas mandated by today's youth market. Certainly in the US, from the end of the Second World War until the mass-marketing of harder-core films, European "art" movies meant "adult" movies meant "sexy" movies. . . .

Now, as I have argued in Charlotte Brunsdon's anthology, *Films for Women*,[1] the lesbian romance is an ideal subject for a cinema which takes its sex seriously and in some sense sells on that basis. It provides a sufficient degree of difference from dominant heterosexual conventions to be seen as "realistic," "courageous," "questioning"—all terms from British reviews of *Lianna*—but it does this by offering literally more of the same, more of the traditional cinematic use of the figure of the woman to signify sexual pleasure, sexual problems, sex itself. So it's not surprising to find lesbian characters across the history of art cinema—from Rosellini's *Open City* to various Bergman films to Chabrol's *Les Biches* to Bertolucci's *Conformist*. Of course, these characters weren't employed until quite recently for romantic purposes, but to signify decadence or doom. They didn't even come in pairs usually, but as solitary eruptions into the heterosexual milieu.

Desert Hearts is different from its art cinema precursors in ways that would have seemed utopian, say, ten years ago. The villainous lesbian character and the tragic lesbian romance of even a recent film like the Hungarian *Another Way* (where one lover is paralyzed by her vengeful husband and the other killed trying to escape the country) seem almost magically trans-

Ruth (Jane Hallaren, left) and Lianna (Linda Griffiths) in a lesbian bar in *Lianna*

formed into this comic romance with a happy ending. And certainly sections of the London press hailed it as a remarkable development, attributable in large part to the politics and determination of its director (Donna Deitch, who is characteristically seen as the "author" of the film, rather than its scriptwriter, Natalie Cooper, or even the novelist Jane Rule).

Yet this innovation depends upon a number of familiar cinematic elements:

1. The popular romance. Boy meets girl, boy loses girl due to parental disapproval, boy finally gets girl back. As Annette Kuhn noted in a discussion of *Desert Hearts*, this standard plot line would be highly improbable (and thus uncommercial) in a contemporary film. Make it homosexual, however, and it achieves immediate plausibility. The lesbian romance renews the genre.

2. The seduction of the woman. My use of the boy/girl formula in the previous example wasn't altogether innocent, since *Desert Hearts* is steeped in the heterosexual tradition of the active pursuit of the reluctant woman. It doesn't invoke the literal, commercially off-putting codes of butch and femme, but it does employ traditionally related dichotomies of class (cheeky casino girl pursues shy professor), geography (candid Westerner courts aloof Easterner), sexual history (experienced lesbian brings out previously faithful wife), and appearance (passionate brunette warms up cool blond, who honors a long cinematic tradition by eventually letting her hair down). The brunette/blond: active/passive dichotomy is now an established convention of the lesbian romance—it features in *Personal Best, Simone Barbes, Another Way,* and *Entre Nous,* as well as *Desert Hearts.* (The lesbian vampire film reverses the convention, making the predator a blond in *Daughters of Darkness* and *The Hunger*—a sort of photo-negative of the dark male Dracula.)

What's really remarkable about *Desert Hearts'* adhesion to these conventions is that they were all written into the film adaptation: in Jane Rule's novel there is no parental disapproval. Frances is happy for Cay (called Ann Childs in the novel) to find love wherever she can. The delaying device is the two principals' own guilt and pessimism. Secondly, the characters are not so rigidly skewed between activity and passivity, or between parallel symbolic dichotomies:

1. Far from the dark/blond opposition, the two lovers look so alike people think they're related.

2. They both live in the West (Evelyn teaches at Berkeley, not Columbia).

3. They're both educated (the Cay figure has a degree, works part-time as a political cartoonist, and—like almost everyone in the novel—has a large library and an achingly conspicuous command of English literature).

Where the novel's characters do differ is in age: they're fifteen years apart, not ten as in the film, and people take them for mother and daughter. This age difference relates to the novel's themes of sterility (it's titled *Desert of the Heart,* remember) and maternity, and is discussed in frankly Oedipal terms. Silver refers to Evelyn as "the latest mother figure" and warns the Cay character: "Love, when little boys want to marry their mothers, they have a hárd enough time of it, but they manage. When little girls want to marry their mothers. . . ."

This theme (desire between mothers and daughters) is clearly far too challenging for a popular romantic film, although it might just qualify for film noir or a social problem drama about incest, so the age difference between the characters is reduced, and their status differences heightened instead. (Interestingly, cross-status desire isn't conventionally taboo in the way that cross-generational desire is.) Furthermore, I believe that it would have been much more jarring if Evelyn had left Reno with Cay's stepbrother Walter, who also pursues her in the film. The heterosexual older woman romance is hardly unprecedented in Hollywood melodrama (think of Rock Hudson and Jane Wyman in *All That Heaven Allows,* and Lily Tomlin and John Travolta in *Moment by Moment*), but by now it's probably less conventional than the lesbian romance.

In order to succeed as a popular romance, *Desert Hearts* was divested of any social or political ramification or context that would restrict its generality. As Donna Deitch herself argues, "I didn't want to put it in seventies' New York. It's not about lesbian custody or any particular issues, it's essentially a love story." This principle of universal applicability is conventionally seen as a mark of artistic success. Thus British reviews of *Lianna* repeatedly praised the film for dealing not just or primarily with lesbianism or coming out, but with "the problem of [establishing] an independent life," "starting over," and—my all-time favorite—"the endless mystery of love and sex." Such universality requires a distance from particularities of politics and history which makes Lianna seem exceptionally naïve for a faculty wife in contemporary New Jersey. Similarly, *Desert Hearts* is set in a fantasized Wild West (where anything goes, pardner) in an idealized retro-chic fifties, without any of the fifties' circumstances which could have contributed to the guilt and pessimism represented in Rule's novel.

The final cinematic convention I want to examine brings us back to the scene in the bathroom. It's axiomatic in feminist film theory that mainstream cinema tends to eroticize the female body rather (or much more) than that of the male. And that it organizes its camerawork and editing so that the spectator's point of view coincides with that of the hero, who looks with us at the erotic spectacle of the woman.

Now consider the poster image for *Desert Hearts:* on it Evelyn (the Eastern professor) stands awkwardly in the foreground in her city suit looking out

The poster image for *Desert Hearts:* Vivian Bell (Helen Shaver, front), flanked by Cay Rivers (Patricia Charbonneau), her brother Walter, and his girlfriend Gwen

past the spectator, while Walter, Cay, and her girlfriend Gwen lean languidly against Cay's phallicly finned convertible and stare appraisingly at Evelyn. Like many film poster images, this shot was staged—it's neither in the film, nor was it Deitch's first choice, an image of the two principals meeting for the first time on the highway. This image was set up at the behest of the marketing department of the film's distributor, the Samuel Goldwyn Company, who asked for a shot which would include more characters than just the two lovers.

In London, advertisements for the film surrounded this poster image with critical quotes like: "brilliant and steamy . . . extremely erotic," "Touching, erotic and fresh," "A passionate and beautifully controlled drama." Despite its fabrication, I think the poster represents a most appropriate "narrative image" for *Desert Hearts*. On the one hand, the male spectator—via Walter in the poster and Joe in the bathroom scene—is invited into an identification with lesbian desire (an interesting reversal on the psychoanalytic presumption that lesbians identify with male desire!). Deitch's own remarks about a male spectator at the Toronto Film Festival ("I think it's a compliment that he is drawn to them and their experience") seems to touch on this. So, more emphatically, does the praise of the *New Musical Express:* "The film totally accepts the existence of lesbian relationships, and manages not to alienate the male audience."

On the other hand, the female viewer is invited into the place which feminist film theory (crudely speaking) assigns to the male viewer: that of the voyeur gazing at the erotic spectacle of the woman, actively desiring her seduction and identifying with her seducer. I think that's true of other recent lesbian romances, notably *Lianna,* which includes a sequence at the lesbian bar with marked close-ups of eyes and eyeline matches in which *Lianna* learns to look erotically at other women. So much so that the next morning she can hardly take her eyes off women passing in the street.

In *Films for Women,* I asked what the consequences would be of a cinema which frees the woman's look in order to vindicate that of the spectator? What does it do to our aspirations for that challenging lesbian film—often described as one which would disturb the pact between the voyeurism in the cinema and that in the narrative? Instead of answering that question, I'll close with a note from film history, one which suggests that even the pristine reaches of the past may be implicated in this regime of looking. Take the supposed epitome of antipatriarchal, antifascist, antihomophobic "challenge"—whose production supervisor, Carl Froelich, decided to alter its title from that of the stage original, *Yesterday and Today:* "We want to get back the money we're investing. We'll call it *Girls in Uniform*—then they'll think, there'll be girls in uniform playing about and showing their legs"—and whose Romanian distributor cabled urgently for a new print, with twenty more meters of kissing. . . .

Note

1. Mandy Merck, " 'Lianna' and the Lesbians of Art Cinema," in *Films for Women,* Charlotte Brunsdon, ed. (London: BFI Books, 1986), pp. 166–75.

Security Blankets:

Sex, Video and the Police[1]

JOHN GREYSON

Over the past thirty-five years, Linus has waged a heroic and dignified battle to hold onto his security blanket, despite the sustained taunts of Lucy, and the rearguard attacks of Snoopy. The urge to interpret Linus's relationship with his blanket is overwhelming—so let's succumb. Just for fun, let's propose a reading which probably wasn't foremost in the mind of author Charles Shultz when he first launched this epic narrative of property, identity, and self-worth. Let's propose a reading which has something to do with the complacent suburban values of the *Peanuts* gang but arguably much more to do with sex, spies, and videotape. Let us think of Linus as a gay man living in North America. Let us think of his blanket as the gay community, both social and political, a context in which he can find identity, relationships, and consciousness. Let us think of Snoopy as the police, an arm of a hostile state apparatus that is intent on destroying that community, and hence Linus's identity.

In October 1990, the Toronto chapter of Queer Nation planned a lunchhour kiss-in at the Eaton Centre, a large shopping mall in downtown Toronto, perhaps best known for the Michael Snow installation of stuffed Canada geese that fly permanently southward over shoppers' heads. The occasion was International Coming Out Day. The strategy was to promote lesbian and gay visibility within this bastion of middle-class heterosexual privilege. Queer Nation, like its affiliated chapters throughout the US and Canada, was formed in 1990 by dyke and fag activists committed to combatting the rise of antigay violence and promoting queer visibility.

The kiss-in was a humorous failure. Only three dozen people showed up, and we seemed more committed to gossiping than smooching. I'd volunteered to videotape it, along with fellow video pals Colin Campbell and Stuart Marshall (in town for the weekend from London), and we had a hard time getting any decent footage of actual lip-to-lip activity. The hundreds of shoppers seemed oblivious, more intent on the sales at Stitches and the Gap.

The cops and security guards were another story, however. Over a dozen of them circled our group, repeatedly asking us to leave, clearly frustrated that they had no legal means of moving us. The chief security guard attached himself to me. He was obviously upset about the kissing and displaced his anger onto my camcorder, insisting over and over again that videotaping on private property was against the law. Knowing the legal precedent, I argued back that the courts, just six months earlier, had legislated that malls were indeed public areas, despite private ownership. I also pointed out that a CBC news crew was filming a few feet away and asked why he wasn't harassing them? The answer was predictable: I wasn't a journalist, I was a demonstrator. Well, I admit I'd done a bit of kissing myself, making me somewhat less than an objective reporter, but why draw the line? Hadn't he heard of Tom Wolfe, the new journalism, the *Village Voice*? The situation degenerated as he grew more and more aggressive. Eventually I was arrested—the only demonstrator to be arrested that day. My camcorder was confiscated because he claimed it could be used as a "dangerous weapon."

That such a lackluster demonstration could be so threatening to the cops, and that it's recorded image had to be confiscated so arbitrarily and paranoically, serves to illuminate just how jumpy the state gets when dissent and desire meet. The demonstration sought to promote visibility through intimacy—in short, to kiss and tell. This combination flies in the face of the state's accelerating project over the past two centuries to regulate sexuality—to do all the talking. As Michel Foucault and others have observed, the state's many tentacles (in particular its legal and medical arms) don't seek to choke or repress the sexual conversation. They merely strive to monopolize and control it. Deviant dissenters threaten this monologue with their own voices, and are thus prime targets of state censorship—and surveillance.[2]

State surveillance is never, of course, passive, never the neutral observation of behavior. Instead, it is always active—state surveillance seeks to discover what people are saying and doing, in order to . . . well, lots of things. Silence voices and suppress activities, of course, but also mold opinions, shape communities, or transform resistances, depending on the issue and context.

The surveillance of gay desire stretches back centuries, finding its mandate in the law books and religious precepts of most societies. Indeed, our knowledge of queer history would be unthinkable without the wealth of court, police, and medical records, which recount again and again the collection of evidence by cops, nuns, priests, state officials, and functionaries, and so on, which "proved" our crime against nature. Surveillance, indeed, was, usually vital, because unlike other sins or crimes, there weren't any victims ready to squawk, only consenting parties.[3]

The emergence of a visible gay community in the last century, with its bars, baths, and social spaces, corresponds to a litany of police raids, entrapments, and prosecutions aimed at keeping a lid on such manifestations of public and collective identity. More often, however, state surveillance has focussed on individuals, with doctors and cops actively collaborating, to seek out, pathologize, and criminalize those deviants who stray from the approved family plan.

The past twenty years have seen a narrowing focus in the field of such surveillance: these days, doctors rarely try to cure "queers" and cops generally do stay out of "the bedrooms of the nation."[4] As the state conceded more and more of what it deemed *private* space back to the homo, it simultaneously accelerated its surveillance of those *public* places where men seek anonymous sex—parks and public washrooms.

In 1988, I completed *Urinal,* a hundred-minute film which explores this policing of public sex, focussing in particular on the prosecution of washroom sex. I was particularly interested in how cops, through entrapment and surveillance, must *create* the crime. Because of the excessive lengths washroom queens go to to preserve their privacy (and to ensure that they don't get caught by either cops or straights), the police have an almost impossible time catching them in the act. As the character Langston Hughes in the film says: "The cops know something is going on, but every time they go in the washroom, it's just a bunch of men, standing around and combing their hair." Throughout the eighties, police forces in Ontario used two methods to make the crime visible: undercover entrapment and video surveillance.

Entrapment is an effective but hardly glamorous way for cops to make a bust. The undercover cop will stand at a urinal, pretending to play with his cock, until another man signals interest. Sometimes that interest can be as little as eye contact or the nod of a head. According to some reports, the really zealous cops even flash their own hard-ons. It's a simple arrest, the cop's word against the man's in court, and it boosts the cop's monthly arrest quota. Promotions, after all, are based on the number of arrests, not convictions.

Geography seems to divide the two practices. While entrapment (and no video surveillance) is commonly used in downtown Toronto, just the opposite seems to be true elsewhere in the province. Regarding the lack of undercover entrapment in smaller communities, it may be that police chiefs in smaller towns dislike the idea of their dicks standing around with their dicks hanging out for hours on end. Imagine! Such squeamishness! Don't they understand that such protracted diddling is a vital and valid use of taxpayer's dollars?

In the early eighties, the Ontario Provincial Police (OPP) purchased an expensive video surveillance system. Contrary to public opinion, the applications of such a system for police forces are extremely limited. The very factors that make video effective for property protection, and therefore widely used by the private sector, make it less than efficacious for crime detection by a public police force. Video surveillance by the police requires a location that is regularly resorted to for crime, one where the police can install the equipment and monitor the results. Crime by its nature tends to rove around, not wanting to stay in any one place too long. The surveillance of washroom sex, in fact, is one of the few applications for such a system. Once the OPP had the system, they had to use it.

Throughout the eighties, the OPP lent the system to various small-town police forces, who would launch a typical surveillance operation of two or three weeks in a local public washroom. Highly publicized mass arrests would follow, with the police often issuing press releases naming the names of the men charged. In St. Catherines in 1985, one of the thirty-two men charged committed suicide on the day his name was printed in the local paper.

The documentary side of *Urinal*'s experimental docudrama format ex-

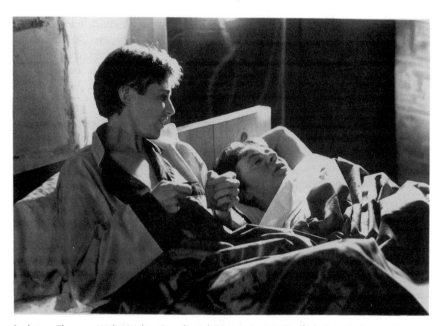

Sculptors Florence Wylie (Keltie Creed) and Frances Loring (Pauline Carey) discuss the group of infamous guests that has assembled to investigate the problem of police surveillance of men's washrooms in *Urinal*, John Greyson

plores the dynamics of these small-town and big-town crime-creation programs in various ways, utilizing a range of conventional and not so conventional documentary strategies. The six narrators, all closeted dykes/fags/ bisexuals and famous dead artists from 1937, each present a mini-documentary that speaks to an aspect of the subject, and often implicitly contradicts or challenges the analysis of the other five. Thus, Toronto sculptor Frances Loring commences with a social history of the public washroom, noting that gay washroom sex as we know it only developed with the creation of the sex-segregated public washroom in the late nineteenth century. Japanese novelist Yukio Mishima (a precocious teenager in 1937), presents a reading of what he terms tea-room texts: various conflicting voices across cultures (legal, pornographic, literary) which describe the practice, including his own, as-yet-unwritten novel *Forbidden Colors*. Harlem Rennaissance poet Langston Hughes travels through south-western Ontario to Guelph, St. Catherines, and Orillia, and his lonely, subjective voice-over captures some of the alienation of the men arrested in those small-town raids. Toronto sculptor and lifelong "companion" of Loring, Florence Wyle, interviews gay activists who have attempted to fight against this abuse of police power, in the courts and in Parliament. Mexican painter and flamboyant bisexual Frida Kahlo delivers a Foucauldian analysis of how the modern state has accelerated its project of infiltrating the private spaces of peoples lives, while at the same time creating the illusion of granting ever more freedom and privacy to individuals under capitalism. Soviet filmmaker Sergei Eisenstein conducts a guided tour to Toronto's hottest tea rooms, and interviews two tea-room queens, one of whom was caught in a video surveillance bust. A social worker in his fifties, he describes how his name was published in a local paper, prompting his boss to summarily transfer him to a purely administrative job with no contact with the public, away from the direct-service work he loved. He decided to fight the case, and the video surveillance footage of himself and the other man having sex was introduced into court as evidence. I asked him to describe his response, assuming this further violation of his privacy would have been a horribly traumatizing experience. His answer caught me completely off guard:

> I didn't expect to see myself behaving sexually on tape. It was a very self-affirming experience. I was rather surprised by how good I felt, even given the anxiety-provoking circumstances, even given that, it was a very self-affirming experience to have to watch yourself behaving sexually on tape. I was delighted by how human and how physical and how sexual and how beautiful I was, and I was surprised."

During this monologue, audiences are often extremely quiet, anticipating, as I had done, a tale of degradation, of visual victimization. When he finishes speaking, having reclaimed this surveillance in such a graceful and surprising way, audiences often burst into spontaneous applause.

In researching *Urinal* and the culture of surveillance, I had to analyze which came first, and which produced which: the technology or the practice? On the surface, it seemed as though the Ontario police force had bought their video system and then had to find a use for it. Their application of video surveillance seems to prove the McLuhanite formulation that the technology produced the social practice. The surveillance of washroom sex became the vehicle for justifying the expenditure, for putting this otherwise worthless equipment to work.

A history of such practices actually suggests the opposite. As Gilles Deleuze and Claire Parnet assert:

> Never is an arrangement-combination technological, indeed, it is always the contrary. The tools always presuppose the machine, and the machine is always social before it is technical. There is always a social machine which selects or assigns the technical elements used. A tool, an instrument, remains marginal or little used for as long as the social machine or the collective arrangement-combination capable of taking it in its phylum does not exist.[5]

The actual practices of Ontario police forces bear this out. Gay historian Gary Kinsman has uncovered several cases in the sixties and seventies when cops would create peepholes in washroom ceilings in order to do live surveillance. The most notorious case of this was in 1969, when a man died in police custody after two cops spied on him through a ventilation grill in the washroom of a Toronto gay bar.[6] The practice of such surveillance was simply modernized through video equipment, not created by it.

Nevertheless, many attempts by artists to represent surveillance tend to get stuck in this rut of techno-determinism. The 1988 Surveillance Show at the artists space LACE in Los Angeles, a multimedia group show addressing issues of surveillance in society, featured too many works which dealt solely with the technology of surveillance. The physical fact of the equipment seemed to be identified by the artists as the problem or crisis, and few of the featured artists seemed interested in the social practices (which admittedly aren't as sexy or visual as the display of high-tech) that actually constitute the experience of surveillance in our society. I'm talking about the taxation procedures, the credit checks, the census-taking, the social agencies who review your refugee status or decide whether your kids are eligible for dental care. I'm talking about the million-and-one ways the experiences of community and autonomy have been eclipsed by the free market's kinder, gentler version of Big Brother. Walking through the exhibit, surrounded by infrared detectors, audio monitoring systems, and electric eyes triggering lights and bleeps, the seduction of all this fetishized high-tech seemed to outweigh the denunciation.

When I was making *Urinal* I was faced with a similar problem: how could I resist the seductive spectacle of the video surveillance image? You all know what I mean: the aesthetics of surveillance imagery are now securely enshrined within popular culture, cropping up even in the January 23, 1991 episode of *All My Children*. One of the characters, suspecting his wife was cheating on him, contracted a private investigator to shoot video evidence of her affair: the black-and-white, Orwellian TV monitor, alienated, cold, sinister, revealing some awful truth that can help one party by hurting another. In the case of washroom sex, the monitor would feature a grainy, high-angle shot of two men having sex. How could I make a film on the subject and not include such an image?

Urinal is full of grainy video imagery transferred to film, but none of it is of washroom sex. All the documentary sequences use the gritty veracity of video to foreground their so-called distance from the filmic dramatic scenes (of course, they are just as much constructions as the dramatic scenes, and their "truths" are just as subjective). Two of the mini-documentaries in particular (Florence's and Langston's) use shots of small-town life that roughly replicate the angles and interests of a leisurely tracking video surveillance camera. In this way, I wanted to point to the broader and more banal implications of surveillance in society.

Questions of portraiture (painted, photographic, filmic, televisual) run through *Urinal,* visually problematizing both the famous dead artist narrators and the documentary interviews subjects. I appropriated Oscar Wilde's *The Picture of Dorian Gray* as the poetic master narrative of *Urinal* for several reasons. The Wilde original is a story about the problems of portraiture, and the picturing of deviant sexuality: though Dorian Gray looks pure and innocent in the flesh, his painted portrait reveals his true and perverse character. In *Urinal,* I shifted the problematic: when we construct a picture of washroom sex, who should we look at, what should we see? Do we see the men having sex, or should we instead shift our gaze to focus on the police practices which make the sex visible in the first place? In Dorian's original story, his picture hid the secret of his "deviant" (gay) life. In *Urinal,* his portrait instead becomes a picture of the police, and their deviant practices.

Given this agenda, of shifting the focus away from private sexual acts and towards public policing practices, I hoped that the *absence* of the grainy surveillance sex image would speak much louder than its presence. Thus, in the film this "surveillance of desire" is documented, analyzed, examined, and interrogated by the characters and subjects, but never visualized—its

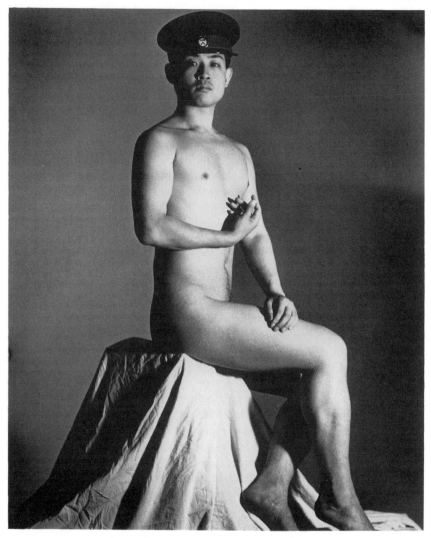

Dorian Grey (Lance Eng) sits for his portrait in *Urinal*

literal illustration is refused. Instead, the police in the narrative use video surveillance to spy on the characters—they practise the "surveillance of dissent."

Unlike the surveillance of gay desire, the surveillance of gay dissent by the state has a much more contained history and trajectory. Dissent in this case refers to lesbian and gay political organizing; surveillance suggests the monitoring, disruption, and sometimes destruction of such organizing.

Examples occur through the century: the burning of Magnus Hirschfeld's Institute for Sexual Science by the Nazi's in 1933; the infiltration of the Mattachine Society in the fifties; the disruption and infiltration of gay rights rallies and demonstrations during the seventies and eighties.[7]

The mountie and the cop in *Urinal* turn Dorian Gray into a double agent, in order to spy on this unwieldy group of famous dead artists. Not completely trusting him, however, they also install a video surveillance system in the house where the group is staying, the better to monitor their activities. Thus the dynamics of video surveillance are reintroduced as a political issue, not simply as spectacle. Amplifying the already established themes of portraiture, these dynamics help drive this appropriated narrative to its unique variation on the Wildean conclusion: in the cops video surveillance monitor, we see Dorian rush towards his portrait and stab it. When the cops arrive at the house, they find the painting intact, beautiful once more—but Dorian lies on the floor, a dead cop.

It's significant that the state's practice of surveillance works hand in hand with the state's project of censorship: while one hand creates pictures, the other destroys them. Surveillance strives to produce a picture of lesbians and gay men as pathological, deviant, dangerous, and diseased, again primarily through its legal and medical arms. Censorship attempts to suppress any autonomous pictures, produced by dykes and fags themselves, which threaten the hegemony of the state's own pictures.

The ideology of free speech, which supposedly allows for the expression of political dissent, exercises an extreme double standard when it comes to sexual dissent. That the work of artists addressing issues of queer sexuality is disproportionately singled out for suppression is hardly a recent phenomenon. Though the recent notorious cases (Mapplethorpe, Riggs, Haynes, Miller, Hughes, et al.), are specific to the particularly dreadful and tawdry place in history we find ourselves in right now, they are also predicated on past struggles in different contexts and moments.

In Ontario, queers have had no choice but to spend a great deal of energy fighting censorship over the past two decades, the two obscenity trials of the *Body Politic* magazine being only the most notorious examples.[8] The provincial Film Censor Board, which came to fame in the late seventies by banning *The Tin Drum* and *Pretty Baby,* has demanded much of our attention, and diverse coalitions of feminists, queers, artists, and community activists came together to fight its rulings. One particular effort, the *Days of Resistance* in 1985, provoked a unique confrontation with both state censors

392 / SECURITY BLANKETS: SEX, VIDEO AND THE POLICE

and undercover cops doing surveillance. This provincewide festival of film and video was conceived as a civil disobedience action, protesting the Censor Board's attempts to prior-censor *all* film and tape in Ontario, regardless of venue, context, or audience. Yes, a documentary about farm animals being shown to a kindergarten class could technically have been raided, if it hadn't been approved (just think what those goats and sheep might be up to!). We quite reasonably argued that if our poems, sculptures, and dances didn't need to be precensored by the government, then neither did our tapes and films. Over forty screenings were organized in eleven cities over a two-week period.

Before each screening began, organizers would ask any cops present (undercover or not) to identify themselves and then ask them to leave. Each audience member would also be asked to turn to the person beside them and ask that person if they were a cop. By law, cops must comply with this request. Since they couldn't see the tapes or films, they couldn't therefore lay charges. In fact, only a handful of the forty screenings contravened the criminal code's puritan notions of obscenity, but *all* the screenings were by definition illegal, since they hadn't received the clearance of the Censor Board—which was of course the point.

The cops soon realized how our exclusion strategy worked and started trying to blend in with the audiences by disguising themselves as artists. Their idea of how artists dress was certainly imaginative. When overweight white men in their mid-thirties would show up at the door wearing gold chain medallions and brown leatherette vests, it wasn't too hard to figure out who they were and refuse them entry. Of course, there were inevitably borderline cases, as some artists do fit that description, but they would quite good-humoredly sign a form stating they weren't cops—only the real cops wouldn't sign the forms.

To say that this process was exhilarating understates the case—Mary, it was divine! We had created completely public screening spaces, open to anyone, which could legally exclude the agents of both state surveillance and state censorship. Were those boys ticked off! Since that time, several changes of government have resulted in a very different scenario, with a very different relationship between the cops and the censors. Under the New Democratic Party government, the Censor Board has stopped its harassment of noncommercial groups and has relaxed its standards considerably, for the first time allowing real porn into the province's home video stores. The Toronto police, as out of control as ever, have taken to raiding home video stores and charging them with peddling filth under the federal criminal code, despite the fact that the tapes have been cleared by the province. Thus, these two arms of the state (the one that makes pictures of us and the one that suppresses *our* pictures), once hand in hand, are now locked in an arm wrestle over who's got the power. Yet another anticensorship coalition, responding to this, among other issues, has had to mobilize the troops yet again.

It's already become a truism to note that a new wave of activism, epitomized by such groups as Queer Nation, Outrage, ACT UP, and AIDS Action Now, is sweeping through the lesbian and gay movement. Spit-in-your-face tactics have been declared appropriate to combat the rise in antigay violence, homophobia, censorship, AIDS discrimination, and surveillance. Lesbian and gay artists are at the heart (some like to pose as the cutting edge) of this new militancy. Not just making banners, not just coordinating the color scheme of a new poster campaign, not just doing video documentation and countersurveillance at demonstrations, not just establishing fashion trends for the next demo . . . but also producing works which explore the boundaries and parameters of sexual dissent. Just as Linus became militant about his right to his security blanket, so, too, do dykes and fags resist outright the attempts of the state to make pictures of us, and resist outright the state's attempts to suppress our pictures.

Last October on International Coming Out Day, when the surveillance of desire, the surveillance of dissent, and the practice of countersurveillance all convened in the Eaton Centre Mall, the results were somewhat anticlimactic. The charges were thrown out of court because the arresting officer had forgotten to sign the warrant. I was only detained for half an hour before being let out on my own recognizance and was able to rejoin the demonstrators on the corner. And, yes, they did return my "dangerous weapon," my camcorder, with the tape still intact. With great excitement, I rushed home and played the tape back. Imagine my disappointment: the footage was unusable, there were only a few seconds of the arrest, and these didn't seem to adequately capture the true extent of my suffering at the hands of a brutal and repressive state apparatus! What would Linus have done? I reached for my blanket. . . .

Notes

1. Adapted from a paper presented at College Art Association Conference, Washington, February 23, 1991. Panel: "Photography, Surveillance and Democratic Movements."

2. See Michel Foucault, *History of Sexuality: Volume One, An Introduction* (New York: Random House, 1980) pp. 7–13.

3. For example, Jonathan Katz's groundbreaking *Gay American History* (New York:

Thomas Y. Crowell Company, 1976) is a compilation of four hundred years of state discourse about queers, a fascinating record of the records that made us visible.

4. In 1969, then Federal Justice Minister Pierre Trudeau declared that the state had no place in the bedrooms of the nation and effectively decriminalized queer sex between consenting adults, but only "in private," a key distinction. See Gary Kinsman, *The Regulation of Desire* (Montreal: Black Rose Books, 1987), p. 164.

5. Gilles Deleuze and Claire Parnet, *Dialogues* (Paris: Flammarion, 1977), pp. 126–27.

6. Kinsman, p. 145, and also, independent research for *Urinal* by Kinsman and Greyson.

7. See articles by John D'Emilio, James Steakley, and Michael Lynch, in *Flaunting It: A Decade of Gay Journalism from the Body Politic,* Ed Jackson and Stan Persky, eds. (Vancouver: New Star Books, 1982).

8. Jackson and Persky, ibid., pp. 4–5.

Homosexuality as Dissent/Cinema as Subversion:

Articulating Gay Consciousness in the Philippines

NICK DEOCAMPO

The time I am now living in is one of the most tortured moments in my country's history. It seems every form of human suffering and nature's wrath has been felt by our people: a country full of sorrow. Living nowadays is not really living, especially when one is growing up *gay*.

Gay life in the Philippines is one that cannot be dissociated from a whole gamut of sociohistorical determinants which continue to stunt the growth of the Filipino people. A people's sexual life cannot be distanced from its economic-political-social-cultural well-being. Hence any discussion of homosexuality needs to consider how homosexuality fits into the whole fabric of the social struggle. It is quite evident that this social struggle seeks not only sexual liberation, but rather a liberation in all levels of social life, counting sexuality as only one of the sites for such a struggle.

Failure to do so, meaning to deny issues of sexuality in the process of the social struggle, would mean the failure to account for the oppressive conditions suffered by almost half of the country's population, as in the case of women. The impact that could result from this failure to respond to the needs of this major sector of the labor force cannot be demeaned. Or, as in the case of the gay and lesbian populations, failure by society to consider other shades of human sexuality could mean a denial of the plurality of lifestyles and options which must be made accessible to and responsible for a people if indeed they are to live in a truly democratic society. A claim to homosexuality then becomes a political, not merely a sexual, option. In times of great repression, as history shows, being gay may even be tantamount to being subversive.

The context that has given rise to the sudden explosion of homosexuality in the Philippines is one that has also given homosexuality a stigma which it must overcome. Since its outrageous coming out in the sixties, peaking in a rampant growth in the eighties, homosexuality gained wider acceptance at the time when social corruption engulfed much of Philippine society. This was the time when poverty, sex tourism, media exploitation, political repression, economic collapse, and moral decay formed a nexus of historical determinants which endowed Philippine society with a disreputable image in general and gave the homosexual community an uphill battle to climb in terms of recognition in particular.

Nowhere in our history has homosexuality been more pronounced, and yet more corrupted, than during the twenty-year regime of Ferdinand and Imelda Marcos. Displacement in social life spurred confusion in values. The rule of the Father, turned vicious, created reversals in identification. Repression brought out avarice in some, but internalized weakness in others. It is not hard to surmise how political coercion spelled irreparable damage in the psychic life of the Filipino people.

Among the major influences shaping homosexual identity and replicating homosexual behavior on a massive scale is media, particularly film and television. In a sense, homosexuals have a lot to thank media for, if only for the vast mileage media has given in terms of public exposure to all sectors of society. Yet many now realize that instead of making the gay issue understood, the result has been one of confusion and caricature. The acts of both representation and signification of gay characters and gay issues have become questionable in the light of the patriarchal ethos that dominates the whole system of production in media and the whole system of reception by the public.

There is a world of difference between what is represented on screen and how homosexuals conduct their lives in reality. And, mind you, this is not begging for a discourse on art and reality. Rather, we must realize how media becomes an instrument in the service of the dominant ideology that is in place in society, and how this ideology seeks to perpetuate itself at the expense of other emerging, thus deemed threatening, forces in society.

As we unmask this ideology, we find that the root cause of this antagonism is one that is sexually motivated: patriarchy. This is further reinforced by the feudal system we live in. Lamentably, patriarchy thrives well among us not only because of the traditional hold on power by men but more so because it has remained unchallenged by women and those belonging to other contending forms of sexuality. The society's culture of silence, undoubtedly, has bred the history of violence that now forms part of our consciousness as a people, and which we must now break.

Looking closely at how media produces images of homosexuals according to a set of stereotypes, it is important to unmask the hidden ideology responsible for such image production. Our society, despite all the trappings of a matriarchal, caring society (including the phenomenal rise of a woman, Cory Aquino, as president), remains beholden to a patriarchal ethos. It is this ethos which spurs male governance and spins the history of violence.

Within the specificity of cinematic construction, for example, none reveals as much about patriarchal values as the way films contrive their closures, or endings. In many films, and these are always slapstick comedies, where the main protagonist is gay the film often ends and all conflicts are resolved through the magical transformation of the gay character into a straight one, where, you guessed it, he then marries the heroine. Order is once more restored in the diegesis and the film may now end. But only because the male order has been restored.

It is evident through this kind of closure how patriarchal values of the society shape the production of meaning favoring the preservation of male chauvinism. Any threat to sexual dominance constitutes a threat to the entire social fabric. A homosexual is deemed to be one such threat, and this threat must be stopped, hence the ending. Cinema embodies the male population's collective wish fulfillment and performs the function of sublimating the fear of the male from his perceived castration.

Very few among the country's artists have expressed voices of dissent in the mainstream cinema in terms of representing the true condition of homosexuals. In the commercial cinema, films by Lino Brocka and Ishmael Bernal tackle gay themes as perceived in their actual milieu *sans* fallacies. In their films gays end up as gays, and not fairies who end up as gladiators.

But for whatever contributions Brocka and Bernal have made in terms of articulating issues of homosexual concern, they stayed in a precarious position of being censored by the state-controlled censorship board, or face the risk of being shunned by commercial producers for being too serious, when what the public "wants" are images of homosexuals audiences can laugh at. Cinema, as it was in the entire sphere of cultural production, was caught in a situation where artists could no longer freely express their convictions.

Thus did the eighties come like a double-edged sword for the Filipino artist. In the early years, there was a rapid politicization of media, as the country reeled under the tyranny and violence of the Marcos dictatorship. In retrospect, the emergence of a radical cinema, a time when an intense confluence of social tension and monolithic dominance in all forms of public articulation could only beg for a revolution to happen, also served to manifest how alternative models of thinking and praxis were being waged outside the state-controlled media networks. The latter half of the eighties, however, separated by the rupture brought about by the people-backed revolution of 1986, soared to a climax with Cory Aquino's rise as Asia's first woman president only to be dashed into disappointment and frustration when social reforms failed to live up to the expectations earlier charted by her phenomenal appearance in the country's political firmament.

This period of struggle provides the context for the emergence of a new generation of Filipino filmmakers who, young as they are, seek new ways of defining Philippine cinema. Existing outside the commercial practices of the mainstream movie industry, they have eagerly sought expression in gauges and genres other than those conventions dictated by the narrative cinema, which had come to assume the popular form of 35mm film. The oppositional struggle voiced in the society had likewise sought expression in the oppositional nature of short, independent films.

The phenomenal emergence of the country's alternative cinema is not without its history and function. It was an eighties phenomenon; by this is meant its growth was an event signalled by dissent towards a political history peculiar to that time. Its characteristic nature to be radical was tempered by the radical impulse that gripped much of the society. As a reaction initially triggered by the dictatorial machinations of the Marcos government, a new generation of filmmakers sought release from the established system of iconographic representations and thought perpetuated during the twenty-year regime and entrenched within a cinema, and a media, which had become subservient to the dominant ideology of the dictatorship.

It was no accident of history that the young filmmaker tried to rediscover the cinematic medium, and it was not by chance that this had to happen within the walls of academe. The efforts at radicalizing the form and function of cinema by young filmmakers were in the tradition of student militancy, which became a major force of dissent in society. Efforts at making cinema attuned to the pressing needs of the times led to a pluralization of filmic articulation. No longer was film expressing only a narrative mode of articulation, but it soon found expression in nonnarrative, abstract, experimental, subjective forms. This radicalism sought to disengage the young filmmakers from the crippling malpractices demanded in the commercial medium. The upsurge of radicalism that guided the efforts to arrive at a new cinema may be seen within the contextualizing framework of the *revolution,* and how, in its historical patterning, it has served to periodize the evolution of cinema in the country.

When cinema was brought to the Philippines in 1897, it came at the heels of our revolution against Spain. In the ensuing years, America bought the country from Spain and held us spellbound, this time not with the miraculous icons which Spain had used to mesmerize us for three centuries, but, more appropriate to the modernizing revolution happening at that time, we were hypnotized by the electric shadows of cinema. Our thoughts, our will, our aspirations to become a people were shaped by that distant factory of myths and illusions—Hollywood. Thus did the movie house connive with the church as places for mass idolatry and as vehicles of illusion which had very direct consequences in ideology formation.

A good ninety years later, in 1986, another revolution was sparked, this time to oust a dictator. This is where we now find the immediate roots of the struggle to attain reforms in cinema. As found in the efforts of young filmmakers, we now demand a redefinition of the cinematic medium which, as a people, we publicly cherish, but, in some distant corners of our hearts, we inwardly resent. Cinema has grown to assume such draconian proportions, its behavior and stature in society have likewise evoked the odious temper of that mythical creature—the hydra. Commercial cinema has continued to decline in recent years.

Here now, at the end of the century, a band of young filmmakers is expressing dissent towards the industrial cinema, hoping, if they can, to chase the spectres manning the gates of their mechanized dreams. What makes this voice of dissent sound convincing is that it comes from a concert of other voices that demand change to happen in all levels of society.

What the young filmmakers are doing, then, is no trivial matter. They belong to a whole nexus of economic, political, social, cultural determinations that, with their intersecting grids of cause and effect, have defined a historically specific period unlike any other in the history of their country's art and culture. With their work in the oppositional cinema, they extend the long tradition of struggle in the medium that has long been a tool of their country's oppression.

I have come to identify myself with this radical cinema as both its practitioner and its chronicler. In the eighties, at the height of the Marcos dictatorship, I found myself articulating gay issues through super 8 films—a medium that, together with video, has become a locus of dissent against the state-controlled media. In 1983, a landmark year for the wind of change which brought us all the way to the 1986 People's Power Revolution, I made a film on a homosexual named Oliver.

Oliver was also called "the Spiderman" because of the lengths of thread he inserted inside his anus which he then pulled out to create a web all across the dance floor. All this to survive. But I saw in his bizarre performance a metaphor for the kind of life all of us were living under the Marcos regime. All of us were weaving our own webs, day in and day out, getting entangled by them and going in circles without really knowing where we would end up.

Making a film on Oliver made me follow the entrails of poverty and into the dissection of illusion as an escape from harsh reality. Unwittingly, the film gravitated around two major themes: poverty and prostitution. Oliver was no isolated particular. He did not exist in a space, in a life all his own. It mattered that he existed among us, in our society. His presence created a spell, even if he only made people shiver and nauseated to know how far a member of our tribe has degraded himself in order to survive.

Oliver's condition can be seen as an aberration and his act evil only because evil can be seen as "other." People don't see it in themselves. Evil exists outside one's own being. It is the nothingness that one sees in another's eye. They shiver at the sight of it because they do not want to be contaminated by it. It is gross. It is superfluous. No one wants to partake of evil. They who have three square meals. They who have nothing to care for but the security of their money in the banks. They who have a family, a religion, a stable job, a wonderful life. They!

Evil is that which commonly—and at all times—becomes something that can be deciphered in another's face. But has anyone realized how poor people think? That the rich for them are evil? That those who are mighty and powerful are evil? That a put-on Christianity is a false religion? Therefore, evilness can be seen by whose eyes?

For all its difference, the documentary I made on Oliver ushered me into world that far exceeded the confines of sheer filmmaking. I was ushered beyond the concerns of aesthetics into matters of social and ethical concerns, into a world of commitment, into the act of articulation. In making the film, I asked myself whether I was merely describing a particular lifestyle. But I found out that I was not just telling. I had some points to make: about poverty, homosexuality, acts of survival—matters that were close to my heart because I had seen them, I experienced them, they were a part of me.

If there was truth in the saying that kind begets kind, then working with Oliver meant an act of solidarity. Together, at the age of twenty-four, we saw how events shaped our lives, how it mean to go on despite the dictates of some realities much bigger than our own. In the end, betrayal became inevitable. Betrayal not in the sense of Judas's kiss but a betrayal that turned night into day, like the way film delivers from the darkened chambers of the apparatus a world conceived in light. Something lay hidden in the dark, and it was brought to light. But what was it that compelled me to look at things hidden in the dark? Would it not have been better if things were kept in the dark?

Oliver and I and a thousand more shadows like us have stayed too long in the dark. We still do. But in making the film, in projecting our moving shadows on the wall, in seeing our lives on screen, there was comfort in knowing where we were, why we were there, and maybe, where we will be going. Redemption would not be far. After the betrayal, one is either filled with anger and revolt, or one resigns and accept things as they are. That was why I considered Oliver's act of survival—that of spinning a web and breaking loose—a death-defying act. He braved conventional norms in order to assert his individuality, his will to live, even if it were but a wish spun in nylon thread.

Thus did the film become a pioneering effort at representing a homosexual in all his complex ramifications. Little did I realize that the film would carry my message across in terms of truth and honesty in the actual depiction of homosexuals, despite their poverty, corruption, and the dehumanizing condition which society has compelled them to inhabit.

My journey into homosexuality climaxed with my film *Revolutions Happen Like Refrains in a Song*. In this autobiographical film I traced my own personal history set against the backdrop of a raging revolution. My awakening to my sexuality coincided with the unfolding of a social upheaval which defined our struggle to survive as a people. As I journeyed into my self-consciousness, I realized that my search for a personal history paralleled the search for identity in the political and social life of our people. My individual search reflects the communal search for identity.

Twenty years of living under the Marcos dictatorship was long enough for me to see the patterns of patriarchy turn malignant. The ugly fangs of unrelenting violence sank deep into my unconscious. I was left with no other choice but to raise my voice and construct an ego, or else face the risk of personal and moral annihilation. For all the anguish and misery I saw happening around me, living was like living inside a volcano's belly.

But unlike the spectacular eruption of Mount Pinatubo, which after being dormant for six centuries disemboweled itself of its gaseous and lethal impurities, no one knows exactly how long the process of social disruption in our society will go on, until the social volcano we are living in erupts and finally gives peace to our people. It has been a long, interminable suffering that has ravaged us for centuries at the hands of our colonizers. Up to now our souls are rocked with viciousness, ever since the enemy sought refuge under our skin. Through all these years, we have almost seen the face of hell in our fight against feudal lords and dictators, in every threat posed by coup d'étàts, in every rise of the dollar, in every disaster that has shaken our will to survive. There is now a heavy air of despondency and despair hanging over our city, Manila, and over the islands hangs an air thick with our people's cries to survive.

For the Filipino homosexual, his struggle is his society's struggle. The homosexual is the society he is living in, or worse. By living under a regime of silence, the Filipino homosexual has failed to recognize himself in the midst of society's confusion. It can only become worse if, now, as the Filipino homosexual is beginning to waken into a new consciousness and a new perception of his identity, he succumbs once more into the abyss of silence and ignorance and fear, which, not unlike the silence of volcanoes, becomes a silence of centuries. It is this silence that we Filipino homosexuals must break. Because in it is inscribed the heavy weight of judgment by a society uncertain of itself. If we become the society we are living in, we will become no more than blind men leading the blind, marching our way into our hellish perdition.

By articulating our condition, by vivifying the sordid experiences we are going through, by putting landmarks in places where we have fallen, I am sure our society will learn from our experiences. It is time for Filipino homosexuals, both male and female, to free themselves from the bondage imposed upon their sexuality, even at the grave danger of being tagged as subversives. After all, like the society we live in, Filipino homosexuals must strive for our own self-determination.

Lesbian Home Handicraft Series #1

TAKE BACK THE LIGHT:
A LESBIAN VISIBILITY LAMPSHADE

by

Donna Evans
and
Jean Carlomusto

Follow these instructions, supply some of your own panache, and you will have a handsome Lesbian Visibility Lampshade bound to please family, friends and lovers. A constructive project for anyone who has ever wanted to take a pair of scissors to a book of theory.

To Construct Lampshade:

fig. 1

Carefully cut along dotted lines to re-move 3 lampshade sections. Don't cut too hard or you may lose some adjoining essays.

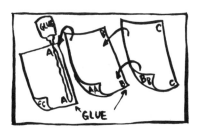

fig. 2

Join 3 sections of shade by gluing along the edges. Match A to AA and B to BB . Allow glue to dry completely before assembling. Good time for a nice, non-alcoholic caffeine-free beverage of your choice.

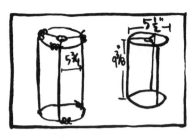

fig. 3

fig. 4

Construct a drum-shaped
frame from thin wire coathangers.
First, form 2 circles, 5 1/2"
in diameter. Then cut
3 vertical braces 10 1/2"
long. Wrap braces around circles
evenly, 5 3/4" apart.
The frame height should be
no more than 9 3/8".
Hate us yet? Try step 4!

Bind top + bottom rings
tightly with narrow
cotton tape, glued down
to frame at beginning and
end.

fig. 5

fig. 6

Carefully spread glue
along the inside of top
and bottom edges of shade.
Roll shade around the frame,
lining up the 3 side braces
of the frame with the 3 seams
in the shade. Secure the paper
to the top and bottom rings with
large paper clips. Glue the last
side seam closed. Let the glue
dry completely. Virgo leanings?
Try step 6!

Stitch the paper to
the top + bottom rings
of the shade frame.
Cover the stitching by
sticking lampshade bead,
(available at department
stores), around the top
and bottom edges.

You're done! Mount your completed shade on a lamp,
turn it on and be proud you are a lesbian.

Coming Soon: Lesbian Home Handicraft Series #2.
Make Your Own Dildo Harness For Under A Dollar.

DO·NOT·HIDE·YOUR·LIGHT·UNDER·A·

BUSHEL; BUT·PUT·IT·ON·A·STAND·SO·THAT·

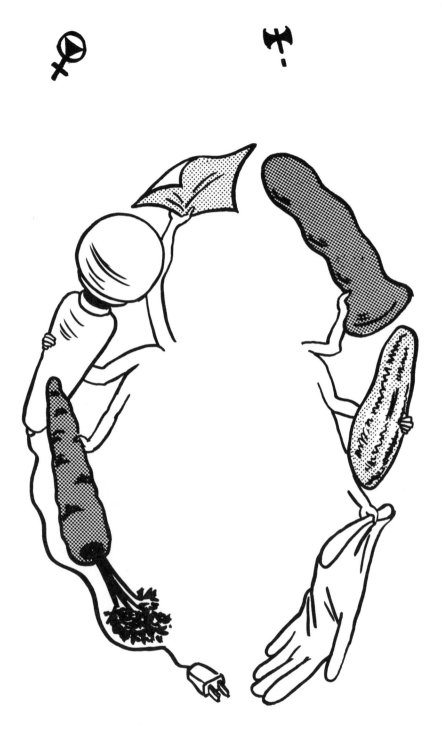

ALL·WHO·ENTER·MAY·SEE·THE·LIGHT▼

DONNA-JEAN 9:28-91

Contributors

MARUSIA BOCIURKIW is a video and filmmaker and writer whose credits include *Playing with Fire, Night Visions,* and *Bodies in Trouble.* She has written extensively on lesbian representation and spectatorship for various publications and anthologies, and teaches lesbian and gay studies at Concordia University in Montréal.

GREGG BORDOWITZ is an activist videomaker who for the past six years has been active in the struggle to end government inaction concerning AIDS and to establish equitable health care in the US.

KAUCYILA BROOKE is a faculty member at the California Institute for the Arts. She has exhibited her work in the US, Canada, and Great Britain. She is coproducer, with Jane Cottis, of *Dry Kisses Only,* a videotape about lesbian subplots in classic cinema.

ALISON BUTLER has worked as an arts administrator and a university lecturer. She is a member of the editorial advisory board of the journal *Screen.*

JEAN CARLOMUSTO has worked with ACT UP, GMHC, and the Testing the Limits Collective to produce AIDS-activist media. Her videotape *L Is for the Way You Look* explores lesbian identifications. Currently she is working on projects concerned with lesbian history.

DARYL CHIN is an artist and writer from New York City. He is in the process of preparing two books, a collection of his critical essays and a collection of his plays and performance texts.

LAWRENCE CHUA produced the video *How Many Eurasians Does It Take to Screw in a Lightbulb?* He is Managing Editor of *Bomb* and a commentator for the weekly National Public Radio news magazine *Crossroads.* His writing has appeared in the *New York Times, Rolling Stone,* the *Village Voice, Transition,* and *Premiere.*

DOUGLAS CRIMP teaches lesbian and gay studies at Sarah Lawrence College. He is the author of *AIDS Demo Graphics* (with Adam Rolston) and *On the Museum's Ruins.*

NICK DEOCAMPO is a filmmaker, poet, theorist, and chronicler of underground cinema in the Philippines. Based in Quezon City, Philippines, his super 8 films include *Revolutions Happen Like Refrains in a Song* and *Oliver.*

SARA DIAMOND is a critic and video artist whose tapes include *Keeping the Home Fires Burning* and *The Lull Before the Storm,* which deal with issues of women's history. An anticensorship activist and independent video advocate, she is currently Director of Television Programming at the Banff Center for the Arts.

JOHN DI STEFANO is an artist and videomaker from Montréal, presently based in Los Angeles. His work has been exhibited internationally, and his videotape *(Tell Me Why) The Epistemology of Disco* received the New Visions award for video at the San Francisco International Film Festival.

411

DONNA EVANS is a printmaker who makes prints that are kind of melancholy, not to say grim. She lives in New York City and also illustrates for progressive publications.

MARK FINCH is a freelance writer and has previously programmed the London and San Francisco Lesbian and Gay Film Festivals.

RICHARD FUNG is a Toronto-based video producer whose titles include *Orientations, Chinese Characters, The Way to My Father's Village, My Mother's Place, Fighting Chance, Steam Clean,* and *Out of the Blue.*

MARTHA GEVER has written critical articles for *Afterimage, Art in America, The Independent,* the *Nation, October,* and other publications. She is coeditor of the anthology *Out There: Marginalization and Contemporary Cultures* and the papers of the conference entitled *How Do I Look?: Queer Film and Video.*

JACKIE GOLDSBY is a doctoral student in American Studies at Yale University.

JOHN GREYSON is a Toronto-based film/videomaker whose works include *Zero Patience, The Making of Monsters, Urinal,* and *The ADS Epidemic.* He cocurated *Video Against AIDS,* a six-hour compilation of alternative tapes about AIDS, and taught at the California Institute for the Arts from 1986 to 1989. He has been active in the gay media arts communities since 1978.

SUNIL GUPTA is an artist who works with time-based media. He edited *An Economy of Signs* and coedited *Ecstatic Antibodies.* Currently he is curator for the Institute of New International Visual Art in London.

BARBARA HAMMER believes that abstraction does not suffice to challenge the extreme political repression of the status quo. Her fiftieth film and first feature, *Nitrate Kisses,* interrogates how lesbian and gay history is made, intercut with images of contemporary sexual practices that could disappear. The film was made with funds from the National Endowment for the Arts.

LIZ KOTZ is a New York-based critic and curator. She has written on film, video, and visual arts for *Artforum, Art in America, Afterimage, The Independent, The Advocate,* and other publications. She is a graduate student in comparative literature at Columbia University.

RICHARD KWIETNIOWSKI is a filmmaker based in Bristol, where he recently split up with the singer in a "grunge" rock band and is counting the *Cost of Love.*

KOBENA MERCER was active in the Gay Black Group in London in the early eighties, and currently teaches in the Art History and History of Consciousness Departments at the University of California, Santa Cruz.

MANDY MERCK teaches, writes, and makes television programs. She is a former editor of the film quarterly *Screen* and Channel Four's *Out on Tuesday,* and the author of *Perversions: Deviant Readings.*

RAY NAVARRO, a founding member of DIVA TV (Damned Interfering Video Activists Television), also produced personal artwork, wrote media criticism, was an AIDS educator working with community organizations, and curated programs of films and tapes dealing with AIDS.

When he died in November 1990 of an AIDS-related illness, he was in the midst of production on a video entitled *Defect.*

MICHELLE PARKERSON is an African American lesbian writer and filmmaker currently directing a documentary on poet-activist Audre Lorde.

PRATIBHA PARMAR is a writer and independent video and filmmaker. She has made numerous videotapes and films for the art gallery and museum circuit, and for broadcast television. Of these, *Khush* has won three awards and public prizes at international film festivals; *Sari Red, A Place of Rage,* and *Double the Trouble Twice the Fun* have also received acclaim at festivals worldwide.

ANDREI PLAKHOV is a critic, theorist, and programmer for the Moscow Film Festival. Based in Moscow, he also served as the Secretary of the National Filmmakers Union.

YVONNE RAINER came to filmmaking from dance and choreography. She has been making feature-length films since 1972, of which the best known are *Film About a Woman Who. . ., Journeys from Berlin/1971, The Man Who Envied Women,* and *Privilege.*

B. RUBY RICH is a cultural critic based in San Francisco. She is a regular contributor to *The Village Voice, Sight and Sound,* and numerous other journals. Currently a Visiting Professor at the University of California, Berkeley, she is preparing a book of collected essays.

CATHERINE SAALFIELD, a writer, videomaker, and media consultant, is the Project Coordinator of Media Network's Seeing Through AIDS Media Workshops. Her collaboratively videos include *Bird in the Hand, Among Good Christian Peoples, Keep Your Laws Off My Body,* and *Bleach, Teach and Outreach.*

WEILAND SPECK is a Berlin-based filmmaker and assistant organizer of the Panorama section of the Berlin International Film Festival. His work includes the film *Westler—East of the Wall* and a series of six videos for Safer Sex Promotion.

JERRY TARTAGLIA is an experimental filmmaker who lives and works in New York City. His film *Ecce Homo* is part of a trilogy which includes *A.I.D.S.C.R.E.A.M.* and *Final Solutions.*

MATIAS VIEGENER teaches critical studies at CalArts and is completing his Ph.D. at UCLA. He has most recently published fiction and criticism in *Bomb, Art Issues, Dear World, Afterimage, High Performance, Framework, Christopher Street, Fiction International,* and the anthologies *Men on Men 3* and *Discontents.*

THOMAS WAUGH teaches film studies and gay and lesbian cinema at Concordia University, Montréal. A frequent lecturer on the queer film festival circuit, he is the author of *Hard to Imagine: Gay Male Erotic Photography and Film from Their Beginnings to Stonewall.*

PATRICIA WHITE is a doctoral student in the History of Consciousness program at the University of California, Santa Cruz. Her dissertation explores the conditions of lesbian representability in classical Hollywood cinema and in feminist theory.